SPAIN, THE JEWS, AND FRANCO

SPAIN, THE JEWS, AND FRANCO

HAIM AVNI

Translated from the Hebrew by Emanuel Shimoni

The Jewish Publication Society of America
Philadelphia   5742 | 1982

Library of Congress Cataloging in Publication Data
Avni, Haim.
   Spain, the Jews, and Franco.
   Translation of Sefarad veha-Yehudim bi-yeme ha-sho'ah veha-emansipatsyah.
   Bibliography: p.   Includes index.
   1. Jews in Spain—History—20th century.   2. World War, 1939–1945—Jews—
Rescue.   3. Spain—Ethnic relations.   I. Title.
DS135.S7A9413   946'.004924   80–39777
ISBN 0–8276–0188–3

The publication of this book was made possible by a gift from
Robert P. Abrams
in memory of his father
Peter Abrams
industrialist, civic leader, philanthropist
1889–1963

To the memory of my parents
ADELA and ISAAC STEINDLING
whose foresight enabled them
to evade the Ides of March

CONTENTS

ACKNOWLEDGMENTS

The Holocaust and the Emancipation, the two extremes of modern Jewish life in the Diaspora, assume a special poignancy in the context of Spanish history.

Spain—where the Inquisition persisted until late into the nineteenth century, where the expulsion of the Jews continues to be regarded as one of the major events of the nation's history—how did this Spain behave toward the Jewish people when, from the late eighteenth century on, the rest of the Western world accepted them as equal citizens? And what was its attitude toward the Jews, during the brutal years of World War II, when most other nations in Europe either participated in the onslaught or turned their backs on them?

My quest for answers to these questions began during a trip to Spain twenty years ago. The poor synagogue of Madrid, hidden in an apartment house in a decaying neighborhood, with no sign or any other outward indication of its existence, fitted perfectly the image of a deeply Catholic and palpably hostile Spain. In contrast was the absolute confidence with which Spaniards, young and middle-aged from all walks of life, lost no opportunity to assert that "Spain was different during the Holocaust," that "Spain saved Jews."

Is Spain the benign land of the Golden Age of medieval Jewish history? Or is it the malevolent nation that promulgated the Edict of Expulsion? Is it still the same Spain that aligned itself with Fascism? Has it really changed?

These questions plagued me then and years later, and were the stimulus for this work. Thus my first acknowledgment goes to those Spaniards who through their self-confidence prompted me to undertake this research.

My primary aim was to gather all the material available in Israel. The Central Zionist Archives, the Yad Vashem records, and the files of other specialized archives, as well as dozens of eyewitnesses interviewed and recorded by the Oral History Division of the Institute of Contemporary Jewry at the Hebrew University in Jerusalem, all provided extremely important documentation. Then followed the search for material abroad: at the Centre de Documentation Juive Contemporaine in Paris; the World Jewish Congress headquarters and the archives of the YIVO Institute for Jewish Research in New York; at Haverford College near Philadelphia, where the American Friends Service Committee's papers are kept; and at the Spanish Foreign Ministry in Madrid. The willing help and generous guidance I received from the librarians, archivists, and directors of these institutions were indispensible to my work. I express my deepest gratitude to every one of them.

Special thanks are due the following people, without whose particular aid this study could never have been completed. My mentor, the late Israel Halperin, guided my initial steps in this research, and Moshe Davis, head of the Institute of Contemporary Jewry, helped me with the English publication. Haim Beinart advised me and through his many contacts in Spain helped me to obtain permission to use the Spanish Foreign Ministry's archives. Yehuda Bauer took a keen interest in my research and as the head of the Holocaust Research Unit of the Institute of Contemporary Jewry and a student of the history of the Joint Distribution Committee assisted me by supplementing my own resources with a number of important documents. Haim Beinart, Bela Vago, Hayyim Cohen, Nathan Lerner, and Jacob Tsur read sections of the manuscript with whose subject matter they were familiar and clarified certain passages. Juan Bautista Vilar of the University of Murcia, Spain, helped by sending several important documents. The late Zosa Szajkowski assisted with certain materials in the YIVO archives in New York. Gerhart Riegner, general secretary of the World Jewish Congress, placed important documents at my disposal, supplementing the material provided by the late Yitzhak Weissman, representative of the World Jewish Congress in Lisbon. Abraham Polonsky of Tel Aviv, commander of the Zionist underground in Toulouse during the war, placed the Armée Juive's archives in his possession at my disposal.

I owe special thanks to my teacher Shulamit Nardi, who was of invaluable assistance in reviewing the English translation, and to my friend Moshe Goodman, director of publications at the Institute of Contemporary Jewry, who devoted much energy to the publication of this book. Emanuel Shimoni translated the text; Graciela Samuels helped me to translate some of the Spanish documents; Raquel Ibanez and Manuel Hierro provided several important photographs.

Finally, the Memorial Foundation for Jewish Culture in New York assisted me with a grant. Research for this book was conducted at the Institute of Contemporary Jewry through support from the late Joseph Levine of Chicago.

To all these I extend my heartfelt gratitude.

SPAIN, THE JEWS, AND FRANCO

INTRODUCTION

On May 16, 1949, only a few days after the State of Israel was accorded membership in the United Nations, the General Assembly entertained a proposal by several Latin American countries to rescind the diplomatic boycott that was imposed upon General Francisco Franco's regime in 1946. Israel was not a member of the U.N. when this matter was discussed previously, but at the May 16 meeting Israeli Ambassador Abba Eban made the following statement:

> The United Nations has arisen out of the sufferings of a martyred generation, which included six million Jewish dead. One million Jewish children had been thrown into furnaces or gas chambers. So long as the history of Israel lasted, it could not for one moment lose sight of that frightful crime of organized inhumanity. That memory alone will determine Israel's attitude.
>
> While the Israeli delegation would not for one moment assert that the Spanish regime had any direct part in the policy of extermination, it does maintain that Franco Spain had been an active and sympathetic ally of the regime that had been responsible for that policy and thus contributed to its effectiveness. . . .
>
> For Israel, the essential point is the association of the Franco regime with the Nazi-Fascist alliance that corroded the moral foundations of civilized life and inflicted upon the human race its most terrible and devastating ordeal. . . .
>
> There are therefore the most compelling reasons, both universal and particular, why Israel is bound in all conscience and responsibility to vote against the draft resolution.

Israel thus joined the fourteen nations voting against Spain. The United

States, France, and Great Britain, who in March 1946 jointly expressed their hopes that the Spanish people would overthrow Franco's regime, abstained.[1]

Israel's association on behalf of world Jewry with the nations boycotting General Franco's regime cut the Spanish government to the quick and prompted it to react to what it called the Jewish attack on Spain. In a pamphlet titled *Spain and the Jews*, the Spanish Foreign Ministry described the contribution of the Nationalist government to the rescue of Jews during the Holocaust, quoting extensively from a letter by Rabbi Maurice L. Perlzweig, an official in the World Jewish Congress, to Spanish Ambassador Juan F. Cárdenas in Washington in March 1943. Perlzweig wrote:

> In the name of the executive committee of the World Jewish Congress, I address myself to Your Excellency to beseech you to express kindly to the Spanish government our deep gratitude for the refuge that Spain has accorded to the Jews coming from the territories under the military occupation of Germany. We understand all too well the difficulties of the situation, and we know the great effort that this war represents for the economy of Spain. We are doubly grateful for the permission given to the refugees to remain in Spain until such time as permanent residence is found for them, a problem that could be long and difficult to resolve during the conflict.
>
> The Jews are a race that possesses a great memory. They will not forget easily the opportunity that has been given to save the lives of thousands of their brothers.

In contrast to the painful memories of the Holocaust on which Eban based his support for the boycott of Spain, Spain presented a reminder of its rescue of Jews, bitterly pointing out that Israel's vote was an act of ingratitude.[2]

In the years following the U.N. debate, the belief that the Spanish government saved tens of thousands of Jews during the Holocaust gained currency, despite the overt and covert alliance between Spain and the Axis powers. Material in the Spanish Foreign Ministry's pamphlet found its way into books about Franco's Spain and subsequently was quoted in a work purported to be the comprehensive study of the history of the Jews in modern Spain.[3] The enthusiastic, albeit somewhat general, evidence of historian Carlton J. H. Hayes, who served as United States ambassador to Spain, also indicated that the Franco government had acted to save Jewish lives.[4]

The significance of these facts faded from memory with the passage of time. Press reviews during the 1950s tended progressively to inflate the numbers of those rescued from the Holocaust. In 1963 one journalist concluded that in the Balkans alone, Spain through its diplomatic representatives saved about 40,000 Jews. In 1970 a somewhat higher estimate was published under the name of Chaim Lifschitz, a New York rabbi, who claimed that about 60,000 Jews were saved by Spain, many of them the result of personal intervention by General Franco.[5] The scattered information and exaggerated estimates did little to clarify all the facts regarding Spain's attitude toward the Jewish people during the darkest period of their history. Comprehensive studies on the Holocaust published until now contain only hints of certain rescue attempts in which Spain was involved; a good press monograph, published in 1973 in Spain and based on important archival material from the Spanish Foreign Ministry, suffers from tendentiousness and, because of incomplete material at the author's disposal, does not encompass all the relevant details.[6] No study published so far has brought to light all the facts in their true perspective.

The pamphlet from the Spanish Foreign Ministry not only describes rescue operations but also links Spain's activities to its historic relationship with the Jews. Jewish groups who came into contact with the Spanish authorities time and again stressed the special bond that existed between the two peoples. As with other cases of rescue, here too there is significance in the relationships that developed between Spain and the Jewish people before the Holocaust. The golden age of Spanish Jewry, the expulsion in 1492, and the Inquisition that continued for centuries afterward etched a deep scar on the national memory. Any examination of Spain's position regarding the Jews during the Holocaust and of the possibility that it rescued Jews therefore must also consider the time of the emancipation of Jews in other European countries.

Did liberalism and the principles of civil equality that applied to the Jews in nineteenth-century Europe also apply in Spain? Was any Jewish presence established there? What were the attitudes of Spaniards: did they retain their hostility, or were there groups sympathetic to Jews? Were Spaniards expected to join in the work of rescue, and was the true situation known to world Jewish organizations? These complex questions remove instances of the rescue of Jews through Spain from the exclusive province of the Holocaust period; they are criteria for a wider historical perspective of the relationship between Spain and the Jews. The Holocaust and the rescue are a flash of lightning that suddenly illuminates the darkness and reveals silhouettes in their stark reality, giving these events a meaning that extends far beyond the bounds of time and place.

1

THE EMANCIPATION AND MODERN ANTI-SEMITISM

EQUAL RIGHTS IN SPAIN

The controversy over Jewish emancipation that raged throughout western and central Europe at the end of the eighteenth and the beginning of the nineteenth centuries in countries with Jewish populations left Spain virtually untouched. The reason was manifest, for the Iberian state, including its vast colonial holdings in Latin America, had no legally recognized Jewish presence; the Edict of Expulsion of 1492 was still in effect, and the Inquisition remained poised to implement the laws of religious persecution. Nevertheless, even in secluded Spain there took place in 1797 a discussion on the Jewish question. The arguments put forth on that occasion were to be repeated frequently in the nineteenth century and continued to reverberate as late as the first decades of the twentieth.

In 1797, Spain was in serious political and economic straits. On February 14, the country suffered one of its most shameful defeats. Near Cape Saint Vincent, in the south of Portugal, a small English flotilla overcame a large and powerful Spanish fleet making its way to the port of Cádiz. As a result, Spain lost the island of Trinidad, off the South American coast, and Minorca, in the Mediterranean. This was only two years after the armies of the French Republic had defeated the Spanish army on its own soil and forced the government to surrender another colony, Santo Domingo, on the island of Hispaniola in the Caribbean. These setbacks signaled the first stage in the swift deterioration of Spain's status as a world empire.

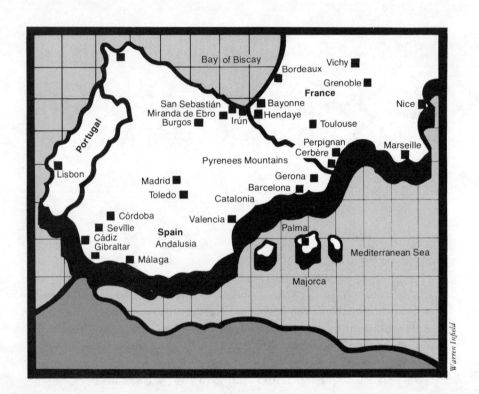

On March 21, the Council of Ministers of King Carlos IV heard a proposal by one of its members, Don Pedro Varela, on how to improve the economic plight of the country. "According to general opinion," Varela postulated, "the Jewish nation possesses the major wealth of Europe"; the admission of Jews into Spain therefore would serve to alleviate the country's fiscal distress. Spain, he suggested, should consider inviting a few important Jewish merchants of Holland to establish branches in Cádiz and other Spanish ports. Only in this manner, Varela claimed, could Spain compete with other countries in commerce and industry. To this end he proposed that a royal decree be issued, stating: "In the wake of the admission to Spain of several houses of commerce, there could follow the acceptance of the whole Hebrew Nation, which has never forgotten the advantages and conveniences that they enjoyed in Spain in the past."

Carlos and the Council of Ministers rejected the proposal. Moreover, five years later, in 1802, the king signed an edict reinforcing the prohibitions against the admission of Jews into any territory under Spanish control. The edict ordered all national and local officials to notify the authorities of the Inquisition immediately of the entry of any Jew, and threatened judicial authorities with severe punishment if they did not provide full cooperation to the Inquisition in its struggle to prevent Jews from coming into Spain.[1]

Varela's abortive effort was an isolated episode. Indeed, it represented Spain's only attempt during the time of the first wave of emancipation in Europe—that is, the period from the French Revolution to Napoleon—to deal with the Jewish question. The changes that subsequently occurred in Spain—the deposing of King Ferdinand VII and his replacement by Napoleon's brother, the war of independence, and the first constitution drafted by the Cortes, the representative assembly, in 1812—were decisive in the country's history; some of them may have influenced certain attitudes toward the Jews, but none affected the Jewish problem directly. Under the article in the constitution regarding religious status, Spain remained a Catholic state, closed to members of all other religions. On February 22, 1813, by order of the Cortes, the Inquisition was abolished. Neither Spain's Catholicism nor the end of the Inquisition had much significance for the Jews, however, for both laws arose out of party polemics.

In March 1814, the House of Bourbon resumed the throne in Madrid. Two months later, in Seville, the capital of Andalusia, church bells rang out as a religious procession passed through the streets, culminating with a pronouncement from the steps of the cathedral declaring the reimposition of the Inquisition. On July 21, a royal decree ratified the pronouncement in Seville and reinstated the Inquisition's authority throughout Spain. On

August 21, 1816, the king issued another decree, which renewed all the prohibitions included in the order of 1802 and reiterated the Edict of Expulsion decreed by the Catholic kings in 1492.[2] The persecution of the Jews in Spain and the efforts to keep Spain free of Jews thus continued into the nineteenth century, as they had done for many centuries before, and the Inquisition was once again charged with implementing them. The fact that during the forty years between 1780 and 1820 there were only sixteen cases involving the "crime" of Judaism (out of more than five thousand heard by the courts) may indicate some diminution in the power and prestige of the Inquisition; it may also prove the success of the age-old determination to prevent Jews from entering Spain and to extinguish every spark of Judaism among its inhabitants. In any event, the very existence of the Inquisition indicated the nature of official Spanish policy on the Jewish issue.[3]

Forty years passed after the restoration of the Bourbons until the return of the Jews to Spain was proposed again in 1854. This period in the history of Spain was rife with political turmoil and civil disturbance. The liberals played an active part in these events even though the struggles were essentially dynastic, with the royal house agreeing from time to time to certain liberal concessions to achieve other ends. One concession was the abolition of the Inquisition in 1834, which took place only after some of the most important powers of the Inquisition (such as the censorship of religious and moral tracts) had been allocated to other branches of the Catholic church and after a special criminal law had been passed empowering the courts to punish anyone attacking Catholicism. During this period a number of laws were passed, stressing in varying degrees the fact that the Catholic religion was not merely the state religion but the only legally permitted faith in Spain.

In 1854, as a result of one of the many political crises, liberal influence increased once again, and Queen Maria Luisa Isabella II was about to convene the Cortes in order to change the constitution. For Rabbi Ludwig Philippson of Magdeburg, editor of the important Jewish weekly *Allgemeine Zeitung des Judentums*, this seemed an opportune time to try to influence Spain to reconsider its position regarding the Jews. He approached the Jews of Marseille, Bayonne, and Bordeaux, France, urging them to join him in attempting to persuade the prime minister of Spain and the members of the Cortes to include guarantees of religious freedom in Spain's new constitution and to promulgate a special law rescinding the 1492 edict. This law was vital to Philippson, for the granting of religious freedom without rescinding the Edict of Expulsion would not solve the Jewish problem.

Rabbi Philippson supported his appeal with detailed historical evidence, most of which he drew from the well-known Spanish historian José Amador de los Ríos. His main contention was that the cruel uprooting of the Spanish Jews, their persecution, and their exile for hundreds of years were terrible injustices for which the new Spain should atone. According to him, Jews were not demanding the restoration of the large amounts of property taken from their forefathers since the days of the expulsion, nor were they asking for the return of the magnificent synagogues that were still standing and had been converted into churches; their only request was that Spain should acknowledge the error of the Catholic monarchs Ferdinand and Isabella and the right of those Jews who wished to return to Spain to do so. Philippson stressed that his appeal was unselfish, and that the Jews of Germany, in whose name he spoke, are "far from the Iberian Peninsula, and belong to another beautiful and beloved homeland, and to another wonderful and esteemed Nation," and they have no intention of moving to Spain. Their approach was motivated by the fact that as a part of world Jewry they felt obliged to demand amends for the injustices committed against "their coreligionists" and that they owed a debt of honor to the memory and suffering of Jews in generations past.

Rabbi Philippson expressed these sentiments in a proposal that was translated into Spanish by the vice-consul of Spain in Berlin and printed in handsome script. Hundreds of copies were sent to the Jewish consistory in Bayonne, which undertook to send them, through channels, to the members of the Cortes. Another document, similar in content, was sent to Prime Minister Baldomero Espartero. The Bayonne community also presented its case to the Consistoire Central des Israélites de France and to the Board of Deputies of British Jews, the representative body of British Jewry, which appointed a special committee to discuss and act on Philippson's appeal. The consistory in Marseille was enthusiastic, but the Bordeaux community was passive and even cold.

The proposal was received favorably in Spain. Liberal newspapers commented sympathetically; one newspaper published it in full. Some of the municipal delegates to the Cortes were empowered by their electorate to support the doctrine of religious freedom.[4]

The Cortes met at the end of 1854 and, after some discussion on the question of religious freedom, voted on February 20, 1855, on article 2 of the constitution, which stated that Catholicism was to continue as the official religion of the state, the only faith permitted in Spain. Foreigners and non-Catholic Spaniards were allowed to maintain their religious beliefs but were not allowed to give public expression to them. The request to rescind the Edict of Expulsion was brought before the special committee that discussed freedom of religion, which rejected it. The appeal of Rabbi Philippson and the Jews of Germany was "a voice in the wilderness."[5]

At this time, a limited Jewish presence had begun to establish itself in Madrid. Mostly merchants and financiers, many came from the south of France, especially Bayonne, and were associated with government officials as a result of their businesses. When their numbers increased, the Consistoire Central asked the Spanish government for permission to establish a cemetery. On October 16, 1865, Spain granted permission and informed the Jewish body in Paris that "if the French Jews living in this kingdom" wanted to purchase land in which to bury their dead and even to surround it with a wall, "there is no impediment to authorizing such constructions," but only on the condition that they do not build on that land "a house of prayer or any type of synagogue, or [hold] any private or public rites." French Jews thus were permitted what had been allowed since 1855 to the English Protestants, without Spain's having to alter its traditional position on the Jews.[6]

Three years later, in 1868, a military insurgence in Cádiz became a general revolution in which most of the army and navy took part, along with liberal forces throughout Spain. Isabella was forced to seek refuge in France, and it began to look as if the rule of the House of Bourbon had come to an end. A declaration published October 8 by the provisional government stated that religious freedom was to be one of the foundations of the new Spain. In a letter sent to all the diplomatic representatives in Madrid, the government expressed the bitterness of the Spanish people toward the Church and its deeds, and promised to expunge from Spanish law all prohibitions and discriminations that applied to members of other religions. Many local councils throughout Spain adopted resolutions calling for freedom of religion, and some of them even began to grant Protestants the right to build houses of worship.[7]

These events provided the opportunity once more to raise the question of Spain's position on the Jews. On this occasion, the matter was taken up by one of the most prominent members of the Spanish-Portuguese community in London, Haim Guedalla, who was a cousin of Sir Moses Montefiore and who knew General Juan Prim, one of the leaders of the revolution, from the period of his exile in London. In a letter of congratulation, Guedalla exhorted the general to attempt to cancel the 1492 expulsion edict.

Repercussions of the events in Spain were heard in France too, spurring the heads of the consistories of Bordeaux and Bayonne to similar action. Unlike Rabbi Philippson, who acted as the spokesman of all Jewry and demanded that Spain repent for its history of sins against the Jews, the heads of the consistories presented themselves as Spaniards and Portuguese, the direct descendants of the exiles. "Our ancestors labored for many centuries for the welfare and glory of Spain," they wrote in their appeal, "and when they were exiled they brought with them to France, England, and Holland the culture, language, and literature of Spain. It is true to say that their descendants in these lands enjoy a prestige that brings honor on their ancient homeland." Like Philippson before them, the heads of the consistories sought no personal profit by their request. On the contrary, being French citizens they never intended to abandon the country that had sheltered them and their ancestors for hundreds of years. Their request to cancel the Edict of Expulsion was merely an effort to collect a debt of honor owed to their forefathers, who were torn by this act from their beloved homeland. "The names of the signatories are Spanish names. Permit us to hope that this will serve as another reason for us to enjoy your patriotic sympathy."

On December 1, 1868, General Francisco Serrano, head of the provisional government, responded sympathetically to the appeal of the Jews of Bayonne and Bordeaux. Because the revolution had committed itself to religious freedom, among other human rights, he said, it had in effect canceled the Edict of Expulsion of the fifteenth century. "As a result, you are free to enter our country and practice your religion like the members of all other religions."[8]

This response was more comprehensive than the request, for it did not confine itself merely to the descendants of the Spanish exiles. To all intents and purposes, this official declaration apparently served to rescind the expulsion of the Jews from Spain. The principle of religious freedom on which it was based, however, still had to be enshrined in law and accepted by all Spaniards, or at least by most of them. In 1869 the article concerning freedom of religion was brought before the Cortes, and in May of that year, after stormy debates, it was adopted by a majority vote. In accordance with article 21 of the constitution, Spain undertook to maintain and support the Catholic religion and its clergy, but foreigners as well as Spaniards were assured the right to practice any form of worship, both privately and publicly, on condition that it did not conflict with universal law and morality. Those who supported this law, including the statesman Emilio Castelar, undoubtedly represented the liberal trends that had become part of the political atmosphere of nineteenth-century Spain. But the fact that the liberals attained a majority among the representatives elected in the wake of the revolution did not diminish the importance and power of the defeated opposition.

The clergy, supported by the proponents of absolute monarchy and the moderate monarchists who feared extreme liberal reforms, opposed this declaration of religious freedom. They rallied to the slogan "Catholic unity" and fought against the principles of religious freedom and human rights. In 1870, one year after the vote on the constitution, the Carlists adopted a political platform that sought to restore to the Catholic religion its exclusive status in Spain and prepared to reinstate the Inquisition.[9] Hostility to the Spanish republic became even more extreme because of the difficulties in its first year of existence and its failure to establish a constitutional monarchy under law. Opposition to religious freedom served as the banner uniting the conservatives in their struggle against liberal forces. The strength of the resistance to the 1869 constitution increased to the point where the Church questioned not merely the religious freedom that had been introduced by the revolution but even the principle of religious tolerance that had been accepted previously.

In 1875, political instability resulted in the return of the monarchy; one year later, new representatives were elected to the Cortes for the purpose of formulating a new constitution. Despite prevalent reactionary trends, the Board of Deputies of British Jews tried to influence legislation concerning religious matters. The board appealed to King Alfonso XII, asking that the law state expressly that Jews be allowed to live in Spain, to practice their religion, and to enjoy equal rights with all other citizens. This appeal fell on deaf ears. After a bitter, protracted debate, the Cortes adopted, by a majority of 221 to 89, article 11 of the constitution concerning the status of religion. Catholicism was declared the state religion, and the Spanish people were obliged to promote Catholic worship and to support its clergy. Non-Catholics were promised that they would suffer no interference as a result of their religious beliefs, provided they respected "Christian morality." Nevertheless, "no religious ceremonies or manifestations will be permitted in public, other than those of the state religion." Article 11 was passed despite vehement protests from the republicans, who tried in vain to base religious legislation on the principles of human rights. Spain once more became a Catholic state in which tolerance toward members of other religions was qualified. Its policy on the Jews, which in 1868 was based on a general idea of religious freedom, remained very uncertain.[10]

In 1881, five years after the constitution was adopted, Haim Guedalla asked Prime Minister Práxedes Mateo Sagasta to make it clear to the Jews that the Edict of Expulsion was in fact canceled. Sagasta's response was that article 1 of the 1876 constitution defined who was a Spaniard and who was not; it stated that all foreigners who had settled in Spain and become citizens, or had acquired permanent resident status in one of the towns, were Spaniards. As the article did not differentiate among foreigners on the basis of religion, it applied also to Jews, and there was thus no need for special legislation or declarations in their case. On the contrary, if such a special law were promulgated, it would reflect upon the overall liberal interpretations of the constitution. "Thus, all those of your coreligionists who wish it can come to Spain without any obstacle whatever, being sure that the Government, interpreting the opinion of the country, will receive them with kindness and sympathy." When he was asked again about religious freedom, Sagasta quoted article 11 from the constitution, adding that this permitted the members of all non-Catholic religions to establish places of worship and cemeteries for themselves; "these are the only guarantees that the Government can provide you and your coreligionists, who should not have any fear whatsoever." Six years later, on February 11, 1887, in response to a question in the Cortes, Sagasta repeated this interpretation of the constitution. He added that the second article, which permits foreigners to settle in Spain and engage in trade, applied to Jews as much as to members of other religions, provided that they adhered to Catholic morality, which was, according to him, universal morality.[11]

This interpretation of the Spanish constitution, which was published in the western Jewish press in 1881 and 1887, was received by the Jewish leadership with understanding but with reservations. The head of the Board of Deputies found it necessary, in 1881, to point out that until Spain abolished the limitations it placed on religious freedom with an appropriate amendment to the constitution, the future of Jews was not secure in that country. Rabbi Philippson adopted a more extreme position; in his view, Sagasta's statement that the first article of the constitution in effect canceled the Edict of Expulsion did not provide sufficient guarantees for Jewish life in Spain, and no Jew who valued his safety would regard it as such.[12]

Isidore Loeb, the general secretary of the Alliance Israélite Universelle in Paris, elaborated upon the constitution and Sagasta's interpretation of it at greater length than did others. In an article published in 1877, soon after the adoption of the constitution, and republished in 1887 with significant addenda, he analyzed the legal implication of the articles of the constitution and of other laws applying to the Jews and drew conclusions that were unemotional and reserved. Loeb wrote that there was indeed a contradiction between the Edict of Expulsion and the first and second articles in the Spanish constitution, which permitted Jews to enter and settle in Spain. But, Loeb continued, as the edict was never repealed by law, there would always be the possibility that a reactionary government, relying on the primacy of the edict, could forbid the entry of Jews into Spain or even their residence there. The constitution apparently guaranteed Jews the right to citizenship in Spain; the implementation of that right, however, was by law dependent upon the goodwill of the authorities, and the article concerning religious freedom was subject to their interpretation. A liberal prime minister, like Sagasta, could create favorable conditions in which non-Catholics could worship and establish communities, but a more reactionary regime could make life difficult indeed. Loeb concluded:

> This legislation does not place serious obstacles in the way of Jewish immigration, but neither does it provide absolute guarantees. The solution of many extremely serious questions relating to the existence of Jews and their communities in Spain depends in large measure upon the sympathy of administrative and judicial authorities and can change in accordance with the regime.[13]

The constitution adopted in 1876 remained in effect for fifty-six years, until it was abolished after the formation of the Second Republic in 1931. Its longevity came about largely because, with the increasing polarization of the Spanish political spectrum and the widening gap between the republicans and the left, on the one hand, and the Carlists, the conservatives, and the Church, on the other, many liberals and moderate republicans and monarchists regarded the legal status quo as the most efficient for Spain. Hence, even a venerable republican such as Emilio Castelar, who had fought for a republican regime for many years and headed one for a time, adopted a position of tacit acceptance and eventually reconciled himself to a regime based on the constitution. The matter of religious freedom became a secondary consideration compared to the other internal problems that beset Spain, which had lost, in the final decades of the nineteenth century, the last vestiges of its empire in the Western Hemisphere and the Far East. For this reason, during the long period that the constitution was in effect, questions of Jewish policy arose not in the context of constitutional or human rights discussions, but as the result of the initiative of a few individuals or groups, most of whom were close to moderate republican and monarchist circles.

A survey of the main events in this context will reveal the diverse trends that dominated the relationship between Spain and the Jews until the establishment of the Second Republic in 1931.

SYMPATHY AND HOSTILITY

In 1881, Spain's attitude toward the Jews was tested dramatically in the wake of the pogroms in Russia. On June 4, Juan Antonio de Rascón, the

Spanish ambassador in Constantinople, reported to the Foreign Ministry in Madrid that a delegation of Jews from Odessa had arrived in Constantinople to make a plea to the sultan on behalf of Jewish immigration to Turkey. The ambassador described the Russian Jews' distress over the fact that the borders of Romania and other Balkan countries were closed to them and stated that Germany, whose consuls in the Turkish Empire had at first protected many Russian Jews there, had decided to limit drastically the number of Jews registered in its legation and to withdraw its protection of them. Rascón's report contained no proposal regarding the Jews; but the ambassador apparently met later with the members of the Odessa delegation when he proposed to the Spanish minister of state that Spain shelter the persecuted Jews within its borders.

Rascón's reports reveal that he maintained close contact with at least several leaders of the Jewish community in Constantinople. It is possible that his proposal arose from sincere humanitarian feelings stirred by the plight of the Jews. In his letters to Madrid, however, he preferred to stress the material advantages that Spain would reap in the wake of Jewish immigration. In his view, such immigration would stimulate commercial ties with thousands of Spanish Jews scattered throughout the Turkish Empire, allowing Spain to establish a permanent shipping line reaching from its ports to the shores of Turkey and the Black Sea, like those of France and England. Moreover, the existence of large Sephardic communities in Constantinople and Salonika would be good reason to establish Spanish secondary schools in these cities, similar to the German schools that had existed there for some time. The ambassador felt that Spain should be interested in disseminating among these Jews a knowledge of modern Spanish, "because in this manner Spain will have in the East the most immediate and the easiest means of increasing its commercial interests and enhancing its influence propitiously." In his few published reports, Rascón made no note of the fact that the Russian Jews who were seeking refuge were Ashkenazim, or eastern European Jews. He expressed fervently his belief that the mass immigration of thousands of Jews to Spain was not only possible, but also desirable.

Rascón's proposals reached attentive ears in Madrid. Foreign Minister Marques de la Vega de Armijo presented them to the king and obtained his agreement. The Council of Ministers, headed by Sagasta, discussed the proposals and voted to empower Rascón to inform the Jews that they were permitted to enter Spain and settle there permanently.[14]

On June 15 the foreign minister informed Rascón of the decision of the Council of Ministers. The next day the story was published, and the news spread far and wide. According to a Reuters dispatch from Madrid, based on the information in the Spanish press, the request to settle in Spain had been made to Rascón in the name of 60,000 Russian Jews; the Spanish government decided, after consultation with the king, that "all Jews desirous of coming to Spain would find the protection they sought in the country in which dwelt so many of their ancestors." The English press—the *Daily News*, the *Daily Telegraph*, and the *Times*—printed this item with their own commentary; in Austria and Holland, too, the news was proclaimed. In France, one newspaper provided amazingly detailed descriptions of Rascón's plans concerning Jewish immigration, while another told of a large campaign supposedly organized by French Jews to present tokens of gratitude to the king of Spain and his ministers. The western European press thus reflected, sometimes accurately and often with exaggeration, the expectations aroused by Spain's response to the appeal from its ambassador in Turkey.[15] News even spread to Argentina, which began to pursue an energetic immigration policy. At the suggestion of one of its citizens living in Europe, and following Spain's decision to accept Jews, the Argentinian government also made plans to channel Russian Jewish immigrants to its shores and to appoint a special immigration agent for this purpose.[16]

The news from Spain found enthusiastic response among British Jews, as well. The London *Jewish Chronicle* in an editorial announced that "an event has occurred which marks an epoch in the modern history of the Jews" and considered the Spanish king's plan to invite Jews to his country "a tardy requital for one of the greatest acts of injustice known in history." The paper compared this event to the return of Jews to England in the seventeenth century, hundreds of years after they had been expelled, and promised that, apart from the economic advantages that would accrue from Jewish immigration, Spain would also benefit from the "support of grateful Judaism in the world of commerce." In the London City Council, two Jewish members proposed that the City should express its support and sympathy for "the spirit of true liberality and religious tolerance" that the king of Spain and his ministers had manifested in their decision to invite Jews from other lands "to establish for themselves a home in the Spanish peninsula." This resolution was adopted unanimously and conveyed to the Spanish ambassador in London.[17] The prospect of the return of Jews to Spain inspired the imaginations of rabbis and preachers; it became the subject of sermons quoting from the weekly portion of the Law and richly spiced with expressions of gratitude to the king of Spain.[18]

The Anglo-Jewish Association, the veteran organization of English Jewry, enthusiastically suggested that several of its members should thank Alfonso XII officially by letter. But even here some skeptical voices were heard. Frederic D. Mocatta, the chairman of the association's council, doubted that the appeal to Rascón actually had come from any authoritative Jewish body. Another council member acknowledged the limitations upon non-Catholic religious worship that still existed in Spain. A third council member supported the chairman's doubts and asked whether it was sufficiently clear with whom and for whose sake the association was supposed to identify itself.[19] At a meeting of the Board of Deputies, to whom the Anglo-Jewish Association appealed for joint action on the proposed appeal to the king of Spain, the voices of skepticism grew louder. The point on which the discussion turned was that as long as Spain had not abolished limitations upon religious freedom, the future for Jews there was not secure. In order to dispel these doubts, Haim Guedalla asked Prime Minister Sagasta to specify the legal status of those Jews who were to settle in Spain; the skeptics were not satisfied by Sagasta's response. But Guedalla, who had worked fervently in the past for the return of Jews to Spain, did not despair.

Guedalla believed in the possibility of widespread Jewish settlement in Spain. Rascón spoke of thousands of Jewish immigrants who would come to Spain shortly. In the press the figure 60,000 was mentioned. Sadly, these hopes were soon dispelled.

Rascón, to whom many refugees from Russia turned, was forced to announce time and again that the Spanish government never intended to assist in the transportation and resettlement of Jews wishing to emigrate to Spain. Nevertheless, with the help of the directors of one of the shipping companies that linked Marseille and Odessa and the guidance of the Spanish consul in Marseille, on his own initiative Rascón assisted dozens of Jewish refugees to set sail for Spain. By September 14, Rascón had arranged the transportation of only thirty-eight Jews, with another twelve waiting their turn. In Warsaw also, the Spanish Embassy announced that Madrid would not provide any assistance to immigrants. The Spanish Embassy in Vienna, to which many Jews applied for aid, turned all of them away. Another fifty-eight families, who in July 1882 asked the government for land and financial assistance in order to settle in Spain as farmers, received the same rebuff.[20]

The public response that Rascón's proposal aroused thus brought no effective results. This fact, however, did not preclude a similar effort five years later. On this occasion, the initiative was taken by Isidoro López Lapuya, a lawyer and senator who edited the liberal *El Progreso* and had connections with newspapers and journals outside Spain. Lapuya discovered a brief letter from a Romanian Jew in one of these journals, calling upon Spanish writers to affiliate themselves with Jews of Spanish origin.

This appeal, coupled with the news of the emigration of many Jews from Romania and Russia to the countries of the New World, prompted Lapuya to think in terms of diverting part of this stream of migration toward Spain. In his letters to the Jewish press in Germany and France, Lapuya emphasized that the age-old ties of Spanish Jews to their ancient homeland, from which they had been exiled, and the decline of religious fanaticism in Spain made it possible, even mandatory, to attempt to correct the injustice perpetrated against the Jews in 1492. Lapuya did not conceal his hope that the immigration of Jews—who were known for their affluence, diligence, business acumen, and experience—would bring enormous benefits to a Spain greatly in need of these talents. Moreover, the return of Jews to Spain would prove to the whole world that Spain's cultural retardation, obscurity, and religious fanaticism were merely "dark fables" having no basis in truth in modern Spain.[21]

To bring his plan to fruition, Lapuya thought it necessary to establish a center to gather knowledge about the economic and legal problems inherent in the settlement of Jews in Spain and to bring this knowledge to the attention of interested Jews. Such a center would also publish reliable information about the Jews to prepare the way for their resettlement. He felt initially that this center should be established by the handful of Jews already living in Spain, but he soon realized that it should have a Spanish national character and therefore must be undertaken by prominent public figures. Lapuya hoped to generate enthusiasm among people from all the liberal parties so that the effort would not be tainted by partisanship. He especially tried to make sure that senators and monarchist delegates in the Cortes would be represented. He thus delayed the creation of the center until enough people connected with Sagasta's party and in agreement with his ideas had been convinced that it was in no way opposed to government policies.

After these preparations were made, senior officials agreed to join the venture, including the state auditor, the director general of public education and a member of the Supreme Education Council, the chief editor of the Bureau of Commerce's journal, a delegate to the Cortes, bankers, businessmen, professors, and journalists. All these gathered on December 30, 1886, in a private home and announced the establishment of the Centro Español de Inmigración Israelita (Spanish Center for Jewish Immigration). The declared aims of the center were to attract Jewish immigrants to Spain "and particularly the descendants of Spanish families who had been expelled in 1492"; to publish reliable information about Jews in Spain, their lives and occupations, and to disseminate information about Spain among the Jews; and to determine, with the aid of European

Jewish organizations, which Jews would be most suitable for immigration and to provide these Jews with financial assistance in all matters involving their civic integration in Spain. The members of the center chose Haim Guedalla as honorary president; Lapuya, who was appointed president, sat on the executive committee with three journalists.[22]

Even before the establishment of the center, Lapuya started to flesh out his ideas. In several articles, he demonstrated the successful involvement of Jews in the politics of France and Italy and their contributions to the development of these countries. He described anti-Semitism as a narrow-mindedness that proves nothing about Jews themselves. In his letters to the western Jewish press, he invited anyone interested in commercial or legal information about Spain to write him directly; he received responses from hundreds of Jews and Jewish organizations. Once the center was begun, Lapuya and his colleagues attempted to dispel the fears concerning the impending legal status of Jews in Spain; accordingly, one of them, Eduardo Baselga, a delegate to the Cortes, asked Sagasta for clarification on the subject. The prime minister answered that the Spanish constitution promised Jews complete tolerance; Lapuya and his colleagues were satisfied that this response dispelled any doubts. Nevertheless, Lapuya did not ignore the strong resistance shown by the Catholic church and its clergy, who were in close daily contact with the public.

The Church's opposition to the sort of tolerance that would facilitate the return of Jews to Spain already had been expressed in 1869 during the debate in the Cortes on religious freedom, when Church representatives rejected the idea that Jewish settlement would save Spain from its economic ills.[23] Lapuya knew that the Church's position had not changed since then; he gauged the lower clergy's anti-Jewish stance from their reactions to Rascón's 1881 proposals. In the wake of the news of the king's decision to allow Jews to return to Spain, a Franciscan monk published a pamphlet in which he explained to his congregants that the admission of Jews would merely increase poverty, decrease food supplies, raise prices, and, most important, spread dissension among Spaniards, who would complain bitterly. Not only are the Jews Christ-killers, wrote the monk, but their sins cause them to be expelled from every country they inhabit; allowing the Jews to return to Spain as a gesture aimed to counteract the dictates of former Catholic kings would be an insult to their memory and in conflict with the very essence of Spain.[24]

Lapuya knew the influence such words had on Spanish Catholics. He attacked similar arguments in the Catholic press, which also sharply criticized his plan. But from them he was able to derive some practical advice regarding the types of immigrants that should be brought into Spain, their numbers, and especially their place of settlement: the immigrants must have financial means that would enable them to open businesses upon their arrival, their numbers should be limited, and they should settle only in large cities, where religious fanaticism had waned. "If the Jewish immigrants will behave with the reserve anticipated from them, it will be possible to wait until the laws [concerning freedom of religion] change, too," he wrote in one of his articles.[25] Lapuya qualified his recommendations further: anyone who was neither well off financially nor an expert in one of the crafts needed in Spain should not emigrate; simple laborers barely earning a living in their present countries would be unable to do even that in Spain, and poor people would leave a very bad impression. The center was equipped to offer limited financial assistance only to those capable of relying upon their own means, and only after they had been integrated would the foundation be laid for the entry of those without money.[26]

These restrictions were in accord with all the Jewish organizations with whom Lapuya spoke. All warned against creating the illusion among poor Russian and Romanian immigrants that they would find succor in Spain. But Lapuya's plan aroused a variety of reactions. Haim Guedalla, who was enthusiastic about the idea of resettlement in Spain, and Hirsch Hildesheimer, the editor of Berlin's *Die Jüdische Presse*, both welcomed the plan, believing that with proper care it would succeed; Hildesheimer regarded Lapuya's attempts to change Spanish attitudes toward the Jews as a blessing. The *Jewish Chronicle* and the Anglo-Jewish Association in London and Rabbi Philippson in Berlin felt that, despite his good intentions, Lapuya should not be encouraged because he could not possibly succeed in the hostile Catholic atmosphere prevalent in Spain. In Paris, Isidore Loeb joined the opposition; in his view, economic conditions in Spain suggested emigration, not immigration, and it was thus illogical to expect Jews to settle there without difficulties. The sympathy of the Spanish intelligentsia was not questioned, but their ability to control public opinion was. The entry of many Jews would cause public unrest, of which the chief victims would be the Jews themselves. Before Loeb's article could be published in the bulletin of the Alliance Israélite Universelle and in the Jewish press in western Europe, however, the first group of immigrants had arrived. Their appearance sealed the fate of Lapuya's plan.[27]

On April 16, 1887, Lapuya announced that thirteen Russian Jews, refugees from the Austrian border town of Brody, had suddenly reached Madrid, penniless and unskilled, and had approached the center for assistance. Their outward appearance was doubtless a far cry from the sartorial elegance, social graces, and superior skills he had envisioned. Lapuya offered to help them at his own expense—partly out of pity for their plight but also out of fear that these refugees would take to the streets of Madrid, causing his reputation irreparable damage. He appealed to the editors of the Jewish newspapers with whom he maintained contact, demanding that they expedite the establishment of local committees to support Spanish immigration and that they immediately provide him with sufficient funds to send the first group out of Spain and back where they came from. Before he received any answer, a second group of thirteen arrived, this time from Morocco. Dressed in common Moroccan garb, destitute, they too appealed to the center for aid. With the help of friends and neighbors, Lapuya managed to care for these two groups, but this was as far as he went. After June 1887, the Jewish press no longer carried news of his plan, and in December of that year Lapuya himself spoke of it in the past tense.[28]

The story of the Spanish Center for Jewish Immigration marked an instructive episode in the history of the relationship between Spain and the Jews. Its chief lesson was that liberals and moderate monarchists had shown sympathy and support for the idea of the return of the Jews to Spain—especially Jews of Spanish origin, who were wealthy and resembled the modern, progressively educated Spaniards. It also proved undeniably the force of popular opposition to Jewish immigration, which served to convince the Jews of western Europe that the renewal of the Jewish community in Spain was a hopeless venture.

No further plans to encourage Jewish immigration to Spain emerged in the following years,[29] but the tendency of liberals to discuss the academic and cultural aspects of Spain's position on the Jews was not eliminated entirely either. During the first two decades of the twentieth century, these efforts were linked with the name of another senator, Angel Pulido Fernandez.

Pulido's first encounter with Spanish Jews took place by accident at the beginning of the 1880s, and except for a brief description of the meeting in a liberal paper, it bore no further fruit. At that time, Pulido was just entering public life, a young doctor with little means and some political ambitions, but with no solid backing. Twenty years later, in 1903, after he had traveled throughout the Austro-Hungarian Empire and learned of the existence of large Sephardic communities in the Balkan lands and Turkey, he met a Sephardic Jewish teacher from Bucharest, Enrique Bejarano. Through discussions with him in Spanish and Ladino, Pulido decided to examine the conditions of Spanish Jews and to try to attract them to Spain. Upon his return home he began a propaganda campaign that quickly brought him fame as the apostle of Spanish Jewry.

This was not Pulido's only public struggle. As a doctor and a delegate to the Cortes, he struggled to introduce reforms for the care of the insane, fought against the public executions then still common in Spain, and tried to introduce substantial improvements in the health programs of which he was in charge between 1901 and 1902. His influence in all these areas was the result of his proximity to the seat of power after he took the advice of his mentor, Emilio Castelar, to abandon the Republican party and cross over to the ruling liberal Monarchist party of Sagasta. His personal connections with José Canalejas Méndez and Alvaro de Figueroa, conde de Romanones—both were leaders of the Liberal party and both had served as prime minister—assured him entry to the highest circles of Madrid politics. His candid personality and his quixotic character, his capacity to throw himself wholeheartedly into a cause in which he believed, assured him a wide audience for his ideas.[30]

Pulido's inspiration came from three sources. The first, theological, he drew from Emilio Castelar's famous speech during the 1869 debate on freedom of religion. A believing and practicing Christian, he did not blame modern Jewry for the crucifixion of Christ; he believed that Christianity is the religion of mercy and grace, which imply religious freedom, brotherhood, and equality for all. Pulido never wavered from this theme, just as he continually emphasized the fact that he was a Catholic and an orthodox Catholic at that. The second source of his inspiration was his admiration for the preservation of the Spanish language and the adherence to Spanish tradition and custom among the Sephardic Jews. The fierce expressions of loyalty he so often encountered in the letters and conversations of many of the Sephardic Jewish intellectuals with whom he came in contact left such a deep impression upon him that he tended to ignore the open declarations of others, who unabashedly and unhesitatingly proclaimed their alienation from Spain and emphasized their exclusively Jewish identity.[31] Pulido's third source of inspiration, and undoubtedly the most important of the three, was his patriotism. He estimated that at the beginning of the twentieth century there were, throughout the Balkans, the Middle East, and the New World, at least two million Jews who were exerting much influence in the commerce and politics of their countries. Recognizing them as members of the Spanish "race" who were forcibly exiled from Spain would provide Spain with new sources of trade, which could compensate at least partially for the loss of the last remnants of its empire in the New World and the Pacific. Moreover, Spain's efforts to expand its influence in Morocco, which increased at the beginning of the century and especially after 1907, would be enhanced significantly if Spain could enlist the sympathy of the Jews of North Africa.

The first step in Pulido's campaign was to publish a series of articles in a Madrid newspaper, all of which he then collected in a book titled *Los Israelítas españoles y el idioma castellano* (Spanish Jews and the Castilian Language), which he sent, accompanied by a questionnaire, to Jews throughout the Sephardic diaspora. He asked the recipients to write to him, in Ladino whenever possible, about the situation of their Sephardic community, the degree to which Spanish was spoken, what newspapers and journals were published there, and what cultural centers existed. The replies he received provided material for a second book, *Españoles sin patria y la raza sefardí* (Spaniards without a Homeland and the Sephardic Race). This voluminous publication, written quickly, presented the knowledge he had gathered about the Judeo-Spanish dispersion and advocated that Spain should attempt to adopt these communities and make them an integral part of its power. Pulido suggested that Spain should allocate funds to foster the teaching of Spanish in Jewish schools and cooperate with the Alliance Israélite Universelle, which ran a group of schools throughout the Near East; the Spanish government should establish contact with several of the most prominent Jews by awarding them decorations and by appointing local consuls and diplomatic representatives from members of Jewish communities; and the Academy of the Spanish Language, the Union of Writers and Actors, and the Union Ibero Americana (Spanish Cultural Relations Organization) should disseminate books, newspapers, and plays in Jewish cultural centers and encourage the Jewish Ladino press to abandon the Hebrew script and replace it with the Latin script. Further, the Spanish bureaus of commerce and industry should develop export lines with Jewish merchants and take advantage of their experience to improve productivity and commerce in Spain.

Pulido also suggested that the procedures for the naturalization of aliens—including Jews—should be simplified for those who wished and deserved it. He concerned himself with the return of the Jews to Spain only as a response to complaints that Spain was in danger of being flooded with Jews who would rush to replace Spaniards in key positions in the economy; he did not ignore the contention that this is precisely what happened in other countries, quoting the Spanish ambassador in Vienna on the causes of anti-Semitism in Austria. Still, because the success of Jews was rooted in the talents, diligence, and energy inherent in their nature, he regarded the entry of a limited number of Jews into Spain as an incentive for Spain's weak economy. If the entry of 15,000 to 25,000 Spanish Jews—including one or two thousand who were especially talented and who would take their proper place in society—led to an increase in productivity and exports and the expansion of Spain's political influence (which were Pulido's main objectives), then the country could only benefit. The competition and hostility that would result were far outweighed by the significance of the contributions of industrialists, bankers, philosophers, and even statesmen who would be among the newcomers.[32]

To achieve these ends, Pulido proposed the establishment of an organization in Spain "composed of people from all parties and persuasions but united by their love of homeland and human advancement." But like Lapuya, he started to act impulsively, eager for the organization to begin. Using his membership in the Academy for the Spanish Language, he demanded the appointment of a number of his Jewish acquaintances as honorary members and advisers to the Academy; his request was granted. As a member of the Cortes, he systematically exploited every opportunity to raise problems associated with Jews of Spanish origin. He continued to expound his ideas concerning Spanish-Jewish rapprochement in the press, and attempted through his connections with Jews in many lands—and especially in Spanish Morocco—to attract them to what he saw as their ancient homeland.

His efforts were successful among members of liberal circles in Madrid and in due course led to the establishment of organizations intended to promote his ideas. In 1910, the Alianza Hispano-Hebrea (Spanish-Hebrew Alliance) was created at the initiative of Carmen de Burgos, editor of the weekly *La Revista Crítica*. This apparently enjoyed the support of radical liberal Prime Minister Canalejas Méndez, as well as others. About two years later a new group was formed, which included such figures as historian Miguel Moryata, president of the League of Human Rights Luis Simarro, writer Rafael Cassinos Assens (a close aide of Pulido's who regarded himself as the scion of a Marrano family), some members of the Cortes, and a long list of journalists from *El País*, *El Mundo*, *El Liberal*, *El Mundo Latino*, and others.[33]

This atmosphere of goodwill created by Pulido and his friends was given concrete expression in 1913 when Abraham Shalom Yahuda, the noted Jewish scholar and Orientalist, was asked by the Spanish government to deliver a series of lectures on the Jewish contribution to Spanish thought and culture. In 1915, the government made plans to establish a chair of Rabbinical Language and Literature at the University of Madrid, in addition to the chair of Hebrew Language that had existed there since the sixteenth century, and to appoint Yahuda to this chair. Zionist leader Max Nordau, who as an Austrian citizen was forced to leave France during World War I and take up residence in Spain, called this event a "Spanish surprise." He considered the announcement of the creation of the chair tantamount to a royal decree, and the widespread publicity surrounding it was as good as a pronouncement abolishing the Edict of Expulsion, "because it is patently clear that the king of Spain cannot invite a Jew to perform official functions without thereby canceling the decree invoking the death penalty upon any Jew who dares to enter Spanish borders." Liberal newspapers responded similarly, especially those with which Pulido and Assens were associated. In Nordau's view, it was most significant that Fidel Fita, the venerable Jesuit priest who headed the Academy of History, was a most enthusiastic advocate of Yahuda's appointment; this proved that supporters of the Jewish cause could be found in Church circles too.[34]

During World War I, Spanish Judeophiles had an opportunity to express their sympathy for the fate of various groups of Sephardic Jews beyond Spain's borders. The state of war between the Ottoman Empire and the Allied powers transformed Jewish expatriates from Turkey living in France and Italy into enemy aliens. The only protection available to them was their association with a neutral country. A large group of Spanish intellectuals therefore sent moving letters to French and Italian leaders explaining the special attachment of Spain to Sephardic Jews of Turkish nationality, and stressed that these Jews regarded Spain as their homeland. It is not clear whether it was in response to this plea or for other reasons that the French and Italian governments chose not to treat most of the Turkish Sephardim inimically and so spared them the indignities imposed upon other enemy aliens. The letter of thanks sent to the prime minister of France in June 1916 was signed by such notables as writer Benito Pérez Galdós; honorary rector of the University of Madrid Gumersindo de Azcárate; historian Rafael Altamira; Republican party leader Melquíades Alvarez; Radical party leader Alejandro Lerroux; the president of Ateneo, the most important Spanish literary society, Rafael de Labra; its secretary, Manuel Azaña; and many other politicians and men of letters.[35]

It was more difficult to assist the Jews living in the Ottoman Empire, particularly Palestine, during World War I. For this the personal intervention of King Alfonso XIII was necessary.

Until America's entry into the war, U.S. Ambassador in Constantinople Henry Morgenthau dealt with all matters of aid provided to the Jewish community in Palestine. As it happened, Spain was one of the few neutral countries capable of rendering assistance to the Palestinian Jews, either directly in Constantinople or indirectly through the German Kaiser. In May 1917, rumors began to reach Spain that Jews were being expelled from Tel Aviv and Jaffa, that terrible cruelties were being perpetrated, and that there was great fear for their future. All this prompted Yahuda, acting under Nordau's advice and the support of Eduardo Dato e Iradier, leader of the Conservative party, to ask Alfonso to intervene.

Yahuda found no difficulty receiving an audience with the king, whom he begged to intercede for the beleaguered Palestinian Jews under the pretext of the many historical associations between Palestine's Sephardic Jews and Spain. "Your Majesty, please have regard for the thousands of Jews of Spanish origin who are in such dire straits and who address you in the same tongue that they have safeguarded for centuries," Yahuda implored. The king responded affirmatively, despite the fact that there was no legal precedent for intervention. Unlike other powers, Spain had made only limited use of its capitulations treaties with Turkey, which permitted the extension of judicial protection to aliens living in the Turkish Empire, including Jews; these treaties, signed in the eighteenth century, led to the formation of a small group of Spanish nationals who were immune from local Turkish jurisdiction. Moreover, the vying of France and Italy, both strongly Catholic states, threatened to undermine the guardianship of several Franciscan monasteries that Spain possessed in Palestine. Because of its neutrality in the war, Spain represented the Catholic interests of these states too, but the difficulties it experienced in protecting the Spanish properties in Palestine were only an indication of Spain's inability to exercise any real influence over the behavior of the Turkish authorities. For that reason, Alfonso appealed to his friend Kaiser Wilhelm rather than to the Turkish sultan. He sent a personal letter in which he expressed his anxiety and instructed the Spanish ambassadors in Vienna, Constantinople, and Berlin to convey his concern to their respective governments. Alfonso thereby added his voice to the vigorous demands being made at that time on other neutral countries and the world press to prevent what appeared to be a plan to eliminate the Jewish community in Palestine. Germany was forced to deny the rumors and even suggested that the king send a neutral commission of enquiry, led by a Spaniard, to examine the situation. In the meantime, the plans of Jemal Pasha, the head of the Turkish military administration in Palestine, were abandoned and the Jewish community was saved.[36]

Following the war, the movement to strengthen Spanish-Jewish relations attained greater momentum than at any previous time. In 1920 an organization was established, calling itself the Casa Universal de los Sefardís (Universal House of Sephardim), which intended to deal with all the matters Pulido had written and spoken about: fostering economic ties with the Sephardic diaspora, handling the political and legal problems of Sephardic Jews, maintaining close touch with the Jewish press, conducting a world census of Sephardic communities, and disseminating the Spanish language and literature. The Sephardic societies that had arisen among the Jewish communities in Spanish Morocco, which had already founded the

Federación de las Asociaciones Hispano-Hebreas in Madrid, joined this new organization and established contacts with Jewish personalities throughout the Sephardic diaspora. Ignacio Bauer, an active member of the organization and grandson of one of the richest and most prominent Jews in Spain, represented the Casa Universal at the conference of the International Federation of League of Nations Societies that met in Brussels in 1920; the conference noted the objectives of the organization and its willingness to support the struggle for Jewish rights everywhere.

The list of people who lent their support to the Casa Universal was most impressive, including almost all the leaders of the major political parties: Antonio Goicoechea and Antonio Maura, leaders of the Conservative party (the latter had served as prime minister); Conde de Romanones; Melquíades Alvarez; Alejandro Lerroux; Juan de la Cierva; and Niceto Alcalá Zamora, who would become president of the Second Republic. The organization was also supported by military figures such as Marques de la Viesca and commander of the navy Lopez de Perea, among others. There were parliamentarians spanning the political spectrum from the extreme left to the moderate right, and a long list of intellectuals, writers, and philosophers, some of whom had been active in previous times in support of the same cause. Manuel L. Ortega, the writer, was elected secretary of the organization; the Moroccan Jewish writer and journalist José de Farache served as president, and the elderly Pulido was elected honorary president.[37]

How effective were these efforts? There is no doubt that the ideas Pulido propounded as self-appointed apostle were later espoused by a very wide circle. It is equally apparent, however, that opposing forces were also at work in Spain.

Pulido's son Martin, who worked with him for a long time, tells of some of his father's experiences. Many people with whom he had associated before he began his campaign for the Jews drew away from him; all his Catholic friends failed to understand his enthusiasm for an alien race, and eventually began to suspect that Pulido must be of Jewish descent himself. His insistence that he was a faithful Catholic, the son of Catholics going back many generations, failed to dispel this suspicion, until his family had no choice but to live with it. According to Martin, the opposition to Pulido's struggles for the Jews caused his political career irreparable damage.[38]

The creation of the chair of Rabbinical Language and Literature and the appointment of Yahuda to that chair were strongly opposed, indicating the hostility toward Jews that pervaded Spain. "Some of the clergy's bulletins, expressing the worst kind of political and religious reaction, snapped at Yahuda like a pack of wild dogs," was how Max Nordau described the anti-Semitic reaction. Even though he tended to minimize its significance, Yahuda himself admitted that there was vehement resistance. Long after his appointment, the attacks and criticism against Yahuda persisted, and in 1920, despite the esteem he had earned, he was forced to resign. The minister of education and the university senate refused to accept the resignation, providing his supporters with an excuse to demonstrate their enthusiasm both for the chair and the man holding it. Yahuda eventually left the post, and no other Jewish professor was appointed in his place.[39]

The opposition to formal relations between Spain and Spanish Jews abroad had been expressed most forcibly a few years before in connection with certain events affecting the large Jewish community of the port city of Salonika, in Macedonia. Because that part of the Ottoman Empire was populated mainly by Christians, it served as the focus of struggles between Greece and Turkey and subsequently between Greece and Bulgaria and Serbia. The Jews of Salonika, who at the beginning of the twentieth century numbered about 80,000 out of a total population of 173,000, were generally loyal to Turkey, with whom they had been associated for hundreds of years, being somewhat in fear of the fanatic nationalism of the Greeks. In 1912, when the city was conquered by the Greeks, the Jews were exposed to the attacks of Greek civilians and soldiers alike, and many of them sought the protection of foreign consuls. On the face of it, here was an opportunity for Spain to invoke its capitulations treaties, extending protection to the large Jewish community that not only spoke the Spanish language but also imparted a strong Spanish influence to the city and its vital port. Unlike the consular officials of other countries, who made use of the extraterritorial rights that the treaties with Turkey conceded to them, the Spanish consul did not rush to exploit the advantages enjoyed by foreign states, and few Jews received his active protection. The hopes that others nurtured for Spanish protection after the fighting ceased and normal life was restored also were disappointed. One year later, Greece rescinded recognition of the rights of foreign powers to protect nationals in Macedonia, and the status of the Spanish nationals, as well as that of others, had to be resolved in a bilateral agreement with Spain. When the agreement was signed in April 1916, many of the new nationals discovered that the Spanish consul was most conservative in providing Spanish protection. Those who were affected by the consul's inaction then sent a special emissary to Spain to lay their petition before the central authorities. The emissary, Isaac Alcheh y Saporta, approached Angel Pulido and his friends in Madrid and made contact with the heads of the Foreign

Ministry and other authorities. Despite the warmth with which he was received and the fact that he was invited to lecture on "Spaniards without a Homeland in Salonika," Alcheh was forced to conclude that what had appeared to be the personally hostile position of the consul in Salonika originated in and was supported by the government in Madrid. The delay in acting on the petition of his group—which numbered no more than thirty families, and not the masses as some Jewish sympathizers in Madrid erroneously thought—demonstrated that the forces opposing the improvement of relationships with Spanish Jews were greater than those in favor.[40]

This conflict was particularly serious when Jewish communities directly dependent upon the goodwill of Spain were involved, such as the communities in Spanish Morocco. A desire to expand its influence in Morocco beyond the two small ports of Ceuta and Melilla, which had been under Spanish control for hundreds of years, drew Spain into many wars and much bloodshed without any real gain in territory. Only in 1907, when the representatives of the European powers met in Algeciras and agreed to divide the Moroccan kingdom into spheres of influence, was the way cleared for Spanish expansion in Morocco. In subsequent years, and as the result of changes in relationships between the powers, the towns of Tétouan, Larache, Alcazarquivir, Arcila, and their environs came at various times under Spanish control. Spain was forced, however, to share its influence with the other powers in Tangier, the large port city opposite Gibraltar, a city it long had wanted to control. Uprisings against Spanish rule—some the result of the competition between Spain and France—never ceased during this period. Consequently, events in Morocco were often the center of public attention, and they occupied a central role in the history of Spain in the twentieth century.

Ancient Jewish communities existed in Ceuta and Melilla; as they were considered part of Spain, the Jews were considered Spanish citizens by birth. About 19,000 Jews lived in the area of the Spanish Protectorate of Morocco and Tangier at the beginning of the twentieth century, about 10,000 in Tangier, and the rest were scattered in other towns. Most of them had come originally from Spain; they spoke Ladino and maintained various Spanish customs and traditions. Insofar as their legal status was concerned, they were citizens of the Sultanate of Morocco, which was represented by a caliph in the Spanish sector who governed by permission of the Spanish authorities. The Jews, like the other Moroccans, were politically subject to the Spanish high commissioner, the Spanish consuls, and the large army permanently located in the region. Spain's efforts to expand its influence in the area were welcomed by the Jewish community before it came under Spanish jurisdiction and of course even more so afterward.

Pulido and his associates sought to foster these hispanophile tendencies. Spain, they felt, should have made the Jews one of the foundations of its rule in the area. The Sephardic community was, in their view, an authentic offshoot of Spain that lent weight to the Spanish presence in Morocco and legitimized Spanish rule. Pulido and his friends thus expanded their contacts with prominent Jewish leaders in Morocco, and at their initiative Judeo-Spanish societies were established for the purpose of generating sympathy for Spain.[41]

This policy of encouraging the Moroccan Jews was supported by some of the Spanish local rulers but encountered opposition among others.[42] The principle objection was that this could lead to the estrangement of the local Moslem population, which would be angered by the fact that the Jews, who were of inferior status, suddenly enjoyed the favor of the Spanish authorities. The frequent wars and uprisings in Morocco forced the Spanish authorities to tread carefully, taking this objection into serious account. From time to time, the regime gave vent to outbreaks of hostility stemming from anti-Semitic impulses. In one instance, in 1920, there was a direct confrontation with Pulido and his group in Madrid, in which they emerged second best. The incident involved the Spanish consul in Tétouan—a post of great importance in the Spanish hierarchy in Morocco—who adopted a consistent policy of discrimination and persecution toward the Jewish community. The complaint of the Judeo-Spanish society came to Pulido's attention, who sought to intervene by publishing an article mildly critical of the consul. The military censor, however, suppressed the article, which only served to increase the consul's hostility. In February 1920, the representatives of all the societies in Morocco met with the heads of the Casa Universal in Madrid—and through them with the prime minister, the minister of the interior, and other officials—and voiced their complaints. The Jewish delegates were even received by King Alfonso, who was encouraging; they returned home with strong hopes that the consul would be transferred and the policy changed. To help his friends and enhance their prestige, Pulido decided to visit the Jewish community of Tétouan as head of a delegation of the Cortes. Members of the Sephardic societies began frantic preparations to make the visit a great success, until senior Spanish government officials intervened in open support of the consul and prevented the visit. Pulido protested vigorously, accusing those responsible of anti-Spanish sentiments and raising the matter during an audience with the king. Except for expressions of support for his activities, no further sentiments were expressed other than a warning to take the greatest possible care not to anger the Moslems of Morocco.[43]

The consul remained at his post for some time before being transferred, and there were further instances of discrimination against Jews in the protectorate. Pulido sent an anguished letter to the high commissioner in December 1922, protesting these actions and demanding redress.[44] His appeal came after Spanish Morocco had been shaken by a series of wars, one of which ended with a shameful and decisive defeat of the Spanish army, on July 21, 1921, undermining the very foundations of parliamentary rule in Spain. In September 1923 the army staged a coup d'état, led by General Miguel Primo de Rivera, and assumed authority with the king's consent, dissolving the Cortes and declaring a state of emergency. Spain was now a military dictatorship.

The support many Spanish leaders expressed for rapprochement with Jews of Spanish origin and the attendant activities of scholars and public figures were overshadowed during the days of the constitutional monarchy by forces hostile to the Jews and deeply rooted in the traditions of Spain. Those who raised their voices in support of the Jews, regardless of their civic prominence, influenced events but little. Spain did not undertake to disseminate its language and culture among the Jews, did not create the instruments to expand industrial and commercial relations with them, and did not encourage them to accept Spanish citizenship and tutelage. Nevertheless, during the first quarter of the twentieth century the emigration of Jews from Spanish Morocco increased, no doubt the result of the government's indifference. This in no way detracted from the commendable actions of dozens of citizens, including many journalists, who supported Spanish-Jewish rapprochement. Thanks to them, the subject was brought to the attention of the authorities, sometimes to the benefit of the Jews. One such outstanding occasion took place, paradoxically, at the time of Primo de Rivera's rule.

In 1923, Spain signed a peace treaty with Turkey, which brought the capitulations treaties to an end. In several states belonging to the Ottoman Empire, such as Greece, the question of the legal status of people under Spain's tutelage but without Spanish citizenship already had arisen, as has been shown, and had been resolved from the point of view of the states involved. Now, however, the situation was more complex and required a solution that would define the status of the nationals in terms of Spanish law. In theory, the Primo de Rivera government could disown all those not possessing Spanish citizenship in the Balkans, the Near East, and even in Latin American countries because, in the absence of certain rights that the capitulations treaties granted the protectors, these people likely would place an unnecessary burden on Spain. But the military regime did not behave this way.

On December 20, 1924, Primo de Rivera chose to grant citizenship to Spanish nationals, "not only in response to the repeated requests of those appearing before foreign governments as almost naturalized citizens and unable to remain in this uncertain status indefinitely, but also for the patriotic reason that these people, who generally know the Spanish language, will, after their naturalization, help to disseminate our language and cultural relations with distant lands, in which they constitute colonies that can bring real benefit to Spain." To effect this order without requiring the nationals to come to Spain to swear an oath of allegiance and register in the population registry, as required by the citizenship law, the military government allowed them to undergo the requisite formalities in the presence of a local Spanish consular representative. For this purpose they were put in a position similar to persons born in Spain of alien parents but who attained adulthood outside the country; if such persons wished to keep their Spanish citizenship, they had to appear before a Spanish consul to make the appropriate declarations. This special concession was to remain in effect for six years, until December 31, 1930. Thereafter, the citizenship option would terminate and with it any form of Spanish tutelage. The order, signed by General Antonio Magaz y Pers, acting president of the military government, introduced a royal decree with the force of law, signed by Alfonso XIII. Those who stood to benefit from the special regulations were defined as "people of Spanish origin who have been protected by the Spanish agents as if they were Spaniards." Each had to document his claim and background and provide proof of his good reputation. This was repeated in a letter sent by the Spanish Foreign Ministry to all its representatives abroad immediately after the issuance of the decree, in December 1924, and later in regulations of the Ministry of the Interior in May 1927.[45]

Although the order did not mention Jews specifically, there is no doubt that the military government was aware that a considerable number, and perhaps even the overwhelming majority, of those involved were Jews. The 1924 decree therefore must be regarded as an event of some significance in the history of Spanish-Jewish relations. In the absence of reliable documentation on the immediate circumstances that prompted the adoption of the order, it is difficult to make the proper attributions. Nevertheless, it is clear that the happy developments—identification of the interests of Jews under Spanish tutelage with the interests of Spain and provision of the option of obtaining Spanish citizenship from abroad— were consonant with the positions of members of the Casa Universal and Angel Pulido. It may be assumed that they and others were involved with these decisions.[46]

The royal decree, however, should not be regarded as granting Spanish citizenship to the Sephardic Jews indiscriminately and ubiquitously, as was claimed later by official sources and repeated even in knowledgeable publications, for the decree and its accompanying regulations deny such a possibility. Moreover, a thorough examination of the Spanish press of the period reveals no indication that any Spanish source gave this broad an interpretation to the policies of the military government. A similar investigation of the important Jewish journals in the West shows that they too attributed no great historical significance to the event. Indeed, the royal decree, even in its narrow interpretation, caused hardly a ripple.[47]

Be that as it may, the fact remains that the royal decree of 1924 created a legal opportunity for Jews enjoying Spanish tutelage to obtain citizenship and perhaps made it possible for others in extraordinary cases to receive Spanish protection.

The terminal date for eligible Jews to avail themselves of the decree's privileges was, as noted, December 31, 1930. In January of that year, however, the Primo de Rivera regime fell, and after a stormy transitional period, a Republican uprising forced Alfonso XIII into exile on April 14, 1931. Soon after, the Second Republic was formed and a new phase began in Spain's evolving attitude toward the Jews.

UNDER THE REPUBLIC

The political structure on which the constitutional monarchy was based had collapsed before Primo de Rivera assumed power in 1923. Because a military regime seemed to King Alfonso XIII the only means of saving his monarchy, he did nothing to defend the constitution. Many moderate Monarchists and Conservatives became Republicans, one of whom, Niceto Alcalá Zamora, was instrumental in effecting a compromise between the opponents of the military regime and the supporters of the Republic. The revolutionary committee he presided over included all political factions, from the moderate Republicans to the Socialists, as well as representatives from Catalonia who fought for local autonomy for their province. In April 1931, this committee became the provisional government of the Second Republic, and in June elections were held for the Cortes, in which the Republican and leftist parties won by an overwhelming majority.

The new constitution drafted by the Cortes addressed itself to the demands of these nonmonarchist parties. In the first article, Spain was defined as a "democratic Republic of workers belonging to all classes organized under a government of freedom and justice." Article 25 stated that all citizens are equal before the law and that the state will take no account of differences arising from birthright and nobility. Articles 8 through 22 granted the provinces the right of political autonomy. Articles 46 to 48 concerned the state's obligation to ensure a decent standard of living for workers, farmers, and fishermen, and to provide social, educational, and cultural benefits to all citizens equally. In articles 44 and 45, the state was made sovereign over all natural resources and art treasures in Spain, without regard for private ownership; these articles also gave the state the right to nationalize essential services and property and to take over the means of production for the good of the economy. All these stipulations were intended to win the support of the leftists—Anarchists and Socialists—who had formed a powerful force in Spain's politics since the beginning of the twentieth century and to appease the advocates of independence for Catalonia and other provinces.

One of the rallying points of the struggle for the constitution was the debate over the relationship between the Catholic church and the state, which was similar in many respects to the debate at the start of the First Republic in 1869. Now, however, it was characterized by leftist and Republican hostility directed against the power of the Church in Spain and its institutions and leaders. The strength of the Republican and leftist parties in the 1931 Cortes gave them the authority to legalize religious status, which had an effect on the status of the Jews in Spain.

Article 3 of the constitution declared that "the Spanish State has no official religion"; article 27 stated that "freedom of conscience and the right to maintain and worship any religion freely are assured on Spanish soil, save the respect owed to the demands of public morality. . . . No one will be forced to declare officially his religious beliefs. Religious affiliation will not determine civil or political status." These articles rescinded the prohibitions of the constitution of 1876, and the Jews—like the Protestants—were granted rights equal to the Catholics. But the drafters of the new constitution did not stop there: a series of additional articles undermined the Church's influence on the state and on the private lives of its citizens. Articles 70 and 87 prohibited priests and religious functionaries from holding the offices of prime minister and president of the Republic. Article 27 proclaimed the state sole arbiter in matrimonial affairs and personal legal matters, removed cemeteries from the control of churches, and legalized divorce. In article 48, education in Spain—which was mostly in the hands of the Church—was secularized and placed under government control, and religious denominations were permitted to teach their doctrines in their own institutions under government supervision.

Having removed from the Church its principal functions, Republican legislators next addressed themselves to the economic privileges enjoyed by the major Catholic orders and monasteries, a source of frequent public dissent during the period of the monarchy. Article 26 of the constitution stated that all Church institutions were subject to the law, and all privileges henceforth were revoked. Further, monastic orders whose members were required to pledge loyalty to authorities other than the state, or whose activities threatened the security of the state, would be disbanded and their property confiscated and turned over to welfare and educational agencies; the property of other orders was to be nationalized.

This attack upon the Church did not go unchallenged. Catholic President Alcalá Zamora, along with many other moderate Republicans, fought article 26 vehemently. Even after their opposition was overruled, the anticlerical articles in the constitution still remained the subject of fierce debate between moderate Republicans and the left, and had their effect on the Jews as well.

The article in the constitution concerning Spanish nationality also affected the Jews. Following an order issued by the new government, before the Cortes convened, special concessions were given to citizens of Latin America, Portugal, and Morocco, who were living as aliens in Spain and wished to acquire Spanish citizenship. Unlike others, who were required to live in Spain for ten years—or, in special cases, five years—before they could become citizens, these aliens needed no more than two years. Articles 23 and 24 in the constitution regarding citizenship legalized the order. Thus, the door was opened for some Jews, particularly from Spanish Morocco, to acquire citizenship in Spain more easily. Even more important was the promise contained in the same article of the constitution, according to which "a special law will lay down procedures that will facilitate persons of Spanish origin living abroad to acquire Spanish citizenship." In contrast to the Primo de Rivera decree, which concerned only Spanish nationals, this promise implied a significant increase in the number of Jews of Spanish descent likely to benefit from Spanish citizenship. It also canceled, in effect, the final date for handling citizenship requests determined in that decree. Even though this law was never passed, the promise alone was sufficient for some Jews in the Balkan lands to acquire Spanish tutelage.[48]

Under the new constitution, Jews enjoyed full legal equality; their existence in Spain was now apparently fully legitimate. But the political struggles that shook the Republic between 1931 and 1936 crippled the constitution and eventually caused its collapse.

The efforts of the Cortes to satisfy the Republicans did not succeed.

Immediately after the constitution was adopted, on December 2, 1931, it was criticized by both the right and the left. Moderate Republicans, under the leadership of Alejandro Lerroux, quit the government over a dispute on the Church's status, among other arguments, and Prime Minister Manuel Azaña formed another government with leftist support. The Socialists and Anarchists also criticized the constitution for its ambiguous articles on economic and social problems. The difficulty in implementing agrarian reform and other social advancements, on the one hand, and the serious fears aroused among Conservative circles, on the other, undermined the stability of the government. In September 1933 the government resigned, and in the November election the rightist forces (Conservatives and Monarchists) obtained 207 seats to the 99 seats of the extreme Republicans and leftists. The moderates, headed by Lerroux, won 167 seats in the Cortes and, holding a balance between the two camps, established a new coalition with the right.

Social and economic reforms were paralyzed, and special legislation was passed to restore to the Church the property that had been confiscated and to renew payments to the clergy. Provincial autonomy, the principal achievement of the Catalonians during the Azaña government, was also jeopardized. This gave rise to an armed revolt in Catalonia in October 1934, which was cruelly suppressed; as a result, provincial autonomy ceased. During the same month, the miners in Asturias revolted; their uprising was quelled, with much bloodshed, only after forces were sent from Morocco.

The end of 1935 marked four years since the new constitution had been established and the end of the moratorium on amending it. The intentions of the rightist parties to do so were no secret, which frightened the Republicans and leftists into establishing a unified Popular Front led by Azaña to protect the constitution. The weakening of democratic governments in Europe, the success of Fascism in Italy and Germany, and the Popular Front established that year in France—all these influenced the creation of the Popular Front in Spain. Basque and Catalonian nationalists, moderate and leftist Republicans, Socialists and Trotskyites joined this alliance, which also gained support from the Communists, Anarchists, and Syndicalists.

On February 16, 1936, elections were held, and the Popular Front won 256 of the 473 seats in the Cortes. The victory of the Popular Front signaled outbreaks of violence against the Catholic church and its institutions, and in many regions landless farmers began to implement agrarian reforms on their own. The Socialists and Communists, who together held 103 seats, did not join this new government, although they promised it parliamentary support. The newly formed leftist-Republican government was thus a minority, and its ability to control the violence of political factions was limited. Armed clashes took place in the streets of Madrid, Barcelona, and other cities among the followers of the Falange Española, the petty Fascist party, and Communists. Prestige, political status, and budgets of army officers had been curtailed drastically. Dissent spread and a conspiracy was being plotted.

In the months between February 16 and July 17, 1936, Spain underwent a series of political upheavals. President Alcalá Zamora was dismissed and replaced by Manuel Azaña. The government was beset by a wave of general and wildcat strikes, and incidents of arson aimed at churches, monasteries, and homes of the wealthy spread through many Spanish cities. Assassination and murder were daily occurrences. The government's inability to find a balance between opposing political forces prepared the field for an armed clash. On July 13, after the execution of José Calvo Sotelo, a prominent Conservative leader who had served as minister of finance under Primo de Rivera, the alarm was sounded. Four days later, the army revolted and civil war broke out.[49]

Many prominent figures of the Second Republic—President Alcalá Zamora, Prime Minister and former President Manuel Azaña, Prime Minister Alejandro Lerroux, and others—were sympathetic to Jewish interests. The intermittent political storms that beset the Republic did nothing to change this. Although the government's position on Jewish matters during the period of the Republic is still not fully documented, a number of incidents indicate a positive approach toward the Jews on the part of the Republican administrations.

In May 1933, during Azaña's regime, this sympathy was shown when the Council of the League of Nations heard a complaint registered by the Jews of Upper Silesia against Nazi Germany, which was at that time taking its first measures against the Jews. The Spanish delegate, Luis de Zulueta, supported the demands of the Silesian Jews and laws defending minorities in general. He stated:

> Spain, with that wisdom which was learned in the hard school of experience, today viewed with deep sympathy and to some extent with maternal interest those thousands of families who, in centuries past, had been obliged to leave Spanish territory, and who, in several countries and territories of the Levant, still spoke the Spanish tongue and carried on the traditions and preserved the memory of the country of their forefathers.

Another representative of Spain, the historian and writer Salvador de Madariaga, who was subsequently elected Rapporteur on Minorities of the Council of the League of Nations, also spoke out on the issue, observing that "Spain's attitude on that question had been dictated solely by her great respect and deep friendship for the German nation."[50]

The lesson from Spain's "hard school of experience" that Zulueta wished to teach the Nazis was repeated in another public event, sponsored and organized by the government, marking the 800th anniversary of the birth of Maimonides, in March 1935 in Córdoba. The celebration enjoyed the patronage of President Alcalá Zamora, who participated personally, and featured lectures on the character of Maimonides by Spanish men of letters and Jewish guests from abroad. A highlight of the occasion was the unveiling of a memorial plaque that read, "Spain, through the government of the Nation, expresses its homage to the immortal genius of Judaism. Córdoba, his native city, adores his memory." In official speeches by the mayor and the representatives of the local academy of science and art, the Republic sought to atone for the expulsion of the Jews from Spanish soil and warned that those European countries who expelled Jews would regret it, just as Spain had.[51]

Pro-Jewish sympathies were demonstrated again when Spain signed agreements with Egypt and Greece, in 1935 and 1936 respectively, guaranteeing that all Jewish families under Spanish tutelage would continue to enjoy this protection in the future.[52] During the time of the Second Republic, the number of Jews who availed themselves of this protection to settle in Spain increased.

While the government was demonstrating these pro-Jewish feelings, however, popular anti-Semitism was on the rise. Indeed, anti-Jewish feeling had been increasing ever since the 1880s, when the works of the French anti-Semite Edouard Drumont and others had begun to penetrate Spain. These soon found a receptive audience, and under their influence many anti-Semitic pamphlets were published in Spain at the end of the nineteenth century.[53] The enormous attention given in the 1920s to that infamous piece of literary bigotry, the *Protocols of the Elders of Zion*, further served to fuel the fires of anti-Semitism. Once the monarchy was abolished and the Republican challenge to the Church's power increased, Spaniards began to associate these political defeats with the "authentication" provided by the *Protocols*. Various tracts in the 1930s sought to prove that the establishment of the Second Republic was nothing but a Jewish plot planned well in advance and abetted by the Freemasons and Communism. "It is the intention of the Jews that this Republic—which they organized from the outside through the Freemasons and which they support and direct—is to reduce Spain to the state of slavery in which Russia finds itself today. . . . Because of Jewish influence, the shackles binding Catholicism will tighten to make life impossible for the Catholics"—so concludes a typical diatribe, with the added warning to readers that their children will be taught to hate Jesus and their property will be transferred to Jews, "as is the case in Russia."[54]

Fear that the fate that befell Russia "because of the Jews" would overtake Spain and the belief that all Jews openly or secretly supported Communism was underscored in several articles by Pío Baroja, one of the best-known Spanish writers at the turn of the century. According to Baroja, Jewish hostility to the social order in Europe and thirst for power account for the Jewish predilection for democracy, equality, and Communism. The Jews' desire to rule the world is proved, in Baroja's view, by the *Protocols*, "which, although their authorship is unknown, originate doubtless in circles associated with Jewry."[55]

The myth of the Jewish control of Spain was widespread among opponents of the Republic even before the Nazis rose to power in Germany. Anti-Semitism was fueled subsequently by propaganda and perhaps financial assistance from Germany. A Jewish journalist who visited Spain at the end of 1934 noted anti-Semitic articles in the press of rightist and conservative circles, Nazi books and pamphlets in bookstores, and the growing presence of Germans in Madrid. Another Jewish visitor in Spain at the beginning of 1935 reported that the Jewish issue had come to serve as a pretext for rightist opposition attacks on the government and that increased anti-Semitism was worrying the Jews. The "Jewish question," which had already emerged in election rhetoric at the end of 1933, became even more prominent in the stormy election held in February 1936. Pronouncements containing extreme anti-Semitic remarks, pasted on billboards in Madrid by the Falange party, prompted heads of the Jewish community to protest to the governor of Madrid and the prime minister and to request their intervention.[56] After the elections, the outbreaks of violence increased. The fact that much of the arson and looting was directed at the Church and its institutions and was related to the debate on the status of religion only heightened the friction between leftists and rightists, turning the military uprising of July 1936, at least in the eyes of its supporters, into a crusade. The "liberation of Spain" from the "Reds"— which was how the Nationalist rebels described their war—was aided by direct military aid from Fascist Italy and Nazi Germany. From the point of view of the Jews, two central motifs in the hostility emerged from this camp: traditional fanatical Catholicism and racist anti-Semitism.

The Civil War and the success of the Nationalists now began to threaten the Jewish presence that had developed in Spain.

THE JEWISH PRESENCE

A handful of French Jews—members of the Bayonne and Bordeaux communities who had lived in Madrid and some Spanish cities in the Bay of Biscay since the early nineteenth century—were the first Jews to settle permanently in modern Spain. In 1859, when Spain fought against Morocco and briefly conquered Tétouan, many Moroccan Jews fled. More than six hundred of them found refuge in Spain; they were brought in Spanish ships to Algeciras and Tarifa, where they were welcomed by the local authorities, given modest financial assistance by the Spanish government, and permitted to practice their religious customs. A year later, most of them returned to Morocco; those who chose to remain in Spain settled, for the greater part, in the coastal cities. Between 1869 and 1875, under the constitution of the First Republic, twenty-five Jews received Spanish citizenship. According to their names, most were of Spanish origin, having come to Spain from various North African towns.[57]

A census was taken in Spain in 1877 in which 406 people, scattered across twenty-one towns and villages, declared they were Jews—276 men and 130 women. The largest single group, comprising 125 men and 84 women, lived in the southern tip of Spain in the port of Cádiz. Few Jews lived in the large cities—31 in Madrid and only 21 in Barcelona;[58] their limited numbers precluded any organized Jewish communities in these two important cities. A visitor to Madrid in 1877 described the prayers on the eve of Yom Kippur in the community of German and French Jews he found there: 7 men and 5 women gathered in a private home, and as dusk descended each man in turn began to read the prayers in French. This was the manner in which the participants had prayed for many years. In 1886, a traveler passing through Madrid wrote that the Jews there lacked even the simplest needs of a synagogue—a Torah scroll, prayer books, and someone who could read Hebrew—and that prayers were conducted only on Yom Kippur. The Jews who came from Gibraltar, Tangier, and Tétouan thus would have to return to these communities for the High Holy Days.[59] It may be assumed that the permission granted in 1865 to the Jews of Madrid, at the request of the Consistoire Central in Paris, to establish a cemetery was never put into practice because there was no Jewish communal authority able to organize and maintain a cemetery.

Despite their small numbers, a few Madrid Jews enjoyed important economic status. Bankers, contractors of the railway line, members of the Pereire family, and the merchants of the Gommes, Benoit, Comondo, and Salcedo families from Bayonne and Bordeaux were already flourishing during the 1850s and 1860s, and the financial activities of the Weisweiller and especially the Bauer families from Austria (who represented the House of Rothschild in Spain) were well known. Some of these Jews integrated successfully into Spanish high society; the Bauer family home was particularly famous as the meeting place of politicians, philosophers, and even churchmen. The status of these wealthy Jews prompted Isidoro Lapuya to expect their support for his Spanish Center for Jewish Immigration; it may be assumed, however, that it was precisely because of this status that Lapuya found it difficult to convince the Jewish banker Alberto Salcedo to join the center.[60]

During the last two decades of the nineteenth century, the Jewish community of Spain increased little. The number of Jews from eastern Europe who were attracted to Spain by the news of Lapuya's and Rascón's programs was limited; in fact, it is very doubtful these programs had any effect upon the growth of the Jewish community. Nevertheless, Jews from North Africa continued to settle in the cities of the south. A traveler who visited Seville briefly in 1889 related that the Jewish families living there numbered a few dozen, that they had a ritual slaughterer and circumciser, and that they maintained regular prayers in a private home. Evidence of the crystallization of this small community, which was apparently the only organized Jewish community in Spain at the turn of the century, also emerges from the information acquired by Angel Pulido in 1904, when he was investigating the conditions of Spanish Jews throughout the world. The community amounted to about twenty families who had come originally from various towns in Morocco and especially from Tétouan. All the Jews of Seville lived in the same modest suburb, earning a livelihood from shoemaking, the jewelry trade, and the manufacture and sale of sweetmeats. They were headed by a rabbi, appointed from within the community, who attended to matters of charity and welfare and saw that no one went hungry. In 1904 the tiny community enthusiastically joined in the welcome that the city of Seville extended to King Alfonso XIII. The decorated balconies on which all the members of the community gathered to cheer the king included a placard written in Hebrew. A Seville newspaper, in describing the event, mentioned the names of seventy men and women of the Jewish community who had participated; the total number of Jews in Seville was probably not much more than that.[61]

In contrast to Seville, the number of Jews in Cádiz, and perhaps in other towns in the south of Spain, decreased. A. S. Yahuda stated accurately that when he came to Spain for the first time in September 1913, there was only one organized Jewish community, that of Seville. If Jewish communities in Spain had grown in other cities, including Madrid, from

1900 until the outbreak of World War I, this growth was not accompanied by the creation of any Jewish community organizations.[62]

This situation changed during World War I. Many Jews sought refuge in neutral Spain when they found themselves far from home at the outbreak of the war and were considered enemy citizens in their places of temporary residence. These included Turkish nationals living in France, to whom the special concession granted by the French government to Jews of Spanish origin did not apply; Russian Jews who did not wish to return to serve in the Czar's army; and Jews from the Austro-Hungarian Empire, who were also not eager to return. As the war continued, the desire of many of these refugee Jews to establish community associations in Spain increased, and they joined with those Spanish Jews with the same desire.

With Yahuda's assistance, and perhaps at his initiative, fifty-seven Madrid Jews organized themselves into the Judeo-Spanish Congregation. These included the banker Salcedo, in whose home the Yom Kippur prayers had been recited for many years; José de Farache, who later was appointed president of the Casa Universal; and the young Ignacio Bauer, grandson of the representative of the House of Rothschild in Spain, who became interested in Jewish community affairs for the first time. In addition, people from twenty countries in the East and West were represented in the budding Spanish Jewish community. The only Jews who remained aloof were those from Germany, whose patriotism prevented them from joining a community organization created by people who were citizens of or sympathetic to the Entente countries. After various interventions, permission was granted for the establishment of a non-Catholic religious organization. Facilities were rented on the second floor of an apartment house, and on February 3, 1917, members of the community gathered with their guests, including representatives of the local authorities and the British and French embassies, to celebrate the opening of the first synagogue in Madrid.

During the same time, the first synagogue in Barcelona was being established. Many Jews found refuge in this large port city close to the French border. According to one source, there were approximately one hundred Spanish Jews with Turkish citizenship and about fifty families from Russia. There were also a small number of German Jews, most of them wealthy, and a few persons from other western countries. In Barcelona a Centro de Sefarditas (Center for Spanish Jews) had already been established, but now some of the older residents, together with most of the temporary arrivals, set about establishing a permanent, official community. After permission had been granted, a large apartment was rented with space for a synagogue, a Hebrew school, and a clubhouse. The synagogue was dedicated at a ceremony in which the mayor and governor of Barcelona participated.

When the war ended, Spain had three organized Jewish communities—in Seville, Madrid, and Barcelona—able to serve as a framework for a proper and stable Jewish life.[63] A Zionist society called Yehuda Halevi, celebrating the first anniversary of the Balfour Declaration in November 1918, sent a delegation to extend greetings to the British ambassador in Madrid. In Barcelona a special committee was formed to offer aid to immigrants. In 1920, the Federación Sionista Hispanica (Spanish Zionist Federation) was formed and sent A. S. Yahuda, its representative, to participate in the Zionist conference that met in London; one year later, it became the Ibero-Moroccan Zionist Federation and was recognized officially by the Spanish authorities. The Spanish writer Manuel L. Ortega, who was active also in the Casa Universal, was elected general secretary.[64]

Unfortunately, these Jewish and Zionist activities soon lapsed. Many Jews who had lived in Spain temporarily during the war left soon after it ended. These included such important community organizers as A. S. Yahuda, who left Spain in 1921, and Max Nordau, who had left some time before. Economic and political developments that led to the establishment of Primo de Rivera's military dictatorship also affected the pace of immigration. The war in North Africa and the defeat that Spain suffered at the hands of the rebels might have been expected to influence many Jews to seek refuge in Madrid, but the size of this immigration and the arrival of a few Jews from Turkey was outpaced by Jewish emigration.

The decline of community activity was shown in the difficulties experienced by Barcelona's congregation—the largest in Spain—in balancing its small budget. In 1921–22, they collected and spent 17,000 pesetas; in 1922–23, this decreased to 15,000 pesetas; they anticipated an overdraft of 6,000–7,000 pesetas in 1923–24 in order to maintain the same level of expenditures. To cover this, the community appealed to the Jewish Colonization Association (JCA) for aid; because they maintained a school for thirty to forty pupils and helped immigrants, the JCA provided 3,000 pesetas.[65] Zionist activity in Barcelona and Madrid also declined. In 1920, 400 annual membership fees (shekels) were collected; in 1922–23 the Zionist Federation could not collect any. The income of the Keren Hayesod (Palestine Foundation Fund) in Spain was £518 between March 31, 1921, and March 31, 1929; this sum was less than the amount raised by the tiny Jewish community of Gibraltar.[66]

Efforts during the 1920s to stimulate Zionist activities in connection with the Jewish National Fund (JNF) reflect the inertia that afflicted the small Jewish community in Spain. For a few years, despite small contributions received in Jerusalem, there was no significant Spanish Zionist activity. Even when a Jew from Palestine who had settled in Barcelona was prepared to initiate activity, a long time passed because of the "complete disinterest here in anything to do with Judaism."[67] All Zionist activity in Madrid ceased; JNF boxes that had been distributed privately and in the synagogue lay idle for years, some of them filled with coins and never emptied. When the Second Republic was formed, the central office in Jerusalem thought that a "new era had begun for the small Jewish community of Spain" and that enthusiasm for Zionism would flourish. But these words, which were addressed to Ignacio Bauer, who as head of the Jewish community had shown some signs of interest in Zionism, arrived just when he, a Monarchist, was considering leaving Spain permanently.[68]

The establishment of the Second Republic did not cause any real change in the community lives of Spanish Jews. Stories concerning the preponderance of Jews in the Republican regime were nothing more than anti-Semitic myths, and those who were involved in the political struggle through the leftist parties were detached from Jewish life. The avowed willingness of the Republican government to attract the Sephardic diaspora to Spain did indeed strike a chord among some Greek Jews; several Jews from Salonika moved to Spain in 1932, but their number was small and insufficient to exert any real influence upon the Jewish communities of Spain. Eastern European Jewish immigrants who arrived in Spain during the first two years of the Second Republic made no real impact either.[69]

When Hitler took power at the beginning of 1933, Jewish refugees began arriving in Spain from Germany and Poland, changing the size of the Jewish community and its organizations. The need to assist refugees brought the JCA and the Hebrew Immigrant Aid Society (HIAS), through HICEM, their combined immigration association, to extend systematic aid to refugees in Spain. For this purpose official societies called Ezra were established in Barcelona and Madrid, receiving their total budget from HICEM. In the course of two years, until the beginning of 1935, the number of Jewish immigrants had reached 3,000, of whom 900 received aid. Most of these came to Barcelona, an industrialized port, expanding the Jewish community there. Relatively few settled in Madrid, and even fewer in other, smaller towns such as San Sebastián, Bilbao, Málaga, Valencia, Alicante, Seville, Granada, and Palma. Spanish legal restrictions concerning the work of aliens hindered the economic integration of the newcomers. According to a law passed on September 8, 1932, aliens working for wages were required to have a special annual work permit provided by the minister of labor; the granting of this permit depended upon the goodwill of the respective trade union. Because these aliens competed in the labor market, the authorities were generally loath to provide permits. Members of the free professions also could not work until they became citizens and had been reexamined in all areas of knowledge necessary for their profession. Commercial pursuits, however, were open to them. Thus, many of the refugees who had brought money with them turned to commerce, some of them introducing new methods in retail business hitherto unknown in Spain. Their increasing participation in trade and their competition with other commercial enterprises provided welcome material for anti-Semitic propagandists.

Increasing distress in Germany prompted the JCA to send a special emissary to Spain to examine the possibilities of resettling additional refugees there. His report discussed the many difficulties inherent in a mass immigration of Jews as a result of the tense political situation and the economic crisis. The report did not minimize the anti-Semitic propaganda and the basic organizational weakness of the immigration committee. Despite all these difficulties, the emissary recommended that fifty to one hundred families of artisans should be carefully screened and sent to Spain and that Ezra should assist them in establishing independent workshops. The recommendation was accepted, and in 1935 sixty immigrants were sent to Spain, most of them heads of families.[70]

Until July 1936, the Jewish population in Spain had increased steadily. In 1934, the number was 4,000, and during the two years following 2,000 more were added. Many of the arrivals refrained from emphasizing their Judaism; some of them even denied it and pretended to be Protestants or Catholics. Others, however, especially those who had been active in Jewish affairs in their former places of residence, brought new blood into existing organizations and helped to create new ones.[71]

In Madrid, where only 150 Jewish families lived in 1936, this revival was felt too little and too late. At the end of 1934, a Jewish journalist visiting Madrid reported that the tiny congregation numbered forty-five, the synagogue was still in a rented apartment and stood empty most days of the year, and the congregation had neither rabbi nor cantor nor the money to hire them. But there was some change in Zionist activity. Zionists from Germany reactivated the Jewish National Fund; a small band of forty women was organized by the wife of Ignacio Bauer and affiliated itself with the Women's International Zionist Organization (WIZO); attempts to distribute the Zionist shekel were renewed; and in April 1936 the Ibero-Moroccan Zionist Federation was revived. Federation president Bauer suggested that they apply the official sanction granted in 1921 to revive Zionist activity. Fifty to seventy Jews, most of them from Germany and central Europe, joined the Federation, whose program was to disseminate Zionist ideals, coordinate the various campaigns, and act on behalf of the Hebrew University and the National Library in Jerusalem. The Federation held weekly meetings and managed to publish a bulletin— until the military uprising in July 1936.[72]

In Barcelona, where the Jewish population was 5,000 in 1936, Jewish life was slightly more colorful. The congregation, established in 1918, numbered only 162 in 1936, and although Ashkenazic Jews were among its leaders, most of its members were Sephardic. It maintained for many years a small Hebrew school, where a couple from Palestine taught. There were prayers in the synagogue every day; the congregation employed a rabbi, Bechor Yitzhak Nahum, who came from Smyrna in 1930; and as the congregation expanded, the possibility of establishing a rabbinical court in Barcelona was discussed. In 1934 efforts were made to establish another congregation in Barcelona; a Hungarian rabbi who arrived in the city offered his services to the existing congregation, but he was rejected. Although the congregation maintained a charitable fund, its welfare activities on behalf of immigrants were transferred to Ezra by Jules Gerzon, a wealthy industrialist from Holland who was prominent in the community. There was also a small mutual aid association, Agudat Ahim, whose members were petty merchants, most of them Spanish Jews.[73]

The increase in the Jewish population in Barcelona and its great ethnic diversity intensified Zionist activity. A circle of women from Germany formed around Mrs. Gerzon and identified themselves as the local branch of WIZO. Ernst Necheles, a Zionist from Hamburg, began a drive for the Jewish National Fund in 1934, and within a short time he achieved results that the local veterans, who were more intimate with the Spanish Jewish community, had never approached. He also succeeded in stimulating other immigrants from Germany, both veterans and newcomers.[74] Another immigrant, Berlin journalist Walter Goldstein, arrived in Barcelona in 1935, intending to move from there to Palestine. He organized Zionist sympathizers among the German immigrants into a small Zionist group of about seventy members. A few of the younger members of this group formed a local cell of the pioneer Hehalutz movement and in 1936 launched a campaign in Barcelona to raise money to purchase a farm that would serve as a training ground prior to their emigration to Palestine; some wealthy German Jewish immigrants pledged financial aid. The Jüdischer Kulturbund, a leftist Jewish group organized in Barcelona and supported by leftist Catalonian elements, embraced the idea of establishing a Jewish autonomous region in the Soviet Union.[75]

Early in 1936, Joseph Fischer, the JNF representative in France, visited Barcelona to broaden Zionist efforts in Spain. At his suggestion, Jules Gerzon agreed to serve as the head of the JNF in Spain, assisted by Maurice Stern, a JNF official from France who served as general secretary and organized all Zionist activities. This was the first time a salaried worker was employed in Zionist activity in Spain, which stimulated hope regarding the amount of money anticipated from a healthy Zionist fund-raising campaign.

Maurice Stern, a thirty-one-year-old Transylvanian-born teacher, arrived in Spain in April 1936 and began working vigorously. He started Zionist youth groups, opened an office that also served as a youth club, made contact with all the existing groups in the city, called meetings, distributed JNF boxes to collect contributions, visited Madrid, kept in touch with a Zionist Actions Committee in Bilbao, and gathered information about the possibilities of Zionist activities in other cities. On June 6 he called a meeting of all Zionists in Barcelona in order to formulate a new organization for their activities. The Zionist Federation of Barcelona was established at that meeting, officers were elected, and the distribution of the shekel and educational activities began.[76]

It was at this time that preparations for the Popular Olympics, scheduled to take place in Barcelona in protest against the holding of the Olympic Games in Nazi Germany, reached a peak. Hapoel, the workers' sports organization in Palestine, was invited to the event, which was supported by anti-Nazi and leftist groups in many countries. This placed the Barcelona Zionists in a predicament: on the one hand, they feared that the leftist Jüdischer Kulturbund would adopt the delegation and thereby undermine the Zionist character of the Jewish community in Palestine, which the delegation was intended to represent; on the other hand, they were afraid that the identification of Jewish Palestine with the leftist forces that had organized the Popular Olympics might harm Zionist connections with other movements in Spain. Before they could resolve their dilemma, even before the Hapoel athletes arrived in Spain, the military revolted and the Popular Olympics were canceled.[77]

On the evening of July 17, 1936, the Spanish army staged an uprising against the government. Within a few days, the rebellion was successful in Andalusia and the western provinces of Spain, but it failed in the eastern and southern regions, especially Madrid and Barcelona. Spain now was divided between two hostile camps, and a cruel, bloody struggle began that was to last more than two and a half years. During this period the Jewish communities of Barcelona and Madrid, who were in the area held by the Republicans, suffered a different fate from those communities of

Spanish Morocco and Seville and the small pockets of Jews living in other Andalusian towns and the island of Majorca, all of which were in the hands of the Nationalists.

Havoc and fear reigned in Madrid and Barcelona in the wake of the rebellion. The government armed the urban proletariat and hastily organized a civilian militia to defend the regime. Armed workers helped to suppress the rebellion in the capital and in Catalonia. There was much confusion in these towns and in many others as armed forces began to pursue and execute supporters of the Fascist party, the Falange Española, and the thousands of monks and nuns who fell into their hands. "What characterizes these days," wrote an eyewitness in Barcelona four days after the revolt began, "is the number of churches that have been set on fire. It is true to say that not a single church remains in Barcelona. Opposite my house a church is still burning; the fire brigade is there—watching the fire and the smoke. They came to protect the adjacent houses. Friends telephone me to say that churches are burning in every suburb."[78] The chaos that suddenly beset the cities of Spain; the fighting between armed workers of different parties, who while supporting the government did not forget their own differences; the stories about confiscation of property and fear concerning collectivization of branches of the economy—all these cast terror into the hearts of the wealthy and the foreigners, many of whom fled in panic from Madrid and Barcelona.

Those fleeing included many rich Jews, some who had lived in Spain before 1933 and others who had arrived later, among them a few people active in Jewish organizations. Ignacio Bauer from Madrid was in Geneva participating in the founding conference of the World Jewish Congress when the revolt began; he did not hurry home. In view of the situation in Spain, he offered his services to the Zionists as a multilingual lecturer on Zionist matters, and for this purpose he traveled to Palestine, "for an extended visit to many places in Palestine to study its problems and institutions." The Gerzon family left Barcelona, as did the head of the local congregation and many other Spanish and German Jews. Maurice Stern, convinced that no Zionist activity would be possible for many months, also left Barcelona and returned to France. Thus in Madrid and Barcelona, the shaky Zionist organization that had just begun to function soon collapsed.[79]

The swift passage of events caused particular distress among the Jewish refugees from Germany who had been living in Spain only for a short time. Before they had managed to integrate socially, they were exposed to suspicion and hostility because of their German background, and the members of Ezra and the Jewish congregation who had not fled were obliged to come to their assistance. A cheap kitchen for the needy was established, according to one source, with the help of the authorities, and everything possible was done to help them leave Spain. HICEM organized and financed the evacuation of refugees, initially through Ezra, and later, when Ezra was disbanded, through a direct representative. Between July 1936 and April 1938, they helped 394 refugees leave Spain at a cost of £8,700. Many other Jews left Spain on their own. Some German Jews, both veterans and newcomers, even agreed to be assisted by the German consul, who arranged for the transportation of German citizens back to Germany. Despite promises that they would be treated no differently than Aryan Germans, upon their arrival in Germany they were given an ultimatum: leave the territory of the Third Reich within forty-eight hours or be imprisoned in concentration camps.[80]

Many Jews stayed in Spain. Most of these, originally from Turkey, were the poorest of the poor, eking out a living as peddlers, petty merchants, and artisans, unaware that their livelihoods were in jeopardy. The anti-Fascist policy of the government, its declarations of sympathy for the Jews, and its willingness to absorb additional refugees after the war secured their political status and their lack of financial means precluded any thoughts of emigration. Among these Jews, as well as among the German refugees who preferred to remain, were many who sided with the Republicans and even some who joined the leftist militias. But the continuing war diminished the size of the Jewish community in the area of the Republic and undermined its institutions. The Barcelona community persisted; despite the anticlerical atmosphere, the synagogue continued to function, and on occasion cattle were allocated for ritual slaughter. When the fighting on the outskirts of the city intensified, the community dispersed in fear of the shelling.[81]

The situation of the Jews living in areas under the control of the Nationalists, however, was very different. The small Jewish community of Seville found itself in an area dominated by General Gonzalo Queipo de Llano, commander of the Carabineros and one of the most outspoken anti-Semites of the rebel leadership. "Our fight is not a Spanish civil war, but a war for Western civilization against world Jewry," he declared in one of his radio broadcasts, which often included anti-Semitic tirades reminiscent of the Nazi press. In January 1938 he imposed a fine of 138,000 pesetas on the small Jewish community of Seville.[82] When these excesses aroused comment in the Western press, Franco's press officer issued a statement denying that the Spanish Nationalist movement was anti-Semitic. "I have been authorized to state that this is entirely untrue," he wrote to the *Jewish Chronicle.* "An anti-Jewish policy in Spain presumes the existence of a Jewish problem, which does not exist in this country. Besides, a mere glance at General Franco's speeches of October 1, 1936, and January 19, 1937, will show you that there is but one exclusion in the program of the New Spain—Bolshevism." But this denial hardly could obviate the fact of widespread suffering in the large Jewish communities under Nationalist control in Spanish Morocco. Moreover, the automatic identification of Bolsheviks with Jews that was current among uninhibited anti-Semites in the Nationalist camp and that appeared constantly in publications of the Falange Española, the party Franco adopted as his own, gave further lie to the denial. The Jewish press abroad continued to publish details of the Nazi presence in areas held by the Nationalists and reports of hostile acts regularly perpetrated against Jews living there.[83]

As to the general Jewish reaction to the Civil War in Spain—a subject outside the scope of this inquiry—suffice it to say that very few Jews anywhere felt open sympathy for the Nationalists, whose dominant elements blamed "international Jewry" for the Civil War and whose Nazi allies had declared open warfare on the Jewish people. Nevertheless, a certain restraint must be noted. For example, at the outset of the war Jewish religious functionaries in France held special prayers on Yom Kippur in memory of Catholic priests and nuns who had been murdered by the Republicans. The *Jewish Chronicle* of London, the official voice, so to speak, of British Jewry, for a long time refrained from taking a position in favor of either the Republicans or the Nationalists, and even its reaction to the bombing of Guernica was muted.[84] On the other hand, as is well known, many Jews, particularly of the left, rallied to the Republican cause. Indeed, such Jews—mainly Communists or members of the Socialist Bund, and coming from all countries—were prominent in the International Brigades that fought on the Republican side. In the course of the war their numbers reached from 3,000 to 5,000, roughly 10 percent of the 40,000 foreign volunteers.[85]

When the Nationalist forces gained the upper hand and the Republicans surrendered, Jewish supporters of the Republic felt that they too had suffered defeat. The thousands of Jews who remained in Spain were cut off from any contact with the rest of the Jewish world. From the point of view of the international Jewish organizations, Spain, in the wake of the Nationalist victory, once more became a land beyond the pale.

LIGHT AND SHADOWS

"It would be difficult to find a country in which clericalism is more rigidly inimical to all reasonable compromise with the Zeitgeist than contemporary Spain," wrote historian Salvador de Madariaga in his book on the Church and clericalism in nineteenth-century Spain.[86] This circumstance resulted in the growing polarization between religion and the state in Spain; the wars of the right and the left took on the aspects of a crusade. The special place that the Catholic religion assumed in the formation of Spain's national character from the days of the Catholic kings onward, the influence the Church wielded for hundreds of years, the Church's alliance with the existing social establishment while ignoring the severe social and economic problems of the masses—all these contributed to the severity and pervasiveness of the constitutional struggle. The question of religious freedom in Spain, in which the Jews (like other non-Catholics) were interested because of its affect on their legal status, was subsumed into larger matters of contention, such as the existence of Catholic orders and their educational activities. For this reason, the attainment of full Jewish emancipation in Spain depended upon the success of certain forces that tried to limit (or eliminate) the influence of the Church. As these forces never comprised the majority of the Spanish people even at the height of their power, their failure affected the status of the Jews in Spain.[87]

The relationship between Spain and the Jews in modern times was affected further by the memory of Jewish contributions to Spanish progress and advancement in the generations preceding Ferdinand and Isabella. This historic consciousness served to inspire a group of Spanish liberal intelligentsia whose views could not be ignored even by those negatively disposed to the Jews. Such Jewish "sympathizers" tended to regard the Sephardic diaspora in the Balkans, North Africa, and the Near East as a part of Spain itself and considered its members Spaniards of the Jewish faith who should be recompensed by Spain for the persecution of their forefathers and who, in turn, could bring to Spain economic and political advantage. The influence of this intelligentsia led Spain to adopt several measures that brought to its borders or under its protection limited numbers of Jews from various countries; it was not powerful enough, however, to force Spain to adopt a consistent policy of support for the Jews, even for Jews in areas under Spanish control.

The Jewish presence that developed in Spain during the period of the First and Second Republics thus bore the brunt of this prevailing inconsistency. In the beginning, its legal basis had the stamp of tolerance, but when full equality was achieved in the eyes of the law, the existence of Jews in Spain was based on contradictions that were difficult to ignore. Sympathy for the Jews, rooted in history, was not shared by most of Spanish society and was not shown toward Jews from eastern Europe. In everyday life, sympathy was overshadowed by traditional Catholic hostility encouraged by the Church and by political conservatives and deeply rooted in the prejudices of the masses. Aside from their normal legal status, Jews living in Spain had to adjust to the fact that the majority society was Catholic and that a permanent legitimacy of the existence of non-Catholics was doubtful. The tendency of many Jews who recently arrived in Spain to hide their Jewishness arose from this fact, which also hindered the creation of Jewish organizations. After decades of a tenuous Jewish presence in Spain, routine events, such as public prayers and marriages, were still described as if occurring for the first time since the expulsion.

During the final days of the Second Republic, the political powers that encouraged the establishment of a Jewish settlement in Spain were undermined. Polarization of views between the left and the right forced the moderates to choose sides; it may be assumed that some of those sympathetic to the Jews found their way to the Nationalist camp. The forces of clericalism and Fascism emerged triumphant, and Spain now found itself in league with the Axis. The skies of Europe darkened as another war loomed on the horizon. A critical period was about to unfold in the history of the relationship between Spain and the Jews. Its events would be determined by Spain's special position among the powers that were to vie for supremacy in World War II.

2

SPAIN AT THE START
OF WORLD WAR II

FROM GUERNICA TO OPERATION TORCH

As the world stood on the brink of international conflagration for a second time, Spain approached the end of perhaps the greatest tragedy in its history. On April 1, 1939, General Francisco Franco Bahamonde, commander of the Nationalist forces and head of state, announced the end of the Civil War, which had continued unabated for three years. On one side were the Nationalists, supported by the additional strength of the regular army, Moroccan fighting units, an Italian volunteer army, and units of the German Air Force. On the other side were the Republicans and the popular militia, which had been hastily mobilized and reinforced by international units of volunteers, the Communists most prominent among them. Each camp was composed of a very loose coalition of various political forces, often warring among themselves, but each fought with a doggedness that wreaked death and destruction. The Fascist states in Europe gave their full support to the Nationalists, but the democratic nations on which the Republicans relied maintained a policy of nonintervention. Paradoxically, this policy was initiated by the Popular Front, which was then in power in France.

The aerial bombings calculated to demoralize the civilian population (a form of warfare used for the first time in history), the political murders perpetrated by both sides that took the lives of tens of thousands, and the starvation caused by the wholesale destruction of supply sources and the burning of crops—all these severely crippled the civilian population. At least 170,000 were killed or wounded on the battlefield.[1] Even after the fighting ceased, blood continued to be shed. Galeazzo Ciano, Mussolini's foreign minister, who visited Spain in July 1939, spoke of nearly 200,000 Republicans interned in jails and concentration camps, of whom hundreds were executed daily in Barcelona and Madrid.[2] According to official figures, the number of prisoners in 1940 was 270,719; this decreased to 74,095 in 1944. Some prisoners were released, but many others, including leaders of the Republican and leftist parties, anarchists, and citizens who became unwitting victims of revenge and slander, were executed. The political murders committed during World War II that were disguised as executions following military tribunals were far more numerous than during the Civil War itself. Conservative estimates gave the number killed at 100,000.[3]

These executions and harsh police surveillance were intended to enable the Franco regime to suppress Republican partisanism. After the Civil War there remained in Spain three million Anarchists, Socialists, trade unionists, members of the various Republican parties, and former supporters of the Republic. Because these comprised one-third of Spain's economically active population, police terror aimed to break their morale. The Nationalist regime succeeded, not only through its oppressive measures, but also because those Republicans who engineered the revolt—and the factions that continued a guerilla war in the mountainous regions—were helpless against Franco's armies. The most striking proof of this was the treatment meted out to 300,000 Republican soldiers who fled to French soil after the fighting had subsided. Instead of aid, rehabilitation, or help in emigrating, these refugees were placed in concentration camps in which subhuman dietary and sanitary conditions prevailed. Thus, Spanish refugees were the first to inhabit the same detention camps in which not long afterward thousands of Jews would be imprisoned prior to their deportation to the death camps in eastern Europe.[4]

This oppression of Republican supporters, which continued in Spain during and after World War II, was necessary to the Nationalists because of the severe economic distress in which the country found itself after the Civil War. Half a million unemployed walked the streets. Agricultural production, the pride of Spain before the war, declined sharply. Industrial production, which had already been among the poorest in Europe, took almost ten years to return to even that low level. The reconstruction of private property, public buildings, railways, and highways required large financial support that could not be obtained internally, and the world war that followed in the wake of Spain's Civil War eliminated any chance of securing it externally. Consequently, controls were imposed on the importation of raw materials and on wages and prices. Shortages of food led to severe rationing, which created a flourishing black market. Large segments of the population went hungry. In May 1940, front-page headlines announced: "Soon the daily ration of bread for each inhabitant of Madrid will be increased to 250 grams."[5] Supplies increased during the course of the war, but at the end of 1943 an American visiting Spain testified that for many months there was practically no oil, butter, rice, or potatoes, and that the prices of the most basic foodstuffs, as well as coal and electricity, increased by almost 60 percent between 1939 and the end of 1942.[6]

During most of the 1940s Spain was a police state, torn and bleeding, with much of its national wealth destroyed and most of its population hungry. Throughout that period, and indeed until his death in 1975, its destiny was determined by one person, General Francisco Franco. Franco's rise to power among the Nationalists in the early days of the Civil War was neither the result of his political following nor of the military revolt he led. Throughout his career and before the revolt, Franco subordinated himself to civilian authority, often to his personal detriment. When the Republic was declared in 1931 and Manuel Azaña canceled the promotions granted by the previous Primo de Rivera regime, Franco's rank was also affected, but in August 1932 he would not support his colleagues who hatched a plot against the government. In May 1935, a coalition of rightist parties ruled the Republic, and Franco was appointed chief of the general staff; he was soon removed, however, when a coalition of leftist parties won the February 1936 election. Regardless of whether he tried to prevent this transfer of power, Franco again subjected himself to civilian authority and was exiled to the post of commander of the garrison on the Canary Islands.[7] Franco did not join the rebels until they were at the height of their preparations; his chief value to them was the prestige he enjoyed among the select units garrisoned in Morocco. Only after the revolt had begun was Franco appointed, on October 1, 1936, generalissimo and head of state. The deaths of generals José Sanjurjo and Emilio Mola, who were the principal instigators of the rebellion, left Franco in the position of sole leader.

From then on, he retained leadership mainly because the Nationalists were split into factions and needed a strong leader. The Nationalists included the Carlists (noted in Spanish history for their extreme reactionaryism, their Catholic fanaticism, and their loyalty to the descendants of Don Carlos), as well as other Monarchists, more moderate than the Carlists and still loyal to Alfonso XIII, who was deposed in 1931. Another division in the Nationalist camp was the Falange Española, composed of several smaller groups; their goals included Fascist national syndicalism, a revolution that would bring about social justice, and an economic system different from either capitalism or Communism. In addition to these were the remnants of the parties defeated in the 1936 elections, particularly the nonmonarchist Catholics and Conservatives and army personnel looking after their own interests. Under pressure from Franco and despite deep ideological differences, the Carlists and Falangists joined forces, forming a united political faction that Franco adopted as his own political base, although he no more intended to implement the social objectives contained in the Falangist platform than he intended to bring a Carlist candidate to the throne of Spain.[8] He was also careful to ensure that other Nationalist factions were properly represented in the government he formed and took great pains to guarantee that the internal balance of power would allow each group to neutralize the influence of the others.[9]

The support the Nationalist forces had received from Germany and Italy during the Civil War created a strong bond between Franco Spain and the Axis powers. The thousands of Italian and German airmen and soldiers who fought and died in Spain created a comradeship in arms and a debt of honor toward Hitler and Mussolini. Despite the basic differences between the Franco regime in Spain and those in Italy and Germany, there was much ideological affinity between the Falange Española and Fascism and Nazism; as the official party whose leader was head of state, the Falange left its mark on Spain. In any event, contempt for Republican ideals and Western democracy was shared by Franco and his Italian and German counterparts.

This was demonstrated in a series of agreements formulated prior to the outbreak of World War II. One agreement, signed with Mussolini on November 28, 1936, obliged Italy and Spain to coordinate their policies in the western Mediterranean and to refrain from siding with each other's enemies; it also provided for mutual, preferential rights in commerce and shipping. On March 20, 1937, a similar pact was signed with Germany, and a few months later the Nationalist regime undertook to pay back Germany in mining and quarrying rights for the equipment and aid it had provided. At the end of the Civil War, on March 31, 1939, another pact was signed with Germany, bringing the two countries together in political friendship and the development of close military, economic, and cultural ties; further, each side committed itself, in the event of war, to refrain from any act that would be detrimental to the other. Four days earlier, on March 27, Franco had secretly signed the Anti-Comintern Pact, linking Germany, Italy, and Japan against Communism, and on May 8 he announced Spain's departure from the League of Nations as a sign of solidarity with the Axis powers.[10]

At the start of World War II, Spain thus found itself closely bound to Nazi Germany. But the very cause that had created this association—the Civil War—made Spain reluctant to be dragged into another war. This became apparent in September 1938, during the Czechoslovakia crisis. General Franco hastened to inform England and France that in the event of war Spain would remain neutral. This step had not been coordinated with the Axis powers and left a bad impression on Germany and Italy. When the war began, Spain was true to its declaration. The evacuation of German and Italian forces from Spain had been completed the summer before, and bases that had been under their control in the Canary and Balearic islands and Morocco were handed back to the Spanish. Except for military officers and teams of technical advisers, when the war broke out there were no regular units of the Axis forces on Spanish soil; Spain's declaration of neutrality was welcomed by France and England. Italy, which had proclaimed nonbelligerence and not neutrality, was still out of the war, and Germany was preoccupied at that time in northern and eastern Europe. Hence, Spain's status in the war was of secondary importance. A new pact signed between Spain and Germany in December 1939 guaranteed Spain all possible advantages as a result of its policy of benevolent neutrality.[11]

The fall of France radically changed Spain's importance in Hitler's war plans. Had Franco declared war against England, it would have dealt a harsh blow to the morale of the British defenders, who would be faced with an extended front encompassing almost the whole of Europe. As a full member of the Axis, Spain would have placed its ports, as well as those of the Spanish islands in the Atlantic, at the disposal of the German navy, thereby contributing decisively toward the naval blockade against England and cutting off British supply lines. As a German ally, Spain would have helped overtake the British fortress on Gibraltar, thus securing for the Axis control of the entrance to the Mediterranean. From the bases in the Balearic Islands, the Axis in effect would have dominated the entire Mediterranean, and England would have been cut off from the British Empire in the Near East and India in the Far East. This isolation would have assured loyalty from Marshal Henri Pétain and his Vichy government; all the French colonies in Africa and the Near East under Pétain's control eventually also would have come under German rule. Furthermore, the Axis would have had exclusive access to the natural resources of Spain—its copper and tungsten mines—part of which was exported regularly to England.[12]

Entering the war on the side of Germany and Italy offered many advantages to the Nationalist regime in Spain, a fact not ignored by its leaders. A victory of the Axis powers undoubtedly would have contributed to the continuity of its rule, whereas an English success very well could have resulted in renewed attempts to restore the Republic. The pact signed in the summer of 1939 between Germany and the Soviet Union—Spain's great enemy—shocked Franco and his ministers. The Russo-German pact, however, did not preclude the possibility of an alliance with the Axis powers, an association that could have afforded Spain the opportunity to retake Gibraltar, a Spanish ambition since the colony's capture by England in 1704. The closing of the Strait of Gibraltar also would have enabled Spain to lay claim to French colonies in North Africa and to the Bay of Guinea, conditions Spain set forth as prerequisites for joining the Axis. Such a large expansion might have assuaged Spain's injured pride after the loss in 1898 of the remnants of its empire in the Caribbean (Cuba and Puerto Rico) and the Pacific (the Philippines).

But in the summer of 1940, in addition to these attractive possibilities, the Nationalist government was faced with the realities of hunger, death, and destruction in the wake of the Civil War. Spain desperately needed a period of rehabilitation and hardly could afford to become involved in another war. Moreover, Spain imported certain vital imports, such as wheat and oil, from the West, and unless alternative sources were assured, a declaration of war would have endangered the future of these supplies. The Franco regime thus was forced to seek the means of acquiring the advantages that entering the war would have provided without risking the dangers such a move inevitably would have entailed.

The first step in this direction was the announcement on June 12, 1940, that Spain was changing from a position of neutrality to one of nonbelligerence. Two days later, on June 14, Spanish forces occupied the North African city of Tangier, which had been under the joint protectorate of England, France, Italy, and Spain since 1928, on the pretext that warring powers could not share the same jurisdiction. Regardless of the pretext, the Spanish populace was told that this heralded the realization of Spain's dream of expanding its empire. In November, Spain replaced the existing administration in Tangier with an exclusively Spanish one.

In June 1940, Spain formulated for the first time conditions under which it would be prepared to join with Italy and Germany, done apparently without pressure from the Axis powers. These conditions now became the subject of intense negotiations during August and September and were discussed at a meeting between Hitler and Franco in the border town of Hendaye on October 23. Spain consistently made three demands:

French colonies, modern military equipment, and oil and food supplies.[13] Only after Germany and Italy had accepted these demands and had begun to supply goods and equipment would Spain enter the war. Every effort by Hitler and Mussolini, including personal appeals to reduce Spain's demands or delay their implementation until after war had been declared on England, failed to move Franco. Whenever the subject was discussed, Franco missed no opportunity to express his loyalty to his colleagues and the Axis countries. On several occasions he went so far as to say that his forces were preparing for the anticipated attack upon Gibraltar, always emphasizing that Spain could not be expected to act until its demands were met. These expressions of support accurately reflected Franco's attitude toward Germany and Italy and his absolute faith in their final victory, but his steadfast conditions demonstrated his disinclination to enter the war and his desire to hold this option until the moment the balance was tilted unequivocally. Franco did not risk much. When the blitz over London failed to accomplish its purpose, and as Germany's ability to invade England weakened, the Nazi strategy now turned to an effort to paralyze Britain's vital supply lines. This fact, aggravated by Mussolini's failures in Greece, only served to prolong Franco's hesitation.

In November 1940, Hitler applied every coercion at his disposal upon Spain. German batallions began to train in the Jura mountains for the assault on Gibraltar, and a delegation of officers was sent to Spain to conduct observation sorties in the areas adjacent to the fortress. The Spanish foreign minister was called to Germany and action was demanded of him; he was warned that Germany knew how to deal with unfaithful allies. In December, Franco was informed by Nazi head of intelligence Wilhelm Canaris that Hitler ordered an invasion by German units to take place in January 1941. Franco refused, and in February, Hitler sent him a letter promising to accommodate Franco's requirements, to compensate him for any damage done, and to accede to his territorial demands after the war. But Franco stood firm, claiming that Spain was not yet ready. In the meantime, the entanglement in Greece forced Hitler to reassign the troops originally intended for Gibraltar. Germany's intensified preparations for the invasion of Russia soon reduced the Gibraltar episode—and Spain's entry into the war—to a matter of secondary importance.

During the discussions concerning Gibraltar, it was proposed that Germany undertake the conquest without Franco's consent and then invade Spain. Because the presence of the German army at the Spanish border made this idea conceivable, Spain had to consider it a possibility. But the Germans themselves shelved any notion of taking Spain by force, knowing full well that such action would encounter opposition and that a

German victory would not prevent a long guerilla struggle. The Germans had not forgotten Napoleon's failure to overcome irregular resistance in conquered Spain, nor were the Spanish oblivious to the historical precedent. For this reason Spain was able to adopt a fiercely independent position, although vital German interests were at stake, at a time when German power was at its height.

The German invasion of Russia temporarily eased the pressure on Spain to enter the war. Franco now chose to depart from his position of nonbelligerence. From the moment of the invasion, he informed British Ambassador Sir Samuel Hoare, the war was no longer one conflict but two, and although Spain continued to regard itself as a nonbelligerent against the West, it was a full partner in the war of the Axis powers against Russia.[14] In this way, Spain hoped to avenge Russia for the aid it had given the Republicans and to participate in the destruction of what it perceived as its greatest enemy—Communism.

Spain mobilized a division of volunteers to fight in Russia; the mobilization was so swift it may have been that many of the volunteers were inducted by force. By the middle of July 1941, the Blue Division (La División Azul) was on its way. The Spanish soldiers underwent a short period of training in Germany, received German uniforms to which they affixed the insignia of Spain, and swore allegiance to the Nazi Führer for whom they set out to do battle.

On August 21, 1941, two months after the attack on Russia, all preparations had been completed, and the Blue Division left for the front. "What prompted the German command to order the division to march nearly one thousand kilometers on foot was not clear then and is still unclear to this day," wrote General Emilio Esteban Infantes, the commander of the division and its historian. The division reached the front on October 14, relieving German units on the northern sector of the line between Lake Ilmen and Leningrad.[15] The Spanish soldiers, accustomed to the moderate climate of the Iberian peninsula, were quickly exposed to the full force of the Russian winter, as well as to Russian counterattacks. During the course of three winters and two summers in the same area, the Blue Division participated in heavy fighting that took a high toll and resulted in no significant territorial change. By December 1943, when it returned to Spain, the division, which had originally numbered 17,000, listed 12,726 of its men killed, wounded, or missing. In order to fill the ranks, Spain continued to send volunteers to the front; the numbers eventually reached a total of 47,000. Even after the division was returned to Spain, a legion of volunteers remained at the Russian front. This unit, known as the Spanish Legion, was composed of 2,133 men, who continued to fight until the northern front collapsed in the spring of 1944. In addition to these divisions, a small Spanish squadron participated in the fighting, and some Spanish volunteers served in the German SS.[16]

The longer the war against Russia continued and the more Spain's involvement deepened, the less Franco was inclined to waver from the position of nonbelligerence he had adopted toward the Allied powers. Germany, which had postponed the conquest of Gibraltar until victory in the East had been attained, could no longer pressure Spain to alter its position, because Germany's ability to satisfy Spain's requirements was rapidly declining. For this reason, the question of Spain's entry into the war became more remote during the latter part of 1941 and most of 1942, although Allied political and military strategy considered it a possibility. This situation changed drastically in 1942.

THE END OF THE BEGINNING

German successes on the Russian front forced the Soviet Union to demand that England and the United States attack Nazi Germany to open a second front. In the spring of 1942, the Allies discussed various plans of action and offered two proposals: invade France to create a bridgehead in the northwestern sector or invade North Africa and take over Algeria, Morocco, and Tunisia. On July 24, 1942, it was decided to invade North Africa. The plan was for American forces to land simultaneously at Casablanca on the Atlantic, at Oran on the Mediterranean, and at the coastal cities of Tunisia. The conquest of the large French colonies in North Africa would result in Rommel's defeat (he was in Al-Alamein, threatening the Suez Canal) and would also alleviate considerably the Allied problem of shipping in the Mediterranean. The entire campaign, called Operation Torch and entrusted to General Dwight Eisenhower, hinged on one assumption: that the Allies would be able to use Gibraltar as their principal base of support. This depended, of course, on the continued nonbelligerence of Spain.

The great secrecy that shrouded the preparations, the subterfuges, and the camouflage was intended to prevent disclosing the real intention of the forces amassing in the small bay at the foot of Gibraltar. Intensified fighting around the convoys to Malta created the impression that the Allies were merely sending reinforcements to that small Mediterranean island. But as the critical time approached—the night of November 7, 1942—fear of Spain's hostility increased. "Spain's entry [into the war] instantly would entail the loss of Gibraltar as a landing field and would prevent our use of the Strait of Gibraltar until effective action could be taken by the Allies. In view of available resources, it would appear doubtful that such effective action is within our capabilities," wrote General Eisenhower in one of his reports seven weeks before the landing. Fears arose not only from the possibility that the whole campaign might be nipped in the bud but also from the fact that Spain, or German forces permitted to attack from Spain, would intervene in the war and inflict a decisive naval and land defeat against the Allies.[17]

Luckily, the subterfuges and secrecy suceeded. Operation Torch completely surprised both Germany and Spain. At 1 A.M. on November 8, 1942, American Ambassador Carlton Hayes awakened the Spanish foreign minister and asked him to contact General Franco immediately to arrange a meeting. The awestruck foreign minister called the palace, and the following morning Hayes presented himself to Franco and handed him a personal letter from President Roosevelt. The letter stated that the Allies promised not to infringe upon the sovereignty of Spain or its territories in North Africa. A similar letter was presented by British Ambassador Sir Samuel Hoare to the Spanish foreign minister. That day the cabinet met; representatives of the Falange and the army demanded that they intervene in the war before the Allies succeeded in consolidating their hold on Morocco and Algiers. Franco, however, preferred to bide his time until the situation cleared. When it became apparent that the invasion of North Africa had succeeded, any thought of intervention was shelved.

The Spanish government resisted all attempts to infringe upon its sovereignty, a political decision that was aimed more at the Germans— who on November 11, 1942, overran unoccupied France and widened the boundary with Spain to the coast of the Mediterranean—than at the Allies. Indeed, as long as the campaign in North Africa continued into the winter of 1942–43, the danger existed that Germany would attempt to alter the situation by a counterattack in northwest Africa and, in the course of this effort, would attack Spain. Even as the chances of repelling the Allies in North Africa lessened, suggestions to invade Spain—or at least portions of it—continued to be raised, but Hitler rejected them all. The fear of becoming involved in a drawn-out war in the Iberian peninsula over-shadowed every other consideration.[18]

Spain's new geopolitical position enabled the Allies to extend their influence. Spain's import of essential commodities had been dependent, from the beginning of the war, upon the West. The blockade of Europe by the British fleet required every ship to carry Allied navicerts (navigation certificates), which continually underscored the dependence of Spanish vessels on the goodwill of the Allies. At the beginning of the war, the grain supply—of which Spain required a million tons each year—and especially the oil supply served as a political lever to keep Spain from joining the Axis. During the latter stages of the war, the Allies exercised their economic influence to gain additional advantage over Spain. So, for example, when in April 1943 the Iberian national airline was grounded because of lack of fuel, the United States after some hesitation agreed to provide Spain with 320 tons of aircraft fuel each month in exchange for supervision of the passenger list on the Madrid-Tangier run; this made it difficult for German agents in North Africa to use the airline.[19]

The struggle for the purchase of strategic materials from Spain, especially the tungsten required for the production of forged steel, was another example of Allied influence. The United States and England sought to prevent Germany from buying these materials in the Spanish market, so they offered double and even triple Spain's asking price. Because the Allies set a high price on the products they were selling to Spain—the United States took twice the normal market price for oil— they had large reserves of Spanish currency that Germany, with its nega- tive balance of trade with Spain, could not match. This competition between the powers brought tremendous profits to the mineowners, traders, entrepreneurs, and smugglers and provided employment to many workers. The Spanish treasury, which imposed heavy duties on exports, also benefited. But as the Allies did not need Spain's tungsten, the com- petition proved burdensome; they began to pressure Spain by cutting off its oil supply to force an embargo on the export of tungsten. Although this measure hurt Spain's economy, it succeeded in reducing drastically the number of export permits Spain provided the Germans.[20]

This measure was accompanied by others no less important: the withdrawal of the Blue Division from the Russian front; the freeing of Italian cargo boats captured by the Spanish after the surrender of the Pietro Badoglio government; the promise to close the German consulate in Tangier, as it served as an important base for German agents in North Africa; and the promise to expel German agents from Spain. The fulfill- ment of these promises was the subject of many diplomatic notes and protests by the British and American ambassadors in Madrid, but the fact that they were made at all is evidence of the Allied ability to impose demands upon the Spanish government.

The change that occurred in Spain's position in the war was given clear political expression by Franco himself on October 1, 1943, the Day of the Leader. Dressed in army uniform and not in the costume of the Falange Española, in a speech to the members of the diplomatic corps Franco defined Spain's position as neutral; he did not return to the term "nonbelligerent," which was how Spain had described itself since June 12, 1940.[21] The emphasis clearly was to indicate the weaning of Spain from the Axis just when German interest in Spain had become most vital.

In addition to strategic materials such as wool, hides, furs, and especially tungsten—produced by Spain and required by Germany because they were available only from sources on the European continent—Germany had enjoyed many services that only Spain could supply. Ambassador Hoare mentioned some of these services when he complained, in a detailed letter of protest, of Spain's divergence from the policy of neutrality. Spain's long and broken shores on the Mediterranean and the Bay of Biscay and the many ports stretching along them served Germany in the naval war. German submarines found shelter there, and maintenance teams were permitted to make repairs; oil and supply vessels anchored in Spanish coastal waters and served as bases for German ships and submarines in the Atlantic and the Mediterranean; observation points on the Spanish coast followed naval movements in the Strait of Gibraltar. The Axis air forces flew undisturbed in the skies over Spain on their way to sorties against the Allies, and crews forced to land in Spain were returned without let or hindrance to Germany. Furthermore, the German secret service had complete freedom of action; many espionage and counter-espionage agents operated in Spain with the obvious cooperation of the Spanish security forces. This was confirmed by Walter Schellenberg, chief of German counterespionage, who claimed that in the German Embassy seventy to one hundred people enjoyed full diplomatic immunity while engaging in espionage and broadcasting. The more the Allies succeeded on the battlefield, the more important were these intelligence bases in Spain, and the Germans asked and received permission for them to continue operating until the end of the war. Germany also exercised influence on the news media in Spain and on the branches of internal security, which received professional guidance from the Gestapo. Close ties with Germany were voiced and perhaps solidified during Himmler's visit to Spain in 1940. The significance of Spain's relationship with the Nazis is illustrated by the fact that they could arrest on Spanish soil and deport to Germany anyone they wished.[22]

This manifold network of vital German interests obviously depended on the compliance of elements in the Spanish leadership. The army representatives in the government, who had designs on German military equipment, tried to ensure that the provision of these supplies would not be interrupted. Representatives of the Falange (and particularly Franco's brother-in-law Ramón Serrano Suñer, who supported Fascist ideology) were antagonistic toward the West and based their hopes on an Axis victory. Their control of the Interior Ministry and the press, and for a long time the Foreign Ministry as well, assured Germany of the same advantages it had enjoyed previously. In contrast, the friends of the Allies in the Spanish government were very few at the beginning of the war; their numbers did not change much as it progressed. During the second half of the war, however, the post of foreign minister was held by a fierce opponent of Axis influence in Spain—Count Francisco Gómez Jordana y Sousa.

Jordana's appointment on September 3, 1942, followed one of the more serious clashes between the diverse political elements that comprised the regime: a bomb thrown at Minister of War Varela Iglesias, a Carlist, wounded many of his entourage, and subsequent investigation revealed that the assassins were members of the Falange. When Serrano Suñer's enemies succeeded in connecting him with the assassins, tension mounted between the Carlists and the Falange. In order to cool tempers without disturbing the balance of power, Franco fired Serrano Suñer and Varela Iglesias and appointed General Carlos Asensio, a Falangist and Nazi sympathizer, as minister of war, and Jordana, a Carlist, as foreign minister. Because Franco assumed the leadership of the Falange himself, Serrano Suñer in effect was removed from public office.[23] These changes, which were intended to maintain the internal balance of power, were extremely significant in terms of foreign policy. For whether Serrano Suñer really tried to hitch Spain to the Axis bandwagon, as British Ambassador Hoare believed, or whether his sympathy for Germany was only a ruse, as Vichy Ambassador François Piétri believed and as Serrano Suñer himself attested, it was understood that he was a friend of the Germans.[24] Jordana, on the other hand, was agreed generally to be pro-West: his attitude was clearly manifested in the two years he served as foreign minister until his death in San Sebastián on August 3, 1944. At the most critical moment in the relations between the Allies and Spain—during Operation Torch—and throughout most of the latter part of the war, the Allies found an attentive ear in the Spanish cabinet.

The more defeats Germany suffered, the more prevalent became the position adopted by Foreign Minister Jordana. Even though he did not succeed in implementing the agreements he signed with the Allies, Jordana was able, with Franco's support, to adopt a more aggressive line toward Germany. Even after Jordana died and was replaced by José Félix Lequerica (an Axis sympathizer who as Spanish ambassador to Vichy had played an active part in mediating between Hitler and Pétain when France surrendered), Spain would not alter its policy. When the south of France was liberated and the territorial contiguity of Spain and Nazi Germany was broken, public opinion in England and the United States demanded that Franco be regarded an ally of Hitler's; Franco then had to face the possibility that these demands would prompt the Allies to attempt to overthrow his regime. One way to forestall a takeover was to make obvious gestures of goodwill toward the Allies. Nazi interest in Spain as an eventual place of refuge could present Franco with the means of extracting concessions from the Germans—and saving Jews could be one of those concessions.[25]

THE POTENTIAL FOR RESCUE

The economic and political situation in Spain during World War II and its status vis-à-vis the Axis and the Allies were decisive in determining Spain's capacity to offer refuge to Jews. Hunger, rationing, and the destruction wrought by the Civil War were factors limiting Spain's ability to absorb large numbers of immigrants over a long period of time. Internal struggles and the suppression of Republicans that resulted in the imprisonment of tens of thousands of Spaniards normally would have made refugees suspect and prevented them from finding permanent residences and moving about unrestricted. As general conditions improved, however, especially during the latter stages of the war, these difficulties decreased and the potential for absorbing the victims of Nazism increased.

Spain's relationship with Nazi Germany throughout the war was not that of a vassal showing fealty to his lord. Even when the Germans threatened Spain with force, Franco succeeded in maintaining his independence. Later, when the military threat from Germany diminished and then vanished altogether, Franco's independent status was strengthened and his ability to extract concessions enhanced. This undoubtedly fostered Spain's power to aid in the rescue of Jews. Moreover, as Allied influence over Spain grew, Spain was forced from time to time to make concessions that would restore its neutral status. Under these conditions it was possible for the Allies to encourage Spain to act to save Jewish lives.

Two widely held beliefs might have reinforced Spain's ability to undertake Jewish rescue. One concerned the supposed Jewish origins of Franco, which for the Germans would have made Spanish intervention on behalf of the Jews understandable. The other concerned Jewish influence in the West, which was fanned by German propaganda. As the Allies gained the upper hand, Spain, eager to curry favor, for that reason could have sought to provide assistance to Jews wherever asked to do so.[26]

This condition was particularly important as Nazi Germany stepped up its war against the Jewish people. The Holocaust machinery was put into high gear in the summer of 1942. From then on, the annihilation of all Jews in the countries under Nazi occupation became Germany's only means to achieve what it termed "the final solution to the Jewish problem." Thus, in contrast to the "end of the beginning" of World War II that started in November 1942 with Operation Torch, the process of the destruction of the Jewish people signaled the "beginning of the end" by July 1942. This gap between the course of the Allies' war against Hitler and Hitler's war against the Jews—a gap that was never bridged—was crucial in the perspective of the Holocaust. The progress of the war and the world political situation created circumstances whereby during the most critical stage of the Holocaust Spain's capacity to rescue Jews was at its greatest.

3

TRANSIT AND PATRONAGE

JEWS IN NATIONALIST SPAIN

At the height of the Civil War, the Nationalist government took measures
to rescind Republican legislation concerning religious affairs. On March
12, 1938, all civil marriages, past and present, were annulled, and divorce
was outlawed. Regulations restored legal status to Spanish Jesuits, removed limitations on other orders, and returned to Church institutions
the economic privileges—such as salaries for the clergy that were paid out
of the treasury—they had enjoyed before the Second Republic. These
enactments were intended, in the words of one law, "to repeal secular
legislation and thereby restore to our laws their traditional significance,
which is Catholic."[1]

The Franco regime repealed the 1931 Republican constitution but
did not restore the 1876 Monarchist constitution or its article guaranteeing religious tolerance to non-Catholics. As no regulation in the complex
network of laws and doctrines on matters of religion defined the legal
status of members of the Jewish faith and their organizations, the Jews
who remained in Spain were left in legal limbo. There was no room in the
new Catholic state for an organized Jewish community, openly conducting
its prayers, circumcising its sons, and providing a Jewish education to its
children. Synagogues in Madrid and Barcelona were closed, the community
disintegrated, and religious worship was forced underground. The sense
of terror that pervaded the post–Civil War period prompted many Jews

to convert. According to one witness, twenty out of twenty-five families of German Jews in Madrid converted, and few Jews remained in the capital. In Barcelona too, where thousands of Jews still resided, many sought refuge in conversion. But there were others who, despite prohibitions and the danger of imprisonment for illegal gatherings, assembled in private homes each year to conduct prayers on the High Holy Days and other holidays.[2]

Things were different after the Civil War in the Spanish protectorate of Morocco. In 1935, according to official statistics, there were 12,918 Jews in Tétouan, Larache, Alcazarquivir, and other towns. By 1941 their number had decreased to 11,686, a decline of 10 percent despite the high birth rate of Moroccan Jews. Spain's occupation of Tangier brought at least another 8,000 Jews into its domain—840 of them refugees and the rest long-standing members of the Jewish community. The legal status of these older communities was not determined by the religious laws of Spain but by the laws of the kingdom of the sultan of Morocco; hence, their communal lives went undisturbed by the changes that occurred in Spain. Religion, education, and community continued to function, and the heads of the Tangier Jewish community even maintained close ties with the Franco regime.[3]

Jewish daily life in Spain during the first days of World War II was overshadowed by the activities of the Falange Española and the presence of Nazis. Angry parades and marches accompanied by Fascist rites, radio and press that slanted the news in favor of the Axis, and streets crowded with German civilians and visiting army personnel were all part of the atmosphere that pervaded Spain. Anti-Semitism fitted smoothly into this pattern. Hitler's *Mein Kampf* and Henry Ford's *International Jew* were reprinted in many editions and found wide readership, in addition to the vicious propaganda contained in the many anti-Jewish pamphlets circulated at the time. Frequent incitements in the daily press against North African Jews by their Moslem neighbors also gave Jews undue prominence.[4]

This hostile mood awakened fears of acts of oppression against the Jews. Rumors spread to the Jewish community in the United States in 1940 that Spain was about to expel all Jews who had arrived there after 1931. One of the leaders of the Jewish community in Lisbon was asked to investigate the matter. In his report, written after a visit to Spain and Morocco, he mentioned serious discrimination against the Jews in Spanish Morocco and Falangist anti-Semitic propaganda in Spain, encouraged by Interior Minister Serrano Suñer. But the Lisbon investigator could find no signs of expulsion or any legislation directed specifically against the Jews. This was verified in 1941 by a Jewish refugee in Madrid who had been reporting on the situation in Spain since the outbreak of the war. The fact that Jews—like everyone else—were required to register with the police and declare their religion aroused some concern, and isolated instances of police brutality against Jews did occur. But this refugee could point to no laws directed against the Jews in particular. On the contrary, there were rumors in Madrid that Franco had refused the German demand to enforce the Nuremberg Laws in Spain, and Jewish business activity went on unrestricted.⁵

Although anti-Semitic hostility did not result in general, systematic attacks against Jews, there were a few localized incidents. Such was the case of several families of German refugees who had lived in peace on the island of Majorca throughout the Civil War. When Gestapo influence increased at the beginning of World War II, Jewish men were separated from their wives and were ordered to leave Spain. When they refused, they were placed in a Spanish concentration camp, and their families were forced to live under the threat of deportation to Germany. Similar instances occurred in Madrid and other cities. Spanish Jews from Turkey and the Balkans also suffered arbitrary acts of hostility. In June 1943, the Barcelona bureau that administered work permits canceled several dozen permits held by Jews. According to a report filed by the representative of the Joint Distribution Committee (JDC) in Barcelona, 184 of these Jews applied for economic assistance because their source of livelihood was suddenly cut off. Although the cause was never fully explained, it is evidence of the tenuous existence of those Jews who remained in Spain.⁶

Against this background of flagrant anti-Semitism and Nazi pressure, another Jewish matter dealt with by the Spanish government during the first years of World War II is significant. In 1941, the Ministry of Education opened the Escuela de Estudios Hebraicos (School of Hebrew Studies). In the first volume of its scientific journal, *Sefarad*—the Hebrew name for Spain—the purpose of the institute was explained as follows: "To collect and inventory the Hebreo-Spanish cultural treasures, to determine their relationship with other civilizations, and to emphasize the Spanish roots that Sephardic Jews still keep alive." But it appears that in the Spain of the 1940s the connection with Sephardic culture—and indirectly with Spanish Jews—still required justification and rationalization. Thus, the following appeared in the description of the institute and its aims: "It was not in Spain that Judaism acquired the materialistic character that some of its segments evince; it was in Provence, in the pagan Italy of the Renaissance, and finally in the frozen valleys of the Batavian coast, under the rationalistic north wind, that this havoc began." Stated plainly, materialism and rationalism, the sources of all evil, depicted by anti-Semites as "Jewish" philosophies, were not characteristics of Sephardic culture or of Spanish Jews, but applied to Ashkenazic Jews and to them alone.[7]

This distinction between Sephardic and Ashkenazic Jews, exalting the former and denigrating the latter, was to be discerned also among Jews in Spain before the days of the Second Republic. That the emphasis on the dichotomy reemerged under the Nationalists, to be articulated by the authorities of an institute for the study of Jewish culture, is a telling indication of the spirit of the times that demanded such lip service. Still, the very establishment of a scientific center for Jewish studies—which for forty years has had to its credit impressive achievements in research into Spanish Jewry—is evidence of the special attitude toward Spanish Jews and their culture among the leadership of the Nationalist regime.[8] Even Spanish anti-Semites believed that the evils attributed to Jews referred to Ashkenazic and not to Sephardic Jews. In an article written by Pío Baroja during the Civil War, Sephardic Jews are described as a community of beautiful, homogeneous noblemen, whose life is exemplified by impressive and respected orderliness. Ashkenazic Jews, on the other hand, are described as an unruly, power-hungry mob. Baroja asks finally, "Is it possible that Sephardic Jewry can integrate into Spain and live in harmony there?" His answer is yes. But Ashkenazic Jews, who are, in his view, the spreaders of Communism, will never succeed in assimilating into their countries. These and other writings were collected in a book whose Fascist editor called Baroja the herald of Spanish Fascism, thereby informing Falangist supporters that an authority on Fascism considered Sephardic Jewry a positive element.[9]

This lack of ideological consistency did not go unnoticed by the Nazis. When German Ambassador Eberhard von Stohrer was asked to report on anti-Semitic legislation in Spain, he wrote in November 1941:

> Since the historic persecution of the Jews that ended in their expulsion in 1492, no new laws have been promulgated against them. Insofar as the people are concerned, and insofar as the official ideology of the State is concerned, there is no Jewish problem. For the last few years, it is noteworthy that as a result of German propaganda there have been some anti-Jewish outbursts in the press and in literature, and there are a number of books on the Jewish problem, but on the whole the attitude of the Spaniards has changed but little.[10]

The Nazi ambassador's disappointment regarding Spain's attitude toward its Jews was verified by the ambassador from Romania. On December 19, 1940, Romania officially asked Spain about anti-Jewish legislation likely to apply to Romanian Jews living as aliens in Spain. The significance of the question was ostensibly to bring harm to Romanian

Jews in accordance with anti-Jewish laws that had been in effect in Romania for some time. Serrano Suñer, now foreign minister, replied, "There is no discrimination in the Spanish laws against Jews living in Spain."[11] (See Appendix, document A.)

The leadership of the Franco regime adopted a policy that would ignore the existence of Jews in Spain but still was disposed favorably toward the cultural tradition of Spanish Jews. To what degree was this ambivalent position maintained as thousands of European Jews attempted to enter Spain in their flight to the West, and as Spanish Jews—flesh and blood and not abstractions—needed the aid and protection of Spain? During the first years of the war, the reply to this question was given through Spain's policies regarding entry permits to Spanish territories and diplomatic patronage abroad.

SPAIN'S VISA POLICY

The Civil War eliminated the possibility for Spain to be a land of Jewish refuge. This continued for about nine months after the start of World War II. In the late 1930s, the massive wall of the Pyrenees guarding the border of the Iberian peninsula seemed at once like the last frontier of free Europe and an impregnable barrier.

This situation changed suddenly on May 10, 1940, when Hitler invaded Holland and the Nazi scourge spread into western Europe. With aerial bombardments of Dutch cities and the aid of airborne infantry and groups of fifth columnists, the Germans overran Holland in a few days; by May 28, King Leopold of Belgium surrendered and Dunkirk was being evacuated. On June 14, the Germans entered Paris. Less than ten days later, on June 22, Marshal Pétain signed the surrender of France.

During this period, streams of refugees fleeing from the scenes of fighting filled the French roads. Some were from Holland and Belgium, but most came from the northern towns of France. Terrified by the German parachutists and the fifth columnists, harassed by the shooting and bombing, they blocked the routes leading south, dragging with them the remnants of the disbanding French army. In the confusion, the news of the surrender and cease-fire was received by most Frenchmen with feelings of humiliation and despair mixed with relief. It appeared that the old Marshal had again saved France and brought their agony to an end.

For the thousands of alien Jews who lived in France or who had fled there recently, as well as those who had assumed French citizenship between the two world wars, the cease-fire was no guarantee of safety.

This they well understood, whether the cease-fire found them fleeing or confined to French concentration camps as enemy citizens. In company with thousands of Frenchmen and citizens of other Allied nations, they took to the few remaining roads still leading out of France. The main arteries, and ultimately the only ones, led through the Pyrenees to the Iberian peninsula and the Atlantic. Thus, the Pyrenees were converted overnight from a far-flung European boundary into the destination and last hope of tens of thousands of refugees.

At this stage, those migrating south had no intention of finding a permanent haven in Spain for several reasons, among them the uncertainty of Spain's status in the war and the fear that this hungry and ruined nation, in which German influence was so strong, could not serve long as secure refuge. The refugees, Jews and non-Jews alike, planned to cross the Iberian peninsula and from there seek the shores of the free world. In June 1940 and for many months after, masses of refugees mobbed the various consulates, hoping to obtain entry visas that would enable them to leave France. Until October 1941, the Nazis still allowed Jews of the Third Reich to leave Germany and the other countries that had been annexed and even encouraged their exodus. This organized migration was supposed to pass through Spain; the rescue of thousands of Jews therefore depended upon Spanish goodwill.

What was Spain's reaction to the requests for transit visas that flooded its consulates and embassies? Spanish representatives initially were generous: transit visas were provided to anyone possessing a Portuguese transit or immigration visa. But the consulates also attempted to examine the identity of those applying in order to prevent the entry of enemies of the Nationalist regime. Republican refugees from Spain piled up along the French border; because of their affiliation with leftist parties, they were in a serious predicament vis-à-vis the Germans in France. This apparently had considerable influence on the pace at which Spanish visas were granted, to the point that some refugees despaired of ever receiving them. The French border town of Hendaye and the Spanish town of Irún on the Bay of Biscay were the main transit points.[12] After the first few weeks, there was an interval when the Pyrenees boundary was closed until Spanish policy could be formulated and the situation in France had stabilized. In the wake of the establishment of armistice lines, the focus of flight moved from the area of the Bay of Biscay, which remained under German control, to the Pyrenees region closer to the Mediterranean, which was part of Vichy France.

On September 4, 1940, the border point of Cerbère was reopened and railway service between France and Spain was restored. Spanish border guards were instructed by the governor of the border provinces of Gerona to permit anyone carrying a valid passport and proper visa to pass through to Spain. Exceptions were army personnel (that is, men between the ages of 18 and 40) of Allied countries that either had been conquered or were still fighting. The number was limited to twenty-five per day, allegedly because of accommodation problems in Port Bou, where the refugees had to await Spanish wagons. Only in special cases were fifty persons allowed to pass through in one day.[13]

Another restriction soon was added to those already detailed by the governor of Gerona: Spanish transit was made conditional on the possession of a French exit visa. During the confusion of the first days after France fell, this was not a serious problem, perhaps because the shattered French government provided exit visas to anyone requesting them, or because Spain had no moral obligation to France that would cause it to scrutinize those visas carefully. When the Vichy government became firmly entrenched, however, this quickly changed. Obtaining a French exit visa in many of the areas held by Vichy became the most complicated of all problems relating to emigration; people who had obtained entry visas to the countries of their transit and destination had to wait many months before they could secure a French exit visa. French hesitation especially affected citizens of occupied countries and made the situation of Jewish refugees much more difficult than was necessary under paragraph 19 of the Franco-German armistice, which ordered France to transfer to German soil any citizens of occupied countries whose extradition was demanded by the Nazis.[14] Due to the hostility of the French administration, or because of pressure from the Germans, Vichy authorities made it difficult for those who wished to leave France, and Spanish authorities, out of loyalty to a close or a distant neighbor, prevented anyone without an exit visa from passing through Spain.

On November 11, 1940, Spanish transit regulations became even more strict. Until that date, the Spanish Consulate in Marseille, the main consulate in Vichy France, was authorized to issue transit visas and needed permission from the central authorities in Spain only in special cases. When this changed, every visa eventually had to receive approval from Madrid. According to the Spanish Consulate, the time required for this was between three and six weeks; even when the applicant was prepared to pay for a response by wire, he had to wait ten to twelve days.[15]

These rules guided Spanish consular authorities and border guards throughout the war. The authorities were particularly careful not to allow the entry of men of military age unless they were able to provide thorough documentation that they were unfit for service. Additional instructions were added from time to time: toward the end of 1941, all border stations in the Pyrenees were closed temporarily; six months later, currency regulations were changed and travelers were not permitted to exchange American dollars for pesetas. As a result, some refugees with visas who arrived at the Spanish border possessing only dollars could not finance their passage in Spain and had to return to France.[16]

Spanish policy regarding visas excluded certain groups of refugees and imposed burdensome procedures upon others, but the rules did not discriminate between Jews and non-Jews. Applicants requesting Spanish transit visas were asked to state their religion, which doubtless aroused fear and suspicion in many Jews. Although the Spanish authorities knew the religion at least of those who declared themselves Jews, there is no evidence that Jews were rejected because of their religion. Even when certain consuls were hostile, they did not refrain from providing visas to Jews who satisfied the formal requirements. During the brief time that these permits were granted without limitation, and despite the limitations that were imposed later, tens of thousands of Jews succeeded in passing through Spain openly and legally, and they were saved.[17]

At the end of July and the beginning of August 1942, the period of legal rescue through Spain ended. The Vichy government issued orders on July 20 and August 5 canceling exit visas to French and alien Jews and instead undertook to extradite alien Jews to Germany, where they would be exterminated. French Jews, like other French citizens, were forced to join labor units that would be sent to Germany.[18] These orders also prevented Jews from obtaining Spanish visas.

Limitations on transit through Spain of necessity led to attempts at circumvention. One less prevalent method was to forge personal information on certificates or to obtain completely fictitious documents that conformed with Spanish regulations. Those few who already held Spanish visas tried this method before the age limitation concerning citizens of belligerent countries went into effect; it was also attempted by those who produced documents proving their inability to serve in the military.[19] Many more tried to get around the regulation by avoiding border patrols; during the summer of 1940 it was relatively easy to cross the frontier into Spain illegally. In some instances, French border officials turned a blind eye to the hidden passengers who boarded the train leaving for Spain in the French town of Cerbère and made every effort to avoid the Spanish patrols when they arrived. More popular was a seven-kilometer mountain pass, which circumvented the border stations and could be managed even without experienced guides. Other more difficult means of escape became frequent, and those fleeing France had to seek the services of professional guides, who exacted a high price for their services. These devious methods were, of course, resorted to only by those refugees who were in danger in France. They knew in advance that they had no chance of obtaining French exit visas and feared that the very request would put the Germans on their heels and eventually would lead to their capture.[20]

As time passed, the number of illegal refugees in Spain increased for still another reason. Refugees holding valid visas encountered various difficulties during the few days they were permitted to remain in Spain. One of the conditions for obtaining a transit visa was that the applicant would travel directly to Portugal, or if he intended to sail by Spanish vessel, he would not stay at the port for more than a few days. On more than one occasion in 1940 and 1941, refugees arriving at the Portuguese border found that the immigration visas in their passports, acquired at a high price from one of the consuls in France, had been canceled by the respective government, and so Portugal refused them entry. Other refugees missed their boats, or the sailing was delayed beyond the validity of their immigration visas.[21]

According to law, Spain at this time did not recognize the existence of refugees staying for an extended period. Those refugees who were to board a Spanish ship within a few days, who possessed valid transit visas and entered Spain legally, were allowed to stay in town provided they reported to the local police station. All others were liable to instant imprisonment, after which their fate depended on the whims of an incapable administration in many cases dominated by extremist Falangists under German influence. François Piétri, the Vichy ambassador in Spain and a friend of the Franco regime, describes the nature of this government in his memoirs: "One should not forget that the Spanish administration showed weakness toward the Germans, and certain elements—particularly Falangists—did not look upon the entry of refugees at all favorably, regarding them as a hindrance and even a danger." The ambassador provides a significant example of this arbitrariness: an old friend notified him in March 1941 that when he arrived in Spain he was placed, together with the members of his family, in the jail of the Madrid security police. The vice-consul sent to deal with the case returned and reported that he was promised that the prisoner and his family would be allowed to leave Spain and were to be taken to the Portuguese border that very day. A short time later, his friends were taken to the French border and handed over to the Germans.[22]

During this time it became clear that imprisonment by the Spanish security forces did not lead inevitably to expulsion to France or deportation to Germany. There is no exact information concerning the frequency of these occurrences, the rules governing the incidents, or the categories of refugees destined to this fate; fragmentary evidence exists, however, concerning instances of expulsion and deportation. But there were also cases of refugees who, with sufficient money, exploited the corruption of the Spanish administration and were able to postpone or avoid imprisonment entirely. All others were placed in jail: women were confined for short terms in regional jails, and men sooner or later found themselves in the Miranda de Ebro concentration camp.

Situated not far from the town of Burgos, Miranda de Ebro was established toward the end of the Civil War and was intended for enemies of the Nationalists. It held both refugees and political prisoners. The ugly picture of conditions in the camp is pieced together from letters and bits of information from prisoners and visitors. The food was mostly hunger rations scarcely sufficient to sustain life; prisoners were housed in windowless huts, where their scanty clothing and thin blankets gave no protection from the biting cold; medical care was poor; and the isolation and separation from family was exacerbated by daily fear of the future. Apparently, however, in Miranda de Ebro there was no indiscriminate torture of imprisoned refugees, and this applied also to Jewish refugees. At least one witness in 1941 described the decent attitude of the camp commander and testified that diplomatic representatives of the Allies were allowed to maintain contact with their imprisoned protégés and aid them with money and clothing. The length of imprisonment in Miranda de Ebro was not defined in advance, however, and some refugees imprisoned in 1940 were still there by 1943.[23]

The harsh conditions of imprisonment, which perhaps are explained by the general shortages and hunger in Spain, were even more difficult for the displaced Jewish refugees because of the prohibition against activities of foreign welfare organizations. Since late 1940, Jewish and non-Jewish welfare organizations sought permission to operate in Spain, but to no avail. In October of that year, the director of HICEM reported that the efforts of his organization and the JDC to contact the prisoners of Miranda de Ebro through emissaries and even through a Catholic priest had failed. The American Red Cross had succeeded in obtaining the permission of the Spanish authorities to distribute food, clothing, and medicine brought in special ships to the suffering Spanish populace, but the duration of this project, largely implemented through Spanish welfare agencies such as the Auxilio Social, was limited; when the time limit had expired, members of the Red Cross team were sent out of Spain and could no longer offer assistance to the refugees.[24] The welfare services of the American Friends Service Committee, which had been very active during the Civil War, also showed interest in the possibility of again operating in Spain on behalf of both Spaniards and refugees. In July 1941 their representative, Philip A. Conard, whose daughter was married to one of the attachés in the American Embassy in Madrid, managed to get to Spain on a "family visit." In a series of meetings with American Ambassador Alexander W. Weddell and his wife, Virginia, as well as with the American Red Cross representative, hopes were expressed that the Spanish government would allow Quaker representatives to enter Spain, and various forms of cooperation with Spanish welfare agencies were examined. But all this remained on paper and the visit never made any difference. The hopes of HICEM and the JDC that they would be assisted by the Quakers when they were given permission to operate in Spain thus came to naught.[25]

The only American social welfare activities that took place after the departure of the Red Cross were those conducted by Mrs. Weddell and the wife of the military attaché, Mrs. Stephens. They used their diplomatic status and immunity to provide aid to the needy among the refugees who were imprisoned in Miranda de Ebro. This assistance, financed by welfare agencies, was jeopardized in 1942, this time not because of the intervention of the Spanish authorities but through the excessive caution of the new American ambassador in Madrid, Carlton Hayes. Instructions received from the U.S. State Department forbade embassy personnel to engage in welfare projects, and Ambassador Hayes ordered this prohibition applied to anyone connected with the embassy, including wives of the attachés.[26] The valuable activities of Mrs. Weddell and Mrs. Stephens, through which the JDC had assisted a considerable number of Jewish refugees, were halted. The solution suggested by Ambassador Hayes (namely, that efforts be made to enable welfare agencies to operate in Spain) encountered strong opposition from the Spanish authorities. Conard visited his daughter again in June 1942 and once more tried to obtain permission for the Quakers to operate, but even the intervention of an influential Spanish friend in the Foreign Ministry did not help. In his discussions with the senior personnel of the American Embassy in Madrid he was told that welfare operations on behalf of the stateless refugees arriving in Spain were aimed essentially at Jewish refugees, which provoked Spanish opposition. These discussions concluded that it was not worthwhile for an American or British citizen lacking diplomatic immunity to continue the activities of Mrs. Stephens because

> it is so largely a program of relief for Jewish cases in and out of concentration camps, which has no sympathy from the authorities. . . . All seemed to agree that it is too hot a proposition for any ordinary American or British citizen to handle until he has definite authorization from the government.[27]

This pessimistic appraisal of the potential for rescue in Spain by people who could well have advanced it suspended temporarily the limited base of assistance through the American Embassy. Fortunately, efforts made by Jewish organizations to provide aid did not depend exclusively upon these circles.

Assistance for the passage of Jewish refugees through Spain and Portugal was handled by the offices of HICEM and the JDC in Marseille and Lisbon. Groups of Jewish refugees from the countries of Nazi occupation, especially Austria and Czechoslovakia, who continued to pass through Spain until the end of the summer of 1941 were aided by the local representatives of a German travel agency, which received them at the border town of Irún and accompanied them to the Portuguese border. The JDC provided assistance, through its unofficial representatives, to this transit as well as to Jews who remained in Spain. A young man named Moshe Eizen, who worked as a doorman in a large Madrid hotel, offered assistance to Jews who contacted him. In Barcelona the JDC was aided by the representative of the German travel agency Norddeutscher Lloyd of Bremen, who was given the means to assist refugees in transit as well as the penniless who remained in Spain. This operation was expanded considerably when Samuel Sequerra, the unofficial senior representative of the JDC, came to Spain in 1941. A Portuguese national with the official position of Red Cross representative and a man of great influence, Sequerra had many contacts. He succeeded in setting up a center for Jewish aid in a large hotel in Barcelona. Begun on a small scale, this operation increased in scope and became vitally important in the summer and fall of 1942. But no matter how small, it could not be hidden from the authorities, who apparently preferred to turn a blind eye.[28]

A progressively declining liberalism in all matters concerning the granting of transit visas and a strict policy regarding anyone who did not leave the country quickly were the two principles that governed Spain's behavior toward refugees during the first years of World War II. Although there was no systematic discrimination against Jews, Jewish stateless refugees suffered more than others because Spanish authorities refused to allow private welfare agencies to operate in Spain.

CONSULAR PROTECTION

The Civil War placed Spain's Jewish citizens and its nationals in other countries in an awkward position. Like the non-Jewish Spaniards in Europe and the Americas, each was obliged to side with the Republicans or the

Nationalists. In the beginning, Jewish Spanish nationals managed to avoid this issue entirely; as Nationalist forces strengthened, however, the number of nations siding with them increased, and the number of Nationalist diplomatic representatives increased, too. Support from Jewish nationals thus assumed greater moral significance, and the Nationalist government became more lenient in several matters concerning them.

Early in 1938, General Franco's representative in Sofia first raised the question of compulsory military service for Spanish nationals, suggesting that methods be sought to exempt Jews because "it would appear illogical to demand that they return to Spain after four centuries to spill their blood for the sake of a religion that is not theirs." The representative was well aware that Spanish Jews would not come to Spain to fight, which was why he proposed that the regulation exempting from military service Spanish nationals in Latin America and the Philippines should apply to the Jews as well. This was espoused by the Foreign Ministry of the Nationalist government; the minister of defense concurred, "in view of the urgent need for these people to continue to retain the benefits of their Spanish citizenship, without interfering with their religious sensibilities." Only one problem remained: this exemption applied only in peacetime, and was invalid in a war against a foreign power. For the exemption to remain in effect, it was necessary to term the Civil War internal, which went counter to official Nationalist propaganda. Nevertheless, the Foreign Ministry chose for this purpose to define the Spanish struggle as an internal war, and on June 6, 1938, General Franco consented. Nationalist foreign representatives in Turkey and the Balkans thus were permitted to renew the passports of Spanish Jews without demanding the conscription of those of military age. Instead, a service tax was imposed upon them in accordance with a law that had been in effect in the days of the First Republic.[29]

When the Civil War in Spain ended, in the capitals of several Balkan countries there were Spanish Jews who had maintained political connections with Nationalist foreign representatives and others who had allowed these ties to lapse. Soon after World War II and the persecution of Jews in European countries began, those possessing Spanish citizenship regarded their Nationalist contacts as a saving grace, by virtue of which the hardships their coreligionists suffered would bypass them. This was the time when Spain's true feelings toward its Jews and their cultural heritage was put to the test.

The first country in which Spanish intervention was needed was Romania, the home of the Spanish Jew Enrique Bejarano, who a generation before the Holocaust had aroused enthusiasm for Spanish Jewry in Angel Pulido. The laws against Romanian Jews, severe enough during the period between the two world wars, were made stricter when World War II began, and the status of the Jews was reduced drastically. At that time there were 107 Jews of Spanish nationality living in Romania, all enjoying Spanish protection because of their identification with the Nationalist regime and their contribution toward its military effort. Most of the twenty-seven families in this category were affluent, owning factories and various commercial enterprises.

In July 1940, the Spanish chargé d'affaires in Bucharest announced that these Spanish Jews, like other Jews, were in imminent danger and must be evacuated as soon as possible to Spain. He recommended this in light of the fact that during the Civil War these people had supported the Nationalists, which ostracized them from the rest of the Bucharest Jewish community. In the spring of 1941 the new minister, José Rojas y Moreno, arrived in Bucharest and was summoned to aid the Jews under his protection.

At the end of March 1941, Rojas learned that seven Spanish Jewish families had received expulsion notices from the Romanian government and were ordered to leave the country by May. He immediately requested a meeting with Ion Antonescu, then premier of Romania, and in a long report he demanded that these Spanish Jews—who had proven their loyalty to Spain and had contributed to the development of Romanian industry—be exempt from any laws against Jews. This intervention achieved its purpose; within days, Rojas received promises from both Antonescu and the minister of the interior that no measures would be taken against Spanish Jews. At the beginning of April, the Spanish Embassy provided the Romanians with a list of Spanish nationals, and from that time onward, the safety of the Spanish Jews was assured, notwithstanding certain restrictions on Jewish-owned businesses and occasional outbreaks of anti-Semitism. In August 1942, Rojas asked Antonescu's government, on the basis of an agreement between Spain and Romania signed in 1930, to exempt Spanish nationals from regulations concerning the confiscation of Jewish property. Antonescu again agreed, and methods of safeguarding Spanish nationals from anti-Semitic attacks were implemented. Rojas's actions were later cited by the director of the European department of the Spanish Foreign Ministry as an outstanding example of successful diplomatic intervention.[30]

Another community of Jewish nationals requiring Spain's assistance was in Greece. About 80,000 Jews lived there when Mussolini invaded on October 28, 1940, bringing Greece into World War II.[31] The Greeks at first were able to rout their attackers, but then the Germans came to the aid of the Italians, and in a brief campaign all of Greece was occupied by April 23, 1941. Greece and its Jewish community was thereafter divided into three sectors. One sector, encompassing parts of Thrace and Macedonia, was annexed to Bulgaria, and the fate of its 5,615 Jews hinged on Bulgaria's internal power struggles and its relationships with Germany. The second sector, the south of Greece to Larissa and parts of western Macedonia, was placed under Italian control, and the fate of its 15,198 Jews became that of Italian Jews. The third sector, the rest of Thrace and eastern Macedonia, fell under the German yoke, and its 59,137 Jews soon suffered Nazi oppression.

Although the majority of Greek Jews were culturally and linguistically Spanish Jews (Salonika was the center of Sephardic culture in the Balkans), the number of Spanish nationals living in Greece at the time of the Italian conquest was only 640. These alone concerned the Spanish government, most of whom lived in the German sector.[32]

When German columns entered Salonika on April 9, 1941, the Spanish Consulate there was headed by Vice-Consul Salomon Ezraty, who had held that position for twenty-eight years. According to a list drawn up a year later, which the Jewish community provided the Germans, there were 511 Spanish nationals in Salonika.[33] In 1943, the embassy in Athens provided a list of the names of another 12 citizens in Salonika, 16 in Dhidhimótikhon, and 11 in Néa Orestiás; this list cannot be considered complete, however. The two lists, which included Salonika and northern Greece but not the Athens area, comprised about 550 persons. In both lists were instances where whole families were included—parents, children, and even distant relatives—but there were also cases where only parts of families enjoyed Spanish citizenship; still others, often members of an immediate family, were not registered at the Spanish Embassy and therefore could not claim Spain's protection.[34]

Throughout the first weeks of the occupation, when the Germans intensified anti-Semitic propaganda, disbanded the Jewish community council, and confiscated Jewish property, the protection the Spanish vice-consul was able to provide freed his protégés from these hardships. Ezraty sent a detailed report concerning the Spanish Jewish community in Greece to the Spanish Foreign Ministry, but no course of action was suggested.[35] The Germans had not yet begun to execute their final plans for the Jews of Greece. The economic crisis, looting and confiscation by the Nazis and their cohorts, and the shortage of supplies resulted in much hunger, which prompted some Spanish citizens to attempt to emigrate to Spain. Eduardo Gasset, the spanish consul in Athens, conveyed their request to the Spanish Foreign Ministry. On November 8, 1941, Gasset was notified that the consulate in Athens was not empowered to issue visas and that special permission had to be requested in each case, detailing the personal qualifications of the applicant and stating where in Spain he wanted to settle; only then would the matter be considered.[36] This reply apparently precluded the implementation of a repatriation plan for Spanish nationals, for few Jews left Greece for Spain during the first two years of the war.

As the hunger worsened, the Spanish nationals in Salonika again appealed to the Spanish Foreign Ministry, asking that Spain persuade the occupation authorities to allow the Spanish community to acquire foodstuffs from local sources at official prices. In this manner Spanish nationals would be able to secure more supplies at reasonable cost, as the Italian nationals did as a result of their embassy's assistance. This request also was rejected, this time by the person in charge of the financial office in the Spanish Foreign Ministry, who maintained that, unlike Italy, Spain had no means of monetary compensation and there was thus no place for such a proposal.[37]

By the end of one year, the Spanish community in Salonika had received no significant aid from the Spanish authorities, but fortunately Nazi persecutions had not yet reached their ominous proportions. The consulate in Salonika had provided its protégés with Spanish passports, which served for purposes of identification and enabled the consulate to extend its aegis over them at the local level. Discussions arose regarding the position Spain should adopt vis-à-vis these protégés in view of the possibility that the situation in Greece might deteriorate quickly. On March 13, 1942, Eduardo Gasset offered the following proposal: many citizens, "with all the rights that derive therefrom," were financially stable; however, "in view of the anti-Semitic ferment involved in the present war," Spain must decide whether to continue to defend them or abandon them to their fate. If it should be found desirable to safeguard these people, Gasset thought, it might be possible to exploit their positive feelings toward Spain and their wish to retain their Spanish citizenship by obtaining from them significant contributions to advance the cultural interests of Spain in Greece. By such means, he considered, it would be possible to establish in Athens a center for Spanish culture and archaeological and historical research; thus Spain could compete with other countries, like France, which had maintained such a center for many years.[38]

Madrid's response to this is not known. A year later, however, before Eduardo Gasset completed his term of duty, a branch of the Falange Española was opened in Greece. According to a German source, the branch cost 10 million drachmas and was financed by Spanish Jews. This same source points out that Gasset often intervened personally on behalf of Spanish Jews.[39]

The small number of Jewish Spanish nationals in Greece was due in part to the fact that since the early 1900s, thousands of Jews emigrated from Salonika and other Greek cities to seek their fortunes in the countries of western Europe. Some settled in France, adding a new element to its Spanish community and enjoying Spanish citizenship there.

When France surrendered in June 1940, it was estimated that 35,000 Sephardic Jews were living in France, some in old settlements along the Bay of Biscay but most in Paris and other large cities. Many maintained close ties with Spain. Two thousand were registered in the Spanish Embassy in Paris as Spanish nationals carrying Spanish papers, and another thousand were registered in other consulates in France. Many of these Jews were financially stable; some were obviously wealthy.[40] In the first weeks after the Nazi occupation, the Germans showed tolerance toward the civilian population, creating an illusion among French Jews that was to be shattered later. The first inkling of things to come was the order issued in the occupied zone on September 27, 1940, requiring every Jew to register at a police station so that the word "Jew" could be stamped on his documents. A week later the Vichy government issued the Statut des Juifs, which differentiated Jews from the rest of the population and imposed many prohibitions on them. German attempts to impose these laws on Spanish nationals forced Spain to take a stand.

The first Spanish reaction came from the consul general in Paris, Bernardo Rolland: as there were no racial laws in Spain and Jews there were not discriminated against, it was only right that these laws should not be imposed on Spanish nationals outside Spain. But José Félix Lequerica, the Spanish ambassador to the Vichy government, had doubts. (See Appendix, document B.) At his request the Spanish Foreign Ministry formulated its position, which was that Spanish foreign representatives were to exercise passive vigilance but should not prevent the application of racial laws to Spanish nationals. Although there were no such laws in Spain, the government could not prevent its Jewish protégés from being exposed to regulations of a general nature. Spanish representatives were also expected to demand that, in any instance of personal registration of their protégés or their property, the Jews should declare their Spanish citizenship so that they could be protected as Spanish nationals.[41] The Spanish Foreign Ministry was not prepared to conduct a campaign in support of its Jewish nationals, but it did not completely abandon them or their property either. Rather, it chose to treat each instance individually. (See Appendix, document C.)

The first issue for which Spanish foreign representatives had to negotiate with the Nazis was the property of their protégés. At the beginning of 1941, the confiscation of Jewish property increased, and on April 26 an order was issued in the Nazi-occupied zone prohibiting Jews from conducting business and requiring them to turn over their property to "Aryan" hands. Spanish representatives first tried to exempt their Jewish protégés from this category, claiming that their property was Spanish property and should not be affected. But after further German pressure and negotiations, Spain agreed to an arrangement whereby businesses of its protégés would be handed over to Spanish commissioners, under the supervision of the Spanish consulates. This agreement, similar to the one the Portuguese and Italian governments had regarding their Jewish nationals, was brought to the attention of the director general of the Spanish Department of Foreign Currency, with the announcement that the Banco de España had been asked to handle the sale of all property, as Jews were prohibited from any further economic activity. In order to sell the property at the best price, the Spanish representatives procrastinated as long as possible, trying to remove the force of the expropriation order.[42]

The intervention of the Spanish representatives on behalf of their Jewish protégés stimulated their friends and acquaintances—Sephardic Jews of French nationality—to try to obtain the assistance of the Spanish government for themselves too. Several leaders of the Association Culturelle Sephardite in Paris, who claimed to represent Sephardic Jews in the French capital, sent General Franco a letter (forwarded to Madrid by Rolland) on March 13, 1941, emphasizing their Spanish origins and their deep relationship with the land from which their forefathers had been exiled and requesting permission to return and settle in Spain permanently. The prevailing mood in Nationalist Spain seemed to indicate that this naive request would be rejected summarily by Foreign Minister Serrano Suñer. Either because the letter was addressed to General Franco or for more substantive reasons, this did not happen. Serrano Suñer ordered the appeal sent to Franco's military secretary, from whom it was sent to Undersecretary of the Government Jésus Carrero, the Ministry of the Interior, and the general director of the security police, and then returned to the undersecretary and the foreign minister with the comment: "The General Directorate of the security police thinks that the appeal should be rejected."

If this appeal by the Sephardic Jews of Paris was brought to the attention of General Franco (this is not mentioned specifically in the correspondence accompanying the letter), it was not given his personal consideration. The decision was handed over to the security police, who rejected the appeal for their own reasons and apparently because of their friendship for Nazi Germany. In any event, it was rejected purely for reasons of Spanish policy: neither the question of German reaction nor the position of the Vichy government influenced the decision. So ended the only attempt made during the entire course of the war to extend Spain's assistance to Sephardic Jews beyond the small communities of Jewish Spanish nationals.[43]

There were serious reservations and obvious loopholes even in the defense of Spanish nationals. In order to safeguard their status as Spanish nationals and still comply with the order concerning special registration of Jews in the occupied countries, Bernardo Rolland informed Spanish nationals that they should register in Spanish consulates; these lists subsequently would be passed on to the Commissariat Général aux Questions Juives, established in March 1941.[44] But the preservation of Spanish sovereignty over its Jewish protégés did not save all of them from hardship and imprisonment. In one of the operations in the 11th arrondissement in Paris, fourteen Spanish nationals were rounded up in August and sent to the Drancy internment camp, where they were among the first Jewish prisoners. This prompted Rolland to urgent action: he appealed to the Spanish Embassy in Berlin to approach the German Foreign Ministry and point out that Italian nationals who had been arrested during that operation had been freed; he also reported this to his superiors in Madrid, who received the news "as information noted." He even attempted an ambitious maneuver that received no support whatever: a German memorandum dated September 14, 1941, stated that Rolland appealed to the German authorities in Paris proposing that approximately 2,000 Spanish nationals registered in the occupied zone be transferred to Spanish Morocco within four or five weeks, provided that the Drancy prisoners be allowed to accompany them. The German authorities considered this proposal; the agent of the Sicherheitsdienst (SD; Security Service) in Paris asked for instructions from Berlin because there already were standing orders from Heinrich Himmler that Jews were not to be transferred from one country to another. But these efforts, like Rolland's other appeals to his superiors and to German authorities, were of no avail. The prisoners remained in Drancy even after one of them died.[45]

The insecurity of the Spanish nationals in France encouraged them to seek a permanent solution to their difficulty. In June 1941, some tried to leave France and settle in Spain. Rolland referred to the Foreign Ministry a number of test cases in accordance with which a general policy could be fixed. The matter was brought for consideration before the security police, who returned it to the Foreign Ministry, reasoning that as many Jews were likely to request similar permission to come to Spain, it was only proper that the Foreign Ministry make the decision. The Foreign Ministry chose not to reply for the time being.[46]

The delay in the response from the Foreign Ministry, and perhaps also the rumor that Madrid's hesitation stemmed from the large number of Spanish nationals in France, prompted several Spanish nationals to try a new, different tactic. In October 1941, five of them traveled to Madrid to meet with the foreign minister personally. With letters of recommendation provided by Rolland, the members of the delegation were received in the Foreign Ministry, where they left a declaration summarizing their case. They expressed their thanks for the concessions that they had enjoyed as Spanish nationals until then and stressed the fear and insecurity to which they were subject, as proved by the imprisonment of fourteen of their number. As Sephardic Jews who had come from Spain and wished ultimately to return and settle there, they always held themselves aloof from other Jews, whom they despised and with whom they refused to intermarry. (Even Alfred Rosenberg in *The Myth of the Twentieth Century* and Houston Steward Chamberlain in *The Foundations of the Nineteenth Century* testify that Aryan blood flows in the veins of Sephardic Jews, which is the reason for their superiority.) The delegation also asserted that the rescue of Spanish nationals is much less problematic than was described in official correspondence of the Spanish Foreign Ministry. According to them, the number of Jewish Spanish nationals in occupied France was not even one thousand and perhaps as few as three hundred persons, including some who had converted to Catholicism. These few Sephardic Jews accepted Spanish citizenship according to the law passed under Primo de Rivera's rule in 1924, whereas the other Jews were unaware of this law at the time and hence did not enjoy its benefits. In the name of these few they asked that Spain provide full guarantees for their lives, their personal freedom, and their property or arrange for their emigration to Spain or another country. This was the first time an attempt was made in official correspondence to distinguish fully documented Spanish nationals. This distinction arose later and determined the fate of many Jewish protégés; at that time, however, it did not provide the delegation with any tangible results. The authors of the declaration hoped that by minimizing the number of those deserving Spanish protection and by pretending to accept the racial arguments, they would solve their problem; their hopes were dashed.[47]

During subsequent months, Rolland continued to report on the increasingly severe persecution of Jews in France and the dangers threatening his protégés. When French pressure on Spanish nationals increased, in

February 1942 he offered his assistance to a new effort by these nationals to improve their status and increase the Spanish protection to which they were entitled. This time he fared better. The secretary of the Spanish Bureau of Commerce in France, José de Olózaga, traveled to Madrid at the recommendation of the president of the bureau and with Rolland's encouragement to speak to the heads of the Foreign Ministry about the Spanish nationals. It is learned from the minutes of the discussions that the purpose of Olózaga's mission was to ensure that the Spanish ambassador to the Vichy government and the consul general in Paris would be instructed to base their contacts with the French authorities on the French-Spanish agreement of January 7, 1862, regarding the rights and mutual protection of the interests of the citizens of both countries. These instructions were necessary to stand fast to the French authorities who had conspired against the property of several Spanish nationals, such as Gategno, the large silk manufacturer from Lyon, whose property was valued at 14 million francs. Olózaga was successful; on March 7, 1942, the Spanish Foreign Ministry wrote the following to Lequerica, its ambassador in Vichy (see Appendix, document D):

> The fact that the Spanish government does not prevent its citizens from submitting themselves to certain regulations, such as those that were the subject of more than one note from you . . . does not mean that their rights should be left without proper protection. . . . Upon instructions from the foreign minister and within the guidelines you have received, you are requested to defend the interests of Jewish nationals of Spanish origin by demanding the French authorities to comply with the 1862 agreement.[48]

This new demand was doubtless of great value to Rolland in defending his protégés. In late July 1942, in response to a question addressed to him by the Commissariat Général aux Questions Juives, he repeated the claim he had been stressing:

> Spanish law does not discriminate among citizens because of their religion, and for that reason it regards Jews who originally came from Spain as Spaniards, despite their Jewish religion. For this reason, I should be grateful if the French authorities and the occupying power would be good enough not to impose upon them [the Spanish Jews] those laws that apply to Jews.[49]

In Vichy there was less need to protect Spanish nationals; there were no significant outcomes from the reservations Lequerica showed toward the Jews. The embassy there did have a role, however, in the defense of Spanish Jews in the French protectorate of Morocco, where they suffered persecution and discrimination.

The Statut des Juifs, concerning damage to Jewish property, personal freedom, and economic activity—imposed by the Vichy government in the south of France—was intended to apply also to the Jews in French Morocco. When French authorities in Morocco enforced the statute in 1941, Jews of Spanish nationality living there suddenly found themselves subject to its regulations. Moreover, after the Moroccan Jews had managed to persuade the sultan to mollify the oppressive laws, Jews of foreign nationality now found themselves in worse straits than local Jews. The Spanish consuls in Rabat and Fez began to report back on the distress of their protégés and asked for instructions from the Spanish Foreign Ministry. Unlike the problem of Jewish nationals in other countries, the problem of Jewish nationals in Morocco directly affected the question of Spanish sovereignty there and one of the fundamental laws in the Spanish constitution. Whereas in Greece and France Jews received Spanish nationality as a result of special laws and arrangements, Moroccan Jews were granted Spanish nationality when they became naturalized in Spain or were born in Spanish territory. Because most were born in Morocco, the French claimed that their Spanish naturalization had lapsed; further, as the law was not made under Moroccan agreement, as required by Moroccan law and as stipulated in a treaty of 1880, even those born in Spanish territory of Moroccan parents could not be regarded as Spanish citizens. Essentially, the argument was that the laws of Spain did not supersede the laws of Morocco, and by taking this position the French in effect challenged Spanish sovereignty in areas controlled by Spain.

In view of the strong French position, the Spanish consul in Rabat, Manuel del Moral, doubted whether, in light of the political climate, the Jews were worth defending. The foreign minister received a similar opinion from the Spanish high commissioner in Morocco, supplemented by a detailed description of the situation. His letter carried overtones that evinced no great sympathy for the Jews, such as the fear that the Jews might "swamp" the Spanish protectorate if it suddenly became apparent to them that this area was safer. But he did not ignore the threat of the loss of prestige that was involved in abandoning the Jews, and so left the matter in the hands of the Foreign Ministry.[50]

The Spanish Foreign Ministry responded thus: as the issue of Jewish Spanish nationals in French territory affects the sovereignty of Spain, prejudice against them must be reversed. The consuls in French Morocco were ordered to provide passports and certificates to Spanish nationals in Morocco, and when the French authorities questioned their right to do so and refused to recognize these documents, on January 5, 1942, the foreign minister instructed Lequerica to bring the matter to the attention of the Pétain government. Even though he had no confidence in his success, Lequerica wrote to the Vichy government. He also had a more original suggestion for his superiors in Madrid: the French regarded Morocco as a nation over which they had control; therefore, any act on Spain's part "not supported by threats of reprisal" would have little success. And as Spain held the area of Tangier, it could reciprocate by adopting hostile measures "against the Moroccans and Jews living in that area" who are French nationals. In September 1942, Lequerica repeated the malicious notion that Spain should protect Moroccan Jews who were Spanish nationals by persecuting their French national brethren, even though he could see with his own eyes the attacks on the Jews of France and grasp the full significance of the "measures against the Jews."[51]

The Spanish protests did not alter the circumstances. Lequerica then put forth a compromise proposal, under which Spain was prepared to cancel the citizenship of some but not all Jews. But this proposal was unacceptable to the Vichy authorities, and the situation remained unchanged. The Spanish consul in Rabat continued to provide Spanish documents for his protégés and continued to complain that the French disregard for these documents injured Spanish prestige. The Vichy authorities in Morocco maintained their position concerning Spanish nationals.[52] The problem of Spain's protection of its nationals in Morocco was only solved when, in the wake of the Allied invasion of North Africa, Vichy control ended in this area.

At about this time, Pelayo García y Olay, the director of the Department for European Affairs in the Spanish Foreign Ministry, summarized the predicament of Spanish Jews by mentioning only two achievements: securing the property of the nationals in France and obtaining guarantees for the personal security and safety of the property of the nationals in Romania. In the other Nazi-occupied countries, the intervention of Spanish consuls either brought no results or was not needed.[53]

AN INTERIM BALANCE SHEET

According to a 1941 HICEM census, there were 50,000 refugees living in France who wished to emigrate. Because immigration organizations were still operating in the Greater Reich and the Netherlands, the total number of Jews desperately eager to leave their places of residence was probably at least twice that.[54] The Germans did not object to the emigration of Jews, and according to some sources were even prepared to encourage it. The chief stumbling block then, as during the 1930s, was the unwillingness of other countries to accept all those Jewish refugees who wished to emigrate. The few fortunate who were successful in obtaining entry visas were forced to travel through Spain; despite the uncertainty of Spanish policy, this was possible in most cases.

Even if official Spanish statistics were available, it is doubtful they could provide a complete or accurate picture of the number of Jews who passed through Spain because of the tendency of so many Jews to hide their Jewishness when applying for transit through a Catholic and pro-Axis country. For this reason, it is necessary to rely on Jewish sources—the internal reports and public balance sheets of Jewish organizations assisting refugees and helping them secure passage—namely the Joint Distribution Committee and its partner in immigration, HICEM.

According to public reports of the JDC, it may be concluded that between 53,000 and 63,000 refugees passed through Spain. These numbers appear to be highly inflated, however. Estimates of the size of immigration in the various destinations of the Western Hemisphere indicate that the total number of Jewish refugees between 1940 and 1942 was 83,339. Of these, 42,854 immigrated in 1940, mostly from Holland, Belgium, and France, and the rest immigrated between 1941 and 1942, many sailing directly from Marseille and Casablanca.[55] The chaos after the fall of France and the impossibility of distinguishing between Jew and non-Jew could have confused even those most intimately involved with refugee matters in the Iberian peninsula.[56] The overall figures appearing in public reports of the JDC should be evaluated carefully, as these reports were intended to present as impressive a figure as possible of the extent of work being done in order to stimulate more public support.

From the internal reports and correspondence of HICEM, it is possible to estimate the number of Jews who escaped through Spain and sailed from Portuguese ports with the assistance of Jewish organizations. According to this source, it appears that in the time between the fall of France and September 1942, HICEM aided in the passage of 10,500 refugees through Portugal.[57] To this should be added the number of those who sailed from Spanish ports with the aid of Jewish organizations, which owing to the greater difficulty, was fewer than the former. In addition are the thousands of Jewish refugees who arranged passage on their own; this was considerable during the first months after France fell and before the Jewish organizations had begun full operation from Lisbon. From the above it may be estimated that during the first half of the war some 30,000 Jews were saved by their passage through Spain.[58]

In comparison, the number of Jews for whom Spain served as an extended temporary refuge was very small. The JDC's report for 1941 and the first six months of 1942 counts only 300 dependent refugees in Spain. Even if the JDC did not extend aid to all those requiring it, it is still doubtful that the number of refugees remaining in Spain was much more than 500.[59]

Compared to the relatively large number of Jews who passed through Spain during the first part of the war and whose lives were saved, there were few Spanish Jewish nationals whose lives and safety depended upon the goodwill of the Spanish government. In the Balkans this number might have reached 1,000—640 in Greece, 100 in Romania, approximately 130 in Bulgaria, less than 50 in Hungary, and perhaps 25 in Yugoslavia. In France there were 3,000 protégés, 2,000 in the occupied territory and 1,000 in the "free" sector under Marshal Pétain. In addition to these, some Jews in Germany, Belgium, and Holland possessed Spanish passports and documents, but these totaled less than a few dozen. There was also an unknown number—apparently not very large—of Jewish Spanish nationals in French Morocco. Altogether, the number of Jews who came under Spanish protection in all the occupied countries was not much more than 4,000, and certainly did not reach 5,000. The only attempt made during the first two years of the war to increase this amount was rejected by Spain before the French or the German authorities addressed themselves to it.

Despite the small numbers involved, the manner in which Spain handled these Jews was a barometer of its attitude toward the Jewish people as a whole. On the one hand, issues touching upon the sovereignty and prestige of Spain were involved in its defense of Jewish nationals; important material interests were not completely irrelevant, either, in view of the large assets possessed by many of these Jews. On the other hand, persecutions were directed only at the Jews, and a consistent diplomatic policy was required to save them from such oppression. In this complex situation, Spain tried to have the best of both worlds. It repeatedly stressed that there was no discrimination on the grounds of race or religion in Spain, hence these criteria should not be used to discriminate against its nationals elsewhere; it also demanded that bilateral agreements in existence for some time between Spain and other countries—agreements that dealt with mutual guarantees concerning the personal safety and property of nationals of these countries—should apply to Jewish nationals as well. Spain chose not to try to exempt its Jewish nationals from local legislation unless this affected Spanish sovereignty. Spain maintained its position much more strongly toward the Romanian and French authorities than toward the Germans.

This policy imposed an especially heavy burden on the Spanish foreign representatives in whose areas of jurisdiction these Jewish matters lay. For this reason, their personalities and attitudes toward Jews were important elements in the rescue of Spanish nationals. This weakness did not go unnoticed by the Germans when agents of the SD in France refused to free the fourteen Spanish nationals imprisoned in Drancy. The principle intervention on their behalf depended on the initiative and energy of the Spanish consul in Paris, Bernardo Rolland, who had to rely entirely upon his local contacts. The fact that the ownership and management of much property and capital was connected with the defense of Jewish nationals was always at the back of the minds of the Spanish foreign representatives, but the only ones who acted with vigor were José Rojas, the minister in Bucharest, and Rolland. Although the attention they devoted to the problem of their Jewish protégés indeed might have been tied to material interests, without any deep sympathy for the Jews this concern doubtless would have been less effective.[60] On the other side, the consul in Athens, Eduardo Gasset, was engrossed in considerations of expediency, and José Félix Lequerica, Spain's ambassador to the Vichy government, was hampered by his reservations concerning the defense of Jewish nationals and his cynical plans for the best solution to the problem of Spanish nationals in Morocco.

The personal traits of the Spanish foreign representatives and their feelings about the Jews were therefore important factors in the lives and security of Jews of Spanish nationality. But even the most sympathetic representatives could not resolve the plight of their protégés by allowing them to emigrate to Spain. The reluctance of Spanish authorities to absorb Spanish Jews into Spain was expressed during the first part of the war in at least two instances. It would become critical as the Holocaust intensified during the latter part, when Spain became the last refuge for Jewish Spanish nationals as well as for thousands of Jews from other lands.

4

L ⅂

SPAIN AS A HAVEN FOR REFUGE

JEWISH REFUGEES

Until the beginning of the summer of 1942, Nazi and local authorities in western Europe concentrated on stripping the Jews of their property and economically ostracizing them from society. Mass arrests took place from time to time, as in Amsterdam in February 1941 and in the 11th arrondissement of Paris in August and December. But these arrests, each of which involved hundreds of Jews, did not include mass murder, nor were they frequent or methodical. In May and June 1942, the Jews of Holland, Belgium, and occupied France were forced to wear a yellow Star of David on their clothes. Not long afterward the Nazis finished their preparations for extermination. On June 28, the head of the SD and the Security Police informed his subordinates in western Europe of the arrangements: in July trains would be placed at their disposal to transport their victims to the "work camps" in Auschwitz. At first, 40,000 Jews from Holland, 10,000 from Belgium, and 40,000 from France would be taken.

In France the transport order was limited initially to foreign Jews, which was meant to fan the flames of anti-Semitism among the citizenry. Any activity in Paris against the Jews was postponed until after July 14, so that the ardor of Bastille Day would not be dampened; in the meantime, all details were being prepared meticulously. The day after the holiday, hundreds of French policemen swept through Jewish sections in the Paris suburbs, armed with lists that had been provided them. Although some

Jews had been forewarned, most were taken by surprise and given only a few minutes to pack some belongings before they were taken away. Under heavy guard, thousands of men, women, and children were herded into a sports stadium in Paris. After five days without food, crowded, in stifling heat, and without proper sanitary conditions, they joined those imprisoned in Drancy. A few days later, trains began to leave for Auschwitz.

The abruptness of the imprisonment of 12,874 people, the cruelty of its execution, the heart-rending scenes of children being torn away from their parents, and the fact that an entire community was suddenly arrested regardless of sex or age under the pretext of being taken to the East to work shocked many Frenchmen no less than it shocked Jews. Some Jews then began their flight from the occupied areas and sought refuge in Vichy France.

During the last days of July, leaders of Jewish organizations learned that Jews in Vichy France were also about to be arrested. Indeed, Theodor Dannecker, the head of the SD in France, moved about the detention camps of Gurs, Rivesalte, Les Milles, and others, reviewing the stock of victims that Pierre Laval and his cohorts had promised to supply for the Nazi death machine. The prohibition against leaving France imposed on foreigners was intended to prevent more Jews from fleeing, as they were to be deported, and preparations for a large-scale shipment in August had gone into high gear. A coordinating committee of Jewish and non-Jewish welfare organizations, headed by a representative of the Young Men's Christian Association, which had met since November 1940 in Nîmes, made last-minute efforts to defer the order. A delegation of non-Jewish welfare organizations appealed to Marshal Pétain, asking for his intervention; he was too old and weak, however, and most likely unwilling to help. Laval and his supporters in the Commissariat Général aux Questions Juives hid behind the flimsy excuse that by handing over foreign Jews they were buying the safety of French Jews. Despite all efforts, boxcars crowded with Jews began to move from the Vichy concentration camps in the direction of Germany, and a wholesale hunt for more Jews was unleashed in the south of France.

During July and August the final, crucial stage in the history of the Holocaust in France began—mass extermination. Most Jews still were unaware of what was happening. Even among the leadership of the organizations—and primarily among the activists of the parent organization, the Union Générale des Israélites de France, which had been established in November 1941 at the behest of the Germans—were many who clung to the belief that the promises of Laval and Pétain would help them.[1]

Out of the events of August 1942 and the subsequent arrests and deportations, representatives of the Quakers and the YMCA in the United States tried to organize the rescue of five thousand children by arranging their emigration to the United States. With the heads of Jewish organizations they sent letters of protest to the Vichy government and appealed to public opinion in France and the rest of the world. In the summer of 1942 the Catholic and Protestant churches expressed sympathy for the suffering of the Jews. Monsignor Saliège, the Archbishop of Toulouse, spoke out from the pulpit voicing his shock at recent events; Cardinal Gerlier, the Archbishop of Lyon, joined forces with Marc Boegner, head of the Protestant Church in France, and tried to pressure Pétain to stop the deportations; Abbé Glasberg in Lyon cooperated closely with a Jewish welfare organization, the Oeuvre de Secours aux Enfants Israélites (OSE; Society for the Rescue of Jewish Children), and with others in an effort to save children and hide adults. The plight of Jews unquestionably aroused the sympathy of the Christian community, sometimes even of those who formerly had been antagonistic toward them.[2]

The new situation facing foreign Jews in France forced many to use forged papers and go underground. Jewish and non-Jewish organizations had been engaged in underground activities for some time; with the force of circumstance, their work intensified. Catholic and Protestant church groups aided Jews in finding hiding places. This means of rescue was the least complicated, but it did not ensure the personal security of those in hiding. Another option was to flee to Switzerland. Along the French-Swiss border were places where crossing was not difficult, and by the summer of 1942, German border patrols had not yet been strengthened. Passage to Spain, the other escape frontier, involved a long and arduous journey through rough mountain terrain. Those fleeing to Switzerland could not expect to leave there before the end of the war, and the fact that this country was surrounded on all sides by Axis powers well could have aroused fears for its future. But democratic Switzerland at least appeared to offer some guarantee of decency toward the Jews and their personal security, at least as far as the local Swiss authorities were concerned. Nevertheless, refugees could not know what awaited them in Spain and had to weigh the chance of crossing Spain and reaching the Atlantic coast through Portugal against the risk that they might fall prey to the Germans. For these reasons very few attempted to save themselves from persecution in France by fleeing across the Pyrenees. Those who did so possessed passports and partial documentation, providing them with some possibility of eventually emigrating overseas.

No organized efforts at rescue through Spain had been mounted by the summer and fall of 1942, so no great assistance could have been expected from existing Jewish organizations. One of the few who tried to flee through Spain was the young doctor Joseph Gabel, a refugee from Germany who arrived in France in 1940 after several years in Belgium. Gabel had been mobilized, like many other Jewish aliens, in a French forced labor camp, Groupement de Travailleurs Etrangers. During a short leave granted him by the director of the camp, he applied to the OSE in Marseille for information and aid. There he and three other refugees were given a hand-drawn map describing the crossing into Spain from a point near Perpignan. With this inexact map, the four set out without benefit of professional guides. Although they lost their way, their luck did not desert them, and they managed to cross the border. From the OSE they had also received a small sum of money to cover their expenses in Spain. Although this could not be described as a regular function of the OSE, it was apparently the initiative of Ruby Epstein, the deputy director of the office and a Jewish refugee from Belgium, who used his personal connections for such purposes.[3] This kind of individual assistance may have been given to other refugees as well, but because of the unusual circumstances they were probably few.

Other assistance was available from the Capuchin monastery in rue Croix de Regnier in Marseille, where Abbé Pierre Marie-Benoît worked devotedly to save Jews, according to his own account, immediately after the Statut des Juifs was issued in October 1940. At first he obtained forged documents for his wards and directed them to secret hiding places provided by his associates; later he helped them flee to Switzerland and Spain. "I made contact with welfare organizations and smuggling operations in Spain and Switzerland," relates the abbé. "Some of these operations were placed at my disposal." Persecuted Jews who knocked at the doors of the monastery at all hours of the day and night seeking help were directed by the abbé to temporary hiding places, provided with documents, food, and information, and put in touch with the smugglers. Some of these refugees were sent to the abbé by Jewish organizations who were working with him in Marseille; in other instances he was aided by church groups. With the consent of the Vichy government, the Archbishop of Marseille appointed him official Church comptroller in the Les Milles concentration camp, as well as in one of the prisons in Marseille. The abbé made contact with the prisoners there, and during the deportations of 1942 he was able to assist some of them. His activities on behalf of Jews, including their rescue through Spain, did not cease even when one was captured at the Spanish border in possession of a forged document and admitted, under pressure of the interrogation, that he had received it in the Capuchin monastery.

Friends of the abbé in the French police made certain he was always forewarned when the authorities made plans to stop his activities. His work continued until the Germans entered the south of France in November 1942, after which he concentrated his efforts on helping Jews in the Italian zone of occupation.[4]

Many refugees, unable to avail themselves of the Abbé Marie-Benoît's help or assistance from Jewish welfare organizations, had to rely entirely on their own efforts in their attempts to flee to Spain. They traveled to one of the towns along the Pyrenees, where they tried to make contact with smugglers. Occasionally they were able to solicit help from the local inhabitants who were touched by their plight. In most cases, however, the refugees required the services of professional smugglers, who extracted tens of thousands of francs for their work. Those with enough money reached agreement with a smuggler, paid him cash in advance, and joined the convoys leaving clandestinely for the Spanish border.[5]

By October 1942, hundreds of Jewish refugees had reached Spain in this manner, including entire families and many single men and women. From questionnaires taken of those who wished to emigrate to Palestine, the age of these refugees was very diverse. Of sixty-five questionnaires examined, twenty-four refugees were above the age of 40 and two were over 65. As young people were given preference in the screening for emigration to Palestine, it may be concluded that the proportion of old people among the refugees who arrived in Spain was even greater. Most were stateless refugees who came to France from eastern Europe and some from Germany and Austria; because many had lived in Holland and Belgium between the two world wars, their status in France was much more tenuous than that of the Jews who had become naturalized there but whose citizenship was revoked by the laws of the Vichy government.[6]

This new wave of refugees reached Spain at a time when Jewish refugees and other people in transit who were delayed there numbered not more than 300. Of these, 250 were allowed to stay in Madrid, Barcelona, Vigo, and Bilbao.[7] As almost all those escaping to Spain in the summer of 1942 were Jews, their arrival put to the test the position of the Spanish government on the rescue of Jews.

Meanwhile, independent of their arrival, diplomatic measures regarding refugees were being formulated in Madrid in August 1942. Rumors had begun to reach the World Jewish Congress in New York to the effect that Spain was about to expel 500 refugees from Madrid and Tangier. At the request of the leaders of the World Jewish Congress, the U.S. Department of State instructed Carlton Hayes in Madrid to express to the Spanish government American concern over the fate of these Jews and the hope that they would be allowed to remain in Spain until they were able to emigrate to another country. The American Jewish Congress appealed through intermediaries to the Italian government, requesting that it urge Spain not to harm Jewish refugees. The Italian Embassy in Madrid asked the Spanish Foreign Ministry for confirmation or denial of the rumors concerning Jewish deportations but received no response. Ambassador Hayes, however, reported on August 14 that his intervention was successful: the Spanish Foreign Ministry issued instructions according to which no refugee would be sent back against his will, and in cases of German refugees nothing would be done until the extradition processes were exhausted or without the consent of the Foreign Ministry.[8]

If such a promise was indeed made, it also protected from expulsion those refugees who arrived in Spain at the end of August and the beginning of September. But the validity of this promise was limited because of the Foreign Ministry's lack of influence over the security police and the Ministry of the Interior: refugees crossing the Pyrenees were dealt with first by internal authorities. Further, the bitter struggle between the Falange Española and its opponents in the Spanish government, which reached a peak during the confrontation in Bilbao on August 15, resulted in the dismissal of Serrano Suñer as foreign minister and the appointment in his place of Jordana, whom Axis supporters suspected of Allied leanings. Thus, there was no reason why German agents and their supporters in the Spanish police should honor promises Serrano Suñer made before he was ousted from office. In addition, in August police surveillance of the activities of Samuel Sequerra, the unofficial representative of the JDC, grew more severe. One day the police arrived at his rooms at the hotel and confiscated all documents and materials they found there; it was not until one month later, after having been examined thoroughly, that most of the files were returned. The promises made applied at best to the handful of refugees already in Spain; the entry of additional refugees seemed likely to prompt the Spanish government to take a strict stand against them.

At first, the Spanish ignored the unexpected growth of the Jewish refugee population. Either because events in France that necessitated escape aroused little attention among the authorities in Spain, or because most of the newcomers hid behind false identities, the first waves of Jewish refugees were able to penetrate Spain with relative ease and even to reach Barcelona without incident. Those who were captured at the border were placed in regional prisons and received neither worse nor better treatment than the illegal immigrants of the two years preceding the summer of 1942. In most cases, the border guards were not hostile, although the instructions provided them apparently differed from place to place and from time to time. These conditions continued until October, when police vigilance increased and Sequerra, who aided many of the refugees who avoided imprisonment, was requested by the police to disclose the names and addresses of those refugees. Until October the deportations had been a matter of local initiative, but by the end of the month the Barcelona police began to take measures that appeared to be aimed at expelling all refugees, both old and new. "Situation refugees now Spain becoming more critical daily," cabled Joseph Schwartz, director of the JDC in Europe, then on a visit in Spain, on October 29, 1942. "Regret advise yesterday ten persons including seven from old group transmigrants were sent to France. Many arrests in Barcelona especially among old group." One week later, Schwartz again informed the heads of the JDC in the United States:

> Situation refugees Spain now most acute with mass arrests Barcelona continuing, authorities there threatening deport entire refugee population both new arrivals and old group. Meanwhile new arrivals continuing come increasing numbers creating huge problem financially and otherwise. We continuing make every effort alleviate situation but believe now every possible intervention your end most important. Advise urgently what steps you undertaking this connection.[9]

Either following instructions from the U.S. Department of State or through Schwartz's connections in Madrid, the American Embassy intervened officially on the matter of Jewish refugees. In a letter dated November 9, 1942, the first secretary of the embassy informed Undersecretary for Foreign Affairs José Pan de Soraluce of news concerning the deportation of Jewish refugees from Spain, including some who had been given permission for temporary residence, and expressed hope that something would be done to prevent this so that the refugees could be provided assistance. This tentative appeal, based largely on the warm personal relations between the secretary of the embassy and Pan de Soraluce, was unlikely to alter the fate of Jewish refugees who continued to flee to Spain. But by the time the letter was written, events made the problem of Jewish refugees part of a more general problem, toward which both Spain and the Allies adopted a completely different policy.[10]

FUGITIVES FROM ALL NATIONS

Many Allied soldiers, survivors of the invasion who were not evacuated at Dunkirk, crossed the Pyrenees late in 1940 with thousands of civilians fleeing for their lives. British intelligence had already begun to organize escape operations in Spain, which gained momentum in 1941 after small units in the Dutch, French, and Belgian undergrounds were mobilized. The chief purpose of these operations was to rescue Allied soldiers who had escaped from German prisons or were sent on missions behind enemy lines. Reliable smugglers were hired, and members of the underground accompanied the escapees to the Spanish border and often beyond. These rescues continued regularly throughout 1941, increasing when the Allied bombings intensified and many flyers were shot down behind enemy lines.[11]

In addition to the British operations, underground groups of other nations, operating on French territory, rescued their own soldiers and civilians and helped them cross into Spain in order to return to their army units. In Marseille in 1941, a group smuggled hundreds of Czechs into Spain legally and illegally; although the group soon disbanded, its members and other Czechs continued to smuggle refugees into Spain during 1942. There were, in addition, several special underground smuggling networks for Dutch army personnel that operated in 1941 and later, and similar organizations assisted Poles and Belgians.[12]

The care of these refugees in Spain was important to the British and American embassies. Allied army personnel who succeeded in reaching one of the British consulates, and whose identity did not arouse suspicion, were received by the military attaché's assistants and given financial assistance that enabled them to reach Portugal secretly. Trucks belonging to the British Embassy in Madrid and to the Consulate in Barcelona that regularly brought food from Gibraltar often served to transport British and Allied soldiers fleeing Spain. Soldiers caught at border crossings and subsequently placed in prison or in Miranda de Ebro received assistance from the British Embassy. The American Embassy also worked to free prisoners and made available its personnel and financial resources. Because of the importance attached to the movement of military personnel for intelligence purposes and the military effort in general, Carlton Hayes regarded their assistance as one of the more important functions of his embassy, overshadowing any activities on behalf of civilian refugees. "He thought that any activity to get Jewish refugees out of France across Spain would hinder his program for getting American prisoners of war out," commented JDC director Schwartz. "Therefore he sometimes regarded our activities as a sort of nuisance."[13]

Until the Allies landed in North Africa in November 1942, the rescue of soldiers and military personnel continued on a limited basis. The Spanish authorities, although aware of some of these activities, were not politically embarrassed by them. But in November events changed drastically.

On November 11, 1942, the Germans reacted to the Allied invasion of Algiers and Morocco by invading the south of France, thus eliminating the last semblance of independence maintained by Marshal Pétain. On November 27, they forced the Vichy government to disband the military units that had been permitted until then according to the Armistice of 1940. The commanders of the French fleet anchored at Toulon chose to destroy it rather than let it fall into German hands: sixty-one French ships were sunk by their own crews. In North Africa, Admiral Jean François Darlan, commander of the French fleet, surrendered to the Allies—ostensibly in the name of Marshal Pétain—and then joined with them. This and the prominence given General Henri Giraud by the American forces caused friction with the Free French under General Charles de Gaulle but did not cloud the fact that the "unconquered" France of Vichy had been vanquished while a free France was emerging in Africa. Thousands of young Frenchmen, under threat of being mobilized to work for the Germans, crossed into Spain to join the French forces in North Africa.

So from mid-November 1942 a new wave of immigrants began to arrive in Spain, despite the early winter snows in the Pyrenees. Young men of army age, singly and in small groups, fled to the French border towns in search of connections with smugglers. Among the wave of refugees were also French politicians and army officers who until then had supported the Vichy government and now realized that the time had come to change allegiance. Priests, mayors, and other public servants extended assistance to the escapees, placing at their disposal their local contacts, who were in most cases the professional smugglers who led them through the mountain passes in exchange for exorbitant fees. The movement of French refugees—greatest during the first months after the German occupation of the south of France—continued despite the conditions that worsened during 1943 and throughout the summer of 1944. The exodus of other nationals, such as the Dutch and Belgians, increased and the avenues of escape widened.[14]

When the refugees first set out for Spain they did not know how its government would react to them. They were aware that they might be sent back or handed over to the Germans. The strict measures taken by the Spanish in Barcelona in October 1942 against the refugees who had just arrived and the deportation of those who had come from France were not good omens.[15] Nevertheless, an unforeseen situation influenced the Spanish authorities in their favor. François Piétri, the Vichy ambassador in Madrid, was uneasy over the inconsistency of his government's position. Darlan's surrender and subsequent siding with the Allies, as well as the German occupation of the south of France, prompted him to view his aid to French refugees as consistent with his loyalty to Vichy. Or it may be that he hoped his concern for the refugees would assure his position in what seemed to be new developments in France and North Africa. For these or other reasons he sent an appeal to Foreign Minister Jordana on November 14, 1942, asking that Spain neither return the refugees nor imprison them. When Jordana informed him that this would likely be refused by both the minister of interior and the minister of war, who would insist that the refugees be returned, Piétri appealed to them personally. On November 15, 1942, Piétri met with Interior Minister Blas Pérez Gonzáles and handed him a letter similar to the one he had sent to Jordana; that same day he spoke to Minister of War Carlos Asensio, who received him with greater sympathy than he had expected. As a result of these meetings, the Spanish government consented, on November 17, to the following:

1. No refugee would be sent back at the border.
2. Men of army age would be held in Miranda de Ebro or elsewhere until another camp could be established, pending a decision regarding their status.
3. Officers in active service would be concentrated in a military base and would be treated decently.
4. All others would be freed upon proof that someone was prepared to care for them or that they had sufficient means to care for themselves.

Piétri noted Jordana's statement, and on November 23, 1942, he circulated it to the French consulates in Barcelona, San Sebastián, and Zaragoza.[16]

The news that the government of Spain had agreed to admit refugees quickly reached France, bringing much-needed relief to the hundreds of men and women who, despite the winter conditions, had already embarked upon the hazardous journey through the Pyrenees. Germans and the Vichy militia tried everything possible to capture the escapees. On November 24, 1942, German guards were stationed along the border between southern France and Spain, and for weeks they worked at improving their vantage points and patrols. Often footsteps in the snow gave the refugees away; the pursuers soon used dogs to track their prey. On February 18 and again on April 3, 1943, Vichy authorities and the Germans expelled many Jews from the five French provinces along the Pyrenees and declared an area along the Spanish border closed, in which only local inhabitants and persons with special permits could enter or move about. During the winter of 1942–43, the Gestapo found and destroyed several British intelligence operations smuggling Allied infantry and airmen into Spain. Informers among the smugglers and local French residents in the border towns were responsible for the capture of a considerable number of refugees.[17]

Germany also applied diplomatic pressure to change Spanish policy vis-à-vis the refugees from France. Piétri, who had remained faithful to

Marshal Pétain, went so far as to demand that the Vichy government strengthen its border patrols to prevent the escape of additional refugees. The presence of two German divisions in the southwest of France and the fear that as the war in Tunisia developed Germany would next attempt to conquer Spain gave German pressure added weight. On March 25, the Spanish Foreign Ministry announced that the boundary in the Pyrenees was closed to refugees without legal transit documents. Even before it was decided what to do about those refugees who had already crossed into Spain, the border police of the Barcelona and Pamplona regions, where most of the refugees had arrived, tried to send some of them back to France. The Spanish government reinforced their border patrols and demanded that the French do likewise.

Germany's political success provoked sharp Allied reaction. Ambassador Hayes met with Jordana and warned him that Spain's recent border actions would not be received well in the United States. He demanded at least that American soldiers and prisoners of war who succeeded in reaching Spain should not be expelled and that Spain should continue sheltering refugees from France. British Ambassador Hoare also met with Jordana and demanded that the Spanish government rescind its order. Jordana gave assurances that escaping soldiers would not be expelled and that the refugee question would be reviewed; despite this promise, refugees were still denied entry into Spain. Winston Churchill now took up the cause of the refugees' plight. On April 7, 1943, he warned the Spanish ambassador in London that "if the Spanish government went to the length of preventing these unfortunate people seeking safety from the horror of Nazi domination, and if they went further and committed the offense of actually handing them back to German authorities, that was a thing which would be the destruction of good relations." The U.S. Department of State gave Juan F. Cárdenas, the Spanish ambassador in Washington, a similar warning. To bolster American demands upon the Spanish government, Carlton Hayes appealed to the papal nuncio, Gaetano Cicognani, and to the Argentine ambassador for support; they too appealed to Jordana.[18]

These vehement protests achieved their objective. In April 1943, Jordana informed Hayes that the order to expel refugees was rescinded and that in future all refugees who reached Spain would be allowed to remain there. Thus, after several weeks of hesitancy and contradiction, Spain reverted to its previous positive policy toward refugees and, despite German protests, continued to be a secure haven for those crossing its borders. As the war proceeded, the danger that this policy would change as a result of German pressure lessened, but its effect on the petty officials in the Spanish government was not gone entirely; even after April, Spanish patrols from time to time sent back refugees.[19]

Although Spain agreed to accept refugees, it never allowed them to settle permanently and become a burden on its treasury. Spain's guiding principle now was the same as the one that determined its policy on transit and exit visas in 1940: Spain was prepared to serve merely as a stopover for refugees on their way to a final destination in another country. Jordana hinted at this when he told Piétri that refugees would be arrested "until a decision was made regarding their status," and that they would be freed if someone was found to care for them. For this reason the Spanish government was quick to seize upon Hayes's false claim that the French fleeing to Spain in an effort to reach North Africa should be treated as citizens of a noncombatant nation seeking to cross Spanish territory from one region of their country to another, just as Nationalists during the Spanish Civil War crossed French territory from one region under Nationalist control to another.[20] In order to facilitate control over these people in transit, the government of Spain still had to formulate its position on the representation of French interests in Spain.

At first, Piétri undertook to care for the refugees. He established a welfare organization and raised the necessary funds. By February he had succeeded in arranging the removal of 200 people from Spain to North Africa. It soon became apparent, however, that this faithful servant of the Vichy government could not represent the French in North Africa. In his place were appointed personnel from the French Embassy who had left Piétri earlier and set up a French Mission with Hayes's aid. One member of the mission, Monsignor Boyer-Más, who had been with Piétri previously, also represented the French Red Cross and devoted himself to dealing with the refugees. On March 10, 1943, at Hayes's request, the Spanish government agreed to grant the French Mission official recognition as the de facto representative of France in North Africa. This paved the way for further work on behalf of French refugees.[21]

As for citizens of countries other than France that were under Nazi occupation, Spain had permitted earlier relief committees to function out of their former diplomatic offices; such was the case with Poland, Czechoslovakia, Yugoslavia, Greece, Norway, Holland, and Belgium. Although these committees had no official recognition, they were allowed to maintain contact with their governments in exile and to deal with their citizens who had entered Spain illegally and were imprisoned there. Now further concessions were granted to these committees as well.

As Spain's refugee policy evolved, hundreds of people were entering from France every day. When they descended the Pyrenees, exhausted and frozen, they were received sympathetically, but all of them, regardless of age, sex, or origin, were imprisoned, first in the local jail and eventually in the regional jail in the capital of the province. There they were treated like ordinary prisoners: their heads were shaved, they ate the usual starvation diet in Spanish prisons, they were placed in cells with political prisoners and common criminals, and they were chained in pairs and accompanied by armed guards wherever they went. Personal information was registered—name, citizenship, age—and the officials accepted the details they provided without checking their authenticity. The prisoners were grouped by nationality according to their declarations, and even when many of them claimed they were French Canadians, the Spanish never seemed surprised that so many Canadians had suddenly come down from the Pyrenees. Fear that men of military age would be treated differently prompted many of those between 18 and 40 to falsify their ages; this fact too went unverified.[22]

Women were kept in central jails in Figueras, Barcelona, and Madrid. For most of the men, however, the regional jail served as an introduction to the central concentration camp in Miranda de Ebro, where most refugees arrived sooner or later. In October 1942 there were 1,400 prisoners at the camp, living under very difficult conditions; by December, the number reached 3,500. The harsh conditions that caused the prisoners great suffering—lack of water or sanitation, crowded conditions, poor diet, and disease—increased as the number of prisoners increased. Because of these conditions, the hungry and frozen inmates staged a hunger strike on January 6, 1943. They rejected the camp food and refused the food parcels sent them by various welfare agencies. Despite the fear of epidemics likely to break out among the weakened inmates, they maintained their strike until January 15. They smuggled telegrams out of the camp to generate support from their governments and arouse public opinion. These cables were brought to the attention of Foreign Minister Jordana, who sent his personal representative to the camp to examine the situation. The Spanish authorities moved soon after to reduce the crowding in the camp.[23]

On January 16, the Spanish agreed to accept the guarantees of the consular relief committees and handed over to them 270 prisoners, most of them Poles and Belgians above and below military age. One month earlier, Samuel Sequerra had begged the governor of Gerona to free all women imprisoned in the jails under his jurisdiction and place them under house arrest in a small summer resort. The governor agreed, and dozens of women were placed in Caldas de Malavella hotels. This created a precedent that became the rule regarding the imprisonment of women and children. Once the first prisoners were allowed out of the camp at Miranda de Ebro, others soon followed, especially in March, when the French Mission began operating. As a result, the number of inmates there was reduced to between 1,100 and 1,200 by May.[24]

When the prisoners were freed, the French Mission made feverish preparations to remove its refugees from Spanish soil. The Spanish government, which acted on the principle that all refugees in Spain were merely in transit, assisted them in this effort. At the beginning of March 1943, approximately 1,400 French refugees were waiting in various places to be taken to Cádiz, and two French ships were anchored at Gibraltar ready to set sail for the Spanish port in order to transport them to North Africa. The German ambassador protested Spain's assisting the Free French in North Africa, demanding that the sailing be halted and threatening that if Spain did not comply, German submarines would be sent to sink the ships. In the face of this pressure, Spain withdrew and the sailing was canceled. But Spain did not forgo the actual evacuation; Jordana advised Ambassador Hayes to obtain Portugal's agreement to an embarkation from one of its ports, as the Germans could not object to the exit of refugees from Spain to a neutral country. After brief negotiations, Portugal indeed agreed to allow refugees to embark from the Bay of Setúbal. On April 30, the first convoy set sail. By August, Monsignor Boyer-Más and his aides in the French Mission succeeded in evacuating nearly 4,000 refugees through Portugal. During that month difficulties arose with the transit, and at the height of renewed negotiations with the Portuguese government violence erupted in Barcelona between French refugees waiting to be evacuated and members of the Falange there. Because German pressure had quieted by then, Spain decided that to avoid future incidents it was essential to expedite the evacuation of refugees and again allowed them to leave from Spanish ports. The Barcelona incident thus paved the way for more departures through the port of Málaga; between October and December, most of the refugees handled by the French Mission were evacuated.[25]

Spain's encouragement of the evacuation of refugees did not apply only to the many French citizens within its borders; other nationals enjoying the protection of the British Embassy were also allowed to leave. From Spain's point of view, this permission applied to all regardless of age or sex. In order to justify its actions to the Germans, the Spanish government used the excuse that Dutch and Belgian refugees were in transit and therefore were allowed to leave for Portugal on their way to Surinam, Curaçao, or the Belgian Congo. Polish refugees of army age were attached to the British citizens, as were a few Czechs and others. Those French and other citizens who informed Spanish prison authorities that they were

Canadian and were recognized as such constituted a special problem; as there were men of military age among them, the British Embassy pretended to recognize their nationality, even though it gladly would have relinquished the financial and administrative burden they imposed on it. At one point the British tried to hand the whole matter over to the French and the Americans, but they were unsuccessful. During 1943, British and other delegations organized the departure from Spain of thousands of refugees of various nationalities. Some left in trains for Portugal, others were transferred to the British base in Gibraltar, but the final destination of most of them was England.[26]

The evacuation of refugees who were citizens of Allied countries affected the situation in the prison camp at Miranda de Ebro. After it had been emptied by one-third in May 1943, it was again filled far beyond its capacity during June and July. The Spanish authorities sent to Miranda all the refugees who had been in the various other prisons, as well as those who were under house arrest in small towns, particularly in the Gerona region. The order to reincarcerate those who had previously been allowed to stay in the towns was given in Madrid; despite an attempt by the governor of Gerona to postpone its implementation, it was finally put into effect on July 13, 1943. At dawn, police surrounded the small summer resort hotels in Caldas de Malavella, and approximately 1,000 refugees living there were transferred by train. After a difficult four-day journey, the train arrived at Miranda de Ebro, and the dazed refugees swelled the number of inmates already in the camp to more than 3,000.[27]

The Miranda camp became in effect a sort of transit and selection point; after receiving the necessary guarantees from the consuls, many of the refugees were allowed to leave. Most of them sailed immediately from Spain; a few returned to settle in the towns and cities. Even though the number of inmates remained stable during the last six months of 1943—approximately 3,000 people—the period of imprisonment for most of them decreased because large groups were removed and were replaced from other prisons. Most of the prisoners hoped to leave the camp, for the time they spent there was unbearable. According to a report prepared in October, physical conditions in Miranda deteriorated. The diet that had been improved during the summer worsened considerably, and the lack of water increased illness; the camp's terrible living conditions had not been improved when the autumn chill heralded the suffering that winter would bring. Leaving the camp for house arrest was, given these conditions, like being on holiday. The Spanish authorities did not look kindly on large concentrations of foreigners in the cities, however, and the costs involved in maintaining refugees there were a burden on the budgets of the several consuls. The distress in prisons and in Miranda de Ebro and the immense sums required to alleviate the plight of the refugees were significant incentives in accelerating the rate of their evacuation, which was in tune with the interests of the Allied consular representatives and the Spanish.[28]

Thousands of Jews—soldiers and civilians of various countries who were included in the evacuated groups—also benefited from the transit policy that the Spanish government adopted and that the representatives of the Allies in effect implemented. The proportion of Jews among the escaping prisoners and airmen was perhaps equal to their proportion in the armed forces of England and the United States, but several were prominent in the smuggling operations. One of these, organized by an English Jew, Major Haim Victor Gerson, was called the Palestinian Operation because of the many Jews participating in it. Several Jews were active in a group organized in Holland at the beginning of the war, and there were of course others. No one regarded this resistance activity as particularly Jewish, but their presence most likely helped other Jews utilize these operations to escape.[29]

Many Dutch Jews were saved by passage through Spain with assistance from the units organized by the Dutch army. According to one story, a Dutch Jew found refuge at first in Switzerland, but in September 1943 he was mobilized by the Dutch military attaché and secretly sent to France—together with another Jew and two Christians—to join one of the convoys leaving for Spain. Although the forged documents and addresses the four had received proved unreliable, they succeeded in making contact with the Dutch underground in Toulouse, which was being assisted by fighting units of the French resistance. With another thirty young Dutchmen, including at least five Jews, they crossed the Pyrenees, west of Andorra. Their first connection with the Dutch agency in Spain, when they were brought to the prison in Lérida, hardly helped them. After enduring the harsh conditions and the hunger that characterized this prison, they were removed after six weeks and taken to Miranda de Ebro. The winter was then at its worst, and conditions in Miranda were undoubtedly the most difficult they had ever been; in comparison with the Lérida prison, however, their stay at Miranda seemed much easier. More than a month passed before 120 Dutch inmates were released and sent to Madrid. For six weeks they rested and did nothing, with all their needs provided by the Dutch agency in Madrid. They underwent security checks, were interviewed, and on January 31, 1944, they left by train for Lisbon to sail to Gibraltar and England. According to one witness, between thirty and forty Jews were among this group. This was one of the last convoys of Dutchmen of military age to reach England before the invasion of Normandy. There were already hundreds of other Jews in Dutch units in England who had passed through Spain at different times but under similar conditions.[30]

The Polish Jews were especially numerous, as they were among the first to be exposed to the horrors that awaited the Jews of occupied and Vichy France. But the largest group of Jews was the young Frenchmen who joined the Free French units in London and the French army in North Africa. The French Jews had known for some time about the possibilities of escape through the French underground. Joseph Fischer (later, Ariel), director of the JNF in France, who played a vital role during the war in financing underground rescue operations in France, testifies that early in 1942 his friend Justain Godard, who had been a diplomat and a senator, offered him his connections with the French underground for the purpose of sending Jews to Spain. Shimon Hammel, a leader in the Éclaireurs Israélites (the Jewish Boy Scouts) in France, heard by the end of 1942 from his friends that Jews would be helped to go to Spain if they were willing to serve in the army of Free France; by the summer of 1942 a group of youth leaders from the Jewish scouts had moved to Spain and joined the French army. Jacques Lazarus also made plans to cross the Pyrenees when he accidentally met a friend who mobilized him for the Jewish underground in Toulouse, where he became one of its chief organizers. The German occupation of France eliminated any doubts of many young Jews, so when the opportunity presented itself, they were prepared to leave. After they reached Spain, according to the evacuation agreement that applied to French citizens, they traveled to North Africa. Older French Jews, men of prominence in the public and political life of France, also benefited from the transit regulations that inspired Spain's refugee policy and eventually reached de Gaulle's camp in London or the French forces in Algeria and Morocco.[31]

Unlike the groups of refugees who left Spain through the evacuations organized by the agencies of their various countries, one group remained there unaffected by these activities. These were the stateless refugees, originating in the Greater Reich, and migrants who had become naturalized in Western countries but had been stripped of their citizenship. From its point of view, Spain's refugee policy applied to these as well. But as their exodus from Spain was fraught with difficulties, they became the touchstone for the true position of the Spanish government on the refugee problem. And as most of them were Jews, the problem of statelessness was also the acid test for the attitude of Spaniards and Allies alike toward the suffering of the Jews during the Holocaust.

Angel Pulido y Fernandez,
"apostle to the Spanish Jews."

Ignacio Bauer, head of the Madrid
Jewish community before World War II.

Behor Isaac Nahum, rabbi of the Sephardic
community in Barcelona, 1930–39.

General Emilio Esteban Infantes, commander of the División Azul, accepting the Iron Cross from Adolf Hitler, November 6, 1943. (Editorial AHR, Barcelona)

Capuchin Father Pierre Marie-Benoît, rescuer of the Jews of Marseille.

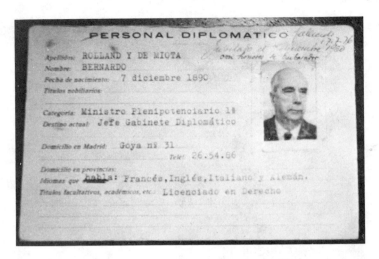

Bernardo Rolland, consul general in Nazi-occupied Paris, 1940–43. (Spanish Foreign Ministry)

Sebastian Romero Radigales, consul general in Athens, 1943–45. (Spanish Foreign Ministry)

Samuel Sequerra, representative of the AJDC in Spain, at his headquarters in the Hotel Bristol, Barcelona.

Joseph Croustillon
in Spain posing with children
rescued by the Armée Juive.

Yitzhak Weissman, representative
of the World Jewish
Congress in Lisbon, 1941–45.

The old synagogue in Madrid dedicated at the Calle de Pizarro in 1958.

The new synagogue in Madrid dedicated at the Calle de Balmes in 1968.

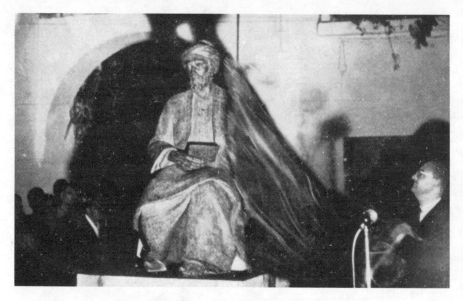

Unveiling of the monument to Maimonides at Córdoba, June 7, 1964. (Instituto Arias Montano)

Members of the Armistad Judeo-Cristiana praying in the Church of Santa Rita, Madrid, February 28, 1967.

THE STATELESS

After the German invasion of the south of France, few avenues of rescue remained open to persecuted Jews in France. Forging documents and hiding among Christians was the least complicated and therefore the most common means of escape, but as surveillance of civilians increased and fear of the authorities grew, these became more difficult and more dangerous. The Milice, formed in France in 1943 to support the German occupation forces and headed by Joseph Darnand, did not make life any easier for Jews in hiding or for those helping them. Although flight to Switzerland was still possible at the end of 1942, the Swiss government eventually clamped down on refugees and began to send them back—in effect handing them over to the Germans. Another means of rescue was related, paradoxically, to the occupation of France. When the Italians overran eight French districts on the Mediterranean coast, they showed fairness and even sympathy to the Jews living there. Thousands of Jews from the German-occupied zone began to make their way to Nice, Grenoble, and other cities in search of refuge, where Italian authorities extended their protection and occasionally came between the Jews and the Milice, which attempted to prove French sovereignty over the occupied zone by assuming the right to arrest Jews and deport them to concentration camps. Jewish security in this area was short-lived, however. After the surrender of Italy in September 1943, the Nazi death machine wound inexorably toward its end, the final destruction of the Jews. Plans to evacuate tens of thousands of Jews by sea from the zone of Italian occupation now had to be abandoned, and the effort to transport many of them overland to hiding places in northern Italy was only partly successful. For thousands of Jews, the Italian-occupied zone became a trap; their very presence made them liable to arrest and deportation to the death camps. Many others, however, were successful in hiding. During the year after Italy's defeat and until the liberation of France in August 1944, Jewish persecution increased, and the distinction between foreign and French Jews gradually blurred. Even the most apathetic French Jews soon perceived that a similar fate awaited all of them and that the need to find refuge was paramount.

As other means of escape became less feasible, flight through Spain became more so. But as time passed, German patrols along the Pyrenees increased, and stealing across the border was no simple task. Nevertheless, between November 1942 and August 1944 there were thousands of Jews, most of them aliens or stateless, who without help from the underground tried and often succeeded in reaching Spain. One of them, a

Belgian refugee who hid in the south of France after he had escaped from a French concentration camp, tells his own story:

> When the Germans conquered the south of France, I sold all my property, took my wife and child, and paid two hundred thousand francs to smugglers who were supposed to get us to Portugal. But the smugglers left us in the Pyrenees mountains, where I was stuck with my wife and child among the mountains and valleys. We wandered around until the Spanish caught us, took everything we still had, and placed my wife in a prison, me in Miranda de Ebro, and my child in an orphanage.

Rabbi Yehuda Ansbacher, who was imprisoned in France in the Gurs concentration camp, was warned just in time by the Jewish welfare organizations that he was on the list for one of the transports that regularly left Gurs for the East and death. With assistance from these organizations, he fled the camp, and with some money he kept, he and his wife contacted smugglers who undertook to get them to Spain. At the height of the winter of 1943, accompanied by two smugglers and one other person, the Ansbachers set out; after three days' wading through deep snow, close to exhaustion, they miraculously eluded the German patrols and reached the border pass. These two stories exemplify the hardships of the hundreds of refugees who managed to cross into Spain of their own accord. In many cases the end was tragic, often because the refugees were betrayed by their own smugglers. These stories also characterize the hundreds of cases of refugees who arrived in Spain and admitted their true legal status, that is, statelessness.[32]

Giora Szenes, another refugee, relates his adventures. After he passed over the Pyrenees near Perpignan with ten other refugees, he was captured by a Spanish border guard and imprisoned. He quickly adopted a false nationality and destroyed the Hungarian passport in his possession. When asked about his identity, he stated that he was a Canadian citizen. The Spanish accepted this, as did the British consulate, which handled his and other "Canadian" cases. Later he joined the masses of stateless people. It may be deduced from the questionnaires of refugees who reached Madrid and wished to emigrate to Palestine that many adopted this procedure. An examination of the questionnaires of those candidates who arrived in Spain before November 1942 indicates moreover that adopting a false nationality was common even before the large waves of refugees arrived after the German occupation of the south of France. Of forty-three refugees included in this category (thirty-one men and twelve women), eighteen declared that they were stateless, and fourteen adopted fictitious citizenships. All were freed from imprisonment by the consular representatives of the countries whose nationalities they had assumed, but they were not helped out of Spain during the operation to evacuate Allied citizens.[33]

In evacuating their own citizens from Spain, the foreign representatives intended primarily to help men of military age. A young refugee's readiness to join the military service of his country was an unequivocal condition for their handling his case. In most cases men of military age were requested to sign a formal guarantee that they would fulfill their obligation. Without this guarantee, their names were eliminated from the list of candidates for evacuation, and they in effect became stateless. Women and children and refugees who could not serve in the army were evacuated only if it was essential; the expense necessary to care for them in Spain was usually a major consideration in such cases. Because of the danger that German intelligence might exploit the escape routes through Spain to infiltrate England and North Africa (of which the consuls were aware), candidates for evacuation were also examined for their trustworthiness. Naturally, those refugees whose nationality was undefined suffered most in this respect.

In addition to these legal considerations, the problems of Jewish refugees were aggravated by anti-Semitic tendencies evident among the diplomatic representatives of several important countries, as well as in the community of refugees itself.

The anti-Semitism rampant in Poland between the two world wars was felt in the Polish units that fought in France and whose soldiers later sought refuge in Spain. Polish consulates in western Europe relied on a law passed on March 31, 1938, according to which the citizenship of anyone absent from Poland for more than five consecutive years could be revoked. This law, intended to prevent the return to Poland of Jews living in Austria and Germany, led to the cancellation of their passports and rendered them stateless. The Polish Embassy in Madrid attempted to apply this law in its policy toward Polish Jews who reached Spain. Samuel Sequerra discovered that the Polish representatives distinguished between their Christian and Jewish citizens and tried to shift responsibility for the Jews to the JDC. The Jews who joined the Polish groups in the Miranda de Ebro camp and those under house arrest in Madrid felt the full weight of anti-Semitism among their Polish compatriots.[34]

Even Dutch Jews found manifestations of prejudice in their fellow Dutch refugees. In Switzerland, Dutch Christians in the refugee camp demanded to be separated from Jews. In Spain, young Dutch Jews found Jew-haters even in their country's official embassy in Madrid. Nor was anti-Semitism unknown in some circles of the Dutch government in exile in England, where Jews were seen in high positions. Army officers—with whom Jews had little contact before the war—were prominent among Christian refugees from Holland, which may explain certain anti-Jewish feelings; it also may explain the hostility of Belgian prisoners, who according to one account tried to attack their Jewish inmates in Miranda de Ebro.[35]

Several Jewish inmates at Miranda have described incidents of anti-Semitism common among French refugees. The epithet "dirty Jew" was hurled at Joseph Gabel by two Frenchmen. When Rabbi Ansbacher was imprisoned there, a French officer incited an anti-Jewish riot. And in August 1943, some French refugees attacked their Jewish compatriots; although the attack was checked by the leaders of the French prisoners, it left its mark on every Jew in the camp. There was also evidence of anti-Semitism among the French refugees who were released from the Miranda camp and moved to Barcelona, where violence erupted in September between French Christians and naturalized French Jews. Even the French Mission was not above discrimination against Jews. After the Barcelona riot (but unrelated to it), the French representative there informed Jewish refugees working with him that he was instructed by his superiors in Madrid to dismiss all of them immediately. Despite their protests, their work was terminated, and they left soon after for North Africa.[36]

As a result of these anti-Semitic actions, the number of stateless Jews in Spain increased. Some Jews were rejected by their fellow nationals, while other Jews chose to reject them, disappointed when those battling Nazism embraced its ideology of racial superiority. Some Jews who sought to avoid military service in the army of their country pointed to anti-Semitism to justify joining the ranks of the stateless.

At first, care of stateless refugees was almost exclusively the domain of Samuel Sequerra and his small band of assistants. With his knowledge of the language and culture of Spain, his personal connections among local authorities, and his talent for capitalizing on an opportunity, Sequerra succeeded in extending valuable aid to many refugees soon after their arrival in Spain. With support from the Portuguese consul in Barcelona, Sequerra was able to strengthen his quasi-diplomatic position; out of his efforts on behalf of non-Jewish stateless refugees, he gained the trust of the British consul in Barcelona and other Allied representatives. Throughout all his activities, Sequerra and his brother Joel never hid the fact that they were observant Jews, which earned the respect of some of their Spanish friends. Despite all his connections, however, Sequerra could not cope with the thousands of refugees who began to reach Spain in late November 1942. Because of the distance from his hotel in Barcelona to Madrid and Miranda de Ebro, he was seldom able to visit these important locations. In Madrid, Sequerra availed himself of the services of Moshe Eizen, who provided financial assistance to refugees who came to him; but Eizen too could not extend his work to the bulk of refugees in the Miranda camp.[37]

Many stateless refugees who adopted false nationalities imposed a heavy financial burden upon the various consuls; the consuls could ease this burden only by transferring it to an official organization recognized by the Spanish authorities. Spain's willingness to receive all refugees—and the fear that this policy might change abruptly—prevented Allied representatives from ignoring the stateless refugees or abandoning those who pretended to be citizens of Allied countries. For these reasons, American Ambassador Carlton Hayes began in 1942 to attempt to persuade Spanish Foreign Minister Jordana of the need to set up some official representation of American welfare organizations that would enjoy the patronage of the American Embassy. In comparison to Hayes's earlier unwillingness to deal with stateless refugees, this step constituted a turning point and shifted Spain's position regarding refugees in general. Jordana uncharacteristically consented to Hayes's proposal and sought to obtain permission for the creation of a joint agency of these welfare organizations. In this manner, the Spanish government hoped not only to find another party to care for refugees during their stay in Spain but also to expedite their swift removal.

In talks with Jordana the name of a candidate to direct this new operation was suggested: David Blickenstaff, a member of the welfare staff of the American Friends Service Committee, who had worked with the Quakers in Spain during the Civil War. As AFSC and JDC leaders agreed, Blickenstaff and his wife, Janine, the daughter of the vice-consul of Uruguay in France, were invited to Madrid for consultations. Hayes requested that they should extend assistance to refugees even in cases where this aid contradicted Quaker principles. In January 1943, Blickenstaff and his wife began their work in one room in the American Embassy, where they functioned until, on April 10, 1943, the Spanish security police authorized the representation in Spain of the American Relief Organizations. Now Blickenstaff was able to rent a house, situated between the American Embassy and the Spanish Red Cross, and to transfer there his team of aides. The JDC and the AFSC determined that the JDC would carry two-thirds of the administrative budget of the new office; when other American welfare organizations joined in 1944, its proportion decreased to 40 percent. Fully supported by the American Embassy, Blickenstaff quickly became a sort of consul general for all those without diplomatic representation.[38]

This improvement in Spain's position toward stateless refugees had swift results: after Sequerra obtained the release of women from prison and the promise that their imprisonment in future would be brief, Blickenstaff's office succeeded in freeing many stateless refugees from Miranda de Ebro. In light of these successes, the Spanish government assumed that the American welfare organizations also would succeed in evacuating all refugees under their auspices from Spain; this was realized very slowly and only much later.

THE EVACUATION

The increasing distress of the refugees in Spain came to the attention of the British and American public almost at the same time as the news concerning the genocide of Jews by the Nazis. After much hesitation, both Allied governments issued, on December 17, 1942, a proclamation condemning the murder of Jews. In the weeks following, pressure from Jewish organizations in England and the United States mounted. Members of Parliament and other prominent British figures demanded that the Allies take action to help the Jews. Among several plans, the most significant proposed that the Allies appeal to neutral countries, guaranteeing financial support for refugees until their evacuation. It was emphasized that promises to evacuate all refugees promptly would encourage the governments of Spain and Portugal to continue to accept refugees.

This proposal was advanced by Moshe Shertok (Sharett), writing on behalf of the Jewish Agency one day after the Germans invaded France, to the American consul in Jerusalem, L. C. Pinkerton. In a letter dated November 12, 1942, Shertok urged the U.S. government to ask Switzerland, Spain, and Portugal to absorb those Jewish refugees who would surely flee from France. To guarantee their swift evacuation from Spain and Portugal, he promised that the Jewish Agency would request the British government of Palestine to transfer to Lisbon the quota of immigration permits originally allocated to French immigrants. In this way the exodus of hundreds of refugees from the Iberian peninsula would be assured. The Jewish Agency in Jerusalem, and later its Executive in London, prepared to send a special emissary to Spain and Portugal to screen candidates for immigration according to criteria established by the British Mandatory government.

Entrusted with this mission was Wilfrid Israel, a prominent German Jew who had found refuge in England. After many delays, he left London on March 26, 1943, and eventually arrived in Lisbon. He met hundreds of stateless refugees in Portugal and Spain and certified many of them as candidates for immigration to Palestine. Because military operations in the western Mediterranean were at their height, Israel's efforts to organize the transport of immigrants to Palestine encountered difficulties he was unable to overcome. On June 1 he left for London to try to increase the number of immigration permits allocated to the Iberian peninsula and to hand over the information he had gathered to another emissary, who was to succeed him. On his return flight, his plane was shot down by the Germans, and all passengers on board were killed. With Israel's death his information was lost, and the offers he had prepared to make in London died with him. Plans for immigration to Palestine were frozen until October, when another Zionist emissary, Fritz Lichtenstein (later, Peretz Leshem), arrived in Spain. Lichtenstein, a member of Kibbutz Yagur and one of the leaders of the Hehalutz movement in England, was forced to repeat the steps taken by Israel in screening all the immigration candidates and coping with the administrative red tape that obstructed their relocation. Not until January 1944 were preparations completed, and the first immigration ship from Spain, the Portuguese *Nyassa*, sailed from Lisbon and Cádiz for Palestine; on board were 170 immigrants from Portugal and 560 from Spain and Tangier. A second group of 425 immigrants from Spain, Portugal, and Tangier sailed on the ship *Guiné* in October 1944. The careful plans and the great expense invested in organizing this immigration resulted in fewer than a thousand refugees taken from the Iberian peninsula to Palestine during 1943 and 1944.[39]

Resettlement in Palestine was only one solution to the problem of Jewish refugees in Spain; because of the war in the western Mediterranean and the White Paper policy of the British government, it was by no means the main solution. The search for other destinations was far more important for the fate of stateless refugees in Spain. Members of Parliament and many public figures in the United States and England urged the establishment of a temporary rescue center for refugees in North Africa (in the French areas freed from Vichy rule) and to transfer there stateless refugees from the Iberian peninsula.

In January 1943, under increasing public pressure, the British and American governments began to organize a special conference to deal with the problem of refugees. After many delays, the conference convened on April 19 in Bermuda. British representatives proposed the creation of a refugee center in North Africa as the quickest and easiest plan to implement. The opening of a refugee camp in North Africa would serve to keep the main escape routes out of the occupied countries open for more refugees. It would also show the world that something had been done to save Jews from annihilation in western Europe. After one week of discussion, the American representatives at the Bermuda Conference were also convinced of the benefits of a center in North Africa. Robert D. Murphy, Roosevelt's personal representative in North Africa, was asked to speak with generals Giraud and Eisenhower, who was then commander of the Algerian and Tunisian fronts; U.S. Secretary of State Cordell Hull offered this plan to the Joint Chiefs of Staff for their consideration.

On April 26, the response of the Joint Chiefs of Staff was received under the signature of Admiral William D. Leahy, commander of the Navy. In their view, a refugee center in North Africa would hamper naval transportation and civilian supplies that were already overburdened and would impose additional, unwarranted responsibility on the High Command in North Africa. Furthermore,

> The influx of a considerable group of Jewish refugees to North Africa might cause such resentment on the part of the Arab population as to necessitate military action to maintain order. For the above reasons the United States Chiefs of Staff strongly urge that the British proposal be rejected.

British representatives met with American representatives to convince them of the benefits of the proposal. But at this meeting, as well as at another with the Joint Chiefs themselves, no minds were changed; on May 7 they informed Cordell Hull of their steadfast position. The Bermuda Conference's resolution to evacuate stateless refugees from Spain to North Africa and its rejection by the Joint Chiefs of Staff were turned over to Roosevelt, who was to choose between accepting the reservations of the Joint Chiefs or ordering the implementation of the Conference's resolution.[40]

On May 14, Roosevelt made his decision:

> I agree that North Africa may be used as a depot for those refugees but not as a permanent residence without full approval of all authorities. I know, in fact, that there is plenty of room for them in North Africa, but I raise the question of sending large numbers of Jews there. That would be extremely unwise.

The President of the United States thereby joined those who raised the specter of anti-Semitism that might have been provoked by the rescue of Jews. Still, Roosevelt implied that the plan to evacuate refugees from Spain would be executed speedily, which would encourage the Franco government to assist in saving Jews. This was not what happened, however. Three obstacles still prevented establishing the refugee center, and a full year passed before the first refugees were evacuated from Spain and reached the transit camp in North Africa.[41]

The first obstacle was the opposition of several State Department officials, headed by Assistant Secretary of State Breckinridge Long. On

June 4, 1943, in a conversation with the British chargé d'affaires in Washington, Sir Ronald Campbell—who was trying to ascertain what had been done so far to implement the evacuation to North Africa—Long explained that as the Bermuda Conference had recommended the convening of the Intergovernmental Committee on Refugees, the United States felt that this committee should handle the evacuation; before it could meet, however, American influence in the committee had to be determined. According to Long, Churchill and Roosevelt had discussed the issue in May 1943, when Churchill promised to raise the matter in Parliament and inform the State Department of its decision; until then and until the international committee could be convened, no action would be taken. Long's deliberate procrastination showed when he disclosed the contents of a cable from Rabbi Maurice L. Perlzweig, in which he questioned the likelihood of evacuating Jews promptly from occupied countries. Long claimed that Perlzweig's cable indicated there had been

> a change of policy and possibly of mind of some of the gentlemen who had been very active in pressing for a swift evacuation. Their new point of view seemed to be realistic and in line with the beliefs of our two governments, as indicated at Bermuda.

Long hoped that in the intervening period public opinion would become more realistic and Jewish organizations would be convinced that nothing could be done to save Jews in the areas of occupation. In his memorandum of June 29, 1943, he attempted to rationalize the resolutions of the Bermuda Conference: the Bermuda Conference was concerned not only with Jews but with all refugees; the problem of stateless refugees is a matter for the Intergovernmental Committee; the Allies are evacuating French refugees, and many of the Jews are French and have been moved to North Africa; this evacuation alleviates the plight of stateless refugees in Spain; and an Allied victory will solve the refugee problem. Although Long did not ignore the need to establish a center for refugees, he never considered the matter urgent.[42]

The U.S. State Department's hesitation came under heavy pressure from the British. On May 22 and June 4, 17, and 24, 1943, British representatives raised questions concerning steps the U.S. had taken to implement the program. When all these inducements failed, Churchill sent a cable to Roosevelt on June 30, in which he wrote:

> Our immediate facilities for helping the victims of Hitler's anti-Jewish drive are so limited at present that the opening of the small camp proposed for the purpose of removing some of them to safety seems all the more incumbent on us, and I shall be grateful if you would let me know whether it has been found possible to bring the scheme into operation.

British eagerness to see their plan implemented is doubtless due in some measure to the fact that, like the U.S., the British government also was under fire publicly and needed to show that efforts were being made to rescue Jews from Nazi-occupied countries. No less important was the British position on another resolution adopted at the Bermuda Conference, whose implementation hinged on British support. This was the plan to save 5,000 Jewish refugees—whose exodus from Bulgaria through Turkey was pending at the time of the Bermuda Conference—and to bring them to Palestine. It is not improbable therefore that England's insistence on the North African refugee camp was related to its inaction on the Bulgarian issue and to its general refusal to rescue Jews by permitting their immigration to Palestine. This was known, of course, to the Americans, who preferred to divert the discussion to the Bulgarian rescue whenever the British raised the question of the North African refugee camp. In this manner the discussions between the two powers on the implementation of the Bermuda resolutions often were reduced to mutual recriminations.[43]

In any event, Churchill's appeal overcame the first obstacle, and Breckinridge Long was asked to prepare a report stating that the camp would be set up and maintained by the Foreign Relief and Rehabilitation Organization, headed by Herbert H. Lehman; the report was sent to the prime minister on July 9, 1943, and was approved. A budget of $500,000 was allocated, to be shared equally by the British and Americans. Generals Eisenhower and Giraud were asked to determine the site for the camp, and the Lend-Lease plan and the U.S. Army were requested to provide necessary food, supplies, and equipment.[44]

Now it seemed possible finally to begin the program without further delay, but another obstacle remained, namely, obtaining cooperation from all authorities in North Africa. Murphy and Giraud at first did not oppose the plan; in their view, it seemed possible provided that thousands of French refugees from Spain were evacuated first. Lehman's elaborations of the practical details were received favorably. On August 11, 1943, Murphy announced that a camp named after Marshal Lyautey had been found at Fedala, near Casablanca, an ideal place for the refugees, and only required ratification by the French.[45] Two months passed while the French delayed their answer, demanding that freedom of movement of stateless refugees be restricted to equalize their situation to that of enemy citizens of military age living in Morocco who, because they would not serve in the Foreign Legion, were imprisoned. The State Department objected, and it was another month before the French agreed to an open camp that would enable refugees to find work and earn a living. Thus in the four months that passed from the time accord first was reached between England and the United States, the plan had progressed no further than an exchange of correspondence between governments. But a third obstacle still remained: the administration and operation of the refugee camp.[46]

In December 1943, the team that was to set up and conduct the camp began to assemble in North Africa. Moses W. Beckelman, a Jewish welfare worker from the United States and a senior official in Lehman's office, was appointed head. Beckelman traveled to Spain; after he negotiated the procedures for screening refugees, it was decided that the actual screening would be handled through Blickenstaff's office in Madrid. The details were worked out, and those refugees interested in moving to North Africa were invited to register. Under instructions from Cordell Hull, Blickenstaff was to disqualify candidates only where security or medical risks were involved. When all preparations had been completed, Blickenstaff's aides began screening immigrants. During January and February 1944, 410 refugees were chosen for evacuation and were transported three months later. By the end of the screening process, the requests of a total of 1,340 refugees had been examined, of which the French authorized 977; of these only 630 actually reached the Lyautey camp.[47]

Mountains of paper—resolutions, diplomatic memoranda, discussions, and reports—had accumulated in the eighteen months since the Bermuda Conference, which was intended to expedite the evacuation of refugees from the Iberian peninsula. All this political maneuvering resulted in the removal of a few hundred Jewish refugees to a temporary transit station; its effect on the plight of stateless refugees in Spain was therefore minimal.

Without a comprehensive plan for the removal of stateless refugees from Spain, there was, at best, hope only for regular immigration permits to countries in the Western Hemisphere. But entry to these countries, which had not been easy during the early part of the war, was no easier now.

The official agency of the welfare organizations in Spain helped those refugees who possessed entry permits to the U.S. by enabling them to make their arrangements at American consulates. Although the already rigid regulations were not changed, the U.S. consented to accept children who had fled to Spain under the latter's agreement to accept 5,000 children from France. Because officials in the American consulates interpreted instructions from Washington to the letter, in effect they disqualified the candidacy of all children who could have been evacuated from Spain. Furthermore, entry permits to adults were conditional upon examination, even in cases where security considerations did not apply. At the end of 1943, when it appeared that progress was being made in establishing the Fedala camp, entry permits to the U.S. were not available to those whose transfer to the camp had been authorized.[48]

The policy of other countries was no better. In 1942, Argentina allowed the entry of 1,000 children, but for various reasons its pledge was never honored. Early in 1943, the government of Chile sent a screening committee to visit the prisons and concentration camps in Spain and choose intellectuals and unmarried persons as candidates for immigration; this affected few refugees, and its motives were unclear. At the end of 1943, Mexico agreed to provide temporary refuge to 160 families, but these would have to be legitimate Polish citizens suitable for agricultural work; in addition, their stay in Mexico was to be in a refugee camp until the war ended. Also in 1943, Canada sent an immigration official to Spain and Portugal to screen candidates for temporary immigration; because the official was instructed to restrict his qualifications, only 350 refugees from Spain and Portugal reached Canadian shores during the whole of 1944.[49]

Processing stateless refugees for evacuation to each of these destinations was the refugees' best guarantee that they would not remain on Spanish soil indefinitely. The lengthy debate over the camp in North Africa and the arbitrary arrangements for immigration to Palestine and other countries forced the Spanish government to face the fact that the time of departure of thousands of refugees from Spain was undefined. In view of this, Spain adopted a refugee policy that changed periodically, often with surprising contradictions.

In the first half of 1943, after women, children, and some men not of military age had been released from prison and were placed under house arrest in towns and cities, Miranda de Ebro still held stateless refugees suitable for conscription. The security police and camp authorities insisted that, like the other prisoners, they should not be freed until 48 hours before they were to leave Spain, which condemned these refugees to remain in Miranda for an undefined period of time. Fortunately for them, however, the Spanish government pursued a somewhat more flexible policy, and refugees who succeeded in leaving the camp, by whatever subterfuge, were able to obtain temporary residence permits when they arrived in Madrid. The problem, then, was to get out of Miranda legally with one of the groups of released prisoners—most of whom were leaving Spain—and to leave the group when it reached Madrid, where the refugees would present themselves in Blickenstaff's office and request (and usually receive) his financial support. In this way, the refugees were issued residence permits to remain in Madrid.[50]

In August 1943, the Spanish government acceded to Blickenstaff's requests, and most of the stateless prisoners in Miranda were allowed to

live in Madrid and Barcelona under police supervision until they left
Spain. This, however, did not prevent the jailing of stateless refugees in
Miranda even afterward. When Blickenstaff visited the prison camp in
October 1943, he found fifty stateless refugees; his efforts to free them
were unsuccessful. Eight months later, Fritz Lichtenstein, the Jewish
Agency emissary, tried to free dozens of other refugees from Miranda;
although he screened and confirmed them for immigration to Palestine,
the authorities refused to free the prisoners until the eve of their departure. Blickenstaff made another visit to Miranda at the end of August
1944; he found 110 stateless refugees still incarcerated, 36 of them Jews.
As German soldiers and officers had begun by that time to request asylum
in Spain, having quit the battlefield in France, the Spanish government
placed them in Miranda de Ebro as well. The Jews still held there now
found themselves forced to live with Nazis. Imprisoning Jewish refugees
in the same quarters as their persecutors was discontinued only after
tension in the camp resulted in violence.[51]

Stateless refugees who for various reasons found themselves in prison
suffered even worse treatment. Even when conditions eased enough for
welfare agencies to send food, prison authorities refused to free stateless
refugees unless they proceeded immediately to the Spanish border, this
despite the fact that they had no time to contact the consuls and other
officials to arrange their departure. These prisoners were trapped in a
double bind: they could be freed from prison only when they could
emigrate, but they could not arrange for emigration because they were in
prison. This illogic assumed its most extreme form in the concentration
camp for forced labor at Nunclares de la Oca, where several dozen stateless refugees were held. On November 3, 1943, the camp commander
informed Blickenstaff that as these refugees were late in arranging their
emigration from Spain, he no longer could grant them special consideration, and they would be subject to the same harsh treatment as the other
prisoners. Nine months later, Blickenstaff visited this camp and found
thirty stateless refugees forced to quarry rocks and build roads, victims of
occasional beatings by the guards. Their only crime was that they had not
responded to the expulsion order (of which none were aware) and had not
left Spain on the appointed date.[52]

Paradoxically, with these injustices came magnanimous gestures on
the part of the Spanish government toward stateless refugees. During the
first months of 1944, the latter were more numerous than the former. In
addition to the permission granted most stateless refugees to live in
Barcelona and Madrid, the government also spared many of them a stay in
prison. Large groups of Jewish refugees arriving during the winter and

spring of 1944 were allowed to live under house arrest in the towns of the Gerona province and later to move to Barcelona. For these refugees the stay in Spain was merely a respite after their tribulations in Nazi-occupied countries before leaving for Palestine or North Africa.[53]

The JDC bore all expenses involved in supporting hundreds of refugees. In the villages, hotel costs were paid, and refugees were given pocket money. In the cities, the refugees received a monthly allowance of 650 to 700 pesetas per person for living expenses, in addition to free clothing and medical care. These amounts were very generous, enabling the refugees to live at a higher standard than the average Spanish government official and freeing the refugees from concerns about earning a living; because they were not allowed to work, they spent their spare time as they wished. As some of the goods and services were provided at the discretion of the staff in Blickenstaff's and Sequerra's offices, there were cases of exploitation and fraud among some refugees and sometimes suspicion and hatred toward them on the part of those providing the aid. Under these conditions of forced but comfortable idleness imposed as a result of the difficulties involved in their exit from Spain, some refugees were tempted to try to extend their transit period as long as possible, in the hope that in the meantime the war would end and they would be able to return to France to seek their relatives and save their property. Even refugees who wished to leave as soon as possible to emigrate to Palestine or elsewhere were affected by the convenience of this temporary residence in Spain.[54]

In this way, Spanish transit policy fostered a rather tranquil existence for refugees in an apparently secure refuge. This conflicted with the declared intentions of the government, but it was accepted with equanimity nevertheless.

ASYLUM IN SPAIN

In October 1942, Spain's refugee policy reached a critical point: the imprisonments and deportations reported from Barcelona could constitute precedents for a move to prohibit additional illegal refugees from remaining in Spain. Although expulsion might have become the rule regarding civilian refugees if such a course had been chosen, soldiers escaping from Nazi-occupied countries were not affected because of special arrangements the Spanish government made with the Allies. During this time, Jews comprised the majority of civilian refugees, but events that followed in the wake of the Allied invasion of North Africa changed all that. Suddenly, the influx of civilian refugees into Spain became an important Allied interest, and American and British ambassadors spared no effort to persuade Spain that it should not send them back. In agreeing to these demands, the Spanish government made no attempt to discriminate against Jewish refugees, as it had not done so in the past; nor did it establish elaborate procedures governing the acceptance of stateless refugees, most of whom also were Jews. Rather, the rescue of Jews became part of its overall arrangements intended to enable European refugees to reach North Africa and England. As a result, Spain became a land of refuge for all Jewish refugees who reached its borders.

As more refugees were evacuated, fewer remained on Spanish soil, improving prospects for the stateless. The hesitation that characterized the Allied evacuation of these refugees—a hesitation partly due to the fact that most were Jews—did not, however, make life any worse for them in Spain. The majority were allowed to wait in the cities or towns until their departure was arranged, and even though they were under police supervision they could spend their time as they liked as long as their needs were taken care of. The harsh treatment of refugees who were not released from prison was apparently the result of differing policies among the various authorities—including local ones—toward aliens staying illegally in Spain. But whether intentional or not, this treatment toward the refugees and their custodians implied that if they did not expedite their exit, the Spanish government soon might terminate its generosity.

From November 1942 until the liberation of France in August 1944, Spain sheltered all Jewish refugees arriving there illegally. The number saved in this manner was not limited by any policy of the Spanish government but rather by the forces of nature and by the Nazis patrolling the rocky, frozen slopes of the Pyrenees. The slow pace with which these Jewish refugees eventually were evacuated from Spain affected the legal rescue of Jews possessing Spanish citizenship.

Exaggerated news published in England and the United States drew attention to rescue attempts through the Iberian peninsula. The total number of Jewish refugees illegally entering Spain at the beginning of 1943 appeared to be in the tens of thousands. In correspondence between several departments in the U.S. government during June and July 1943 regarding the establishment of the refugee camp at Fedala, the number of stateless refugees in Spain—excluding all other categories of refugees— was estimated between 6,000 and 7,000 persons,[55] a figure that continued to guide those handling the evacuation of these refugees for some time. According to information provided by reliable sources, however, their number was much smaller.

Wilfrid Israel, the Jewish Agency emissary, estimated their number in May 1943 at 1,500.[56] Six months later, Rafael Spanien, one of the directors of HICEM in Lisbon, arrived in Spain to collect information on all Jewish refugees then in Spain. He compiled lists of refugees, including their nationality, occupation, and date of arrival in Spain, and found a total of 2,100 Jews, of whom 1,200 were stateless. This census covered all Jewish refugees known to the representatives of the welfare organizations and the consular authorities; those not included could not have numbered more than 150 or 200. As he also counted Jews who had arrived before August 1942 and a small number of Jews of Spanish nationality who had managed to reach Spain legally, it appears that the number of illegal refugees then on Spanish soil did not exceed the 2,100 he mentioned. At that time the evacuation of French citizens reached its peak; according to Spanien's estimate they numbered between 15,000 and 16,000, among whom Jews comprised at most 10 to 12 percent. It appears thus that the number of French Jews who were rescued was not more than 1,500 to 2,000; with them were many stateless Jews who left for North Africa, having adopted French citizenship or volunteered for French units. Spanien estimates their number at 1,200. It appears then that according to Spanien the maximum number of Jewish refugees who passed through or stayed in Spain between the summer of 1942 and the end of 1943 was 5,300.[57] This number is confirmed by Rabbi Yehuda Ansbacher, who from the latter part of 1943 until he emigrated to Palestine in January 1944 worked in David Blickenstaff's refugee aid office in Madrid. According to Ansbacher's figures, the total number of Jewish refugees in Spain until the end of 1943 was approximately 5,000.[58]

In preparing his estimate, Spanien doubtless was aware of the 300 refugees that HICEM had helped evacuate to various places during 1943. It is possible, however, that he did not include the hundreds of Jews who left Spain that year with refugees of other nationalities. Their proportion among the British, including the Canadians and those who became "Canadians" when they arrived in Spain, was considerable. There were also Jews in the Belgian, Czech, Polish, and Dutch groups who left Spain before Spanien conducted his census. In the course of the evacuation of the Dutch refugees, for example, 403 required special assistance, so the JDC agreed to help support them financially in Jamaica and Surinam after they left Spain and Portugal.[59] If all these groups are added to Spanien's estimates, almost 6,000 Jewish refugees reached Spain by the end of 1943 and were saved.

Until September 1944, when flight from France was halted completely, this number swelled by several hundred Jews. They continued to arrive on their own initiative, but especially through the escape route organized by the non-Jewish French underground and other organizations. Monsignor Boyer-Más, who was responsible for French refugees in Spain, estimates the total of those he helped at more than 23,000; this figure is confirmed by other sources, who point out that the number of French refugees who passed through Spain during all the war years was between 28,000 and 30,000. If Spanien's estimate is correct that French Jews comprised 10 to 12 percent of all French refugees, then during 1944 another 700 to 800 Jews were included among the French refugees. That same year, more Jews arrived and were evacuated from Spain. In addition were the Jews among the approximately 3,000 British and American soldiers who were smuggled across the Pyrenees from 1943 until June 1944.[60]

When all these figures are added together, the number of Jews rescued in Spain during 1944 may reach at most 1,500,[61] and the maximum from the summer of 1942 until the fall of 1944 will therefore be 7,500. Especially noteworthy were some 600 young people and children who were smuggled into Spain by the Jewish Army in Toulouse.[62]

5

THE RESCUE OF SPANISH NATIONALS

GERMAN AND SPANISH POSITIONS

The vicious hunt for foreign Jews in Paris in July 1942 and the subsequent deportations in both occupied and Vichy France alarmed the Sephardic Jews living in France at the time. Jews of Turkish and Greek nationality felt the danger closing in on them. Even those Sephardic Jews whose families had been French citizens for many generations—and who, like the Ashkenazic Jews, had deluded themselves that they would not be affected—sensed that their security was threatened. Some even attempted to adopt Nazi racial ideology to divorce themselves from the fate of other Jews, encouraged by the rumor that the Iranian ambassador to France had convinced the Germans that Persian Jews were "Aryan" and thus were exempt from all anti-Jewish decrees in France. In an article written by a scholar of the Pasteur Institute in Paris, some Sephardic Jews found support for their contention that Sephardim are racially different from Ashkenazim. For a considerable sum, they obtained from another scholar anthropological and historical "research," including definitions and quotations from racist propagandists, stating that Sephardic Jews are distinguished from Ashkenazic Jews not only by their features but also by the composition of their blood. On the basis of these findings, they requested that the Nazis and the Commissariat Général aux Questions Juives recognize their right to be considered Aryan. In the course of these efforts, they appealed to Bernardo Rolland, the Spanish ambassador in Paris, in

October 1942. Rolland listened to them, accepted a copy of the research report, and promised to forward it to Foreign Minister Jordana for his consideration. Rolland kept his promise, but Jordana's reply never reached them—and may never have been written. The entire attempt ultimately was foiled by the French and German governments, who ruled that Sephardic Jews were Jews in fact and were to be treated the same as the others.[1]

The panic that spread among the Jews in France during the fall of 1942 prompted other Sephardic Jews—those without Spanish citizenship—to base their hopes on receiving immigration permits to Spain. It was rumored that Madrid had consented to provide entry and residence permits to all Sephardic Jews who could secure from two relatives or friends an invitation to live in Spain at their expense. According to the rumor, this invitation, when verified by local Spanish authorities, would be sufficient for the Spanish Consulate in Marseille to provide permits to all who requested them. Léon Rousseau, former head of the charities of the Sephardic community in Paris, brought this information to the attention of HICEM in Marseille on October 7, 1942; Rousseau also provided the names of several Sephardic families who already had been granted permits. He appealed to HICEM to adopt this precedent for Jews who had no personal connections in Spain through that organization's representatives there.[2] The procedures Rousseau outlined for granting residence permits in Spain were similar to those that the Spanish Consulate in Marseille had issued in November 1940. These regulations may have been the source of the rumor two years later; this time, however, Madrid had no intention of admitting Sephardic Jews for permanent residence in Spain, even when they held Spanish citizenship, as shown in the resolutions the Foreign Ministry formulated in 1942 regarding Jews of Spanish nationality.

A change in the leadership of the Spanish Foreign Ministry in September 1942 apparently brought about a reevaluation of the activities of several branches of that office. The Director of the Department for European Affairs, Pelayo García y Olay, summarized existing policy toward Jewish nationals of Spain in Nazi-occupied countries. In a report submitted October 2, 1942, to Foreign Minister Jordana, García y Olay reviewed the laws under which citizenship was granted to Spanish Jews living outside of Spain and then proposed steps Spain should take in handling their affairs in the future. He suggested that a census be conducted immediately of all Spanish nationals in each country. In each case, legal grounds for citizenship should be examined, and on the basis of the information received, a decision should be made "so that the aims guiding the Royal Decree of December 20, 1924, will not be distorted." Spanish consuls must continue to defend Jewish nationals abroad and improve their status whenever possible. Until their rights are recognized, their plight must be alleviated, such as has been done already by the Romanian government. Nevertheless, the instructions sent to Ambassador Lequerica in Vichy in November 1940 must be followed, according to which Spanish foreign representatives should report attacks on their Jewish protégés and act in their interest but should not interfere with the carrying out of local laws against Spanish Jews.

García y Olay's report did not contribute to the support the Foreign Ministry provided to representatives who continued to work on behalf of their Jewish protégés. Moreover, the report might have served to condone Spanish representatives who preferred to refrain from defending their Jewish protégés. Because the chief purpose of the 1924 decree—which was promulgated in the days of the Primo de Rivera regime—was to legalize those holding Spanish citizenship at that time, it also in effect canceled any citizenships granted before 1924 or after 1930. The report thus reflected Madrid's tendency toward a more severe line regarding those Spanish Jews living abroad as nationals.[3]

Two cases considered by the Foreign Ministry in December 1942 illustrate that the suggestions in García y Olay's report were adopted and became Spanish policy. On December 14, 1942, Bernardo Rolland informed the Foreign Ministry in Madrid of the new prohibition that Pétain and Laval had imposed on November 9 upon foreign Jews living in Vichy France. This new law forbade foreign Jews from leaving their homes without a special travel permit issued by the police. Rolland pointed out that limitations placed upon Spanish nationals conflicted with the Spanish-French agreement of 1862 and asked for instructions so that he could prevent the law from applying to his Jewish protégés. The Ministry's answer was found in the margin of his note: "He should make the request that he indicated." Three days later, the Spanish consul in Marseille wrote the Ministry that several of his Jewish protégés could not show proof of their nationality under the 1924 decree. These included an eighty-year-old man who had left Salonika for France with his wife in 1916; both were registered in the Marseille Consulate in that year and possessed citizenship documents provided by that consulate in 1922 and 1923 and a passport issued in 1929. Also included was a man from Salonika who held a certificate issued in 1918, which testified that all members of his family were registered in the Salonika Consulate and that he was also registered in the Marseille Consulate. The consul in Marseille pointed out that only lack of information had prevented these people from conforming with the regulations set forth in the 1924 decree; they were asking now for authentication of their Spanish citizenship, without which the German and French authorities would cancel their identity cards and food rations. The Foreign Ministry answered: "If they do not have documents that are completely in order, he cannot occupy himself with them."[4]

This response in effect turned these Spanish Jews into Greek nationals or, worse, stateless persons. It meant abandoning them to the Germans, which should have been evident to the Spanish consuls as they witnessed the arrests of foreign Jews. They could not pretend ignorance of the events of the night of November 4, 1942, when the Gestapo, aided by the French police, raided the homes of Greek Jews, most of whom were Sephardim, and arrested many hundreds of them that night and in the days following. Men, women, and children were deported to the concentration camp at Drancy. In a group that left on November 9, 877 Sephardic Jews were sent to their death, most of them of Greek nationality and the rest holding Turkish or other citizenship. Hundreds of Sephardic Jews from Greece and Turkey were also included in transports that left after this date.[5]

Under these new circumstances, the position outlined in García y Olay's report and adopted by the Spanish government regarding its Jewish nationals was wholly unrealistic. Even before the policy shift in Madrid, the Germans had sealed the fate of the Jewish nationals of neutral countries, including those of Spain.

Adolf Eichmann, head of the Gestapo's Jewish office, demanded from the beginning that the Jews of neutral countries be treated no differently from any other Jews. At a conference of Gestapo members from Nazi-occupied countries on August 28, 1942, Eichmann spelled out his plans and set June 1943 as the final date for the elimination of the problem of foreign Jews. The German Foreign Ministry, however, fearing adverse reaction, suggested that neutral countries be allowed to evacuate their Jewish nationals from areas of Nazi occupation. After discussions between the Foreign Ministry and the Reichssicherheitshauptamt (RSHA; Reich Security Main Office), Eichmann himself informed the Gestapo that until March 31, 1943, neutral countries were permitted to evacuate their Jewish nationals, provided there were no security risks.[6]

Even after this agreement, however, the Gestapo and senior officials in the German Foreign Ministry continued to object to the rescue of Jews holding neutral citizenship. In March 1943, Franz Rademacher, the head of the office in the Foreign Ministry that handled the Jewish problem, informed Hans-Adolf von Moltke, the German ambassador in Madrid, of a Reuter's communiqué stating that Spain was negotiating with the Allies for the rescue of Jews holding Spanish citizenship and of Sephardic Jews of other nationalities. Rademacher drew von Moltke's attention to the fact that the German ambassador to Bulgaria had been instructed to oppose negotiations concerning either the rescue of Jews or their emigration. Such negotiations conflicted with German interests, were likely to serve the propaganda needs of the Allies, and contradicted the "position of the Axis in relation to the Arab nations."[7] The assumption that Spain would not save its Jewish nationals was expressed by Günther Altenburg, the German ambassador in Athens, where hundreds of Sephardic Jews lived. Because of the absence of direct communication lines between the Spanish Embassy in Athens and the Foreign Ministry in Madrid, Altenburg allowed the Spanish ambassador to use the German Embassy to send cables regarding Spanish nationals, explaining to his superiors that he did so because he thought the Spanish government would reject the proposal to save its nationals, "and a negative response is in accord with our interests."[8] Altenburg's assumption also guided Gestapo officials, and when it appeared that Spain might abandon its Jews, they were prepared to forgo the murder of a Jewish family for whom the Spanish ambassador had made special representations in Berlin. When the Germans realized that this assumption was pointless, they quickly broke their promise to allow the evacuation of this one family because "this far-reaching concession" seemed unwarranted.[9]

But the Germans did not cancel the permission granted to Spain to evacuate its Jewish citizens from all the areas under Nazi occupation or influence. Eichmann's representative at the German Embassy in Paris opposed the rescue of Jewish Spanish nationals. In the correspondence that followed, the Germans set the rules to identify those entitled to repatriation. In a letter dated June 19, 1943, Eberhardt von Thadden, Rademacher's successor in the German Foreign Ministry, explained to the ambassador in Paris and to the commander of the Gestapo and the SD that "all Jews who possessed their foreign citizenship before the date we demanded that their respective governments repatriate them will be freed." If Jews received their Spanish citizenship only during 1943, however, "then the German Foreign Ministry will inform the Spanish government through its embassy in Madrid that the government of the Reich will be unable to exempt them [the Spanish Jews] from the measures taken against all Jews." Any additional impositions upon the Spanish were to von Thadden "politically undesirable." This was the policy the Germans eventually adopted.[10]

Moreover, even when the Spanish delayed the repatriation of their nationals, the German Foreign Ministry showed flexibility and patience, maintaining this position throughout 1944. This was shown during May and June in the wake of a request by Spanish Ambassador Rojas in

Romania to permit the evacuation of Jews from Bucharest to Spain. The German ambassador in Bucharest, Manfred von Killinger, objected to this request; the Gestapo supported his opposition and demanded that the Foreign Ministry refuse to issue the transit visas through Germany and France that Rojas had requested. Von Thadden reminded his superiors that the Foreign Ministry was the final arbiter in matters concerning foreign Jews, so the Foreign Ministry, and not the RSHA, must decide on this question. Furthermore, as Germany allowed the departure of foreign Jews who lived in the countries occupied by the Reich, there was no justification for preventing Romania from doing the same with its foreign Jews. Von Thadden's position was supported by the heads of the German Foreign Ministry.[11]

The Germans had their motives in allowing Spain the option of evacuating its nationals, even when the Spanish would not likely keep to a timetable. First was the desire not to become involved in a delicate problem with a country whose importance for Germany increased during 1943 and 1944 and whose attitude—including Franco's—toward the Jews was still ambiguous to the Germans. They also believed that the Allies were pressuring Spain to save Jews, and because of this pressure Spain could well demand the release of its nationals, who might in the meantime be murdered. Even though it hoped that Spain would abandon its Jews, the German Foreign Ministry actually was prepared to allow their rescue, provided Spain pressed this demand firmly.[12]

On January 21, 1943, the German Embassy in Madrid informed the Spanish Foreign Ministry that Spain could evacuate its Jewish nationals from the countries of western Europe until March 31. On February 22, von Moltke announced that this also applied to Poland, the Baltic countries, and the other occupied countries of eastern Europe. On April 30 this announcement included, with a change in the final date, the north of Greece. Spain, like the other neutral countries, thus faced an ultimatum: either bring to its borders all its Jewish nationals or forsake them to the Nazis.

This dilemma, repatriation or abandonment, brought the Spanish Foreign Ministry to adopt two contradictory resolutions within one month of each other. At first, in February 1943, the Foreign Ministry decided that Jewish nationals would not be allowed to enter Spain. The German ambassador in Madrid, who spoke on February 22 to José María Doussinague, the director of the Department of Foreign Policy in the Foreign Ministry, informed the German Foreign Ministry that "the Spanish government has decided under no circumstances to allow its nationals of the Jewish race the right to return to Spain. The government of Spain would appreciate it if these Jews were allowed to return to the countries of their origin, particularly to Turkey and Greece." Spain also expressed its willingness to provide transit visas to Jews, enabling them to travel to Portugal and from there to the United States. If these possibilities did not materialize, however, "the Spanish government would leave the Jews of Spanish nationality to their fate." On February 16, 1943, Ginés Vidal, the Spanish ambassador in Berlin, was instructed to try to obtain for Spanish nationals entry visas to Greece, Turkey, or any other country. Vidal then told Bernardo Rolland in Paris, who requested permission for a group of his protégés to come to Spain, that "these Spanish Jews have no authorization to come to our country, and those who wish to leave those territories [France, Belgium, Holland] can not hope that they will be allowed to settle in our territory."[13]

On March 18, one month after this position was taken, Foreign Minister Jordana announced a new policy. In a cable to Rolland, Jordana stated that "entry visas to Spain will be given to Spanish Jews when they prove with complete and satisfactory documents their own nationality and the nationality of each member of their family accompanying them, and when they demonstrate compliance with the requirement concerning inscription in the national registry and the marriage registry (if they are accompanied by their wives) as well as registration of births, if they are accompanied by their children." In each instance, when Rolland requested permission for entry into Spain he had to cable the full name, the document presented in compliance with the above conditions, and the border point where the Jews would enter the country. Jordana asked Rolland to urge the Germans to allow the Spanish Embassy to handle the property of these Jews later. Jordana added: "Advise the applicants for visas that the Spanish authorities will select their place of residence in Spain and that they will not be allowed to leave without prior permission. The visa will be valid for a single entry into Spain at a certain border point from a certain date until a certain date."[14] (See Appendix, document E.)

What happened between mid-February and March 18, 1943, to cause the Spanish Foreign Ministry to alter its hostile position? Did Spain adopt the new position alone, or was it the result of Allied pressure?

U.S. Ambassador Carlton Hayes relates in his memoirs that on March 18, Jordana sent his aide, German Baraibar, director of the European Department in the Foreign Ministry, to meet with the persons responsible for refugee matters in the American Embassy, Miles W. Bond and David Blickenstaff. According to Hayes, Baraibar announced at this meeting that "the Spanish government was anxious to use its good offices to rescue as many Jews as possible from Nazi oppression and persecution and that it was ready to assert a fanciful Spanish citizenship for Sephardic Jews in German-occupied countries as a basis for asking the German government to free this group of Jews and let them join the other refugees in Spain." This surprising description of the legal status of candidates for rescue is found also in a report Hayes sent to Secretary of State Cordell Hull one year after that meeting. The fact that candidates for rescue were Spanish nationals was not mentioned at all, and the entire episode was presented as an agreement between the Spanish and the German governments, according to which those rescued would be brought to Spain in transit, on their way to other destinations. Whether these matters were written—both in his report and in his memoirs—for the purpose of praising Jordana in particular and Spain in general, or whether they accurately represent Hayes's information, they at least testified that the Spanish chose to save their nationals without Hayes's influence. Moreover, Hayes adds in his memoirs: "We were obliged to explain to the Foreign Ministry that there was no immediate prospect of our finding any place outside of Spain where 'stateless' refugees might go, but that we hoped before too long we could find places for them and then, of course, the Sephardic refugees whom Spain was sponsoring could be included." It appears that the American ambassador regarded this rescue as a purely Spanish operation, so much so that he found it necessary to warn Jordana that those who came would have to remain in Spain for a certain length of time.[15]

British Ambassador Sir Samuel Hoare also may have exerted his influence on the Spanish government. Indeed, he relates in his memoirs that he intervened on behalf of Spanish Jewish nationals and tried to persuade Madrid of its duty to accept them, but this applied only to those living in Salonika, and happened apparently later and not between February and March 1943. So it seems that the change that occurred cannot be attributed to Hoare's actions either.[16] It therefore appears that the cause of the shift in Spain's position must be sought in the events that developed and the policies adopted within Franco's regime itself.

When the Spanish representatives in Berlin and France received their first instructions concerning the policy of abandoning the Jews, they began to examine the possibility of transporting their protégés either to the countries of their origin or overseas. These possibilities soon revealed that all other avenues of rescue were closed: Greece and the Balkan countries were under Nazi occupation or influence; Turkey was in no hurry to evacuate its own citizens and was thus less than eager to accept Jews who were not Turkish nationals; Portugal did not wish to absorb Spanish nationals whom Spain itself refused to welcome; and of all the lands in the New World, only Argentina was represented in Paris and, due to immigration limitations, was not prepared to accept Spanish Jews. All Spain's efforts to find an alternative to emigration to Spain were fruitless also because of Germany, which informed the Spanish government on March 6, 1943, that it would not agree to the evacuation of Spanish nationals to any destination other than Spain.[17]

Ambassador Vidal in Berlin apparently understood the seriousness of the situation and tried at least on two occasions to call the attention of the Spanish Foreign Ministry to the consequences of its policy of abandonment. In a letter dated February 26, 1943, he wrote: "In effect, Spanish Jews have no alternative other than to remain where they are, facing the most somber prospects." A week later, when the Germans requested a list of names of all Spanish Jews in western Europe, he wrote to Jordana: "As one can not hide from His Excellency the German objective, permit me to ask of His Excellency to be so good as to give me his supreme instructions whether or not to hand over the names they request." The situation of Spanish Jews brought Vidal to offer a solution that to a large extent contradicted the abandonment policy in effect. "If the government finds it convenient," he wrote in his letter of February 26, 1943, "it could grant them permission to go to Spain with transit visas, which will allow them to wait there the necessary few days until they receive a permit, directly or through the Red Cross, that will enable them to travel to another country."[18]

The Jewish Spanish nationals living in France also took measures to save themselves. On February 18, 1943, several of them sent a petition to General Franco, in which they mentioned the prohibitions already imposed on them and the fear of arrest and expulsion awaiting them. They spelled out the advantages of the protection Bernardo Rolland had provided them and even discussed their efforts invested in an attempt to rely on racist ideology to protect Sephardic Jews from the racial laws. After all this, they were left with only one alternative—seeking permission to come to Spain and settle there, which they were requesting General Franco to grant them. Five Jews signed the appeal—among them one Louis Franco, whose name appeared first among the signatories. The petition was received in the Foreign Ministry on March 1. It was marked for transfer to Franco's adjutant, and if need be to Franco himself; it is possible therefore that the petition reached its destination.[19]

A few days later, Rolland sent Jordana a second petition regarding Jewish Spanish nationals drafted by the Spanish Bureau of Commerce in Paris. In an emotional letter, the heads of the bureau of commerce expressed their bitterness that Spain intended to abandon its Jewish nationals and attached to their appeal a list of 125 names and business addresses, all of them "members of the bureau and honorable people who were always concerned with the interests of Spain." Thus the bureau of commerce placed all its influence behind the effort to save only a small number of the 3,000 nationals of Spain living in France.[20]

The suggestions of Ambassador Vidal, the requests and supplications of the Spanish Jews, and the bitterness of the bureau of commerce doubtless contributed considerably to the change in the position of the Spanish Foreign Ministry. These were perhaps supplemented by others inside and outside the Foreign Ministry who were sympathetic toward Spanish Jews. Some even may have supported Jews in previous years, including perhaps Jordana himself. When he was a military commander and governor in Spanish Morocco, Jordana maintained connections with the Jewish community in Tétouan; in 1930 this community had inscribed him in the Golden Book of the Jewish National Fund as a sign of appreciation. It is possible that these contacts with Jews left a positive impression on him.[21]

But even if all these elements helped to alter the policy of the Spanish Foreign Ministry, they did not induce Spain to act to save all 4,000 of its Jewish nationals. In the cable to Paris dated March 18, 1943, in which Jordana informed Rolland of the new policy, and in other statements issued that same day and the week following, conditions were spelled out that drastically reduced Spain's rescue operation.

The first condition appeared in Jordana's cable. Only full citizens, with complete documentation, were allowed to come to Spain, and all other nationals would be disregarded. The second condition came in a personal letter Jordana wrote on March 22 to Interior Minister Blas Pérez Gonzáles, in which Jordana outlined the problem of Jews of Spanish nationality and the threat, after April 1, 1943, of their being deported to concentration camps like other Jews in Nazi-occupied countries. Jordana later wrote Pérez Gonzáles that it was decided to permit their entry into Spain "under the auspices of an organization that would ensure their swift departure from Spain for their ultimate destination." Their visas would indicate the border point of entry, where Spanish police authorities would accept them and inform them of the town in which they would live under police supervision for as long as they remained in Spain. For the sake of efficiency, Jordana recommended close contact between the security police, which was under the jurisdiction of the Interior Ministry, and his own office; in this way, he claimed, it would be possible to expedite their eventual emigration. Thus, the second condition was that what the Germans called the "repatriation" of Jewish Spanish citizens would be nothing more than their transit through Spain, like all other refugees.[22] (See Appendix, document F.)

Arrangements for this transit—like the assurance of financial support for Spanish nationals if they needed it during the time of their forced stay in Spain—were planned on March 18, 1943 (the same day Jordana cabled Paris) between German Baraibar and those in the American Embassy responsible for handling refugees. At this meeting, David Blickenstaff promised to do his best to assist in the emigration of Spanish nationals; Jordana therefore was able to tell Pérez Gonzáles about the "organization" that would ensure their departure from Spain. A few days later, Jordana asked Blickenstaff to put his promise in writing. Blickenstaff called in Samuel Sequerra from Barcelona, consulted with him, and after obtaining permission from Joseph Schwartz wrote on March 24 to José Pan de Soraluce the following (see Appendix, document G):

> Having been informed by the Spanish Foreign Ministry of the means adopted by the Spanish authorities to facilitate the entry into Spain of certain groups of Jews living in the occupied territories of Europe, the Joint Distribution Committee wishes to assure the Foreign Ministry that its representatives in Europe and outside of Europe will do everything possible to obtain immigration permits for these people. Within the limits of its functions, the JDC will provide these people the necessary welfare and financial services they may need during the period of their transit through Spain.[23]

The representatives of the JDC could make these guarantees because in March 1943 great hopes were placed upon the Bermuda Conference, and there was a general anticipation of concerted Allied action on behalf of Jewish refugees. The problem of the refugees in Spain was then the focus of public interest. The JDC undertaking satisfied the Spanish authorities, and they moved to notify the Germans of their new position. On March 22, Ambassador Vidal officially informed the German Foreign Ministry that Spain was not abandoning its Jewish nationals but instead was interested in bringing them to its borders. For this reason, the Spanish government requested that the final date set for repatriation should be postponed and that Spain be given more time to organize the evacuation. The Germans agreed to the request and set a new date—the end of May 1943. This announcement marked the end of the period of disinterest in the future of Jewish nationals, and repatriation began under the conditions Spain had set.[24]

REPATRIATION FROM WESTERN EUROPE

The conditions limiting those entitled to the Spanish citizenship that Foreign Minister Jordana established affected primarily the number of candidates for rescue from France. The delegation of Spanish Jews that went to Madrid in October 1941 to ask Jordana to allow a small group of Spain's nationals to settle in Spain estimated that the number of people having fully documented Spanish citizenship was much less than 1,000 and possibly was not even 300—only a fraction of the 3,000 nationals listed by the Spanish consulates in France at that time. The representatives of the Spanish Bureau of Commerce in Paris in 1942 and 1943 dealt with this same small group, which according to the list numbered 125 heads of families and so did not amount to more than a few hundred people. It appears that the greatest pressure on the Spanish government to defend its Jewish nationals was applied to only a small segment of those sheltered under its wings.

Jordana forbade increasing this number. In a cable on April 2, 1943, he asked Ginés Vidal in Berlin to inform the consuls under him in western Europe who were examining those entitled to repatriation that "they should proceed with this matter with much attention and the greatest possible care." A few days later, Jordana laid down the rules concerning the establishment of Spanish nationality: anyone who did not receive citizenship—or did not renew it—by means of the Primo de Rivera decree of December 20, 1924, could not be considered a citizen of Spain. Exceptions to this rule were the few cases who came to France from Egypt and who were included in the lists attached to the agreement concerning the defense of nationals signed between Egypt and Spain in 1934.[25]

Bernardo Rolland, who was being exhorted by those of his protégés who were excluded from these categories, did not accept Jordana's instructions literally. Through Vidal he again raised the problem of persons who held genuine Spanish citizenship but for various reasons had not been listed in the citizen's register established under the 1924 decree. His efforts concentrated particularly on a group of ninety nationals, who received their citizenship by virtue of special orders renewed from time to time and who had been given Spanish citizenship in the past through directives from the Foreign Ministry. The embassy in Berlin supported Rolland's efforts and granted permission for their entry into Spain. Rolland quickly transferred their passports and requests for exit to the German Embassy in Paris so that they would receive exit visas. Vidal wrote Rolland that entry visas to Spain would be provided once exit visas had been received by the Germans, but this communiqué reached Paris after Rolland had terminated his period of service, and a new consul, Alfonso Fiscovich, replaced him. Instead of dealing with the Germans and providing the necessary visas quickly, Fiscovich asked Jordana whether it was possible to extend Vidal's instructions regarding the ninety nationals and apply them to all Spanish nationals in similar straits. Fiscovich maintained that this issue was crucial because the Spanish Embassy in Vichy continued to instruct the French consulates to block the entry of nationals into Spain, as a result of which these nationals were likely to come to Paris to request entry; 140 other nationals had already come to his office with similar requests.

Fiscovich's questions indicated not only a contradiction in the manner in which two arms of the Spanish Foreign Ministry were dealing with the same problem but also aroused Spain's fear of increasing the number of people rescued and seemed calculated to undermine the rescue of the ninety Spanish nationals for whom permission had already been granted. In any event, this is what happened. Fiscovich's letter was received at the Foreign Ministry with the letter from the Berlin Embassy, which contained the names of the ninety nationals; from the marginal notes it may be concluded that Fiscovich merely confused the authorities in Madrid. As the continued safety of these nationals depended upon this new consul in Paris, it is most significant that the Foreign Ministry had in its files nothing further concerning the outcome of their rescue. The definition of those entitled to repatriation from France thus was not softened in the wake of this episode; on the contrary, it appears to have been made even more strict.[26] The reasons prompting Fiscovich to behave as he did might have stemmed from the tension between certain branches or persons in the Foreign Ministry, such as between the Vichy Embassy under Lequerica and that in Berlin under Vidal. Most likely they were based on Fiscovich's open hostility to Jews, as evidenced by a report from the time of his service as consul general in Tunis. On March 18, 1942, he sent two official newspapers of the Vichy regime to Madrid, both of which contained anti-Jewish laws. In his accompanying letter he defended these laws, claiming that Jews had supported the popular leftist front and had managed to hide and smuggle their capital out of France. These laws probably would have affected the few Jewish Spanish nationals in Tunis as well. Fiscovich remarked that although "their nationality has not been definitely recognized," he would act according to the directives he had received.[27] The complicated administrative procedure of the repatriation of Jewish nationals to Spain was in Fiscovich's hands from May 1943 onward.

Jordana instructed the Spanish Embassy in Berlin to collect applications from the various consulates and cable them, after examination, to the Foreign Ministry in Madrid, where they were to be checked and sent, when necessary, to the security police for clearance. When approved they would be returned to the Berlin Embassy. Only then would the Germans deal with them. The German Foreign Ministry transferred the applications through von Thadden to Eichmann's office, which in turn sent them to Gestapo agents in areas where the Spanish nationals resided for evaluation of their security status; after receiving Eichmann's approval, the German Foreign Ministry informed Vidal that the exit visa was approved, and he informed the Foreign Ministry in Madrid of the date and place of entry into Spain. This long and complicated procedure—containing no less than eleven stages and depending upon the goodwill of so many authorities—must have been hopelessly slow. As a result, one time limit set for its termination soon passed, and then another passed, with most of those due to be rescued still not moved.[28]

In May 1943, the first of the refugees began to cross the Spanish border, mostly Spanish nationals from Belgium and a few Sephardic Jews from France—a total of twenty people—who passed through Irún in the week of May 10. During the following week, several more Jews of Spanish nationality entered Spain in the same manner that others had been permitted earlier. The repatriation of larger groups, however, continued to be held up. Two months passed before the Spanish Embassy in Berlin found out that all its letters concerning exit visas for nationals from France had gone unanswered. Upon investigation it was learned that the commander of the security police in the German Embassy in Paris had delayed all the permits because he had "discovered" that all the candidates for exit were born and lived in the Balkans or France; he asked the Spanish Embassy to explain the national origin for each candidate. But when the German Foreign Ministry intervened, it became clear even to this Jew-baiter that it was not in the German interest to place obstacles in the way of Spain's rescue of its Jewish nationals. When this hindrance was removed, the way was clear to prepare the first group for its journey.[29]

On August 10, 1943, after repeated delays, all preparations were finally completed and the first group of repatriates went on its way. It contained eighty Jews, including one fatally ill woman who died en route. Despite the promise of Germans to free five Spanish nationals imprisoned at Drancy and to bring them to the railway station in time for their departure, the Germans did not keep their word and the group left without them, accompanied by a French police commissioner and a representative from the Spanish Consulate in Paris. A carriage placed at their disposal at one of the stations on the way was attached to a German military train, which brought the repatriates to the French border city of Hendaye. Those leaving were entitled to take with them much baggage, most of which was sent to Spain separately. At the French border post, German guards searched their possessions; they were allowed to take with them only 300 francs per person in cash. On the afternoon of August 11, the group reached Irún and immediately was placed in the hands of the security police. The travelers were allowed to select one of the Spanish provincial capitals as their place of residence under police supervision; because of lack of financial resources, however, they were unable to leave Irún. Some sold or pawned possessions, but most prayed for help from Samuel Sequerra, who had been called in from Barcelona. Through his intervention their continued passage was arranged, and by August 18 they were taken to seven cities in Spain—from Zaragoza and Logroño and Burgos to Toledo and Granada.[30]

On June 21, 1943, long before the repatriates arrived in Spain, José María Doussinague asked the security police for a detailed report on the number of Spanish Jews who already had entered Spain and their whereabouts, "in order to enable them to leave our country in accordance with what had been agreed upon previously." At the same time, Spain was being asked to remove hundreds of its nationals from Salonika; on August 12, the Spanish Embassy in Berlin informed the Foreign Ministry in Madrid that 366 of these nationals were on their way to the Bergen-Belsen concentration camp and that the Germans demanded they be evacuated from there immediately after their arrival. On August 13, two days after a group of Jewish nationals from France had arrived, Doussinague wrote from his vacation residence in San Sebastián to German Baraibar that he immediately should contact the representative of the JDC to determine exactly how he intended to deal with these Jews. If they could be removed from Spain without delay, Doussinague would agree that the Salonika Jews could come directly from Bergen-Belsen; if not, he would tell Vidal in Berlin not to allow them to come. (See Appendix, document H.)

On August 16, David Blickenstaff received an official request from the Spanish Foreign Ministry. After mentioning the written guarantee made by the JDC on March 24, 1943, the letter established the policy of making the arrival of Jewish nationals from Salonika contingent upon the evacuation of the Jewish nationals from France. "New groups of Spanish Jews will not be able to come to Spain until those recently arrived have been removed from our soil," stated the Spanish letter, and it soon became evident that Madrid would hold fast to this demand. In this way, the Foreign Ministry placed on Blickenstaff's shoulders not only responsibility for the evacuation of Spanish nationals who already had arrived but also responsibility for failing to save additional Spanish nationals.[31]

This double burden fell upon Blickenstaff at a time when his ability to make a real contribution to the evacuation of those who had arrived in Spain was severely limited. This powerlessness was in direct contrast to the extensive assistance Blickenstaff had promised Foreign Minister Jordana in March. It was the result of the general apathy of the Allies in everything related to the solution of the Jewish refugee problem in Spain in the five months since Blickenstaff's promise was given. By August, immigration permits still had not been placed at the JDC's disposal, nor had evacuation arrangements to a temporary reception center for Jewish refugees been made; for this reason Blickenstaff could not keep his promise to expedite the emigration of Spanish nationals. The only help he could offer was to screen the candidates for emigration to Palestine, but their departure from Spain depended upon their sailing on the Mediterranean, and at that time no one from the Jewish Agency capable of handling this could be found in Spain or Portugal.

On September 28 and 29, Blickenstaff sent Paul Block, a refugee who had worked in Blickenstaff's office with Palestine emigration, to visit the Spanish nationals. He traveled to the cities where they were staying and interviewed most of them. The results of his visit were bleak; most of the fifty Spanish nationals interviewed were unsuitable for receiving emigration certificates. Moreover, from his meetings with the refugees it was obvious that they were not interested in leaving Spain. All expressed to Block anger and disappointment at the fact that their stay in Spain was temporary. One of them, Francisco Molho, who claimed to have served as a Spanish consul in Italy for twenty years, refused to cooperate in any arrangements for his emigration.[32] The dwindling possibilities for the evacuation of the nationals and Madrid's stubborn insistence that the evacuation be completed before additional groups arrived resulted in an almost total paralysis of repatriation activity for four months. Except for forty-five people who arrived from the south of France at the end of October 1943, there is no evidence whatsoever that the Spanish government continued to take up the matter.[33]

At the beginning of December 1943, the Spanish Foreign Ministry made the first move; German Baraibar met Monsignor Boyer-Más, who dealt with the French refugees, and asked him to include Jewish Spanish nationals from France in the evacuation of French citizens. Boyer-Más responded favorably to this request, and shortly afterward Spanish nationals began to gather in the port of Málaga for evacuation.[34]

As preparations for their departure to North Africa continued, new and unexpected difficulties arose for some of the Jewish Spanish nationals. Although the Spanish Foreign Ministry and the Interior Ministry treated Jewish nationals like alien refugees who were in Spain in transit, Spanish military authorities regarded them as Spanish citizens liable for military duty. As a result, six were mobilized as soon as they set foot in Spain; three were placed in Spanish units in Morocco, and the others were sent to camps in Barcelona, Madrid, and Cádiz.

Thus, in December 1943, while their families were waiting in Málaga to sail for North Africa, those mobilized were in military camps and unable to join them. The case of one who was about to be separated from his wife was brought to the attention of Carlton Hayes, who attempted to intervene. In a personal letter written on December 8, 1943, to Foreign Minister Jordana—which was stolen by German intelligence and sent to Berlin as definite proof of American interference to save Jews—the ambassador pleaded that the injustice about to be done to this family should be prevented. In the meantime, transportation arrangements from Málaga had been completed, and the sailing of the Spanish nationals could not be delayed any longer. The authorities decided at the last moment to remove the family members of the mobilized soldiers from the transport to North Africa, a total of approximately twenty persons. On December 13, all the remaining Spanish Jews who had come from France—including Francisco Molho, the consul from Italy, and Louis Franco, the first signatory of the petition to General Franco—set sail from Málaga. The avenue that had been closed to the repatriation of large groups of Jewish Spanish nationals was opened again.[35]

At the beginning of December, Spain renewed its efforts on behalf of its Jewish nationals in France. Now intervention was required not only to arrange their exit to Spain but also to free fifty Jews who were candidates for repatriation but were arrested by the Gestapo on the night of November 25, 1943. This was not the first time that Spanish representatives were required to make arrangements to free their protégés from prison. The seventy-nine Jewish nationals who arrived in August included some who had been released from prison; the case of five Jews whom the German authorities did not free in time—and therefore could not leave with their group—was the subject of further intervention by the Spanish Embassy in Berlin in August. The situation changed in December, however, both because of the large number of those arrested and because of German reaction.

On December 22, the secretary of the Spanish Embassy in Berlin met with von Thadden in the German Foreign Ministry to receive the reply to Madrid's note. Responding to demands that the German authorities release the arrested Spanish nationals and allow them to leave for Spain, von Thadden enumerated all the extensions that had been granted to Spain between April and October 1943, some of which the Spanish Embassy had ignored completely. Von Thadden argued that despite these delays, the Germans waited another month and only then began to make arrests. The Spanish Embassy secretary countered that if the prisoners were not released it would create a bad impression in Madrid and the German Foreign

Ministry would be blamed for it. Von Thadden blamed Spanish hesitancy for the ensuing complications. He stated that the release of those who in the meantime had been transferred to a "work camp" outside of France was no longer feasible because they were employed in secret factories. Furthermore, the prisoners would be difficult to locate because certain records, including information concerning their whereabouts, had been destroyed during one of the Allied bombings; the embassy secretary would be able to contact them only after the war ended. Nevertheless, von Thadden promised to intervene to free those Spanish nationals who still were being held in camps and prisons on French soil.

Von Thadden brought these arguments to the attention of the German Embassy in Madrid so that the ambassador there also would be able to respond to Spain's renewed demands regarding its Jewish nationals. The directors of the Foreign Ministry in Berlin discussed this and decided to invite Ambassador Vidal for additional clarifications at a higher level. The hints the secretary of the Spanish Embassy made concerning the negative effect that deportations of Spanish nationals to the East would have in Madrid apparently sparked concern in the German Foreign Ministry.[36]

This renewed Spanish intervention came too late for many imprisoned Spanish nationals. The fate of others who had not yet been transported depended on the efforts that Spanish representatives invested in the struggle to keep them alive. Fiscovich in Paris was the Spanish official directly responsible for handling most of the Spanish nationals in France. In his letter dated July 17, 1944, he summarizes his work on their behalf. On January 12, the Germans informed him that the head of the Gestapo agreed to release nationals who had been in prison, provided Spain would evacuate them without delay. Six days later, Fiscovich presented two lists to the German authorities, one of prisoners to be released from Drancy and the other of Spanish nationals who, according to the citizenship papers in their possession, were candidates for repatriation to Spain. Despite their promise to free the prisoners, and despite his interventions, the Germans deported many of them without notifying Fiscovich of the exact date and place to which they were sent. The rest of the prisoners were freed on February 25, 1944, and from that time, in order to prevent additional deportations, Fiscovich requested the German Embassy in Paris and the Gestapo to provide exit visas from France for thirty-six Spanish Jews. This request was not honored until five months later, when on July 5 they received word from the German Embassy in Paris that the security authorities had given permission for their repatriation; only then did the preparations for their transport to Spain begin.[37]

Fiscovich's letter reached the Foreign Ministry in Madrid on July 24,

1944, informing the Spanish security police of the arrival of these nationals. One month later, France was liberated, and although there is no clear testimony that this group ever reached Spain, it is possible that the German and Spanish authorities did not complete their preparations by the time Spain was isolated from the German areas of occupation. It may be assumed, however, that Spain's attempts to rescue these thirty-six Jews saved them from their death, although they were not repatriated.

What did Fiscovich do in the five months that passed from the time the prisoners were released from Drancy in February 1944? His letter mentions nothing. Nor do German and Spanish documents contain any hint about his activities during this period. It appears that the answer to this question—as well as to the question of why he confined his efforts to these thirty-six Spanish nationals—should be sought in the developments that were taking place at the same time in Greece.

In contrast to occupied France, where all activities on behalf of Spanish nationals were concentrated in the Spanish consulate in Paris, in Vichy France several consulates operated, each one caring for the Jewish nationals residing in its region of activity. All these consulates were under the supervision of Ambassador Lequerica, and matters dealing with exit visas and other questions involving the Pétain government and the German authorities were conducted through the Embassy in Vichy. Active defense of the rights of Spanish nationals on the local level, however, depended upon the initiative and energy of local consuls. Instructions concerning the rights of citizens and Jewish protégés to be considered Spanish nationals were interpreted to the letter by the embassy. Despite this, the number of recognized Jewish nationals who gathered in the south of France increased. The adversity and uncertainty that affected them in Paris and the hope of finding some protection in a different area resulted in their flight from occupied France. Although archival material is too sparse to describe the attitude of each one of the Spanish consuls toward his Jewish protégés and other Jewish refugees, it may be said that the Jews enjoyed the support and vigorous defense of at least some consulates.[38]

The German plan to eliminate foreign Jews from all areas of occupation did not escape the notice of Spanish nationals in the south of France. When the deadline for their deportation approached, ten of them from Marseille sent a petition to General Franco. In their appeal, dated March 9, 1943, they begged Franco to instruct the embassy in Vichy and the consulate in Marseille to allow their immediate entry to Spain. The policy Madrid adopted on March 18 to allow Jews of Spanish nationality to enter Spain was construed as a direct answer to their appeal. Soon Spanish nationals in Marseille, Lyon, Toulouse, and other French cities began preparations to leave for Spain.[39]

One group of Jews from Vichy France was assisted by the Spanish consul in Toulouse and through him obtained entry visas into Spain. This group crossed the border on October 1, 1943, at Cerbère. A second group of thirty-three Jews entered Spain about three weeks later and like the first group was received without Madrid's making their arrival contingent upon the evacuation of the group of Spanish Jews on August 11 from Paris. A third group of seventy-three Jews assembled in June 1944 in Perpignan but did not receive authorization to enter Spain. As the persecutions increased in France, so did the threat of arrest and deportation to Germany. The news of the plight of the seventy-three reached Fritz Lichtenstein in Spain, who appealed to German Baraibar at the Spanish Foreign Ministry to expedite their arrangements. On June 5, Baraibar promised that this would be taken care of, but by July 14 all he knew was that these Jews were being detained at the Spanish border because the German authorities were not giving them exit visas. This is all that is known about this group; it is doubtful whether their situation improved before the liberation of France.[40]

What did the Spanish Embassy in Vichy do to obtain the exit visas necessary to rescue this group of Jews? Sources provide no answer to this question, and because of the lack of information it cannot be established definitively whether these seventy-three Jews were the third and final group handled by the Spanish Embassy. It is noteworthy, however, that during the first months of 1944 there is no evidence of Spanish activity to terminate the processing of their repatriation or that of any other group. The reason for this must be sought in Spain's activities regarding its Jewish nationals in Greece.

REPATRIATION FROM SALONIKA

Germany's period of relative moderation toward Jews in occupied Greece came to a halt in July 1942. On July 11, nine thousand Jewish men were gathered into Liberty Square in Salonika, allegedly for the purpose of being registered for work in the German war effort. In effect, this developed into vicious public mistreatment of thousands of Jews who were crowded for long hours in the burning sun without drinking water and ordered to roll in the dust and perform other "exercises" for the amusement of the German and Greek onlookers. Similar incidents of public degradation continued throughout the following week as the "registration for work" proceeded. The Jews of Salonika were forced to labor under subhuman conditions in various regions of northern Greece while 2.5 billion drachmas (approximately $100,000) were extorted from them as ransom for exempting the rest of the community from this work.

During this period the citizens of neutral countries or countries sympathetic to the Axis, such as Spain, were left unharmed. This immunity availed them also when the Nazis began the final deportations of the Jews of Salonika. On Saturday, February 2, 1943, two of Adolf Eichmann's aides, Dieter Wisliceny and Alois Brunner, arrived in Salonika accompanied by four assistants. On the following Monday, Jews were given three weeks to identify their stores as Jewish-owned, wear yellow badges, and move to one of the surrounding districts that had been designated a ghetto. On February 13, Jews were forbidden to use public transportation, to appear in public places, or to have a telephone. On that day, all anti-Jewish decrees went into effect in the whole of Nazi-occupied Greece. These were merely an introduction to the systematic plunder, deportation, and destruction that began in Salonika on March 15 when the first transport left Salonika supposedly on its way for "resettlement" in the Cracow ghetto. From then until May 9, at intervals of from three to six days, stifling baggage trucks crowded with Jews left the transit camp in the Baron Hirsch suburb, slowly moving to Auschwitz. By mid-May, 42,830 Jews of Salonika and its environs had been deported in this manner. Thus, the Germans destroyed this ancient Jewish settlement as they continued their annihilation of the Jewish communities in eastern Europe.[41]

On February 6, 1943, and in all subsequent orders, the Nazis discriminated in favor of "foreign nationals who could prove their position with a valid passport."[42] But they had no intention of allowing them to remain in Salonika. On the day the deportation of the Jews began, the German consul general in Salonika informed the German Foreign Ministry that it was necessary to deport those with foreign citizenship, a total of 860 people according to estimates. In addition to 511 Spanish Jews, this group also included 281 Jews with Italian, 39 with Turkish, 6 with Portuguese, and 15 with Argentine, Swiss, Hungarian, or Bulgarian citizenship, as well as 8 enemy citizens. The Spanish nationals were thus the majority among these candidates for rescue.

A short time thereafter, the German ambassador in Athens, Günther Altenburg, informed Spanish Consul Eduardo Gasset of the deportation of the Jews of Salonika. Altenburg added that the Germans were also about to deport the Spanish nationals because Spain had abandoned them. "I was amazed to hear this," testified Gasset, "and I told him that as I had not received any instructions in this matter, it was my duty to continue to protect these nationals, whether they were Jews or not. Therefore, any steps taken against them in Salonika by the Germans will be considered a most unfriendly act against our country." As he had no direct line of communication with either Berlin or Madrid, Gasset asked to send a report to Spain and to request instructions through the German Embassy in Athens. To Gasset's surprise, after a few days he learned from the first secretary of the German Embassy, Georg Vogel, that his message had been held up in Berlin and had not reached Madrid. He wrote another report at the beginning of April, sent it by courier to the Spanish Embassy in Sofia, and from there it reached Madrid on April 5. But the Athens consulate never received any reply and had to wrestle by itself with the threat of deportation facing Spanish nationals at the Gestapo's arrival.[43]

On April 30, 1943, the German ambassador in Madrid was ordered to inform the Spanish Foreign Ministry of the intention to deport the Jews of Greece for "security reasons"; further, as Spanish nationals had commercial and social relations with Greek Jews, they too constituted a "security risk," and for that reason Spain should evacuate them. The final date for this evacuation was to have been June 15, after which the Spanish nationals were to be deported with the other Jews. On that day, the German Foreign Ministry sent for confirmation to the Spanish Embassy in Berlin a list of 511 Spanish nationals. Ten days later, the German Embassy in Madrid forwarded the warning to the Spanish Foreign Ministry.[44]

Although the policy Spain would adopt toward its Jewish nationals had been formulated on March 18, news of this had not yet reached the Spanish Consulate in Athens. In the meantime, changes in personnel took place, and in mid-April the new Spanish consul general, Sebastian Romero Radigales, arrived in Athens. From the moment of his arrival, Radigales devoted his best efforts to protecting the rights and the welfare of his Jewish protégés.[45]

The first evidence of his vigorous defense of Jewish nationals is found in German Foreign Ministry documents dated only two weeks after his arrival. On April 30, Altenburg complained that persistent demands by the Spanish Embassy forced him to delay the "coercion" of Spanish nationals; because this could not be allowed to continue, he requested that the German Foreign Ministry ask Madrid to instruct its envoy in Athens to desist from interfering with the deportations. Altenburg also asked for permission to deport Spanish nationals "despite the opposition of the Spanish representation here." As no instructions were forthcoming from Madrid concerning Jewish nationals, on May 18 Radigales asked his superiors to allow him to provide his Jewish protégés with entry visas to

Spain or Morocco. In response he received a copy of the March 18 directives from the Spanish Foreign Ministry. In this way, Spain confirmed for the first time its willingness to accept its Jewish nationals from Nazi-occupied Greece.[46]

In the meantime, the deportation of Jews from Salonika ended, with several Spanish nationals among the thousands of Jews shipped to concentration camps. A total of thirty-eight persons—fourteen Jews from Salonika, thirteen from Dhidhimótikhon, and eleven from Nea Orestiás—were removed from the group of candidates for repatriation and sent to their death. According to the testimony of one of them who survived the death camps, he and his brothers were caught during a hunt through the streets of Salonika; it is safe to assume that others who were deported from Salonika at that time were caught in similar ways. A list of those deported from Dhidhimótikhon and Nea Orestiás reveals that only a few members of the eight families held Spanish nationality. It is thus likely that the Spanish nationals did not want to be separated from their relatives who were without Spanish citizenship, and so went with them for "work in Poland." Hoping to save them, Radigales tried to ascertain when each was deported, compiled a detailed list, and asked the Spanish Embassy in Berlin to secure their release. But by this time most of these unfortunates were no longer alive.[47]

The final date set for the evacuation, June 15, 1943, was fast approaching, and not one of the problems connected with the repatriation had been solved. The Spanish Embassy in Berlin, which was examining the eligibility of Jewish Spanish nationals in Salonika for repatriation, asked for an extension until July 15; the Germans consented to delay only until July 1. On June 17, the screening of the candidates ended, and a list of 510 Spanish citizens in Salonika entitled to go to Spain was handed to the German authorities in Berlin with a request to facilitate their departure. Because the Spanish Embassy in Berlin regarded the repatriation contingent upon instructions from Madrid concerning visas and means of transportation, these two administrative obstacles soon jeopardized the entire evacuation.

The question of passports with which the evacuees from Salonika were to be provided was first raised by the Germans. Following Altenburg's suggestion, the Germans insisted that Spanish nationals travel on a collective passport, which would simplify procedures at the Bulgarian, Hungarian, and German borders and would obviate the need to issue separate transit visas. The Spanish Foreign Ministry objected, and Radigales was told to stamp a Spanish entry visa into the passport of each traveler.[48]

The question of transportation proved even more complicated. The idea of Mediterranean transport was raised first. Altenburg suggested that Spain send its own ships to evacuate its nationals. Radigales, who did not think this was feasible, proposed that his protégés sail for Spain in Swedish ships run by the International Red Cross, which were bringing food to Greece. Radigales spoke with the Swedish ambassador, who agreed, providing Spain approach the Swedish government. But before the Spanish Foreign Ministry could implement the plan, the Germans rejected it. Von Thadden felt it would require negotiations between Spain and Sweden, and then between Sweden and the Allies and the Axis; in the meantime, much time would pass, additional extensions would be required, and the evacuation would be postponed.[49]

Plans for organizing a sea transport therefore were abandoned, and overland arrangements were discussed instead. Once again, there was a wide gulf between German demands and the Spanish position. Germany wanted the repatriation to be organized and financed by the Spanish Embassy; Spain refused to participate in the transportation arrangements or to bear responsibility for them. Altenburg tried to compromise and asked the German consul in Salonika to examine the possibility of the Germans handling the arrangements until the evacuees reached Vienna, where the Spanish Embassy in Berlin could take over. But the Gestapo opposed this plan and demanded that Spain negotiate directly with the railway authorities of the Reich. On July 3, 1943, Wisliceny traveled to Berlin; on his return, he confirmed that the Gestapo would not allow a special train to be run unless it was requested and paid for by Spain. The Spanish Embassy in Berlin informed Radigales that Spain would not accept responsibility for ordering a train. Eichmann and his staff considered the evacuation of foreign nationals a special German gesture toward sympathetic or neutral countries. Spain, on the other hand, viewed repatriation as the consequence of German policy, without which Spanish nationals could have remained undisturbed, so it did not feel obliged to assist in implementing such a policy.

The conflict between these two positions created an impasse that could only be solved by one side's submission. After one week Germany conceded. On July 15, von Thadden told Altenburg of the change in the position of the RHSA: Wisliceny received orders that if Spain did not request a special train, he should discuss with German military authorities the possibility of placing such a train at his disposal. The German Sonderkommando was now prepared to arrange for a special train to the Spanish border, to be paid for by the evacuees themselves, just as they would have to pay for their own provisions for the journey. This would complete the repatriation of all Spanish nationals from Salonika.[50]

Then the situation suddenly changed. One day after Germany had accepted Spain's terms, Spain suddenly refused to accept its Jewish nationals from Salonika. On July 16, Ginés Vidal cabled Radigales from Berlin: "In view of the new instructions (which I have just received from our government) I cannot authorize repatriation of Spanish Jews either en masse or in small groups. You may grant visas only in exceptional cases." This in effect heralded Spain's abandonment of its Jewish nationals in Salonika, which was tantamount to handing them over to the Germans. It seemed a dangerous gamble with Nazi patience.[51]

How did the Germans react? Altenburg took Vidal's message as an inexplicable delaying tactic and proposed to discuss the issue with the Spanish government again to clarify the matter once and for all, so that the Nazis could get on with their deportations. The German Foreign Ministry and the Gestapo, however, were in no hurry to accept this offer. On one hand, Germany was not interested in forcing Spain to accept Jews it no longer wanted; on the other hand, Germany hesitated to send Spanish nationals to their death because of the fear that under Anglo-American pressure Spain would again demand their release. Hence an interim solution was devised: to send the Spanish Jews of Salonika to a camp at Bergen-Belsen, which had been built for the purpose of temporary imprisonment, and to hold them there for at least two months before sending them to the East for extermination. If Spain should demand its Jewish nationals, their return from Bergen-Belsen could be arranged without disclosing "security secrets." Even after this solution was accepted, it was not put into effect as long as there was any possibility of a change in Spain's position. Only when new instructions failed to arrive from Madrid was the German Embassy in Athens ordered to begin deportations.[52]

The silence of the Spanish Foreign Ministry nevertheless did not prevent Radigales from acting. With Ezraty in Salonika, he spoke to his Italian colleague concerning the possibility of evacuating Spanish nationals from Salonika to the Italian zone of occupation in Athens; Radigales obtained preliminary approval from the Italian government. This move angered Altenburg, who was not informed of the matter. He ordered Radigales not to force Italy's hand before an agreement had been reached between Spain and Germany, as Germany would not tolerate the manipulation of one Axis power against another in affairs concerning Jews. Altenburg also insisted that the German Foreign Ministry reject this new plan or, if it was not possible "to place Spanish Jews on a par with German Jews [i.e., to exterminate them], then they should be held in a detention camp and not moved to Italian-occupied territory, because this would undermine Germany's prestige." Von Thadden agreed with Altenburg and asked

Eichmann to instruct the Sonderkommando to halt the planned transfer to the Italian zone.[53]

But the work of Radigales and Ezraty was not in vain. With Ezraty's aid, 150 Spanish nationals fled from Salonika to Athens in an Italian military train taking Italian soldiers home on leave. When the Germans began deporting Spanish nationals to Bergen-Belsen, they found only 367 Spanish Jews in Salonika. Despite their anger, the Germans declined to protest to the Italians. This happened one week after the overthrow of Mussolini and the rise of the Badoglio government in Italy. Because of the relationship between Germany and Italy at that time, the Germans understood that their protest would be futile.

On July 29, 1943, all heads of families of Spanish nationals were called to meet with Wisliceny in the Beth Shaul synagogue. After they had assembled, the synagogue was surrounded by German guards and Wisliceny told them they were to be sent to Germany. They were promptly loaded onto trucks and sent to the transit camp in the Baron Hirsch suburb. That evening, the families of the arrested were ordered to join them.

The arrest of 367 Spanish Jews was the final step in the destruction of the ancient Jewish community of Salonika, the site of the flourishing of Sephardic culture. In the two months preceding, Spanish nationals were the last Jews remaining in the city, after they had witnessed for so long the disappearance of all their relatives and friends holding Greek citizenship and had seen the emptying of Jewish houses, streets, and quarters. Since the end of May, only they had remained, together with a handful of Italian nationals and 820 "privileged" Jews and collaborators, whom the Germans had promised to send to Theresienstadt and not to kill. On June 1, 1943, these 820 had been sent by special transport directly to the death camp at Treblinka; a few weeks later, the Italian nationals were evacuated. Thus there remained in this desolate city, emptied of its Jews, only this handful of Spanish nationals, the last surviving branch of a felled tree, until they too were taken to the transit camp, from which the Jews of Salonika had left on their last journey.

Radigales and his aides did not cease in their last-minute efforts to delay or lessen the deportation order. On July 30, 1943, the translator from the Spanish Embassy, a Greek priest named Father Ireneo Typaldos, arrived from Athens. He tried to persuade Wisliceny and the German consul in Salonika that because negotiations were still under way for the transfer of Spanish nationals to Athens, their deportation to Germany should be delayed. When Father Typaldos was refused, he asked that Ezraty, who had been arrested along with his family, be excluded from the deportation. When this was refused, he requested that he himself, as representative of the consulate in Athens, be allowed to join the convoy; Wisliceny refused this too. But Typaldos succeeded in seeing Ezraty and was able to secure from the Jews about to be deported some of the money that had not yet been extorted from them by the Nazis and the Jewish collaborators. He sent the money to Athens, where Radigales added it to the large volume of assets, including gold, silver, and jewelry, that had been deposited in the embassy earlier by the Spanish Jews.[54] On August 2, the Spanish nationals were loaded onto railway freight cars and arrived on August 13 at Bergen-Belsen.

Two days after the arrest of the Spanish nationals and their imprisonment in the Salonika transit camp, Spain's position shifted again. On July 31, the Spanish Embassy in Berlin demanded that the deportation to camps in Germany be done under the best possible conditions and that the old, the infirm, and children, for whom the journey would be difficult, should be exempted. On August 6, Spain asked that Ezraty and his family be removed from the group of deportees and sent directly to Spain. Finally, on August 9, before the group reached Bergen-Belsen, Spain announced that it was prepared to accept all its Jewish nationals and demanded that they be treated as Spaniards in every respect. In its communiqué, the embassy requested further that a Spanish official be allowed to visit the detainees in Bergen-Belsen in order to prepare their emigration.

How can these reversals in Spain's attitude be explained? What happened in the Spanish Foreign Ministry between July 16 and August 9, 1943?

An official of the German Foreign Ministry who received the cable from the Spanish Embassy in Berlin for the purpose of conveying it to Radigales in Athens claimed he was told that "in view of the unexpectedly large number of these Spanish Jews—more than 500—the Spanish government has serious doubts about bringing them to Spain."[55] Confirmation of this testimony is also found in Spanish sources.

Although not a single group of Spanish nationals had yet arrived in Spain at that time (the first group of seventy-nine people came from Paris on August 11) and the accord reached by the Spanish Foreign Ministry and the JDC on March 18, 1943, had not yet been tested, Spain reopened discussions on the repatriation of Jewish nationals. At a meeting on August 4 in San Sebastián, the government debated the issue of the deportation of Spanish Jews to Germany and decided finally to allow the entry of the Spanish Jews of Salonika. This indicates that some members of the government opposed the entry of Jews to Spain. Moreover, the instructions Foreign Minister Jordana sent to Ginés Vidal in Berlin after the government session apparently included a compromise. Although

Vidal was requested to demand guarantees from Germany that Spanish Jews would be treated in a manner befitting Spanish citizens, he was authorized to provide group passports for no more than twenty-five persons. After one passport had been issued and members of the group were sent on their way, he had to wait for confirmation from Madrid to issue the next passport. According to instructions, Vidal was to make sure that the Jews carried sufficient documentation proving their Spanish citizenship, despite the fact that the candidates for rescue in Salonika had already been checked and approved. All this was doubtless intended to delay the emigration and limit its scope.[56]

On August 13, 1943, 367 Spanish Jews from Salonika reached Bergen-Belsen. They were kept in special quarters so that it would be possible later to transfer them to Spain without exposing them to the horrors of concentration-camp life. As a result, they did not suffer like the other prisoners even when their stay was extended because of protracted negotiations.

These negotiations had begun before the Spanish nationals reached Bergen-Belsen. Following instructions, the Spanish Embassy in Berlin approached the Germans on August 9, 1943, asking that the evacuees be divided into groups of twenty-five, each of which would be sent to Spain at predetermined intervals. Vidal tried to persuade the German Foreign Ministry that this was in the interest of Germany's public relations, but they rejected his proposal as impractical because they thought it would take six months for all the Salonika Jews to leave Germany; in addition, much manpower was needed to accompany them to the Spanish border, and all this would offer no advantage for German propaganda abroad. Thus Spain was required to remove all its nationals in one group, or no more than three groups. After another debate on August 31, Spain agreed to evacuate them in groups of 150. The Spanish Foreign Ministry again demanded that the German authorities treat these Jewish nationals as Spanish citizens and that its representatives who formerly had not been allowed to contact the detainees—on the pretext that they were grouped with other political prisoners—be allowed to meet with them immediately after they left the concentration camp.[57]

In mid-September, Spanish authorities were handed a list of the Spanish Jews from Salonika detained in Bergen-Belsen, which cleared the way for their evacuation to Spain. But once again Madrid was in no hurry to act because Jewish nationals who had arrived from Paris in August 1943 were still on Spanish soil. Despite continued requests by the Germans— and a threat that unless the Salonika Jews were repatriated they would be deported to the East—Madrid chose to wait until the refugees from France were removed. On December 9, after preparations for the evacuation of the Spanish refugees from France had been completed at Málaga, Spain informed the German authorities that it would accept the Salonika Jews in two large groups.[58]

This repatriation was not carried out until February 1944, according to Eichmann's office in the Gestapo, because of the lack of transportation during the Christmas holidays. The first group left Bergen-Belsen on February 3 and, after delays at the Spanish border, entered Spain on February 10. The second group arrived in Spain three days later, exactly six months after their detention in Bergen-Belsen.

When they crossed the border, the 367 refugees from Salonika were accorded a friendly and impressive welcome. They were placed in the care of JDC representatives, who began to prepare for their emigration to Palestine. But it was not until June, when the Fedala refugee camp near Casablanca was established, that a destination was created for these refugees. On June 21, 1944, most of the refugees from Salonika were transferred to this camp.[59]

On October 13, after waiting four months in Fedala, the refugees from Salonika journeyed east from Casablanca. Some reached Palestine via Rafa, and the remainder waited in various camps pending their return to Greece. They wished to regain their personal property, which Radigales was safeguarding faithfully.

REPATRIATION FROM ATHENS

After they fled from Salonika to Athens, the number of Jewish Spanish nationals in the Greek capital was 235, including several married to Christians. Encouraged by the shift in his government's position toward its Jewish nationals, Radigales began immediately to work on their behalf. He knew that if they were not evacuated, sooner or later they would fall into the hands of the Germans. Following his suggestion, the Spanish Embassy in Berlin on August 20, 1943, demanded from the German Foreign Ministry that no measures be taken against those who left Salonika and that the Germans arrange with Radigales to facilitate their departure for Spain. The Germans did not reply. At the beginning of September, von Thadden informed Günther Altenburg that although the problem of refugees from Salonika was still under discussion, Germany would not oppose the emigration of forty Spanish nationals living in Athens. Again, on September 21, von Thadden stated that they had not yet decided how to handle those who moved to Athens "in breach of agreements."[60]

In the meantime, Radigales attempted to implement the repatriation plan. On August 17, he asked the Spanish Embassy in Berlin for clarification of his authority, in view of the change in Spain's policy toward its Jewish nationals. He was told that he could organize repatriation for groups of twenty-five people, but that the transport of each group was contingent upon special permission granted only after the previous group had left Spain. On August 31, Radigales responded that under these conditions it would take two years to evacuate all his protégés; he therefore requested permission to organize the repatriation in one group or in small groups of five persons, utilizing all available means of transportation. He received neither permission for this nor the authority to provide Spanish visas himself. On September 30, Ginés Vidal told Radigales that the Foreign Ministry prohibited sending to Spain Spanish nationals whose transport had not previously been cleared and asked him to forward a list of the names of the twenty-five people he intended to send.[61]

By that time, the situation of the Jews of Athens had changed abruptly. After the surrender of Italy, the Germans controlled southern Greece. In September Wisliceny arrived in Athens with Jürgen Stroop, the general responsible for the destruction of the Warsaw ghetto. They began preparations for the annihilation of the remainder of Greek Jewry.

On October 7 and 8, 1943, on the eve of Yom Kippur, Stroop's first directives to the Jewish population appeared in Athens newspapers and in placards posted in the streets: Jews scattered throughout the city were to be concentrated in one area and registered, and Jews with foreign citizenship were to bring their papers to the offices of the Jewish community center on October 18 for registration. Despite Radigales's protests, those with Spanish citizenship were forced to come at the appointed time and were subject to all the curfew regulations imposed upon the other Jews. The only restriction differentiating them from Greek Jews was that they were not obliged to report weekly to the community center. The Gestapo and the SD in Athens revoked the German transit visas of those who were about to leave for Spain.[62] This was Eichmann's first step in his plan to eliminate Jews of foreign nationality in Athens and Italy. On November 15, Eichmann explained to the German Foreign Ministry that as foreign Jews had sided with the Badoglio government, they should be treated like other Jews in Nazi-occupied countries—they should be deported for extermination. If the German Foreign Ministry considered this politically undesirable, however, Eichmann proposed that those holding foreign citizenship be arrested immediately, placed in concentration camps, and from there transferred to their country by group, insofar as circumstances and means of transportation would permit.

The German Foreign Ministry accepted Eichmann's proposal. On December 10, 1943, the German Embassy in Madrid informed the Spanish government that the Jews of Athens were to be deported. Madrid replied on December 21 that it was prepared to accept all its nationals. It requested that they not be treated as enemies, and that a reasonable length of time be allowed for their free evacuation from Athens, which would be possible only after the departure of the Jews from Salonika who were in Bergen-Belsen. But Spain's request to treat Jews as neutrals and to allow their transport to Spain was rejected by von Thadden. No Jew can be considered a neutral, he insisted, even if he holds a Spanish passport. As a gesture of goodwill toward Spain, however, the German authorities were instructed to act without undue severity while organizing the group transport of the Spanish nationals.[63] Thus, the repatriation of Spanish Jews in Athens under conditions of personal freedom was ruled out.

Throughout these discussions the Jews of Athens enjoyed a respite, albeit temporary. Except for the directives imposed in October and occasional arrests, the Germans created the impression that they would leave the last remnant of Greek Jews alone. This lull ended on Friday, March 24, 1944. On that day, the Germans trapped 350 men when they came to register at the Jewish community center. That evening their families joined them, either freely or by force. At midnight, those holding foreign citizenship—Spanish, Portuguese, and Turkish—were hunted down, taken from their homes, and detained in the Jewish community center. All were deported on March 25 to the concentration camp at Haidari, near Athens. On April 2, 1,300 Greek, Italian, Spanish, and Portuguese Jews were taken to the railway station and loaded onto cattle cars; only those with Turkish and Argentinian citizenships were removed from this transport. On their way north through central Greece, additional trains carrying Jews from various communities, who had until then been left undisturbed in the Italian-occupied zone, were attached to the convoy. In Austria, the cars carrying Spanish and Portuguese citizens were detached; they reached Bergen-Belsen on April 14.[64]

In the hunt for Spanish Jews, 155 were caught. Their arrest surprised Radigales, who on the night of the round-up tried without success to intervene with Altenburg; even so, news of the deportation reached Radigales too late for him to notify his government of the date and the destination of the transport. He bitterly reported to Madrid his efforts on behalf of Spanish nationals who had managed to hide: of eighty Jews with Spanish citizenship remaining in Athens, thirty were in danger of being deported to Poland if apprehended; those who had intermarried were safe for the time being. By July 14 the Germans caught six more Spanish Jews, and Radigales demanded that the arrested remain in Athens or that the Germans at least inform him of their destination so that he could notify the Spanish Foreign Ministry. His efforts succeeded: at the end of September 1944, he reported to Madrid that the Germans had released the six Jews and had promised that nothing would happen to those in hiding if they reported to the police weekly. Did this concession from the Germans come about because they were afraid to become involved with the murder of Jews for whom Spain demanded release? Were there other factors involved? This cannot be established from the information available. Because Athens was liberated from the Nazis only two weeks after his report was sent, however, it may be assumed that those Jews under Radigales's protection were saved.[65]

The fate of the Spanish nationals deported to Bergen-Belsen was less fortunate. On April 11, 1944, before the 155 Jews from Athens reached Bergen-Belsen, Madrid through its embassy in Berlin told the German Foreign Ministry that it was willing to receive its nationals and that it wished to be informed of the location and date of their arrival at the Spanish border. On May 4, the Germans handed the Spanish Embassy the names of the 155 Jews and announced that after the list had been verified by the Spanish authorities arrangements would be made for a date of transfer to Spain. The Spanish Embassy promised to grant permission immediately after instructions were received, but communication from Madrid was delayed, once again apparently because of Spain's policy of making the repatriation of one group contingent upon the evacuation of another. In any event, this is what German Baraibar maintained on June 5, when the representative of the Jewish Agency asked him to expedite the rescue of the Jews of Athens.[66]

On June 21, most of the Spanish Jews rescued from Salonika were transported to Fedala, and Spain's precondition was fulfilled. On June 24, Foreign Minister Jordana instructed his ambassador in Berlin to arrange with the German authorities for the evacuation of the Spanish nationals detained in Bergen-Belsen. The embassy approached the German Foreign Ministry on June 27, and von Thadden relayed this information to Eichmann on July 14. (See Appendix, document I.) But now the Nazis were in no hurry to respond. Germany's position in western Europe was deteriorating rapidly. Allied forces, who had landed in Normandy on June 6, were beginning to threaten Germany's control of France, reducing its ability to guarantee the safe conduct of refugees from Bergen-Belsen to the Spanish border. This might have been why, on July 14, the Spanish Embassy in Berlin asked the German Foreign Ministry to organize the transportation of Spanish nationals to Vichy and from there leave all arrangements for their passage to Spain in the hands of local Spanish consulates. Representatives of the Jewish Agency in Lisbon and Madrid, who had approached the Spanish Foreign Ministry regarding the Bergen-Belsen refugees, were told that an appeal lodged with the Germans had been granted and that their arrival at the Spanish border was expected sometime in July. The representatives quickly informed the Zionist Executive in Jerusalem that Spanish Jews from Athens had been saved, but their message was sadly premature: the 155 Spanish Jews from Athens never reached Spain.[67]

How did this happen? In the margin of a memorandum to Eichmann containing the Spanish demand, dated July 29, 1944, von Thadden remarked that the RSHA wished to move this group to the Spanish border at Hendaye together with nineteen Jews from Athens holding Portuguese citizenship. This was conveyed to the secretary of the Spanish Embassy in Berlin, who telephoned the German Foreign Ministry on August 1. Two additional marginal comments on that same memorandum, however, prove that the Spanish Embassy did not refer to this matter again and that "the transport is not longer practicable." This last comment bears the date August 31, 1944. Despite this, nineteen Jews from Athens carrying Portuguese papers reached Portugal approximately on August 16, 1944.[68] Von Thadden's comments, together with the fact that the Portuguese nationals from Athens who also were in Bergen-Belsen were rescued and eventually reached Portugal, demonstrate that the failure to repatriate the 155 Jews from Athens was the result of insufficient pressure by the Spanish Embassy in Berlin.

Once the opportunity to bring the Spanish Jews from Athens to Spain had been lost, efforts were made during the last months of 1944 to evacuate them to Switzerland. Sally Mayer, the representative of the JDC in Switzerland, and Lazaro Benveniste—who represented himself as a former vice-consul of Spain in Kavalla, Macedonia, living in Lausanne—undertook this project. At their initiative, Salomon Ezraty, who at that time was still in Barcelona, was urged to participate, and some time later the American Embassy in Madrid also became involved. All these requested that Spain enlist Switzerland's help for the rescue of Spanish nationals from Athens. On September 25, the Spanish Foreign Ministry promised Carlton Hayes that appropriate instructions would be sent to the Spanish embassies in Switzerland and Germany. On November 15, the American Embassy in Madrid again informed the Spanish government that the Swiss government had agreed some weeks before to accept the Athens Jews, but that Spain should approach Switzerland officially to establish a precedent for demanding that the Germans release them from Bergen-Belsen.[69]

Spain instructed its embassy in Bern to approach the Swiss government and request its intervention. On November 28, the Swiss Embassy in Berlin informed the German Foreign Ministry that Switzerland was prepared to allow the passage of the 155 refugees through its territory. The JDC gave the Swiss the necessary guarantees for the maintenance of the refugees, and to all intents and purposes their rescue was at hand.

This did not happen, however. Was the time involved in intergovernmental negotiations to blame? Did Eichmann's meddling, into whose hands the Swiss appeal fell, delay the repatriation? There is no evidence here.

The 155 Spanish nationals therefore remained in the "privileged" transit camp in Bergen-Belsen, where conditions continued to deteriorate as the fall of Germany became more certain. On April 6, 1945, as Allied forces approached the concentration camp, the Spanish nationals, along with 2,200 other prisoners, were jammed into trains that began to roll along the devastated railway tracks of Germany. On April 13, after a week of aimless journeying, the train was captured by one of the advance columns of the American Army, and all the surviving prisoners were rescued.[70] Spanish citizenship thus saved the lives of this group of Jews until the eve of their liberation, despite the vagaries of Spain's efforts to rescue them. But only a miracle saved these 155 Spanish nationals from the fate that befell those who died during the last days of the war.

THE SAVING GRACE OF SPANISH NATIONALITY

When the Germans suggested to neutral countries that they evacuate their Jewish nationals from Nazi-occupied areas, they set one fundamental condition: that neutral countries no longer may continue to grant citizenship to Jews beyond those already registered in their agencies. The circumstances under which the German policy regarding foreign Jews was established indicate that many Nazi officials in the German Foreign Ministry, and obviously in the RSHA, would do everything they could to keep the number of survivors to a minimum. In accordance with that policy, however, it may be said with certainty that the number of Jews Spain could have saved was approximately 2,000 in occupied France and another 1,000 in Vichy France. The fact that the efforts to rescue Spanish nationals from France involved only a few hundred Jews was not the result of German restrictions but arose from a policy adopted by the Spanish government in March 1943 to recognize only those Jewish nationals whose citizenship could not be canceled. By the beginning of October 1942, less than six months before this policy was taken, a Spanish Foreign Ministry report summarizing the situation of Jewish nationals indicated that the number registered at the Paris embassy was 2,000. At the end of April 1943, approximately six weeks after the policy was adopted, the Paris embassy reported that the number of registered Jewish nationals entitled to receive entry visas to Spain was only 250. Apparently, 1,750 Jews in occupied France were disqualified by the Spanish Foreign Ministry. Although there are no exact figures concerning the situation in Vichy France, it seems that there the ratio between those qualifying for repatriation and those disqualified by the Spanish government was similar if not worse.[71]

In Greece, too, the number of Jews registered apparently was greater than the total of the various groups handled by the Spanish representatives. According to one source, the number was approximately 830, of which 250 were in Athens, 560 in Salonika, and the others elsewhere.[72] According to Spanish documents, the Spanish authorities only handled 640 cases. Although there is no evidence that the other 190 were lost in the Holocaust, it should be remembered that the Spanish citizenship of those dealt with by the Spanish authorities was not in doubt and that the number mentioned was minimal.

Despite the drastic limitation in the number of candidates for repatriation, the rescue did not include even all of these. Only 365 Jews reached Spain from Greece. According to lists, only a few small groups of Spanish nationals, the largest of which entered through Irún on August 11, 1943, came from France. The total number in all the groups was 194. In addition, there were families from western Europe who were allowed to enter Spain after the Germans ordered their deportation, just as there were some Jewish nationals who found their way to Spain from all parts of the Diaspora during the first years of the war. According to lists drawn up in 1943 by a member of HICEM, the total since the beginning of the war was 165. Taking into account the possibility that not all those having Spanish citizenship were known, it may be estimated that for all these cases there were no more than 250 people. Thus, during all the years of the war no more than 800 persons were repatriated to Spain.[73]

The number of Spanish nationals saved by repatriation is therefore far less than the overall number even of those whose Spanish citizenship was unquestioned. The principal reason for this was the policy adopted by the Spanish government, which stipulated that one group of refugees had to leave the country before another group was permitted to enter. This policy determined the fate of many Spanish nationals in western Europe. It also forced 155 Jews from Athens to remain in Bergen-Belsen for an entire year; their rescue came about only by a stroke of luck during the final days of the Third Reich.

The release of the small group of Jewish Spanish nationals who remained in Athens indicates that in certain circumstances the extent of rescue was not bound exclusively to the possibility of repatriation. In this connection, a special study of the situation of the Jewish Spanish nationals in other Balkan countries is necessary.

6

ℳ ℼ

DEFENDING JEWS IN
THEIR OWN COUNTRIES

BULGARIA

Lured by the territory acquired through its treaty with Germany, Bulgaria joined the Axis. By September 1940, Bulgaria had stripped Romania of the province of southern Dobruja; six months later, it received Thrace and Macedonia in return for its aid in the war against Yugoslavia and Greece. Bulgaria now held vast areas and was ready to serve as a faithful ally to Germany without relinquishing its sovereignty.

One result of its Nazi affiliation was far-reaching anti-Semitic legislation, passed on December 24, 1940. The Bulgarian parliament attempted to isolate 50,000 Bulgarian Jews from the rest of the population, to restrict their business activities, and to remove them as much as possible from public life. Because of this legislation and other laws that followed during 1941 and 1942, the Jews lost most of their property through exorbitant taxation and the forced sale or closure of their businesses. Jews were mobilized for public work, which at its peak employed 10,000 people, approximately one-fifth of the entire Jewish community. In addition, strict limitations were imposed on their freedom of movement. Insofar as the Germans were concerned, all these were only the first steps toward deportation and destruction.[1]

The oppression that troubled the lives of Bulgarian Jews also affected foreign Jews living there, including approximately 150 Spanish nationals, 25 of whom—residents of Skopje—were registered, until the conquest of

Yugoslavia, with the Spanish Legation in Belgrade. Several of these managed, during 1941 and 1942, to secure entry visas and reach Spain. The fate of the rest lay in the hands of the Spanish minister in Sofia, Julio Palencia y Álvarez.[2]

The threats to the welfare and property of Spanish nationals and the injustices they suffered often brought the Spanish Legation to work with the Bulgarian authorities on their behalf. By his efforts, Palencia succeeded in removing some cash from the frozen deposits of his protégés and was careful to avoid any activities that might weaken his future plans. After the Commissariat for Jewish Affairs was established in Bulgaria in August 1942 and new measures had been adopted against Jews, a newspaper published a cable from Madrid stating that the Spanish government had limited Jewish business activities and the hiring of Jews in many enterprises. Because he feared that this false information would provide the Bulgarian authorities with an excuse to impose further anti-Semitic laws on Spanish Jews, Palencia requested an official denial from his superiors in the Spanish Foreign Ministry. But the Spanish nationals in Bulgaria were not harmed and continued to enjoy immunity as a result of their special status.[3]

The German scheme to include Bulgarian Jews in its plans for annihilation was implemented first in 1943. Theodor Dannecker, one of Eichmann's assistants, came to Sofia in January; on February 22 he reached agreement with Alexander Belev, head of the Commissariat for Jewish Affairs. During the initial stage, 14,000 Jews would be deported from Thrace and Macedonia and another 6,000 from Bulgaria itself. After preparations had been completed, hunts began in Thrace and Macedonia, where 11,343 Jews were arrested and sent to Poland on March 22, 25, and 29; in Skopje, 7,122 Jews were arrested and sent by train; and in Lom, 4,221 Jews were arrested and taken via the Danube to Vienna.

On March 16, 1943, one week before the deportations began, Palencia heard what was about to happen from Bulgarian Premier Bogdan Filov. Knowing that the Spanish nationals were also in danger, he cabled Foreign Minister Jordana, suggesting that Madrid inform the Bulgarian government and Germany that "Spain cannot permit its subjects to be deported to Poland because of racial laws that do not exist in our country. Just as Bulgarians live in peace in Spain, so Spaniards have the right to live in the same manner in Bulgaria." Palencia also expressed his opinion to Filov; available documentation indicates that the deportations from Thrace and Macedonia and the arrests in Kyustendil, Plovdiv, Varna, and Ruse did not include the few Spanish nationals there. As many of these nationals lived in the latter three cities and Palencia could not defend them properly from his office in Sofia, he asked Madrid for permission to appoint salaried consular officials who would safeguard the interests of his protégés in those cities.[4]

Before his cable reached Jordana, Palencia was informed of the repatriation policy adopted in Madrid, and he responded joyously. The new policy increased the danger that Spanish Jews would be included among the Bulgarian Jews who were being expelled in May from Sofia to the smaller towns. Because of his sympathy for the Jews, the conditions under which Palencia was working grew unbearable. The Bulgarian police watched the mission building, questioned everyone entering and leaving, and arrested Palencia's secretary, who was Jewish, accusing him of espionage. Palencia tried to surmount these difficulties by appealing to the source of the persecutions, Germany's ambassador in Sofia, Adolf Beckerle. Palencia told Beckerle of Spain's plan to repatriate its 150 Jewish nationals. Palencia expressed his bitterness at the deportation of the Jews of Sofia and sought Beckerle's intervention for a few of his Bulgarian Jewish friends. Like all the others, this request was rejected.[5]

His openly pro-Jewish stance earned Palencia the epithet "the well-known friend of the Jews" in German correspondence. Indeed, the Spanish minister and his wife openly expressed their shock at the persecution of Jews. When Leon Arie, a Sephardic Jew, was sentenced to death for allegedly raising the price of the perfume he sold by a few pennies, Palencia and his wife appealed to various people of influence to prevent his execution. Their efforts were in vain, however; the man was put to death. The Palencias later surprised their diplomatic colleagues by requesting permission from a Bulgarian court to adopt Arie's son and daughter. On June 5, 1943, the official Bulgarian newspaper published the court's decision confirming the adoption of Klodi and Renée, Arie's 21- and 26-year-old son and daughter, by the 58-year-old Spanish minister and his wife, Zoé Dragumiz de Palencia.[6]

The Germans and the Jew-haters in Bulgaria were furious. Palencia was declared persona non grata and was recalled to Madrid. In August he terminated his duties and prepared to leave Sofia with his adopted children. The German Foreign Ministry was alerted to the possibility that the "friend of the Jews" would try to exploit his diplomatic passport and take the children of the executed Jew with him. Von Thadden instructed Hans Dieckhoff, the new German ambassador in Madrid, to inform the Spanish Foreign Ministry that Germany would not provide a transit visa for this passport. Palencia nevertheless completed his preparations, avoided saying good-bye to his Axis colleagues (using excuses that were interpreted justifiably by them as a show of disrespect), and left with his adopted children on August 21 for Bucharest, where their mother, Arie's widow, was awaiting them.[7]

Did Palencia try to rescue his adopted children by taking them to Spain? Sources reveal only that had he attempted this the German Embassy in Bucharest would have refused the Palencias passage through Nazi-occupied areas. Was another avenue of rescue for the children and their mother ready in Bucharest when the Palencias' role ceased? There is no evidence here either. In any event, the mission of Julio Palencia ended as it had begun: identification with the persecuted Jews of Bulgaria and tireless defense of his protégés. As punishment for interfering in official political business, Palencia was reprimanded when he returned to Spain and was suspended from duty for a period of time. But according to at least one source, he was awarded the Cross of Isabella the Catholic for his heroism.[8]

Before he left Sofia, he completed his plans for the repatriation. Three lists of candidates for rescue through Spain, a total of 119 names, were sent to the Spanish Embassy in Berlin; after this list was examined and confirmed, it was forwarded to the Foreign Ministry in Madrid. In the meantime, however, several months passed and the likelihood of repatriation disappeared. Fortunately, as the persecutions declined in Bulgaria, the evacuation of Spanish nationals became less urgent. Spain's readiness to accept its nationals from occupied countries thus was not put to the test in Bulgaria; here diplomatic immunity was sufficient to save the handful of Spanish nationals.[9]

ROMANIA

Spanish nationals in Romania had enjoyed relative quiet since the summer of 1942; the Romanian government promised the Spanish Legation in Bucharest that it would not harm its protégés or their property, and it seemed to be keeping its promise. The problem of repatriating the few Spanish Jews thus did not arise here until 1944. Even then, the need for repatriation apparently did not arise from any threats of extermination by the Germans but rather from the advance of the Russian army, which might well have endangered those who had supported Nationalist Spain. In March 1944, the Spanish Legation approached the German Embassy and requested transit permits through the German areas of occupation for forty-five of its one hundred protégés.[10]

The Spanish were forced to repeat this request many times. Two months later, they received a reply, which stated that because of the invasion of Normandy the Spanish-French border had been closed. In July they were told that crossing the German-French border required a special permit that would be issued only in extremely urgent cases and then only after orders from Berlin. Germany's reluctance to answer a Spanish request that was initiated by German demands might have stemmed from conflicting opinions regarding Jews who were citizens of neutral countries. German correspondence on this subject reveals that the Spanish Legation's request came when the RSHA, through the German Embassy in Bucharest, was pressing Romania not to respond to Allied proposals for the rescue of Jews: granting permission for rescue by emigration to Spain appeared to the Nazis an undesirable precedent. The German Foreign Ministry wanted to handle the repatriation of foreign nationals from Romania itself, just as it had handled repatriation from other countries. The fate of alien nationals thus was in its hands, but because the Ministry did not wish to counteract the work of the RSHA, its representative in Bucharest was instructed to use delaying tactics.[11]

Did the Spanish Legation in Bucharest succeed in exploiting its limited opportunities for saving some of its protégés before Romania was liberated by the Russians? The answer is not known. A secondary source, who perhaps drew on the oral testimony of the Spanish minister in Bucharest, maintains that before the spring of 1944, sixty-five Spanish nationals left Romania for Spain, and the rest managed to leave for Turkey and Palestine that summer. This source also points out that in 1944 Spanish protection was provided for the homes and property of two hundred other Jews. Although these two statements still require authentication and further documentation, it is clear that Spain's willingness to repatriate its nationals in Romania was not put to the test; they were protected without having to move to Spain.[12]

HUNGARY

Approximately 825,000 Jews lived in Hungary and the areas Hungary had annexed with German aid at the end of the 1930s and the beginning of the war. Until March 1944 this large Jewish community remained in relative tranquillity, serving as a place of refuge and transit for refugees from Poland and Slovakia. There were, to be sure, discriminatory anti-Semitic laws, economic prohibitions, and worst of all, forced labor on the Ukrainian front; by the spring of 1944, 63,000 Jews of Greater Hungary had fallen victims to the persecution. Although this suffering did not completely undermine Jewish life in many communities, it was only a small hint of what was yet to come.

On March 19, 1944, the German army entered Hungary, and the pro-Nazi government of Döme Sztójay that was established under their patronage agreed to assist the Germans—or be assisted by them—in destroying the Jewish community, whose very existence had for some time been the subject of complaints from Hitler against Admiral Miklós Horthy, regent of Hungary. Now that the opportunity presented itself, the Germans moved to carry out the deportations quickly. Himmler instructed Eichmann to head a special SS Einsatzgruppen formed to eliminate the Jews of Hungary. On March 19, Eichmann arrived in Budapest and began to put the plan into operation.

The Einsatzgruppen spent the rest of March and all of April traveling to provincial towns, finding convenient places for concentration, and making preparations. They also negotiated with Jewish leaders, trying to extort money while deluding them with false hopes of worthless concessions. These steps were part of a deception that Eichmann planned in collaboration with László Baky and László Endre, who had been placed in charge of the extermination by the Hungarian Ministry of the Interior. Deportation and destruction now suddenly overwhelmed the Jews of Hungary. When Jews were taken from villages and farms and placed in central ghettos (which were only temporary prisons) and when they were detained in factories or in open fields, the Germans had no trouble convincing them that they were being transferred for work in Hungary. This hoax succeeded so well that even when shipments to Auschwitz began—the first group of 4,000 people had left by April 27, 1944—those being deported either did not know or refused to believe that they were about to be murdered. In a period of nine weeks, between the end of April and July 4, Eichmann, with the aid of the German SS and several thousand Hungarian police, sent approximately 500,000 Jews from Greater Hungary to Auschwitz. At the beginning of July 1944, only 247,000 Jews remained in Budapest and its outlying districts.

Word of the deportations of hundreds of thousands of Jews to extermination camps began to reach the West in May 1944. Joel Brand, a member of the Zionist relief and rescue committee in Budapest, arrived in Turkey and provided first-hand information as well as offers to save the Jews of Hungary in exchange for war matériel and equipment that the Allies were to supply to Germany. A detailed report of what was happening in Auschwitz was smuggled through Switzerland and published in the press there at the end of June. The news stimulated violent protests, threats, and pressures against Horthy—who still symbolized Hungarian sovereignty and enjoyed official influence—forcing him to halt the deportation of the Jews of Budapest, sparing them for the time being. At the beginning of July, rumors reached Horthy that units of police, who had been mobilized in Budapest to aid in the deportations, might serve to spearhead an uprising; Horthy ordered these units removed to provincial towns. With the surrender of Romania at the end of August 1944 and the advance of the Red Army into Hungary, Horthy attempted to disengage himself from the Axis, but the coup he had planned failed. He was deposed, and control was seized by the Fascist Arrow Cross party under its leader, Ferenc Szálasi. After October 15, the Jews of Budapest were at the mercy of armed bands of a regime entirely under German control.

The situation on the front had deteriorated meanwhile, and the Russian Army was advancing on the outskirts of Budapest. This did not hinder the Germans in their extermination plans, however. Because of lack of transportation, they forced the Jews of Budapest to march to the Austrian border, allegedly for work on fortifications. In freezing cold, without food or rest, tens of thousands of men and women were marched for more than 125 miles; thousands died from exposure, exhaustion, or starvation. The terrors of this death march shocked the diplomatic representatives in Budapest. Vatican representative Angelo Rotta, supported by Pope Pius XII and his colleagues from other neutral embassies, strongly protested to Prime Minister Szálasi and urged him to stop the deportations. On November 29, 1944, the Hungarian government issued an order forbidding the Jews remaining in Budapest to live outside the two ghettos that had been assigned them. From that time onward, their fate hung in the balance. The Russian Army blockade on Budapest on December 24 almost brought about the complete extermination of the Jews. Horrible rumors concerning preparations by the desperate Arrow Cross to blow up Jewish homes pervaded the ghettos. Only when Russian soldiers burst into the central ghetto on the evening of January 17, 1945, did the torture cease. On that day, no more than 125,000 Jews remained in the capital, of whom 30,000 had been saved by the defense and protection provided by representatives of the neutral countries, the Red Cross, and the papal nuncio.[13]

What part did Spain play in this rescue?

When German forces entered Hungary in March 1944, Miguel Angel Muguiro was serving as the Spanish chargé d'affaires in Budapest. His reports had long been critical of the anti-Semitic position of the Hungarian government. The changes that took place in Hungary as a result of the German occupation were faithfully reflected in his reports after March. In concluding one report he raised the question whether, under the circumstances, Hungary could still be considered a sovereign nation. Muguiro devoted particular attention to the new policies regarding the Jews. The laws that excluded Jews from the Hungarian economy, forcing them to wear a yellow badge, the looting and pillage by the Gestapo—all these, as well as the reactions of the Hungarian people, Muguiro described in great detail to his superiors in the Spanish Foreign Ministry. On May 20, 1944, when the deportation of Jews from the provincial towns was at its height, the Spanish Legation received an anonymous protest from a Hungarian, "a prominent Christian," denouncing the cruelty and robbery and appealing to the neutral countries—including Spain—to raise their voices. All this Muguiro reported to Madrid.

Diplomatic tensions rose in the meantime between Hungary and Spain after the Hungarian minister in Madrid announced that he would not recognize the new regime in Budapest and the Spanish government delayed the appointment of a new Hungarian foreign representative. The Hungarian foreign minister in turn blamed Muguiro for muddying international relationships; this little crisis ended only when a new Spanish chargé d'affaires was assigned to Hungary. Angel Sanz Briz arrived at the beginning of June 1944. The tension and its resolution strengthened the status of the new Spanish representative, who was given the opportunity to utilize Spain's neutral status in order to save Jews.[14]

The first request to exert its influence to save Jews was made to the Spanish government by the Jewish communities in Tangier and Tétouan. Several hundred Hungarian Jews had found refuge in Tangier before and during the first years of the war, and some of them had managed to build successful businesses there. Because of their connections in Hungary they were aware of recent events there, and they persuaded the Jewish community to attempt to enlist Spain's aid in the rescue of Jews. The communities of Tangier and Tétouan maintained close ties with the Spanish authorities in North Africa; a refugee relief committee in Tangier assisted 660 Jews who found shelter in this international city under Spanish rule. On May 22, 1944, several leaders of these communities appealed to the Spanish High Commissioner in Morocco to allow 500 children, ages five to fifteen, to enter Tangier. According to them, 400 to 500 Jewish refugees were ready to leave Tangier; consent to this request therefore would not increase the refugee population. The community leaders promised to bear all expenses in maintaining the refugees, and hoped that transportation to Tangier would be provided by the International Red Cross. A few days later, their request was seconded by the American chargé d'affaires in Tangier, and on June 2 the Jewish community again announced that it was prepared to accept financial and moral responsibility for any children rescued. This guarantee doubtless was offered by the Jews of North Africa in consultation with the JDC, which supported the refugee relief committee in Tangier; it is even possible that it was the JDC who appealed to the American representative in that city.

The High Commissioner in Morocco honored the request but stressed that the children could not be brought to Tangier before the adult refugees had been relocated. The Spanish Foreign Ministry, where the decision ultimately rested, also agreed but again emphasized the connection between the evacuation of earlier refugees and the entry of new ones. On July 20, 1944, Sanz Briz was instructed, together with the Red Cross authorities, to begin screening the children. Sanz Briz contacted the Jewish organizations and requested them to refer to him children who had been orphaned during the war.[15]

The transportation of children to Tangier soon encountered difficulties with the German authorities, in the same way that only 320 of the 10,000 children for whom the Swiss government had provided entry visas had ever reached Switzerland, and these from Bergen-Belsen and not Hungary. Because the very provision of entry visas to Tangier constituted partial protection, the 500 children who received Spanish visas were placed under the protection of the Red Cross and the Spanish Legation.[16]

As news of the events in Hungary spread, concern in the United States and England grew, and demands that the Allies act to save refugees became more persistent. During the summer of 1944, Jewish organizations asked that the Allies work vigorously to rescue Jews either by negotiating with the Nazis following the proposals Joel Brand had received from Eichmann or by bombing the installations at Auschwitz. The Allies rejected both suggestions. The Allies were willing only to increase their involvement in neutral countries, such as Spain, so that their influence could be exploited to save Hungarian Jews.

One such appeal concerned 1,684 Jews for whose release the Budapest rescue committee negotiated with Eichmann in Budapest. When these refugees were permitted to leave Hungary, they immediately needed entry visas to a neutral country. Eliyahu Dobkin, a member of the Jewish Agency Executive on a brief visit in Madrid, obtained the support of British Ambassador Samuel Hoare, who appealed to the Spanish Foreign Ministry to allow these refugees to enter the country; this request later was supported by the American Embassy. Sanz Briz forwarded the plea of the heads of the Budapest rescue committee, Otto Komoly and Rezsö Rudolf Kasztner, to Madrid; Madrid quickly responded and Sanz Briz was told to issue the necessary permits. The fact that the convoy of refugees never reached Spain but was diverted to Bergen-Belsen and from there to Switzerland was the result of German opposition and changes that had occurred in the meantime on the western front.[17]

While dealing with this group of refugees, the American Embassy on July 22, 1944, made a further request of the Spanish Foreign Ministry. According to unofficial information it had received, the Germans were prepared to allow Jews to leave Hungary. The U.S. government therefore asked Spain to provide entry visas for as many Jews as possible and to take full responsibility for them until their evacuation from Spain. On August 11, the American Embassy asked Madrid to provide transit visas without delay to all Jews holding American passports and expired emigration permits; on August 30 it expanded this request to include the relatives of American citizens as well as the relatives of aliens living in the U.S. The British Embassy also joined in the demand to provide Spanish permits to all those asking for them and promised to assist in speedily evacuating those coming to Spain. This pressure on Spain to provide Hungarian Jews with entry visas almost without limitation came at a time when the fighting in France was quickly closing off the territory between Spain and the Axis countries; there was thus great doubt whether the Allies actually intended to organize serious rescue operations in Spain. It is more likely that these efforts were prompted by reports that emigration permits or any neutral documents might provide protection to those who held them. Spain gradually responded to these requests, in the beginning only to those with passports and American emigration permits but later expanding its efforts.

When Jewish leaders from Tangier appealed to Madrid in September 1944, requesting that Spain provide entry visas for 700 additional Jews, Spanish authorities again agreed. The Spanish ambassador in Washington, Juan F. Cárdenas, thus was able to inform the World Jewish Congress on October 25 that the Spanish government had instructed its ambassador in Budapest to protect Jewish Spanish nationals, Sephardic Jews without Spanish citizenship, and eastern European Jews whenever possible.[18]

All these appeals provided Angel Sanz Briz with the full support of the Spanish Foreign Ministry, backing he sorely needed in his efforts to save Jews in Hungary. From the time of his arrival in Budapest, Sanz Briz closely followed events and opinions regarding Jews in the Hungarian capital, from time to time conveying his impressions to his superiors in Madrid. On July 15, 1944, he sent a report on anti-Semitic Hungarian legislation and commented that the authorities were concerned with the Jewish question second only to the war. On July 24, he forwarded a letter from the Hungarian government intending to explain Hungary's policy toward the Jews, but added that the letter "does not mention that among the 500,000 people deported were a large number of women, old people, and children who were completely unfit for work, and concerning whose fate the most pessimistic rumors are circulating in this country." A few days later, he presented appeals from the Pope and the king of Sweden to Admiral Horthy, urging that he halt the deportations of the Jews. In August, Sanz Briz sent to Madrid a copy of the testimony of two refugees from Auschwitz and Majdanek, handed to him by members of the Zionist organization in Budapest, describing graphically what had happened to them from the moment they were sent to these camps in the spring of 1942. Sanz Briz added the following:

> The origin of this report makes it suspiciously one-sided. Nevertheless, from the information I have succeeded in obtaining from people who have no direct interest in the problem and from my colleagues in the diplomatic corps here, it seems that many of the facts described are unfortunately authentic.[19]

The tragedy of Hungarian Jewry, in all its pitiful detail, was known to Sanz Briz. As the representative of a Catholic state, he doubtless had an especially close relationship with Angelo Rotta, the papal nuncio, who had been outstandingly active on behalf of Jews since March 1944. The anti-Semitic legislation and the subsequent deportations—which did not exempt converted Jews, thereby violating the sanctity of the Catholic baptism—forced Rotta to intercede repeatedly with Prime Minister Sztójay and the foreign minister. On March 23 and 30 and April 18 and 24, he demanded that the Hungarian government modify the persecution laws; after the deportations began, he severely condemned the government's actions, and insisted that at least converted Jews should be excluded from the decrees. At the end of July, when there was a danger that the Jews of Budapest would be deported also, he urged the Pope to appeal personally to Admiral Horthy and to ask that the deportation order be canceled. One month later, acting on information that the Hungarian authorities intended to enforce the deportations from Budapest, Rotta convened the ambassadors and representatives of the neutral countries; together they formulated a declaration condemning these deportations. In their protest, handed on August 21, to the Hungarian deputy prime minister, they wrote:

> Aside from the fact that the new deportations will deal a death blow to the good name of Hungary—which has already been harmed by the previous deportations—the representatives of neutral countries feel obliged, because of feelings of human solidarity and Christian charity, to protest strongly against this activity. It is unjust in its reasoning and inhuman in its implementation, for one cannot accept that people should be persecuted and sent to their death merely because of their racial origin. The representatives of the

neutral countries demand that the Hungarian government put a complete end to these actions, which for the sake of the honor of humanity should never have begun.

Sanz Briz participated in the meeting of ambassadors and reported its discussions to Madrid, but his name was not included among those who signed the petition of protest.[20]

At that time, Sanz Briz was attempting to locate the 500 children who were supposed to be sent to Tangier and to offer his protection to 45 Jews who he could claim were Spanish nationals. This was the first step in the rescue he initiated after October 15, 1944.

The arrest of Admiral Horthy after his abortive attempt to remove Hungary from the war and the rise to power of Ferenc Szálasi, leader of the Arrow Cross, strengthened the status of the representatives of neutral countries in Budapest. Internal chaos and the desire of the new government to gain diplomatic recognition made it possible for representatives of neutral countries to extend their protection, under various pretexts, to an increasingly large number of Hungarian Jews. At that time, Allied pressure and Sanz Briz's reports from Budapest prompted the Spanish Foreign Ministry to allow its representative to behave as other neutral ambassadors did, without formal and legal limitations. Sanz Briz approached the officials of the Hungarian Foreign Ministry who remained in office despite the change in the regime and obtained permission to extend his protection over the Spanish Jews in Hungary and work for their repatriation to Spain. He was dealing apparently with only 300 people, but after permission was granted and the fact was established that Spanish protégés were living in Hungary, he extended his protection to more than 2,000 people. He provided 45 Spanish Jews with regular Spanish passports whose validity was limited to three months; another 352 Jews received special, slightly different passports; and 1,898 additional Jews received "letters of patronage," testifying that the bearers were about to emigrate to Spain and were therefore under the protection of the Spanish Legation. To safeguard the lives of all these protégés, the Spanish minister, with funds donated by Jewish individuals and organizations, rented special houses where signs were posted indicating that the buildings constituted part of the Spanish representation and were therefore extraterritorial Spanish territory. By chance Sanz Briz formed a friendly relationship with an Arrow Cross official who was the newly appointed mayor of Budapest. By virtue of this friendship he managed to maintain the immunity of the rented houses and save the lives of their tenants.[21]

His intervention on behalf of Jews did not go unnoticed by the Germans, who followed his activities and those of other representatives.

On October 13, von Thadden informed Edmund Veesenmayer, the German ambassador in Budapest, that the Spanish government had yielded to pressure from the United States and agreed to provide entry visas to thousands of Hungarian Jews to save their lives. One month later, Veesenmayer reported that Sanz Briz had requested from the Hungarian Foreign Ministry exit visas for 300 Jews, justifying his request by stating that these were relatives of Jews living in Spain. Veesenmayer believed that the Hungarian Foreign Ministry was inclined to respond positively to Spanish requests in the hope that in return Spain would recognize the Szálasi government. The Hungarians agreed that negotiations on the question of Jewish rescue should be conducted between the Spanish Embassy in Berlin and the German Foreign Ministry. On December 8, von Thadden informed the German Embassy in Madrid that no requests had been received from Spain to allow the departure of its nationals. This appeal was never considered because the passports and documents were merely intended to save the lives of the Jews of Budapest.[22]

Efforts to safeguard Spanish protégés, as well as the many Jews protected by other countries, involved continuous vigilance. The death march into which the Germans dragged tens of thousands of Jews did not exempt foreign nationals, including some protected by Spain. Through interventions, Sanz Briz managed to save thirty of his protégés from the march and return them to Budapest. On November 17, at the insistence of Angelo Rotta, he participated with other neutral representatives in an appeal to Szálasi to halt the march and order the return of the exiles. After the march was stopped, resistance continued against the members of the Arrow Cross and the Germans who violated the diplomatic immunity of the protected houses by attacking their inhabitants and their property.

The Red Army had, in the meantime, begun to close in around Budapest. Unlike the representatives of Switzerland, Sweden, and the Vatican, Sanz Briz feared for his safety if the city fell into the hands of the Russians. On instructions from Madrid, he left his post in December for Switzerland. On December 14, in Bern, he wrote his last report as the Spanish representative in Budapest, summarizing his attempts to save Jews by providing them with passports and documents.[23]

On December 24, Russian forces surrounded the Hungarian capital and laid siege to it. Now the last chapter in the struggle for the lives of the few remaining Jews of Hungary had begun. Because Sanz Briz left Budapest secretly, his protégés and the protected houses remained undefended but were left untouched. Fortunately, at this stage a new Spanish representative appeared on the scene; although he had been neither appointed nor authorized by Madrid, Giorgio Perlasca undertook the function of the Spanish chargé d'affaires. Born in Trieste, Perlasca was employed at the Spanish Legation, and after Sanz Briz's departure he began to act as the representative of Spain on behalf of the Spanish protégés. These circumstances may have made possible the survival of many of the Jews Spain protected in Hungary.[24]

THE EXTENT OF RESCUE

In the two years preceding World War II, Jews of Spanish nationality in Bulgaria and Romania—and apparently in other countries too—were faced with the test of identifying with one or the other side in the Spanish Civil War. For various reasons, 150 Jews in Bulgaria and 107 in Romania chose the Nationalist side, despite the fact that Jewish communities throughout the world sympathized with the Republicans. Because an unknown number of Spanish nationals did not identify with Nationalist Spain, they lost contact with the Spanish Embassy, which after the Civil War represented Franco's government. Although the existence of these ex-nationals of Spain is confirmed, they did not enjoy the protection that Spain extended to its nationals. Nevertheless, the Franco government owed a debt of honor to these few Jews in Bulgaria and Romania because, aside from their connection to the rebel government at Burgos—and their promoting its image in the countries of their residence when Spain most needed their support—these Jews voluntarily contributed significant sums to finance the Nationalist embassies.[25] Hence, the representatives of Spain in Bucharest and Sofia tried vigorously to defend their Jewish protégés; fortunately, the special circumstances in these two countries enabled them to be rescued without their having to move to Spain.

In contrast to Romania and Bulgaria, where Spanish protection was limited to Spanish nationals, in Hungary protection was extended to a large number of Jews, most of whom were not even of Spanish origin. Several factors that did not exist in other Holocaust countries and that happened to coincide in Hungary were responsible for this. First, the need to rescue the Jews of Hungary only arose in the summer and fall of 1944. German defeat was already apparent by then, and Spain was more inclined to respond to the demands of the Allies. For their part the Allied governments indeed included the protection of Jews in Hungary among the activities they requested Madrid to undertake. Another factor was that the shaky Hungarian regime and the undermining of its internal order prevented it from overseeing the rescue operations of neutral representatives. Their activities on behalf of Jews were no mean challenge for their

Spanish colleague Sanz Briz, who like them was an eyewitness to the destruction of Hungarian Jewry and was moved to act on their behalf. A third factor—and a decisive one—was that in Hungary there was no question of repatriation, which inevitably would have resulted in an increased Jewish presence in Spain, but merely of diplomatic protection. This set of circumstances prompted Spain to extend its protection to 2,795 Hungarian Jews.

The total number of Jews saved as a result of Spanish protection in Hungary, Bulgaria, and Romania was approximately 3,000. To this figure should be added the 235 Spanish nationals from Athens who were saved through the protection that Romero Radigales, in the name of Spain, so wholeheartedly extended to them. Hence, the maximum number of Jews who were protected by Spain and thus might have survived the Holocaust was 3,235.[26]

⌞ ⌟

FACT AND FANTASY

SPAIN'S WORDS AND DEEDS

"Spain, imbued with its universal Christian spirit of love for all the races on earth, contributed to the rescue of Jews, and acted more for spiritual than for merely legal or political reasons. Our government's aid was extended not only to Spanish Jews dispersed throughout the Continent, but also, whenever the opportunity presented itself, to all Jews irrespective of their nationality or place of residence." This is how the Spanish government described its rescue activities in a pamphlet intended to rebut Israel's vote against Spain in the U.N. General Assembly in 1949. These same words had appeared earlier, in 1945, in an article published in Madrid. The article evidently was used by the authors of the pamphlet; it was, of course, not the only one. That year and afterward this depiction of unflagging magnanimity and outstanding accomplishments in the rescue of Jews during the Holocaust was repeated frequently. The chapter concerning the Holocaust in *Spain and the Jews in the Second World War*, published in Spain in 1973, was for this reason symbolically entitled "Don Quixote Faces Hitler," recalling the Spaniards' admiration for their legendary idealistic nobleman. It seems that the notion that Franco's government actually did everything in its power to save Jews has been accepted commonly in Spain.[1]

How does this idealization tally with the results of the present study?

It should be pointed out first that Spain's legal position on Jews was different from that of similar regimes, save Portugal. Unlike the Balkan states, and of course Italy and Germany, Spain had no existing anti-Semitic legislation. Spanish authorities in their relations with other governments never failed to stress this fact and to make it the crux of their demands concerning people of Spanish nationality. Police action and discrimination against Jews, which did occur in Spain, were not based upon anti-Jewish regulations; rather, they were the result of deep-rooted Spanish prejudice. Manifestations of this hostility during the pre-Holocaust period were bolstered by Nazi influence and propaganda. Evidence shows, however, that the attitude of the common people—guards and police and the majority of Spaniards with whom Jewish refugees came in contact—was sympathetic and warm. In their eyes, the satanic image attached to the word "Jew" did not represent the people of flesh and blood who, suffering and persecuted, stood before them and admitted they were Jews. Spanish foreign representatives such as Romero Radigales, Julio Palencia, and Bernardo Rolland, who initiated attempts to safeguard the Jews who depended on them, presumably accurately reflected this feeling. The behavior of these representatives of Spain have justified the title "Don Quixote Faces Hitler."[2]

Spanish authorities refrained from discriminating against Jews, legally or otherwise. This was reflected also in the regulations regarding transit permits, which enabled tens of thousands of Jews to pass through Spain during the first years of the war. The difficulties facing Jews who tried to secure immigration visas and the obstacles that the French and German authorities placed in the way of their escape determined the dimensions of this avenue of rescue. Spain did not aggravate these difficulties, but out of loyalty to and support for the Vichy regime, it did not help alleviate them either.

The matter of long-range refuge in Spain presents a very different picture, however. Although the Jews who reached Spain illegally during the beginning of the war—or those whose transit arrangements failed— were few, Spanish authorities treated them harshly. Refugees were turned back at the border, others were imprisoned indefinitely, and the creation of an official welfare organization that could handle them was prevented. In this respect, these actions characterized Spanish policy toward the Jews. When in the summer of 1942 the number fleeing France increased, Spanish authorities tended to be even more strict, sending back to France those who had managed to cross the border and reach Barcelona. Fortunately, the flight from France after November 1942 became a problem of strategic importance for the Allies. Because of constant pressure and as a result of its new geopolitical position after the invasion of North Africa,

Spain agreed to change its policy. The Spanish border remained open to those escaping German-occupied areas, and major concessions were granted to diplomatic representatives and welfare organizations handling refugees. Spain repeated its demand that the refugees be removed from its territory promptly. The fact that it did not differentiate between Jewish and non-Jewish refugees made Spain a haven for all refugees who were able to cross its borders during the second half of the war.

But the situation of stateless refugees was more critical, because no destination could be found for them outside Spain. During the latter part of 1943, the Spanish government permitted most stateless refugees to settle in the cities until they left Spain. Although many refugees believed they were allowed to remain until the end of the war, the heads of the welfare organizations responsible for the stateless refugees knew that the government's tolerance was contingent upon efforts to evacuate the refugees. Furthermore, this tolerance must be considered in light of the fact that the number of stateless refugees who stayed at any given moment in Spain never exceeded 2,000. Within these limits the Spanish authorities probably would have allowed the entry of many more Jewish refugees if they were removed promptly, but the Allies and Jewish organizations failed to evacuate even these stateless refugees on time. In any event, the Spanish attitude toward a larger presence of refugees well might have been less cooperative. This fact must not be ignored when comparing Spain's position on the rescue of Jews to that of other countries, notably Switzerland.

When the accounts of rescue through diplomatic patronage and protection are considered, there is a considerable difference between the descriptions reported in Spanish publications and what actually took place. The blurring of the concepts "Sephardic Jews" and "Spanish nationals" or "protégés" created the impression in these publications that the Spanish government protected all descendants of the Spanish Jews exiled in 1492 who were living in France and the Balkans. A publication of the Spanish Embassy in Washington in 1949 concludes thus:

> Because of Spanish protection, some 6,000 Jews were able to live, work, and survive Nazi persecution in France. . . . The Spanish Minister [in Romania] was able to obtain for the substantial Sephardic communities in Romania the same or similar advantages enjoyed by the Spanish communities in France. Sephardic Jews were the only Jews not persecuted in Romania.[3]

In fact, except for one case in Hungary, protection offered by Spanish representatives covered only Spanish nationals. In the only instance when French Sephardic Jews asked to be included among those enjoying Spain's protection, their request was denied. Moreover, even the defense of its nationals was half-hearted during the first part of the war; Spain never unequivocally demanded that they be exempted from Nazi decrees. In October 1942, the Spanish Foreign Ministry chose to limit its protection to those holding full citizenship papers. In this way, Spanish protection was removed from large numbers of Jews, mainly in France, even before the Jews—and the Germans—were aware of this withdrawal.

In contrast to this reluctance on the part of the Spanish Foreign Ministry, many of its representatives in various countries showed initiative and determination. The brutal persecution of Jews that they witnessed and their personal connections with many of their protégés prompted the best of them to act on their own. Their success in protecting their protégés was considerable, especially in countries where the rescue of Spanish nationals did not imply repatriation. There were, unfortunately, other Spanish representatives who were unresponsive to the suffering around them.

The Germans made the rescue of Spanish nationals conditional upon their swift evacuation to Spain, which put Spain's attitude toward the Jews to the test. A letter sent by Spanish Foreign Minister Francisco Gomez Jordana to his colleague, Minister of War Carlos Asensio, provides a glimpse of Madrid's real position on this. (See Appendix, document J.) The letter, dated December 28, 1943, and classified "personal and confidential," concerns the question of releasing from the army the Jewish nationals who had been mobilized after their arrival from France on August 11. Jordana wrote:

> I wish to deal once again with the matter of the Jews of military age. As you know, the first consignment of seventy-three Jews from Paris left from Málaga, except for four or five who remain here with their families, comprising a total of twenty-five because some of the members of these families are of military age. Now, the problem is not limited to them alone; it is of a general nature because this was only the first consignment in a program that was created to solve a serious political conflict.
>
> The problem is that the number of Jews holding Spanish citizenship who are in Europe either in concentration camps or destined for them amounts to many hundreds. We cannot bring them to Spain to settle here because it is not worthwhile in any way, nor does the Caudillo [General Franco] authorize it; nor can we leave them in their present situation, pretending to ignore the fact that they are Spanish citizens, because this could create severe criticism in the press overseas, mainly in America, and cause us serious international difficulties.
>
> In light of all this, the possibility of bringing them in groups of approximately one hundred was considered, and when one group had left Spain—passing through our country as light passes through glass, leaving no trace—a second group would be brought and then removed to enable others to come. This being the system, it was obvious that under no circumstances would we allow the Jews to remain in Spain. This is why we did not look for reasons to keep them here; it would eliminate the proposed solution and leave us with the problem pending and unresolved.

Jordana then explained to Asensio the legal procedure through which the repatriated Spanish Jewish nationals could be exempted from service in the army. According to regulations concerning military service, Spaniards in Latin America could make financial payment in exchange for their duty; these regulations also applied to Jews with Spanish citizenship living in the Balkans and Morocco. Because those who came from concentration camps had been robbed of all their property, they could ask the Spanish government to try to retrieve their property or compensation for it, which the government would then accept as payment for military service. But the Jews were to be told nothing, so that dormant claims would not be aroused. "We simply will allow them to leave, while creating the legal fiction of a payment and a reimbursement, which in practice will never come to be."[4]

Examination of this document reveals the following. First, the purpose and the contents of the letter—to prevent Jews of military age and their families from being detained in Spain—show that Jordana eliminated any possibility of providing a permanent refuge for the Jewish nationals in Spain. According to him, Franco also discounted this possibility. Second, Jordana did not question the citizenship of these Jews. Spain chose to save them only because abandoning them would have negative repercussions in the West. Jordana preferred to base his arguments to Asensio on realpolitik rather than on humanitarian feelings or on the loss of prestige and sovereignty that would be involved in the arrest and expulsion of Spanish citizens by the Germans. This might have reflected Asensio's attitude and not necessarily Jordana's, but by raising this point he proved that public opinion, especially in the United States, could have influenced Spain's actions on the rescue of Jews. Third, the "legal fiction" that Jordana suggested as a solution to the problem of army service proves that he was familiar with the disposition of the private property of the Spanish Jews. His suggestion indicates that Spain felt it had a right to this property. Finally, the details of the letter indicate Spain's basic approach in dealing with its Jews, namely, to solve the problems concerning them under existing laws without recourse to special regulations.

The two policies the Spanish government adopted concerning repatriation—the strict definition of those entitled to be considered Spanish citizens in order to enter Spain and the determination that they may not settle permanently in Spain—severely limited the number of candidates for rescue and increased the anguish of those who ultimately were saved. On the basis of these policies, the Spanish government's attitude toward the property of Jewish nationals has a particularly gloomy tone.

Among the Spanish nationals in each country were wealthy Jews, who were often more affluent than the Jewish community as a whole. There is evidence of this in reports from the minister in Bucharest and the consuls in France, and it was hinted at in letters from the Spanish representatives in Sofia and Athens. As the first step in the Nazi extermination of the Jews was to rob them of their property, the first concern of the Spanish representatives was to defend their protégés' belongings. Some of them succeeded in modifying the Nazi decrees by having their own non-Jewish agents participate in the management of Jewish property.

When the Germans forced the Spanish government to choose between repatriating its Jewish nationals and abandoning them, the question of their property arose again. Ginés Vidal, the Spanish ambassador in Berlin, wrote to Madrid on February 11, 1943, that the Germans were about to seize the property of the Spanish nationals, and the matter therefore was extremely urgent. Vidal added:

> I am not unaware that the present situation of our legislation, which does not distinguish between Jewish and non-Jewish citizens, will make it difficult for this property to be confiscated by the Spanish government. This would be the most efficient way to prevent confiscation by the Germans. But perhaps one could obtain with relative ease [from the Jews themselves] agreement to consign their property, under certain conditions, to the Spanish State, which could manage their property and return it to them in due course when a final decision is made concerning them.

When Vidal wrote these words, he did not know that Spain was ready to inform the Germans that it was disowning its nationals; he learned of this five days later. It is thus possible that Vidal really was seeking a method of protecting Jewish property for its owners.[5]

A sad picture emerges from the exchange of letters between Spain and Germany in May 1943. At that time, Spain reconsidered forsaking its nationals but limited the number of candidates for rescue. A letter from the German Embassy in Madrid dated May 10 stated:

> The German government assumes that the Jews who return to Spain will continue to dispose of their restricted property in the Reich. On the other hand, according to the criterion presented until now, it cannot be known for certain who will be the legal successor of said property. Specifically, whether it will be the Spanish treasury—and in this case under which laws or administrative regulations will the treasury take over these assets?—or whether it is Spain's opinion that every Jew who was sent to work in the eastern territories should have the right to determine the future of his property, even though these assets constitute, according to Spanish rules, part of the national property of Spain.

The matter centered on the property of Jews forsaken by Spain who were "sent to work in the eastern territories." Spain's response leaves no room for doubt:

> The assets of Spanish citizens abroad constitute part of Spain's national property. Just as in the case of the death of a Spanish citizen, the state can, in certain circumstances, inherit him. So when an absence is created, as in this case, because Jews are sent to work in the eastern territories, no one has a better legal case than the Spanish State to the right to administer these assets in the name of the absentee during the period of his absence.

At the time of this writing, in late May 1943, Spain knew—as the whole world knew—the real significance of "work in the East." It is thus abundantly clear that Spain had elected to ignore its nationals and protégés, to forsake them to destruction and inherit their property.[6]

Edgar Cori and his wife, Bertha (née Goldschmidt), from The Hague, were two of the many Spanish nationals not rescued through Spain. On February 1, 1943, the Spanish Embassy in Berlin testified that because the Coris possessed valid Spanish passports and their request to enter Spain was under consideration, they should not be deported with the other Jews from The Hague. The Germans responded that the Cori family was scheduled for deportation on the same date as the other foreign nationals, and they would come to no harm. The Germans waited a few months and then deported the husband to the concentration camp at Buchenwald and his wife to the camp at Ravensbrük. One year later, as a result of official Nazi procedure, the Reichskommissar in Holland took the trouble to inform the German Foreign Ministry of these arrests so that the latter could inform Spain. Von Thadden thought this announcement unnecessary, however, because the Spanish Embassy had taken no interest in these nationals during the preceding fourteen months. For some reason, the forty-two-year-old merchant and his wife were forgotten. According to a report concerning them in the Spanish Foreign Ministry, they had received Spanish passports during the 1920s and 1930s, but the documents in their possession did not include a formal registration under the rules set forth in the 1924 Primo de Rivera decree. Did Spain inherit the property of the Cori family? There is no evidence of this, but from the documents it is clear that Spain considered itself entitled to it.[7]

Spain's decisions on how to deal with its Jewish nationals were made unilaterally. Its policies reflect the forces at work in Franco's government on matters concerning Jews. Hostile forces were not sufficiently strong to bring about complete disavowal of these Spanish nationals; they certainly were not powerful enough to discriminate against Jews legally or through police regulations. Nor were the sympathetic forces strong enough to promote a magnanimous policy such as the one Spain subsequently tried to ascribe to itself. In fact, both forces would have united to oppose the formation of a visible Jewish community in Spain. Spain thus did not exhaust all its capabilities in saving Jews during the Holocaust.

Spain's rescue efforts are distinguished by two stages; any blurring of the differences between them will result in a distortion of the outcome. During the first stage, in the first half of the war, Spain was asked to assist in the emigration of Jews by providing transit visas through its territory and responded generously to this request. Had Spain refused, it would have prevented the rescue of nearly 30,000 Jews who held entry visas to Portugal and who eventually reached safety. Had Spain refused passage to these people—most of whom also held transit visas beyond the Iberian peninsula—it would have placed Spain in a position of even greater hostility to the Jews than either the Germans or the Vichy government, who did not, at that time, prevent the exit of Jews. Spain's part in rescuing these Jews at this stage of the war was expressed by not being more anti-Jewish than the Nazis and their collaborators were.

During the second stage, in the second half of the war, Spain was required to take action in order to save Jews. Providing a haven for refugees involved real difficulties for a country that had suffered seriously from a civil war only a few years before. Rescuing Jewish nationals and providing them with protection, as well as extending this protection to other Jews in Hungary, also involved concerted, positive action on their behalf. During the second half of the war, Spain acted to save 11,535 Jews: roughly 7,500 refugees who reached its border under all the national programs; 3,235 who enjoyed various forms of diplomatic protection; and another 800 Spanish nationals who were saved through repatriation. It should be stressed that these numbers are to be regarded as maximum estimates only and that at least the last mentioned was far below Spain's full potential for the rescue of Jews.

The present study of the various rescue operations has shown that the very ideological and political proximity of Spain to Nazi Germany created a potential for rescue; it is possible that if Spain's status during the war had been different, this rescue might never have taken place. Spain's readiness to save Jews, combined with its sensitivity to Allied pressure—even when this pressure was not exerted—resulted in the rescue operations already discussed. This readiness and sensitivity indicate that had pressure been increased, Spain's potential for rescue might have been exploited to a greater extent.

THE JEWS, THE ALLIES, AND THE RESCUE

The pressure on Spain to do everything it could to rescue Jews came, first and foremost, from the Allied governments, who were acting chiefly in response to public opinion. Jordana's letter to Asensio shows that the Spanish government too was not entirely insensitive to the American press. This situation provided Jewish organizations with several areas in which vigorous activity on their part might have influenced rescue through Spain. Requesting the governments of the United States and England, as well as the Spanish ambassadors in these countries, to urge the Spanish government to use its Axis connections to save Jews was one of these areas. Speeding up the emigration of refugees from Spain was also of great importance and might have increased the number of Spanish Jewish nationals rescued. Another area that could have been influenced directly by Jewish groups was the organization and encouragement of emigration— and especially of illegal flight—from Nazi-occupied countries to Spain.

Did the Jewish organizations in the free world know what possibilities of rescue existed in Spain? Did they do all they could to exploit these possibilities? These questions must arise in any examination of the relationships between Spain and the Jews as they unfolded during the Holocaust.

At the start of World War II there were no recognized Jewish organizations in Spain. The tenuous relations that Zionist organizations maintained with Spanish Jews during the days of the Second Republic were not renewed in 1939 after the Nationalist victory. The Franco regime's opposition to the establishment of any official Jewish agency did not change throughout the war; the government did, however, tolerate the presence and activities of Samuel Sequerra as an unofficial representative of the JDC. From the beginning of 1943, an agency of the American welfare organizations headed by David Blickenstaff operated out of Madrid, but although the JDC bore most of the expenses, there were no Jews among its senior staff. Joseph Schwartz, director of the JDC in Europe, visited Spain on several occasions. At various times, representatives of the Jewish Agency—Wilfrid Israel, Fritz Lichtenstein, and Eliyahu Dobkin—as well as Rafael Spanien, the emissary from HICEM, all spent brief periods of a few weeks in Spain. Each was involved in long, complicated procedures to obtain a visitor's permit.

The hope of Jewish organizations to expand their presence in Spain encountered not only opposition from the Spanish government but also from American Ambassador Carlton Hayes, who saw no need for any representatives—Jewish or non-Jewish—in addition to David Blickenstaff, either under the auspices of his office or outside it. Hayes's opposition did not weaken even when, at the beginning of January 1944, President Roosevelt established the War Refugee Board. Given extraordinary power to act both openly and clandestinely to rescue Jews, the board intended to place its own agents in Spain; these agents were to encourage Jews in France to escape into Spain and then to speed their emigration to other destinations, thereby increasing the acceptance of more refugees in Spain. Hayes stubbornly refused to allow any special agents of the board to be placed in Spain, maintaining that his embassy and Blickenstaff's office were already doing everything possible to aid all refugees who arrived in Spain. Special agents, Hayes argued, over whom the embassy would have only limited control, might interfere with the delicate relationship between the United States and the Spanish government and might damage the war effort. Hayes even opposed granting permission to Sequerra or any other representative of an American welfare organization to assist in smuggling refugees into Spain, arguing that such activities would interfere with the rescue of pilots and other military personnel who escaped from France.[8]

In contrast to the other neutral countries of rescue—especially Switzerland and Turkey—there was no senior representation of any Jewish group in Spain. This fact forced Jewish activities to operate under inferior conditions.

The place nearest to Spain where Jewish organizations could exist and function was the capital of Portugal, Lisbon. The existence of a small but well-organized Jewish community, with its own welfare organization, facilitated the establishment of a program to aid refugees who reached Portugal. The activities of the community were financed by the JDC, which moved its main offices to Lisbon at the beginning of the war. The directors of the JDC and HICEM established their bases in Portugal and from there maintained close connection with their offices in Marseille, their representatives in Spain, and their central executives in New York. In addition to these large organizations, the World Jewish Congress also tried to operate from Lisbon in order to save Jews. For this purpose it appointed Yitzhak Weissman, one of the refugees who had arrived in Portugal at the beginning of the war; Weissman's independent activities soon irritated the JDC, HICEM, and the community committee. There was no permanent representation of the World Zionist Organization in Lisbon throughout most of the war, however. The local Zionist Federation was too small and too poor to be of any significance, and the special emissary of the Zionist Movement remained only for short periods of time. A permanent Jewish Agency office was not opened in Lisbon until April 1944.

Under these circumstances, the JDC and HICEM were most important, performing an essential function in all matters relating to welfare and emigration. During the first years of the war, the HICEM offices in the south of France and Lisbon helped thousands of Jews arrange their departure through Spain to the New World. The JDC aided in financing these activities, and through the work of its Trans-Migration program it assisted many Jews in the United States to pay the travel expenses for their relatives. During the latter part of the war, the JDC, through its unofficial representatives in Spain, provided support for needy refugees, thereby fulfilling the condition on which Spain had based its willingness to accept refugees. By virtue of JDC support, thousands of refugees were able to live in Spain on a decent standard of living. The JDC participated in financing HICEM's activities in everything relating to the emigration of refugees from Spain, just as it had financed the charters of the ships *Nyassa* and *Guiné*, which together brought a thousand immigrants to Palestine during the war. Screening potential immigrants, preparing them for immigration, chartering ships, and making arrangements for departure were the tasks of Jewish Agency representatives Wilfrid Israel and Fritz Lichtenstein, with the aid of the HICEM administration. All these activities made a vital contribution to the rescue operation; without them the record of rescue through Spain doubtless would have been much worse.

The welfare and emigration activities alleviated the plight of the refugees who arrived in Spain but did little to increase their number. In order to bring in more refugees, Jewish organizations had to help devise illegal escape operations from France by disseminating reliable information about Spain's rescue policy to Jewish refugees; this might have allayed the fears of many French Jews concerning what was in store for them on the Spanish side of the border and convince them to flee France. In Spain were smugglers who, either alone or in collaboration with friends in France, helped refugees to escape. If from the beginning of the war there had been a Jewish organization with the initiative and means in Barcelona or Madrid to handle these activities, more refugees might have been saved.

When Samuel Sequerra, the only Jewish representative permanently stationed in Spain, was asked whether the JDC there aided in illegal rescue during 1942 and 1943, he answered no, confirming any remaining evidence on this subject. David Blickenstaff, who operated under the aegis of the American Embassy and thus was subject to the directives of Ambassador Hayes, most likely was not involved in any illegal activities. The danger of becoming entangled with the Spanish authorities was clearly the reason these men refrained from such activities.[9]

Wilfrid Israel reached Spain at the end of April 1943 to interview candidates for emigration to Palestine and to examine various means of transportation for them. His plans went far beyond these objectives, however. He devoted much thought to the rescue of Jews from western Europe through Spain and Portugal and tried to take advantage of connections with the International Red Cross and other organizations. Through meetings with refugees in Spain and Portugal he learned how they had escaped; he used this information to formulate plans for smuggling children. He hinted at these plans in a letter, but he did not go into detail because he intended to file a report after his return to London. When his plane was shot down by the Germans, all his plans and the connections he had made were lost with him.[10]

At the end of May 1943, before Israel left Portugal, two emissaries from the Zionist underground in Toulouse crossed the Pyrenees into Spain. Calling itself the "Armée Juive" (Jewish Army), the group proposed to send young Jews to Spain, where they could leave for Palestine and the Jewish units of the British Army there. Before he left, every candidate who wished to come to Spain had to promise that he would make every attempt to reach Palestine, which was at least as vital as the resistance movement in France. Because of sketchy information on recent events in Spain, the emissaries did not have specific instructions for their activities there. They were required only to get in touch with representatives of Jewish organizations, inform them of the situation in France, obtain their help in relaying information back to France, and look after members of the Jewish Army who would follow them later; these instructions did not include creating an escape network on the Spanish side of the Pyrenees.[11]

The two emissaries, Joseph Kruh (who called himself Croustillon and continued to use this name after the war) and Shlomo Steinhorn, were arrested by Spanish border patrols soon after their descent from the mountains and were imprisoned at Lérida. Following instructions, they claimed they were Canadian citizens and so were handed over to the British Consulate. Croustillon was released from prison and reached Barcelona on July 9; Steinhorn arrived three weeks later. Immediately after his release, Croustillon appeared in Sequerra's office, explained his mission, and asked that the JDC place a certain sum of money at his disposal for his activities. Because Sequerra had not heard of any underground Jewish organization in France, and Croustillon had no references from any agencies Sequerra knew, Croustillon seemed to him one of the many refugees he had encountered telling stories and making exaggerated demands. A letter Croustillon wrote to Joseph Schwartz also brought no results; except for the help the British Consulate gave him as a Canadian refugee, he received no support for his activities in Barcelona. Steinhorn met with a similar fate.[12]

On August 11, after a month of delay and inactivity in Barcelona, the British Consulate sent Croustillon to Madrid. There too he sought support for his work, this time from Paul Block, whom Wilfrid Israel had appointed to represent the Jewish Agency in screening candidates for emigration to Palestine through Blickenstaff's office. Block, a refugee himself, also refused to assist Croustillon, who still was unable to carry out the mission entrusted to him and his friend before they left Toulouse. The two emissaries of the Jewish Army—the only people in Spain able to establish a link with the Jewish underground in the occupied countries— were for a long time out of contact with the world Jewish organization.[13]

In December 1943, another two emissaries reached Spain—Rafael Spanien, a director of HICEM in Lisbon, and Fritz Lichtenstein, the Jewish Agency representative. Their object was to assist the refugees already in Spain; both of them soon realized, however, that there were many opportunities to expand illegal escape into Spain. Spanien reported to his superiors that smugglers in Spain would, when provided with an address, bring refugees from France in return for 6,000 to 10,000 pesetas, depending upon the distance from the border and the age of the person to be rescued. He learned from refugees who had just arrived that the persecutions in France were intensifying and that the danger facing Jewish children was mounting daily. Despite the great danger, he proposed that HICEM should undertake illegal rescue, at first on a small scale, and then if it were successful, expand its operations. David Schweitzer, a HICEM official, passed this suggestion on to the Executive in London, where it was endorsed strongly. Claude M. Montefiore, a head of HICEM, approved the expenditures involved, and Arnold Philipson, president of the JCA, promised to find the money required.[14]

Fritz Lichtenstein also reported on the likelihood of expanding illegal rescue. During his visit in Barcelona he made contact with various middlemen and provided them with the addresses of several Jews whose relatives were living in Portugal and who were prepared to pay to have them smuggled into Spain. In his report he complained about possibilities for rescue that had been missed because of the absence of an official representative of the Jewish Agency in Spain. But as his mission was limited in time, he offered these points as "a few facts which are of interest, though they do not concern us and therefore do not occupy me. You cannot, however, escape hearing about them while you are here."[15]

Lichtenstein met the emissaries of the Jewish Army, as well as several more young members of the same group who had managed to reach Spain in the meantime. From them he learned of recent events in France, and Croustillon and Steinhorn expected him to help carry out their mission. But they were disappointed again: Lichtenstein, like Sequerra, was unsure about them; the financial resources at his disposal were limited (he could provide them with only 2,000 pesetas), and the bad relationship between them and Sequerra could not be ignored. Furthermore, Lichtenstein was reluctant to accede to Croustillon's request to appoint him temporary representative of the Jewish Agency in place of Paul Block, who had emigrated to Palestine. Steinhorn, despairing of the chance to accomplish anything, set sail for Palestine on the *Nyassa*, leaving Croustillon behind in Spain—now the only representative of the Jewish Army from France.[16]

The possibilities of illegal rescue through Spain did not escape the attention of Yitzhak Weissman in Lisbon. Despite his weak position as a refugee who was granted only temporary residence in Portugal, Weissman never stopped looking for ways to take advantage of underground connections in France. But opposition from the JDC and HICEM to the welfare and rescue efforts of the World Jewish Congress made his work more difficult, and Weissman's personality and tendency to use unorthodox methods strained his relationships with the directors of the Jewish organizations in Lisbon.

When, in December 1943, he received reports of arrests and deportations of hundreds of Jewish French children, Weissman attempted to create an illegal rescue network for children. He appealed to a Portuguese friend, Manuel Alvez, who was active in opposition circles in Portugal but also had connections in Spain. At that time Fritz Lichtenstein was about to leave for his visit to Spain, and Weissman asked for his help to introduce Alvez to Jewish refugees in Barcelona and Madrid in order to obtain correct addresses of refugees still in France. Lichtenstein met Steinhorn in Barcelona, learned from him of the activities of the Jewish underground in the south of France, and suggested that he should try to connect Weissman and his emissaries with the leaders of the Jewish Army in Toulouse. Steinhorn agreed, although this was not part of his original instructions. In a letter to his superiors in Toulouse dated January 3, 1944, which was given to Alvez, he wrote that if the Jewish Army did not wish to deal with this matter itself, it should hand it to one of the other groups dealing with the rescue of children in France. Soon after he wrote this letter, Steinhorn sailed for Palestine, and Croustillon undertook to continue the connection with Alvez.

The escape of children to Spain began in the spring of 1944. Andrée Salomon, one of the more active members of the Oeuvre de Secours aux Enfants Israélites in France, which was responsible for the rescue and hiding of hundreds of children, chose those she considered best suited for Palestine and handed them to the Jewish Army people in Toulouse. The underground group appointed Gisèle Roman to organize the rescue operation, and together with her young aides, she accompanied the group of children to the French-Spanish border. The convoys traveled along two routes, guided by Spanish smugglers and French underground fighters. Without undue incident they reached the cities of Andorra, Lérida, and Barcelona, where the children were placed in the charge of one of the local refugees. Manuel Alvez arranged their subsequent transfer to Portugal; Yitzhak Weissman obtained permission from the Portuguese authorities to house them temporarily until their departure.[17]

The rescued children had to go a long way from their hiding places in France to the home that Weissman had found for them in Portugal. The success of this venture depended on the close collaboration of various organizations who were unknown to one another. The rivalry between the JDC and the World Jewish Congress added further difficulties that lay in the way of a smooth, effective undertaking. When the first group of children began to arrive, Samuel Sequerra took over the entire operation, ignoring Weissman. The fierce quarrel that ensued between representatives of the Jewish organizations did not hinder the escape of the children from France, but it was typical of the ineffectiveness of the Jewish organizations and their unwillingness to cooperate to exploit rescue possibilities to the fullest. The rescue ended in September 1944, by which time approximately 100 children had reached Spain; 79 of these eventually arrived in Palestine aboard the *Guiné*.[18]

The escape of adults, members of the Jewish Army in Toulouse, became more effective during the months just prior to the liberation of France. In May 1944, Jules Jefroykin, one of the senior members of the underground, reached Spain. He also had been one of the trustees of the JDC in the south of France, and as a result a close association developed immediately between him and Sequerra. Several convoy smugglers who reached Spain during July and August were placed in secret contact with the office of the JDC in Barcelona; in this way supervision was improved and the safety of the escapees ensured. During the whole of the war, the underground in Toulouse smuggled approximately 500 young men and women from France into Spain, most of whom reached Palestine.[19]

The 600 refugees who were saved through the Jewish Army with assistance from Jewish organizations comprised the share of the free world's Jewry in the record of illegal rescue through Spain. The weakness of the acting Jewish representation in Spain, its fragmentation and lack of cooperation, saw that nothing was accomplished in promoting the escape of refugees into Spain in the summer and fall of 1942 and throughout 1943. By the time relations were established among the organizations and a formal agreement was signed, it was July 1944. One month later France was liberated from the Nazis, and there was no longer any necessity for underground rescue through Spain. David Shaltiel, the Haganah representative from Palestine, who arrived in the Iberian peninsula at the beginning of September 1944 to help organize rescue activities, was forced to write his superiors, "There is nothing to do here; we came two years too late."[20]

In another area of activity, the rescue of Jewish Spanish nationals, the JDC had an essential, official function. The Spanish Foreign Ministry placed responsibility on the Jewish organizations to care for refugees from the moment of their arrival and to arrange for their prompt emigration. This agreement, signed with the JDC on March 24, 1943, did not specify the number of Jews involved, but later reports from the JDC's office in Lisbon to the Executive in New York estimated that the number of candidates for rescue in France was 300 and in the Balkans about 2,000. The Spanish Foreign Ministry emphasized in this agreement that the rescue of each group was contingent upon the swift evacuation of the previous group. Jewish organizations thus were made responsible for the rate at which rescue took place. Vigorous efforts to provide destinations for emigration for Spanish nationals could have rescued all of them and might have mollified the inflexibility of the Spanish government in its strict definition of those entitled to repatriation. To what extent did the representatives of the JDC—and subsequently those of other Jewish organizations—meet the challenge that Spain imposed on them?

The first report concerning Spanish nationals was sent by the directors of the JDC in Lisbon to its Executive in New York on May 24, 1943, two months after David Blickenstaff promised that the representatives of the JDC in Europe and elsewhere would do their best to evacuate the rescued Jews from Spain. Herbert Katzki, who signed the report, called the attention of his superiors to a press release concerning the German demand that neutral countries evacuate their Jewish citizens from the areas of occupation, and added that the first group of ten Jews had already reached Spain. Katzki wrote in the report:

> The Spanish Foreign Office had been interested in this, and as a matter of fact has approached our representatives in Spain to see to what extent these people may be provided with maintenance should they be admitted to Spain. We had no idea whether or when any additional Spanish Jewish people will be coming to Spain, but we thought that you would want to know about the situation.

Katzki's report contains no hint of Spain's demand for guarantees in the removal of refugees from Spain. From the text of his report, it may be concluded that Katzki saw no active function for the JDC in this rescue operation beyond routine welfare activity. He also must have assumed that the whole issue was unknown to the JDC Executive in New York.

Three months later, on August 16, Katzki cabled Moses Leavitt, secretary of the Executive of the JDC, the following:

> The Spanish Foreign Office asked Blickenstaff whether we [are] prepared [to] maintain [in] Spain, if admitted there, a group of Jewish people now [in the] Balkans who [perhaps are] able to establish a Spanish derivation . . . and subsequently try their evacuation from Spain. . . . The number of persons mentioned [was] up to 2,000, although all cannot come at once, but they would be [in] our charge since they [are] not permitted [to] work.

This echoed José María Doussinague's letter to German Baraibar, asking him to ascertain whether the representatives of the JDC had prepared a plan for the removal of Spanish Jews who had arrived from France. Katzki's cable stressed the question of financial support, in contrast to the emphasis the Spanish placed on removal. According to Leavitt's reply, which gave financial guarantees and promised that the JDC would do its best to remove the refugees, nothing had been done until then about emigration.

On September 22, James Bernstein, HICEM director in Lisbon, informed the Jewish Agency in Jerusalem of the arrival of seventy-nine Spanish Jews from France and asked that they be provided with immigration visas. Bernstein said that additional Spanish Jews were about to arrive and that the removal of the Spanish Jews from France would expedite the issuing of entry visas for the new refugees. But even here there is no evidence of any special emergency measures by the Jewish organizations to expedite the rescue of Jewish Spanish nationals.[21]

In the autumn of 1943, activities of Jewish organizations on behalf of Jewish refugees were limited to interviewing those who had arrived from France and allocating Palestinian immigration visas to some of them. At that time, and even later, their status was described in internal Jewish correspondence as "Jews of Spanish derivation," despite the fact that any direct contact with the first Spanish nationals who arrived could have determined their true legal status as well as the actual number of those able to claim Spanish citizenship. No documentation has been found to date of any efforts made during this period to persuade the Allies to absorb these Jews, at least under temporary conditions of the type decided on at the Bermuda Conference.

Moreover, information regarding the possibilities of rescue of Spanish nationals under the conditions that Spain mandated did not even reach every Jewish organization. The World Jewish Congress, which at that time was in contact with Spanish Ambassador Juan Cárdenas in Washington, was unaware of these conditions. In May 1944, more than a year after Spain agreed to save its Jewish nationals, Arye Kubowitski, the director of the refugee department of the World Jewish Congress, doubted that Spain was making the rescue of its Jewish nationals from Athens conditional upon the prompt removal of the refugees from Salonika. As he then conveyed these doubts to Cárdenas, it may be concluded that before May 1944 the World Jewish Congress did not ask Cárdenas for guarantees that Jewish Spanish nationals would be received in Spain without preconditions, and it is almost certain that the World Jewish Congress did not address such an appeal to any other authority. The rescue committee of the Jewish Agency in Palestine also was not mobilized for joint efforts on behalf of Spanish Jews. Eliyahu Dobkin, a member of the presidium of the rescue committee, reported in September 1944 on his visit to Spain to his colleagues in the Jewish Agency Executive in Jerusalem; Dobkin still considered the rescue of Spanish Jews a matter exclusively for the JDC, and the refugees themselves as "Jews who claim that their forefathers left Spain 450 years ago and now have the right to expect the protection of the Spanish government."[22]

No emergency measures were adopted by Jewish organizations and no pressure was placed either on the Allies or on Spain to pursue every avenue of rescue for Spanish Jews. The reason for this was a lack of awareness on the part of the organizations regarding Spain's terms of removal for the rescued refugees, aggravated by poor cooperation among the Jewish agencies. Under these circumstances, Cárdenas could hint at a "lack of cooperation" between the representatives of the JDC in Spain and the Spanish government and their failure to keep their promises. Cárdenas also could respond evasively to Arye Kubowitski. He well might have given his answer while deriding the shortcomings of the Jewish establishment.[23] (See Appendix, document K.)

As a result of the absence of any senior Jewish representation in Spain and the weak coordination between Jewish welfare organizations and Jewish political organizations, contact between the American and British Jewish communities and Spain took place primarily through the Spanish ambassadors in London and Washington. Here Jewish leaders felt they could repay Spain for its assistance to Jews by improving its public image. This was suggested by Rabbi Maurice Perlzweig, who told his colleagues in the World Jewish Congress that their appeals to Cárdenas should be based not only on philanthropy but also on specific Spanish interests. In his letters to Cárdenas, Perlzweig emphasized the humanitarian aspects of his appeals and hinted that a response would enhance American Jewish opinion of Spain. The argument struck home with Cárdenas; in his recommendation to José Pan de Soraluce he stated, "The very fact that I received Rabbi Perlzweig and listened to him was enough to elicit a very favorable reaction toward Spain in the important Jewish centers."[24]

The requests that representatives of the World Jewish Congress addressed to the Spanish ambassadors in Washington and London before June 1944 varied in content. They included appeals for the nonexpulsion of Jewish refugees from Tangier and Spain; assistance in persuading the Germans to allow the exit of a thousand Jewish children from the areas of occupation, whose absorption was promised by Argentina; permission to distribute food and clothing to Jewish refugees in Spain through representatives of the World Jewish Congress; aid in saving Jews in Bulgaria; and saving Jews who possessed invalid Latin American passports and who had been arrested by the Germans and sent to the Vitel camp in France. What all these requests had in common was that none of them had any practical results.

The story of the rescue of Spanish nationals from Athens is one example of the ineffectiveness that contacts with Spanish ambassadors had on the rescue operations. When information that the Jews of Athens were being deported and that Spanish nationals were being held in the Haidari transit camp reached Yitzhak Weissman in Lisbon, he alerted the World Jewish Congress leaders in Washington and London. They turned to the Spanish ambassadors in these two capitals, as well as to the Spanish ambassador in Lisbon, Nicolas Franco, brother of Spain's head of state. The Jewish leaders appealed to the ambassadors to act to save the Spanish nationals in Athens. The ambassadors promised to do their best to intervene on behalf of the Jews and sent urgent cables to Madrid, but the Spanish Foreign Ministry replied that appropriate instructions already had been given to save these Jews. These interventions failed to change Spain's position on repatriation, and the Jewish Spanish nationals from Athens were unable to reach Spain in time. Spain's interest in improved public relations was not sufficiently strong to act as an impetus for rescue. Moreover, this interest largely had been served by the warm relationships Spanish ambassadors developed with a number of Jewish leaders, who benefited Spain by promoting the myth of the extent of its activities to rescue Jews.[25]

Rabbi Perlzweig's hopes in May 1943 that rescue through Spain could be increased by contacts between Jewish organizations and Spanish representatives in the West were entirely unfounded. Real achievements in the rescue of Jews could be attained only when the Allies pressured Spain as part of overall Allied interests. Demands from Jewish organizations thus should have been directed principally toward the governments of England and the United States, for only when their pleas moved the Allies to help the Jews was there a chance that this help also would bring about rescue through Spain. Jewish and general public opinion was unsuccessful during the Bermuda Conference in April 1943, but in 1944, after the creation of the War Refugee Board, things finally began to move. In the matter of Hungarian Jews, the British and American governments appealed to Spain and saw positive results.

The poor achievements of world Jewry in the area of rescue were the consequence of a long-held Allied tendency to remain aloof from Jewish suffering. The meager political influence of the Jewish people during World War II, diminished further by the confusion that pervaded Jewish organizations, limited their ability to reverse this tendency. And, in the case of Spain, this was compounded by the ignorance of the Jewish organizations regarding Spain's real potential to rescue Jews. Hence the paucity of efforts invested in moving the Allied powers to convince Spain to save Jews. Franco's Spain, the restored patrimony of Catholic monarchs Ferdinand and Isabella and the protégé of the Axis powers since the days of the Civil War, seemed unlikely to become a significant element in the rescue of Jews. Eliyahu Dobkin, who reported his impressions of a visit to Spain as late as the autumn of 1944, admitted that Spain was "a somewhat new area for us [the Jewish Agency]" and that the possibilities of rescue he found there surprised him. Rabbi Perlzweig, who was prepared to help Spain improve its image in the United States if Spain helped Jews, did not hide his Jewish and political embarrassment at dealing with the Franco regime, but he excused it with his disappointment at Allied attitudes toward the Jews, demonstrated by the Bermuda Conference. Marc Yarblum, the French Jewish Socialist leader, could not overcome his reticence even after it became clear that Spain had helped Jews. In protest at the praise Yitzhak Weissman heaped upon Spain at the World Jewish Congress conference, he threatened to leave the organization in which he had been active for many years.[26]

Was it really the noble and idealistic "Don Quixote Faces Hitler"? In the matter of the rescue of Jews, was the Spanish government an altruistic, innocent knight fighting chivalrously against evil? The present study has shown that this was not the case. It is true that the Spanish authorities did not discriminate against Jews when they were among large numbers of French, Polish, Dutch, and other refugees illegally crossing the Spanish border, but Spain's real attitude was revealed when the rescue of Jews alone was at stake.

Because of Spain's position during the war, the Spanish government could have rescued some groups of Jews, but it refrained from taking full advantage of the opportunity. The Franco regime did not want a Jewish community established either in La Mancha or in any other part of Spain, and so it could never become the modern Don Quixote it pretended to be. Although knowing that abandoning its Jewish nationals and other Jews was tantamount to annihilation, the Spanish government confined its operations to what seemed the most expedient at the time.

The Allies, for their part, did not press Franco's regime on questions concerning the rescue of Jews, thus allowing Spanish rescue operations to be reduced to the barest minimum. Contrary to the belief of many Spaniards, England and the United States did not regard the rescue of Jews an important issue of the war. Only at the very last stage of the slaughter, when Hungarian Jewry was being marched to death, did the Allies use their influence and urge Spain to extend its help to larger groups of persecuted Jews. From the results, the conclusion is unavoidable that if this pressure had been exerted earlier, Spain could have been instrumental in the rescue of many more Jews.

With no sovereignty or power, world Jewry was too divided and too weak to persuade the Allies to change Spain's attitude toward persecuted Jews. History weighed heavily on the relationship between Spain and the Jewish people and limited even more the already meager capabilities of Jewish organizations to work in Spain.

These divergent forces are the background of the history of the rescue of Jews through Spain.

8

IN THE POST-HOLOCAUST
GENERATION

EMANCIPATION

On July 17, 1945, two months after World War II ended in Europe, a series of laws defining the basic rights of Spaniards was passed. The Fuero de los Españols (Statute Law of the Spanish People), as these laws were called, dealt among other things with the status of religion in Spain. Paragraph 6 made Catholicism the official religion, with the full support and encouragement of the government. The law guaranteed that no one would be prevented from holding his own religious beliefs or form of worship, provided this was done privately; public ceremonies and open demonstrations of a religious nature were permitted only to Catholics. This legislation finally brought to a close the legal limbo in which Jews and Protestants found themselves in Nationalist Spain since the abolition of the Republican constitution; it also set them back ninety years to the time of the 1855 constitution.

Spain signed an agreement with the Vatican confirming the inferior status of non-Catholics in Spain on August 27, 1953. The first paragraph stated: "The Apostolic Roman Catholic faith continues to be the religion of the Spanish people, enjoying special rights and privileges in accordance with Divine Law and Church legislation." The announcements following the agreement continued the validity of the 1945 laws. Non-Catholic Spaniards were permitted to absent their children from Catholic religious studies, which once again were made compulsory in all schools.

Another basic law, on the Principles of the National Movement (May 17, 1958), named the Catholic religion not merely the official religion but the very essence and singularity of the Spanish people and state. Repeating one of the principles of Falangist ideology, the law actually excluded all non-Catholics from the Spanish nation.[1]

During the early 1960s, there were signs of a shift in Spain's attitude toward the Jews. The development of economic and military ties with the United States, industrial expansion, and especially the tremendous increase of tourism gradually set the pattern for a greater degree of religious tolerance toward non-Catholics. This process was accelerated by discussions held in the Vatican on the Church's position regarding Jews and other non-Catholics that took place intermittently from 1963 on.

In January 1965, General Franco hinted at the possibility of rights for religious minorities in Spain. The final vote in the Second Vatican Council on the relationship between the Church and the Jews and its ratification by Pope Paul VI in October 1965 paved the way for changes in Spanish religious legislation. After months of preparation, a referendum took place on December 14, 1966, ratifying a new set of laws. Paragraph 6 of the Statute Law of the Spanish People, which concerned the relationship between church and state, now read:

> The profession and practice of the Catholic religion, which is the religion of the Spanish State, shall enjoy official support. The State shall assume the responsibility for protecting religious freedom, which shall be guaranteed by an efficacious judicial machinery, which at the same time shall safeguard morals and public order.[2]

This amendment apparently advanced Spain from a position of tolerance toward non-Catholics who practiced their religion in private to a full recognition of their right to exist and worship in public. In practice, however, it did not recognize religious freedom as a fundamental human right, as had been the case in the 1869 constitution. For now, the Franco regime retained the right to "protect" religious freedom and to impose special legislation upon non-Catholics. Thus, even though the law was amended, it still fell far short of the liberalism that had existed in 1869. The adopted amendment to paragraph 6 nevertheless aroused the opposition of the conservative majority in the Spanish Catholic church and government.

After the amendment was published in December 1966, these forces took up cudgels against it. When on January 10, 1967, the Council of Ministers heard the first reading of the proposed Ley Sobre el Derecho Civil a la Libertad Religiosa (Law Concerning Civil Rights for Religious Freedom), most of the ministers considered it too liberal and rejected it.

Not until the ministers realized at the time of the second reading two weeks later that Franco supported the amendment did the government approve it. The law was published on February 25, 1967. It was discussed until June, when its final version was ratified by the legislators. Several months later, regulations for implementing the law were passed.[3]

Once the amendment was law, the Jews of Spain—and the Protestants as well—found that they still were far from enjoying religious freedom.

> Under a regime of mere religious tolerance we developed our activities unhindered, without giving the civil authorities cause for complaint; I only hope that this regime of religious freedom will not impose new, additional limitations over and above those of the previous regime.

This was the reaction of Max Mazin, the head of the Madrid Jewish community, to the official supervision imposed on non-Catholic organizations by the new law and the requirement to register with the Ministry of Justice. A meeting of the Barcelona Jewish community called in December 1967 to discuss the new law demanded that the government amend the law to guarantee genuine religious freedom called for by the Vatican Council and even by Spain's own Statute Law of the Spanish People. These reactions and those of the Protestants were of no avail; the regulations for the implementation of the law were ratified on April 5, 1968.[4]

December 1968 marked one hundred years since the leaders of the liberal revolution preceding the First Republic told the Jews of Bordeaux and Bayonne that the Republican revolution had in effect revoked the 1492 Edict of Expulsion. In that month, General Franco emulated the actions of Francisco Serrano, his liberal predecessor. On December 16, on the occasion of the dedication of the new synagogue in Madrid, Minister of Justice Antonio Oriol issued an order revoking the expulsion edict of the Catholic kings. In contrast to the earlier government, however, this announcement was not accompanied by an amendment to the existing law in relation to the day-to-day life of non-Catholics. Hence, Jews and other non-Catholics still did not enjoy full equality with their fellow Spanish Catholic citizens.[5]

During this period and in subsequent years, Spain was engrossed in the consequences arising from the beginning of the end of Franco's regime. In 1969, Franco appointed Prince Juan Carlos, of the House of Bourbon—grandson of Alfonso XIII, the last king of Spain—to succeed him after his death as king and head of state. In the summer of 1974, Franco became ill, causing concern about the future of the regime. Franco recovered, however, and continued to serve as head of state, although his health did not permit him to perform all his functions. Political tension rose in the meantime, and the Spanish underground gained strength. The struggle of the Basque separatists against the Franco regime intensified. In October 1975, at the height of an international furor resulting from the oppression of the Basques, the world learned of Franco's mortal illness. One month later, Franco was dead at the age of 82. After forty years under Franco's control, the country stood on the threshhold of a new era. Once again a monarch was to rule Spain.

On November 22, 1975, as soon as Franco was buried, Juan Carlos ascended the throne. Conservative hopes in the government that authoritarian rule in Spain would continue were quickly dashed. Prime Minister Carlos Arias Navarro retained his post, ostensibly ensuring the continuity of the Franco regime. But with his assistance, Juan Carlos gradually responded to the democratic demands that came in the wake of the hopes for change in Spain. During the first eighteen months of his reign, he allowed all political parties to renew their activities: he permitted Communist leader Santiago Carillo to return to Spain, he took steps to appease demands for autonomy in the Basque provinces and Catalonia, and he lifted the severe restrictions on the Spanish press. A referendum was held in December 1976, in which more than 94 percent of the voters expressed their support for far-reaching changes in the laws of the state to encourage democratization of the legislature.

This paved the way for direct elections to the new Cortes, to be composed of a house of representatives and a senate. In 1976 and 1977, Spain witnessed the revival of political groups and leaders dating back to the days of the Second Republic and the Civil War. Dolores Ibarruri, "La Pasionaria," the famous Communist leader who inspired the soldiers of the Republic with her speeches and slogans during the Civil War, returned to Spain in May 1977 after spending most of her years of exile in Soviet Russia and other Communist countries. On June 15, the citizens of Spain, most of them for the first time in their lives, went to free secret elections to elect the new house of representatives and most of the delegates to the senate. As a result of this election, the Union de Centro Democratico (Union of the Democratic Center), a coalition of democrats and moderate conservatives and Francoists under the leadership of Adolfo Suárez, from which the king drew his support, emerged as the strongest party.[6]

These changes did not alter the legal status of Jews and other non-Catholics in Spain, who continued to be subject to the inspection and supervision of the Committee for Religious Freedom of the Ministry of Justice. In March 1976, as these changes were beginning, Max Mazin made the following statement: "We, the Jews, hope this law will be amended, because at the moment it discriminates against other religions in favor of Roman Catholicism, the official religion." His hope was apparently based on the warm reception accorded to the delegation of the World Sephardic Federation by King Juan Carlos on February 27, 1976. The leaders of the Jewish community in Madrid and Barcelona participated in this delegation, along with the heads of Sephardic communities from Great Britain, the Netherlands, and other European countries. Queen Sophia's attendance at a Friday evening service in the Madrid synagogue three months later also was a source of encouragement; this seemed to be related to the visit of the royal couple to the United States a short time later and to their efforts to win the support of American Jewry for the new Spain. Nevertheless, it must be regarded as an exceptional event and perhaps the first of its kind in the history of the Jews in modern Spain.

Despite the sympathy of the royal house, equal rights for Jews and other non-Catholics in Spain was still no more than an unrealized hope a year later. A leader of the Madrid Jewish community, asked in June 1977 for his views on the new government about to be installed after the elections, again expressed the hope that this government finally would abolish the inferior status that Franco's Spain had imposed on members of the Jewish faith and other non-Catholic religions.

This hope became reality when, in May 1978 in a democratic referendum, a new constitution for Spain was ratified. Article 16 ensured all Spaniards that "freedom of ideology, religion, and worship for individuals and communities is guaranteed, with no more restrictions on their expression than may be necessary to maintain the public order protected by law." Contrary to the previously existing "basic laws"—which were repealed— the new constitution declared that "there shall be no State religion. The public authorities shall take the religious beliefs of Spanish society into account and shall maintain the consequent relations of cooperation with the Catholic church and the other confessions." Even though this declaration did not preclude the possibility of preferential treatment for the Catholic church (in the field of education, for example) it clearly reestablished, as in 1931, full constitutional emancipation for the Jews of Spain. Thus, a sound legal basis was provided for organized Jewish life, which had been expanding in Spain all the while.[7]

THE GROWTH OF THE COMMUNITY

Despite their tenuous legal status, the number of Jews in Spain after World War II increased. Ignacio Bauer, the head of the Madrid Jewish community before the war and one of its most outstanding leaders after it, estimated that there were approximately 2,500 Jews in Spain in 1950. Political events in North Africa during the 1950s and the early 1960s caused many Jews from Morocco and Tangier to leave their homes, and several thousand of them were absorbed into Spain. The tremendous economic growth of Spain during the last two decades attracted other Jews, until their numbers reached almost 9,000 by 1969.[8]

Until 1975 the expansion of the Jewish community in Spain increased further. The worsening political situation in such South American countries as Chile, Uruguay, and particularly Argentina forced many Jews to seek their fortunes in Spain. This was accelerated after the death of General Franco. The changes in the Spanish government took place while terror from rightist and leftist underground struggles in Argentina spread. Oppressive measures against the left after a military coup headed by General Jorge Videla in March 1976 prompted an increasing number of professionals and intellectuals to leave Argentina. To many of them Spain appeared a desirable and secure refuge. The number of Jews in this wave of immigration is not known, but there is no doubt that their arrival increased considerably the number of Jews in Spain. At the beginning of 1974 an active member of the World Jewish Congress, visiting Jewish communities in Spain, estimated that there were 10,100 Jews there. At the beginning of 1978, press reports and other unofficial sources began to speak of a Jewish community in Spain numbering 12,000. These two figures are not based on any first-hand, authenticated information; even if these figures were exaggerated, however, there is no doubt that in the late 1970s there were more Jews in Spain than at any time since the expulsion in 1492. As in previous times during the modern era, now too most Jews in Spain were permanent residents who were not naturalized citizens.[9]

The Jewish presence in Spain increased also from the point of view of its geographical distribution. In the beginning, relatively large concentrations were formed in Barcelona, Madrid, and Málaga, in addition to the two old communities in Ceuta and Melilla on the North African coast. In the course of time, partly due to the Spanish tourist industry, Jews also settled in Seville, Valencia, Alicante, Marbella, and Torremolinos, as well as in Palma and Ténérife, the capital of the Canary Islands. Doubtless, Jews were found in smaller cities as well.

As the number of Jews in Spain increased, their community life improved. In 1945, when the Jews of Barcelona wished to reopen their synagogue, they were refused permission by the mayor. When this came to the attention of Yitzhak Weissman, the representative of the World Jewish Congress in Lisbon, he appealed to his friend Spanish Ambassador Nicolas Franco, who promised to look into the matter. By December,

Franco was able to inform Weissman that the Interior Ministry had ordered the mayor of Barcelona to grant the necessary permission, and that same month the first synagogue was opened in Barcelona. Located in a rented apartment, it could be considered, according to Spanish law, a private place of worship.[10] Even when the Jews of Barcelona built their own building in 1954, housing the offices of the community, a youth club, and two synagogues—Ashkenazic and Sephardic—the building was designed to look like an ordinary apartment house. Shortly after the establishment of the first synagogue, the Jews of Barcelona began to concern themselves with the education of their children and other religious matters. In 1946 they advertised for a "ritual slaughterer, teacher, and spiritual leader for the Ashkenazic and Sephardic communities." Community services soon expanded, and as the economic situation in Spain improved, the Jewish community invited teachers from Israel to organize educational services for its youth. By the 1960s, Barcelona had become an active Jewish center, maintaining strong ties with Israel and other Jewish communities throughout the world. On the occasion of the festival of Simchat Torah in 1969, the community dedicated additional wings of the community building, in the presence of many guests from abroad.[11]

Most impressive of all was the development of the Jewish community of Madrid. Because few Jews lived in the capital of Spain immediately after World War II, the organization of the community initially lagged. On January 2, 1949, Moshe Lavenda, a Polish Jew, who had lived in Madrid since the days of the Second Republic, took the initiative and opened the first synagogue. This too was in a residential building, with no external sign to indicate that it was a house of prayer. At that time there were approximately 200 Jews in Madrid, and the modest community organization they established provided only the most basic Jewish requirements: kosher meat had to be brought from the Jewish community in Gibraltar.[12] During the 1950s and early 1960s, however, the number of Jews in Madrid increased, until by the mid-1970s it had reached 3,000. In 1958 the synagogue moved to a more spacious apartment in a residential building in one of the side streets in the center of town. A few years later the community expanded religious services even further, brought in a ritual slaughterer, and began to provide a Jewish education to their children. In 1964 a kindergarten was opened, which soon developed into a day school. A youth organization (Maccabbi), social activities, and summer camps provided youths with informal Jewish educational activities. Adults too were offered a Jewish environment beyond the prayer services on Sabbaths and festivals through various social circles and community activities.

This expansion reached its peak in 1968. On March 10 the community organized a celebration to mark the laying of the cornerstone for a new synagogue building. Inscribed on the scroll was the following:

> This house of prayer is the first ever to be built in Madrid. May it be a symbol and a memorial for the Jewish communities that existed in this land until 1492 and a portent for the revival of Judaism in Spain.

While the building was still under construction, the Madrid Jewish community took another step forward. On the eve of Rosh Hashanah 1968, the president of the community introduced to the congregation assembled in the synagogue its first rabbi, Baruch Garzon Serfaty, a young North African Jew who had recently been ordained in England. Three months later, on December 16, the Jews of Madrid celebrated in an impressive ceremony the dedication of the new synagogue and community center. In the presence of representatives of other religions and government officials and with the chief rabbis of Great Britain and Argentina present, the Torah scrolls were placed in the Holy Ark and mezuzot affixed to the doorposts. The event received full coverage in the Spanish press, which noted that this was the first synagogue built in Madrid—and in all of Castille—since the expulsion of the Jews from Spain.[13]

During the years after the establishment of the community center, the Jewish community in Madrid continued to increase. Unfortunately, during the early 1970s a bitter dispute erupted among its leadership. That sector of the community originally from Tangier and Spanish Morocco, whose influence in the community was continually increasing, ousted the previous leadership and the head of the community, Max Mazin. The process of expansion of the community continued nevertheless, and in December 1977, nine years after the dedication of the synagogue, the Jews of Madrid celebrated the establishment of another community building. A school, erected in one of the suburbs of the capital, was then dedicated with the participation of the Chief Sephardic Rabbi of Israel.

Thus, during the late 1970s there were in Spain two large and well-organized communities in addition to two in Ceuta and Melilla, which dated back many generations but were limited in size and decreasing in number. Other small communities, in Málaga, Seville, and elsewhere, were in various stages of organization; the general feeling was one of expansion and consolidation. A parent organization for those communities, the Council of the Jewish Communities, was established in 1965. This constituted a confederative authority whose purpose was to promote cultural cooperation between communities and represent Spanish Jewry to the authorities. This organization, which changed its name to the

Sephardic Federation of Spain, represented Spanish Jewry in the World Jewish Congress and in the World Sephardic Federation.

In 1976 the Jewish communities of Spain demonstrated their strengthening ties with world Jewry in the form of a resolution inviting the European branch of the World Jewish Congress to convene in Madrid. This event inadvertently was transformed into a disappointing expression of the new relationship between Spain and the Jews and the State of Israel.

CONTEMPORARY SPAIN AND THE JEWISH PEOPLE

Soon after World War II, when Spain was isolated and Franco's regime needed all the goodwill it could find, Spain made several overtures toward the Jews. Permission to open the synagogue in Barcelona without changing the legislation regarding non-Catholic worship was one gesture. Another concerned Spanish consular protection for its Jewish nationals in Egypt and Greece. According to agreements between Spain and these countries made in the 1930s, Spanish nationals were to lose Spanish protection in 1949. As 1949 approached, General Franco issued a decree permitting those affected to appeal to Spanish embassies and request the status of "Spanish citizens abroad." This decree was signed on December 29, 1948, and from the instructions sent by the Spanish Foreign Minister on February 11, 1949, to Spanish ambassadors (to which lists of names of Jewish protégés were appended), it is learned that they dealt with 271 people in Egypt and another 507 in Greece. These names were copied from lists included in the original agreements with Egypt (dated January 17, 1935) and Greece (dated April 7, 1936). No information exists regarding how many of the 271 Jews who lived in Egypt in the mid-1930s were still there at the end of 1948. There is, however, information concerning the fate of Spanish nationals in Greece in the period after the agreement was signed and especially during the war. It is thus quite clear that the number of Jews who benefited from Franco's order was much smaller than the 778 people mentioned.[14]

Despite the limited nature of this gesture, the Spanish Foreign Ministry emphasized it in the propaganda pamphlet published after Israel's vote in the U.N. General Assembly as conclusive proof of the benevolence of the Spanish government toward the Jews. "Franco Provides Spanish Citizenship to Sephardic Jews," read the headline to the quotation, quoting from the order of December 29, 1948; this is also the version that found its way into biased historiographical accounts and even a survey appearing in a reputable yearbook.[15]

Spain's disappointment with Israel's vote in the U.N. did not result in hostile measures taken against Jews. Government support for the study of Jewish culture in the Arias Montano Institute did not cease, and in 1951 the senior scholars of this institute, professors José Maria Millás Vallicrosa, Francisco Cantera Burgos, and Federico Perez Castro, visited Israel. In 1953, Daniel Baruch, leader of the Madrid Jewish community, was granted an audience with Franco; this was used to illustrate the goodwill shown by the government toward the Jews.[16] In 1958, with the agreement of the authorities, a branch of the World Sephardic Federation began to operate in Madrid, and an international exhibition of Sephardic culture was organized there in 1959. Five years later these positive gestures toward the Jews reached a climax. On March 18, 1964, Franco signed an order establishing a Sephardic museum in Toledo, in the beautiful synagogue built by Don Shmuel Halevi around 1357. The same order determined the composition of the executive committee of the museum and the adjacent Sephardic library. Its members included the lecturer on Sephardic history in the Middle Ages from the Hebrew University in Jerusalem, the president of the Jewish community in Madrid, and representatives of world Sephardic organizations. This order in effect provided indirect but official recognition of the Jewish community organization in Spain and established a relationship between the government of Spain and Jews outside Spain. Three months later, in June 1964, an international symposium was held in Spain concerning the cultural heritage and status of Sephardic Jews in the past and present. This event was part of the festivities marking the 25th anniversary of the Nationalist regime and provided an opportunity for many expressions of official beneficence toward the Jews and Israel.[17] On January 20, 1965, the leaders of the Barcelona and Madrid communities were granted an audience with General Franco, and one month later, on February 27, the Jews of Madrid were the first community to receive official recognition by the Interior Ministry.[18] This gesture, which stirred many hopes for true and complete emancipation, was repeated by the authorities when the synagogue was dedicated in 1968, by a specific order based on the Law Concerning Civil Rights for Religious Freedom.

During the 1960s, the government of Spain again had the opportunity to assist Jews in distress and at least on two occasions intervened on their behalf. In one instance, during the mass exit of Jews from Morocco, Jewish organizations dealing with immigration to Israel were able to use Spain for transit purposes. A second time, during the Six-Day War in Israel, Spain helped to make arrangements whereby many Jews were allowed to leave Egypt, sparing them prolonged arrest and brutality.[19]

Throughout these years, until the mid-1970s, Spain had no diplomatic relations with Israel. The consular office that had existed in Jerusalem during the Mandate remained there after it ended, continuing to represent Spain to the British government, as it were. This situation remained throughout the 1960s and 1970s, when Israel worked toward the establishment of full diplomatic relations with Spain. Spain's strong ties with the Arab world prevented it from establishing similar relationships with Israel, and the grievance that Spain bore toward the Jewish State for having voted in 1949 and 1950 against the cancellation of the diplomatic boycott imposed upon Spain in 1946 served as an excuse for not responding to the Israeli overtures. Israel's support in December 1955 of the acceptance of Spain into the U.N. has been overlooked.[20]

After Franco's death there were mounting hopes that Juan Carlos would change Spanish policy regarding Israel. The delegation from the Sephardic Federation that appeared before him on February 27, 1976, included this wish among their requests. In the following months there were occasional reports in the press of Spain's intention to improve its relationships with Israel, but these were either unfounded or premature. In December 1976 the extent of Arab influence over the Spanish government became evident. The conference of the European branch of the World Jewish Congress that convened in Madrid was due to be greeted by the Deputy Minister of Justice on behalf of the government, and a delegation from the conference was scheduled to be received by the king. The very fact that the conference was taking place aroused the ire of the Arab embassies in Spain; the Spanish authorities bowed to pressure and canceled their participation in this event. Even though this was not connected directly with the issue of Spain's relationship with Israel, the incident illustrated the degree of dependence of Spain's new regime on the Arab states, who controlled the supply of oil to Spain.[21] One year later, in December 1977, the Chief Sephardic Rabbi of Israel, Ovadya Yoseph, was received warmly by the king. This benevolence toward the man regarded as the religious leader of Sephardic Jewry in Israel may indeed suggest genuine sympathy on the part of the heads of the government for the Jewish State, which the rabbi represented; it is just as likely, however, to indicate the government's sentimentality for the Sephardic diaspora, whom it regarded as the "lost children" of Spain. This gesture was overshadowed in September 1979, when Prime Minister Adolfo Suárez received Yasser Arafat, the leader of the Palestine Liberation Organization, who came to Spain on an allegedly unofficial visit. Madrid Jewry's protests were in vain and served only to emphasize the pro-Arab leanings of the Spanish government.

Significant changes nevertheless have taken place in the attitude of certain Church circles toward the Jews. The rapprochement between Jews and some members of the Spanish clergy was a direct reaction to the wave of swastikas and anti-Semitic attacks that swept Europe and certain countries in the Western Hemisphere in 1961. Several Catholic clergymen, together with the president of the Madrid Jewish community and his deputy, took the initiative of establishing, on November 14, 1961, the Amistad Judeo-Cristiana (Judeo-Christian Fraternity). One month later this organization received the full support of the Bishop of Madrid; soon afterward, its constitution was approved by the civil authorities and its existence was established by law. In 1967 a similar organization was established in Barcelona, and in the spring of 1970 in Seville as well.[22]

The activities of this organization were intended at first to draw the attention of Christians to the Jewish roots of their religion. These activities encountered apathy and even hostility during the years before the Vatican Council. When the Church began to discuss the Jewish Document, and especially when it was affirmed, the activities of this organization expanded. The Jewish-Christian dialogue resulted in the presence of gentiles at special prayers in the Madrid synagogue on a number of occasions. In February 1967 these activities reached a high point when Jews and Christians gathered together for a common religious service in one of the churches in Madrid. The special liturgy prepared for this event included chapters from Psalms, a prayer for peace from the Jewish Prayer Book, and a special prayer—Christian in form and general in content—composed by the members of the organization. This unusual event was widely and sensitively reported in the Spanish press.[23]

In 1969, the Christian members of the organization took up another task. In order to intensify the understanding of the Jewish principles in Christianity, Father Vicente Serrano and his colleagues in Madrid established the Centro de Estudios sobre Judaismo (Center for Studies on Judaism). Three years later, in September 1972, this center became, by decree of the Bishop of Madrid and Alcalá, an official institution of the bishopric, bearing the name Centro de Estudios Judeo-Cristianos (Center for Christian-Jewish Studies). One of the outstanding functions of this institution was the conducting of seminars on Jewish subjects intended mainly for the Catholic clergy, which were organized both in Israel and Madrid in close cooperation with the Israel Interfaith Committee in Jerusalem.[24]

In the wake of the changes that took place in Spain after the death of Franco, some favorable influence on Spain's relationship with the Jews emerged from the revived political parties. Many leaders of the Socialists, the second largest faction in the house of representatives since the 1977 elections, and similar circles in other parties certainly were not likely to support legal discrimination against Jews in Spain or favor hostility toward them outside Spain. Some of these voiced their support for the Jews during and after the elections, in their contacts with the Jewish community in Madrid and with Israelis visiting Spain.[25]

Despite these signs of beneficence, conservative and hostile forces did not disappear in Spain. Rapprochement with Jews by some of the Catholic clergy in Madrid, Barcelona, and Seville did not mean that the entire Church in Spain identified itself with or supported them. The conflict between liberals and conservatives in the Catholic church is far from settled, and a constant vigilance is necessary to ensure that the declaration of the Second Vatican Council, absolving Jews of guilt for the crucifixion of Jesus, should penetrate all levels of the Church and reach every segment of the Spanish population. The satanic image of Jews, which has been eliminated from the newest editions of the official Spanish dictionary, still pervades the consciousness of most Spaniards. Belief in medieval blood libels is also likely to find some supporters. Much effort was required to expunge from religious services and textbooks mention of the 1491 blood libel concerning the murder by Jews of the Holy Child of La Guardia. The success of these efforts does not prove conclusively that religious hostility toward Jews and other non-Catholics in Spain has disappeared. Neither has sympathy for Nazism and Fascism disappeared. As late as 1973, members of the Judeo-Christian Fraternity were forced to protest the existence of neo-Nazi groups that were openly preaching the annihilation of Jews and Protestants in Spain. Organizations such as Cruz Ibéria (Iberian Cross), Partido Español Nacional-Socialista (National Spanish Socialist Party), and Los Amigos de Europa (The Friends of Europe) published bulletins, attacked libraries, robbed a bank, and held an international brown-shirt gathering where Adolf Hitler was acclaimed brazenly. All this took place in the Instituto Municipal de Educación in Madrid. These and similar groups have not disappeared from Spain but have underscored their continued existence with the political violence that has erupted since the change in the regime, although this was less than had been expected. The stubborn fight of Basque separatists, which in the late 1970s cost scores of lives—during the time the government was granting provincial autonomy, as prescribed in the new constitution— prompted their opponents to use similar tactics in their struggle for preserving a united Spain. Ex-Falangists and neo-Fascists, along with leftist guerrillas of all shades, seemed to have forgotten the cruel lessons of the Civil War. The specter of terror and armed clashes once again haunted the minds and hearts of many Spaniards.[26]

These forces, despite their limited strength, may fan the latent flames of hostility that still glow in the hearts of many Spaniards against the Jews. Anti-Semitic Arab propaganda, propelled by the financial resources at their disposal, is likely to provide much fuel to Jew-haters and their activities. The escalating economic crisis that is overtaking Spain at this writing may also play into the hands of those hostile to the Jews, in view of the existence of a large Jewish community ensconced in the wealthier stratum of Spanish society. This danger obviously will be diminished under conditions of a stable democracy; however, if circumstances result in political polarization and deviations from orderly parliamentary debate, it is likely to increase.

The hopes for the complete normalization of Jewish existence in Spain and the dawning of a new era in the history of the relationship between Spain and the Jewish people thus must be viewed in the 1980s in the context of the darkness and the danger still lurking there.

Twenty-five years passed from the time the Spanish government decided that refugee Jews were not welcome in Spain as permanent residents until the day the cornerstone was laid in the building of the beautiful synagogue in Madrid. The dedication of the synagogue and community center, in December 1968, took place exactly twenty-five years after a minister of the Spanish government explained to his colleague that Spanish nationals from France and Salonika must pass through Spanish territory "as light passes through glass, leaving no trace." Despite the unwillingness of the Spanish authorities to allow the establishment of a permanent Jewish community in their country, it came into existence nonetheless and constitutes another link in the long history of the relationship between Spain and the Jewish people.

Now, after the Franco era, Spain and Spanish Jewry too are on the brink of a new age. The new restoration of the House of Bourbon as a constitutional monarchy recalls the words of Amador de los Ríos at the end of his book on the history of the Jews in Spain, written a century ago, when the House of Bourbon was restored for the first time as a constitutional monarchy. The Spanish historian then wrote:

> Now who can tell the future in such critical and solemn moments? We, for our part, do not possess that ability. But . . . given the special circumstances in which this volume is being published, we do not hesitate in calling the attention of our statesmen to it . . . ; nor do we forget the Jewish com-

munity. If they really cherish the desire to visit the ancient sites of their ancestors [in Spain], they should not lose sight of the many and valuable lessons that history offers so eloquently and generously.[27]

The relationship between Jews and Spain was then, as in earlier generations, stamped with the mark of their history. But in the present generation, this long story has added new fateful chapters, in which light and shadow intermingle: the record of the attitude of Spain toward the Jewish people during the Holocaust and at the time of their renewed independence.

⌐ ¬

APPENDIX

DOCUMENT A

Madrid, 3 de enero de 1941

GC/LV
B1—(s) RU—1
A la Legación Real de Rumania.

Nota Verbal

El Ministro de Asuntos Exteriores saluda atentamente a la Legación Real de Rumania y en contestación a su Nota Verbal número 1909 de 19 diciembre ppdo., tiene la honra de participarle que en la legislación española no existe discriminación alguna en relación con los judíos que residen en España.

DOCUMENT B

Lequerica, Irún, 8.11.1940 Nú. 630

Para los 2,000 sefarditas inscritos en este Consulado y con documentación en regla, las autoridades francesas y alemanas han acordado que las recientes medidas contra los judíos se hagan también extensivas a ellos. En España no existe legislación que establezca diferencia de razas ha contestado el Consulado. Por si estima oportuno comunicar instrucciones someto el caso a la consideración de V.E. Por el Consulado se ha informado a V.E.

Lequerica

DOCUMENT C

2 de octubre 1942

M.A.E. Europa
[Pelayo García y Olay]

Informe
Estado en que se encuentra el problema Sefardita

. . . [en cable número 637 de 9.11.40 al Embajador de España en Vichy], se le decía que se diera únicamente por enterado de dichas medidas y en último caso, no pusiera inconvenientes a su ejecución, conservando una actitud pasiva. Se añadía que aunque en España no existe ley de razas, el Gobierno Español no podía poner dificultades, aún en sus súbditos de origen judío, para evitar que se sometieran a medidas de carácter general.

Esta fue la pauta seguida en cuantas instrucciones se dieron a diferentes consulados españoles, tanto en la zona francesa ocupada como en la libre, Marruecos y Argelia añadiéndose siempre que cuando tuviesen que inscribirse nuestros sefarditas en algún registro especial o prestar alguna declaración en cuanto a sus bienes o de cualquier otra clase, deberían hacer constar su nacionalidad española para que sean defendidos sus intereses como súbditos españoles . . .

DOCUMENT D

Madrid, 7.3.42

Europa.
[El Subsecretario
al Embajador de España en Vichy]

. . . El hecho de que el Gobierno Español no ponga dificultades para que dichos súbditos se sometan a ciertas medidas como las que han sido objeto de más de una comunicación de V.E. y del Consulado General en Paris, no significa que se hayan de dejar sin el debido amparo los derechos de cada uno de ellos dentro de lo establecido en el mencionado acuerdo.

En vista de lo anteriormente expuesto de Orden comunicada por el Sr. Ministro de Asuntos Exteriores ruego V.E. se sirva, dentro de las normas e instrucciones que ya ha recibido, defender los intereses de los súbditos españoles de origen sefardita exigiendo a las autoridades francesas el cumplimiento del acuerdo de 1862 debiendo participar a V.E. que con esta fecha se cursan al Cónsul General de España en Paris idénticas instrucciones.

DOCUMENT E

Madrid, 18.3.43

Se concederá visado de entrada a España a sefarditas españoles cuando acrediten con documentación completa satisfactoria nacionalidad (no carácter protegido) suya y de cada uno de los familiares que le acompañan demostrando cumplimiento requisito de inscripción en el Registro Nacional y Registro Matrimonio, cuando le acompañe esposa y el nacimiento de hijos, si estos le acompañen. En cada caso telegrafie V.E. nombre completo y los documentos presentados acreditando dichas condiciones así como vía de entrada en España y frontera con tres fechas margen por dificultades comunicaciones. Urja Autoridades de Ocupación acepten que los bienes inmuebles de dichos sefarditas sean administrados por los representantes de los consulados españoles. Advierta a los solicitantes de visado que las autoridades españolas se encargarán fijar la ciudad de su residencia que no abandonarán sin autorización previa. El visado será "bueno para entrar en España por una sola vez por la frontera de tal a tal fecha."

Jordana

DOCUMENT F

Madrid 22 de Marzo de 1943

Sr. Carreño:
En el asunto de la venida de sefarditas ordena S.E. que se tomen al máximo toda clase de garantías de que efectivamente han de salir.

J. M. Doussinague

DOCUMENT G

Madrid a 24 de Marzo de 1943
American Joint Distribution Committee

Excmo. Sr. don José
Pan de Soraluce, Subsecretario
de Asuntos Exteriores, M.A.E., Madrid

Excelentísimo Señor:
Habiendo sido informado por el Ministro de Asuntos Exteriores de las medidas tomadas por las Autoridadas Españolas para facilitar la entrada a España de ciertos grupos de judíos residentes en los territorios ocupados de Europa, el A.J.D.C. desea asegurar al Ministerio de Asuntos Exteriores que sus representantes en Europa y fuera de ella harán cuanto les sea posible para conseguir visados de inmigración para tales personas y, dentro de los límites de las funciones de A.J.D.C., les prestará los servicios de socorro y ayuda financiera que puedan precisar durante su tránsito por España.

que D. guarde V.E. muchos años

David Blickenstaff, Representante del A.J.D.C.

DOCUMENT H

San Sebastian 13.8.43

Sr. Baraibar:

. . . Si pudiera [el A.J.D.C.] hacerse cargo de ellos para hacerles salir inmedita-
mente de España, se podría acceder a que vengan en uno o dos grupos. Si sólo tiene
un vago proyecto de fletar un barco sin tener ya éste a su disposición ni haber hecho
otra cosa que concebir la idea, entonces tendré yo que poner un telegrama a Vidal
insistiendo en las anteriores instrucciones.

J. M. Doussinague

DOCUMENT I

Berlin, 14. Juli 1944

Auswärtiges Amt
e.o. Inl. II A 2418

Schnellbrief

Seitens der Spanischen Botschaft wurde telefonisch um Mitteilung gebeten,
ob unter Umständen der Abtransport der 155 in Bergenbelsen sich aufhaltenden
spanischen Juden bis Vichy sich binnen Kürze durchführen liesse. Die Spanische
Botschaft in Vichy sei bereit und in der Lage, für den Weitertransport von Vichy
bis zur spanischen Grenze Vorsorge zu treffen.
Um telefonische Stellungnahme darf gebeten werden.

Im Auftrag
gez. v. Thadden 14/7

1) An
das Reichssicherheitshauptamt,
z. Hd. von SS. Obersturmbannführer
Eichmann, o.V.i.A.
Kurfürstenstr. 116

1) RSHA will Gruppe möglichst zusammen mit 19 Portugesen an Span.
Grenze stellen, sobaldmöglich.

2)

2 Wochen
v. Thadden 29/7

Vermerk durch Anruf
B. Sekr. am 14/7
"   " ruft an 1/8
RSHA wird Gruppe schnellmöglichst
nach Hendaye in Marsch setzen

bald Abreise mitteilen
 B. Sekr. Aruero [?] verständigt
Span. Botschaft ist nicht auf Angel. zurückgekommen.
Transport nicht mehr durchführbar.

v. Thadden 31/8

DOCUMENT J

Madrid 28.12.1943

Personal y reservado
Excmo. Señor General D. Carlos Asensio,
Ministro del Ejercito.

Mi querido General y amigo:
 Vuelvo a tratar del asunto de los sefarditas que están en edad militar. Como sabe Ud., la primera expedición de setenta y tres sefarditas procedentes de París salió por Málaga, salvo cuatro o cinco que se quedaron aquí con sus familias formando un total de veinte y cinco, por estar algunos de los miembros de las mismas en edad militar. Ahora bien, el problema no se concreta en éstos sólo sino que tiene un carácter general, que ésta era tan sólo una primera expedición de todo un sistema montado para resolver un grave conflicto político.
 Consiste éste en que son muchos cientos los sefarditas con nacionalidad española que están en Europa, sea en campos de concentración sea a punto de ir a ellos y nosotros no los podemos traer a España a instalarse en nuestro país porque ésto no nos conviene de ninguna manera ni el Caudillo lo autoriza ni los podemos dejar en su situación actual aparentando ignorar su condición de ciudadanos españoles porque ésto puede dar lugar a graves campañas de prensa en el extranjero y principalmente en América y provocarnos serias dificultades de orden internacional.
 En vista de lo cual se pensó en irlos trayendo por grupos de un centenar, poco más o menos, y cuando un grupo hubiera salido ya de España, pasando por nuestro país como la luz por el cristal, sin dejar rastro, traer un segundo grupo, hacerlos salir para dar entrada a los sucesivos etc. Siendo éste el mecanismo, claro es que la base del mismo estaba en que nosotros no permitiéramos de ninguna manera que los sefarditas quedaran en España y por lo tanto no contábamos con que se había de buscar razones para detenerlos aquí, puesto que ello implica anular la solución propuesta y dejarnos con todo el problema pendiente y sin salida posible . . .

DOCUMENT K

Embajada de España
Washington

May 11, 1944
re: Jewish refugees

No. 477

Dr. A. Leon Kubowitzki
Head, Rescue Dept.
World Jewish Congress
330 West 42nd Street
New York 10, New York

Dear Sir:

In reply to yours of the 9th inst. concerning the situation of several Spanish sefardites in Athens and in occupied France, I wish to inform you that under this same date, I am sending a cable to Spain requesting that, if possible, all aid be tended them.*

In what it refers the last paragraph of the same letter,† I may add that according to information received from our Ministry of Foreign Affairs, Spain has been giving all possible facilities to the Jewish refugees, regardless of whether or not they have Spanish nationality. The Spanish Authorities, in accordance with several Committees within the country working on the subject, have been trying to facilitate their transit through Spain towards the different localities previously assigned to them.

As soon as I have any definite news I shall be glad to communicate with you again.

Yours very truly,

Juan F. de Cárdenas
Spanish Ambassador

* The issues were: "400 Jews of Spanish citizenship, who used to live in Athens, were sent to the Haidari Concentration Camp"; "500 Spanish Jews . . . interned in the dreaded Camp of Drancy near Paris"; "200 Spanish Jews . . . at Perpignan."

† Kubowitzki wrote: "One of our informants states that the Spanish Government objects to admitting any more Sephardic Jews until those who entered Spain in March [from Salonika] have left the country."

ABBREVIATIONS

AFSC American Friends Service Committee files, Haverford College Library, Haverford, Pennsylvania

AJ Armée Juive files (possession of Abraham Polonsky, Tel Aviv)

AJYB *American Jewish Year Book*

AZJ *Allgemeine Zeitung des Judentums*

CDJC Centre de Documentation Juive Contemporaine, Paris

CZA Central Zionist Archives, Jerusalem

IW *Israelitische Wochenschrift*, Magdeburg

JC *Jewish Chronicle*

JCA Jewish Colonization Association archives, London

JDC American Joint Distribution Committee archives, New York

JP *Die Jüdische Presse*

LBI *Leo Baeck Institute Year Book*

OHD Oral History Division, Institute of Contemporary Jewry, Hebrew University, Jerusalem

SFM Spanish Foreign Ministry archives, Madrid

WJC World Jewish Congress archives, American Jewish Congress, New York

WRB War Refugee Board files, Franklin D. Roosevelt Library, New York

YV Yad Vashem central archives, Jerusalem

YW Yitzhak Weissman private files, Tel Aviv

YIVO HIAS-HICEM archives, YIVO Institute for Jewish Scientific Research, New York

NOTES

INTRODUCTION

1. United Nations, *Official Records of the Third Session of the General Assembly*, pt. 2., Plenary Meetings of the General Assembly, Summary Records of Meetings, April 5–May 18, 1949 (Lake Success, N.Y., 1949), p. 500. The draft resolution was submitted by Bolivia, Brazil, Colombia, and Peru. Israel voted against, with fourteen other nations, most of them from the Soviet bloc. The proposal failed because the twenty-six votes in favor did not comprise a two-thirds majority. In a vote on an alternative resolution, calling for sanctions against Spain proposed by Poland and the Soviet bloc, Israel abstained. See summary of previous discussions and resolutions on this question, United Nations, *Yearbook of the United Nations, 1948/49* (New York, 1950), pp. 311–15.

2. Spain, Bureau d'Information Diplomatique, *L'Espagne et les juifs* (Madrid, 1949), pp. 10–11, 17–31. Here Rabbi Perlzweig's letter is attributed mistakenly to the conference of the World Jewish Congress in Atlantic City in November 1944; it was written in March 1943. See SFM, I5-E2 (2), appended to Cárdenas's letter, no. 149, March 9, 1943.

3. Julio Caro Baroja, *Los Judíos en la España moderna y contemporanea*, vol. 3 (Madrid, 1961), pp. 211–16.

4. Carlton J. H. Hayes, *Wartime Mission in Spain, 1942–1945* (New York, 1946), pp. 121–24.

5. *Diario de Barcelona*, October 30, 1963. See also Charles Steckel, *Destruction and Survival* (Los Angeles, 1973), pp. 16–17. In the chapter "Distorted Historiography," Steckel refers to Rabbi Chaim Lifschitz's 1970 estimate. Rabbi Lifschitz, of Yeshiva Torah Vodaath in Brooklyn, went to Madrid to thank General Franco for his alleged personal activity on behalf of the Jews. His gesture gained worldwide publicity, notably in *Newsweek*.

6. Federico Ysart, *España y los Judíos en la Segunda Guerra Mundial* (Barcelona, 1973).

CHAPTER 1

1. José Amador de los Ríos, *Historia social, política, y religiosa de los Judíos de España y Portugal*, vol. 3 (Madrid, 1875–76), pp. 552–54.

2. Ibid., pp. 556–88.

3. Henry Charles Lea, *A History of the Inquisition of Spain*, vol. 3 (London, 1922), p. 311; cf. Cecil Roth, *A History of the Marranos* (New York, 1959), p. 353.

4. *AZJ*, September 25, 1854, pp. 489–94. See also ibid., August 21, August 28, October 9, November 13, December 4, 1854. For efforts in the nineteenth century to renew the Jewish community in Spain and the attitude of the Jews in western Europe toward these attempts, see Joseph Jacob Lichtenstein, "The Reaction of West European Jewry to the Reestablishment of a Jewish Community in Spain in the 19th Century" (Ph.D. diss., Yeshiva University, 1962).

5. Amador, *Judíos de España*, pp. 561–65. In January 1855, Amador wrote an article in which he contradicted several historical points in Philippson's proposal. In a letter dated January 1, 1855, the committee stated that they rejected the doctrine of religious freedom because of fears that it might become a cause uniting antiliberal forces (*AZJ*, October 20, 1868, p. 853). The cause of religious freedom was defeated narrowly by 4 votes—103 opposed and 99 in favor. See Lichtenstein, "Reaction of West European Jewry," p. 108.

6. Henry Léon, *Histoire des juifs de Bayonne* (Paris, 1893), pp. 357–58.

7. *AZJ*, October 20, 1868, editorial; ibid., October 27, 1868, p. 878; ibid., November 3, 1868, p. 899; ibid., November 17, 1868, p. 939. See also Lichtenstein, "Reaction of West European Jewry," pp. 110–53, for a discussion on the days of the revolution.

8. Léon, *Juifs de Bayonne*, pp. 358–59. See *AZJ*, November 3, 1868, p. 900, which quotes General Prim's reply to Haim Guedalla, suggesting that he direct his request to the provisional government.

9. The supporters of Don Carlos, who in 1833 refused to recognize Isabella II and claimed the Spanish throne in the name of her dead father's brother.

10. Amador, *Judíos de España*, pp. 561–67, which concludes that nineteenth-century Spain was not ready to adopt a doctrine of religious freedom and all efforts toward this end were doomed to failure. Cf. Léon, *Juifs de Bayonne*, pp. 359–60. Lichtenstein, "Reaction of West European Jewry," pp. 172–95, discusses the Board of Deputies's appeal to Alfonso XII and the debate in the Cortes on religious freedom.

11. *JC*, July 8, 1881, p. 10; ibid., September 9, 1881, p. 5. See also Isidore Loeb, "L'Espagne et les juifs," *Bulletin de l'Alliance Israélite Universelle*, ser. 2, no. 12 (1887): 89.

12. *JC*, September 16, 1881, p. 5; *AZJ*, August 9, 1881, p. 529; ibid., August 16, 1881, p. 544.

13. Loeb, "L'Espagne et les juifs," pp. 97–101.

14. Documents from the SFM concerning this episode were summarized and published by Manuel Fernandez Rodrigues, "España y los Judíos en el reinado de Alfonso XII," *Hispania* 25 (1965): 565–84.

15. *JC*, June 24, 1881, pp. 11–12; ibid., July 1, 1881, p. 12; ibid., July 7, 1881, p. 10.

16. Victor A. Mirelman, "A Note on Jewish Settlement in Argentina, 1881–1892," *Jewish Social Studies* 33 (1971): 5–6.

17. *JC*, June 24, 1881, p. 10; ibid., July 7, 1881, p. 10. Fernandez Rodrigues, "España y los Judíos," p. 567, writes that the resolution was forwarded to Madrid on July 6.

18. *JC*, July 1, 1881, p. 12. The well-known preacher Adolf (Aaron) Jellinek of Vienna published his sermon on this subject and sent it, with a dedication, to the king of Spain.

19. *JC*, May 17, 1881, p. 6, which contains a report of the meeting of the Anglo-Jewish Association in London.

20. Fernandez Rodrigues, "España y los Judíos," pp. 573, 581; *AZJ*, August 23, 1881, p. 560; ibid., September 13, 1881, p. 613.

21. *JP*, October 28, 1881, p. 445; *AZJ*, December 8, 1881, p. 769.

22. The composition of the Central Committee and the resolutions adopted at a meeting of the members on December 30, 1886, were published in full in *JP*, January 6, 1887, p. 3; ibid., January 27, 1887, p. 37; *JC*, January 21, 1887, p. 9; *IW*, March 3, 1887, p. 77. See also Loeb, "L'Espagne et les juifs," pp. 93–95. These sources are based on Lapuya's statements. The extent of support for Lapuya's ideas in liberal circles in Spain requires further study.

23. Lichtenstein, "Reaction of West European Jewry," pp. 148–51, discusses the denunciation by Vicente Manterola; see also Julio Caro Baroja, *Los Judíos en la España moderna y contemporanea*, vol. 3 (Madrid, 1961), pp. 189–90.

24. Angel Tineo Heredia, *Los Judíos en España* (Madrid, 1881), pp. 33–51.

25. *JP*, October 28, 1886, p. 412, which quotes his article in *El Progreso*; *IW*, March 17, 1887, p. 94.

26. *JP*, March 10, 1887, p. 109, supplement.

27. For supporting views, see *JC*, February 4, 1887, p. 12; *JP*, November 18, 1886, p. 445; ibid., November 25, 1886, p. 453. For dissenting views, see *AZJ*, March 9, 1887, p. 139; ibid., May 19, 1887, p. 308; *JC*, January 21, 1887, p. 9.

28. See Lapuya's letters, January 15, March 16, April 24, April 28, 1887, in *JP*, January 27, 1887, p. 37; ibid., April 21, 1887, p. 155; ibid., May 5, 1887, p. 177. See Lapuya's last article in *AZJ*, December 8, 1887, p. 769.

29. In December 1891, responding to an appeal by a group of Jews from Odessa, the Spanish ambassador in Russia asked Madrid if Jews were permitted to immigrate to Spain. The Spanish government replied the following month that there was no objection to their coming but they could not expect any financial support. See Manuel L. Ortega, *Figuras ibéricas: el doctor Pulido* (Madrid, 1922), pp. 327–28.

30. Angel Pulido was born in Madrid in 1852 to a poor, devout Catholic family. The time of his university studies paralleled the period of the First Republic, and after he was graduated he began his medical practice. He joined the group of moderate Republicans under Emilio Castelar, with whose support he was elected a delegate to the Cortes in 1893. In 1899 he served as senator from the Royal Academy of Medicine in Madrid and from 1903–9 as a senator from the University of Salamanca. Upon recommendation from Canalejas, Pulido was appointed senator for life in 1910. He served as vice-chairman of the Cortes on three occasions. He was a prolific orator and writer, leaving behind 117 books and

other publications on medical, political, and social issues. Pulido died in 1932 at the age of 80. See the biography by his son, Martin Angel Pulido, *El dr. Pulido y su epoca* (Madrid, 1945).

31. For the influence of Emilio Castelar, see Angel Pulido y Fernandez, *Españoles sin patria y la raza Sefardí* (Madrid, 1905), pp. 596–604, esp. pp. 106–30, 180–83, for views of those opposed to his work.

32. Ibid., p. 640. His proposals are detailed on pp. 519–640. The matter of immigration to Spain is discussed on pp. 538–41.

33. Isaac Alcheh y Saporta, *Los Españoles sin patria de Salonica* (Madrid, 1917), pp. 9–10.

34. Max Nordau, "Hafta'ah sefaradit" [A Spanish surprise], *Ktavim tzioni'im* [Zionist writings], vol. 4 (Jerusalem, 5722/1962), pp. 16–19; A. S. Yahuda, "Prakim mi-zikhronotai" [Chapters of my memoirs], *Talpiot* 3 (5707–8/1947–48): 604–5. See also Haim Boger's introduction to Yahuda's *Ha-haganah al ha-yishuv ha-yehudi bi-yemei milhemet ha-olam ha-rishonah* [The defense of the Jewish community during World War I] (Jerusalem, 5712/1952), pp. 4–5.

35. Ortega, *Figuras ibéricas*, pp. 329–31, quotes parts of this correspondence. See Yahuda, *Ha-hagana*, p. 23.

36. Yahuda, *Ha-haganah*, pp. 37–56; cf. Arthur Ruppin, *Pirkei hayai* [My life and work], vol. 1 (Tel Aviv, 5728/1968), p. 272. For the activities of the Spanish representatives in Palestine and their difficulties in maintaining the Franciscan monastery in Ein Kerem, which they owned, see Father Samuel Eijan, *Hispanidad en Tierra Santa: actuación diplomática* (Madrid, 1943), pp. 175–83.

37. Ortega, *Figuras ibéricas*, pp. 331–38, 382–90.

38. Pulido, *El dr. Pulido*, 211–12.

39. Nordau, "Hafta'ah," pp. 16–19; Yahuda, "Prakim," pp. 604–6; Max Nordau, "Dr. Yahuda and the Madrid University," *JC*, April 9, 1920.

40. Alcheh, *Los Españoles sin patria*, pp. 30–43; on the agreement between Spain and Greece, see SFM, I5-E2 (1), no. 61, letter from Salomon Ezraty to Eduardo Gasset, July 2, 1942.

41. Pulido, *Españoles sin patria*, pp. 479–507. See Isaac Laredo, *Memorias de un viejo Tangerino* (Madrid, 1935), p. 328, on the visit of Castelar with the Jews of Tangier in 1891.

42. Baroja, *Los Judíos en la España*, vol. 3, p. 205. Providing protection to the sultan's nationals in Morocco—particularly to the Jewish nationals—was discussed among England, France, Italy, and Spain from 1877–80, and Spain was not alone in opposing this policy. See Lichtenstein, "Reaction of West European Jewry," pp. 196–207.

43. Angel Pulido y Fernandez, *La reconciliación Hispano-Hebrea* (Madrid, 1920), pp. 13–33. For Pulido's interview with the king on March 25, 1920, see pp. 103–15, 129–33.

44. Angel Pulido y Fernandez, *España en Marruecos: penetración, pacífica, y colonización en su protectorado* (Madrid, 1922).

45. The decree and the regulations were published in the official *Gaceta de Madrid* on December 21, 1924, and appeared the following day in all the Spanish newspapers. They recently were republished in Consejo Superior de Investigaciones Científicas, *Actas del primer simposio de estudios Sefardís*, ed. Ya'akov M. Hassan (Madrid, 1970), pp. 583–90. The decree does not bear Primo de Rivera's

signature because he was supervising military action against the rebels in Morocco at the time.

46. On January 25, 1924, a few months after the Primo de Rivera regime came to power, the Spanish government presented a collection of books to the National Library in Jerusalem. It is possible that Judeophiles close to the regime were behind this gesture.

47. Spanish Embassy, *Spain and the Sephardi Jews* (Washington, 1949), p. 1: "In 1924, General Primo de Rivera offered the Sephardi Spanish citizenship." Baroja, *Los Judíos en la España*, vol. 3, p. 205, repeats this claim, as does Gregorio Marañon Moya, director of the Instituto de Cultura Hispanica, in the opening lecture in the symposium on Sephardic Jews, held in Madrid in 1964 (Consejo Superior, *Actas del primer simposio*, p. 336). The title of the Royal Decree of December 1924 and subsequent documents (p. 581) refers to the "concession of Spanish nationality to the Sephardic Jews." In the introduction, the sentence defining those benefiting from the decree is taken from the order of the Military Directorate, but it omits the latter portion, so that it appears to refer to "persons belonging to families of Spanish origin." The original sentence reads: "And generally to persons belonging to families of Spanish origin, who at some time were registered in Spanish registrations." This error was repeated in Jewish publications; see Jeonathan Prato, "Spain," *Encyclopaedia Judaica*, vol. 15 (Jerusalem, 5731/1971), p. 244. The terminology in the last paragraph of the decree provides for Spanish protection after December 31, 1930, in those countries whose laws recognize it.

48. Spain, *Constitución de la República Española* (Madrid, 1931). The law was dated April 29, 1931, and signed by Alcalá Zamora and the minister of justice in the provisional government. See Consejo Superior, *Actas del primer simposio*, pp. 592–94.

49. For the history of the Second Republic and the Civil War, see Gabriel Jackson, *The Spanish Republic and the Civil War, 1931–1939* (Princeton, 1965); Hugh Thomas, *The Spanish Civil War* (New York, 1961); Dante A. Puzzo, *Spain and the Great Powers, 1936–1941* (New York, 1962), pp. 1–51. Figures from the elections of November 1933 and February 1936 vary in different sources; those used here are taken from the *Encyclopaedia Britannica*, vol. 20 (1968), p. 1107.

50. League of Nations, *Official Journal* (Geneva, 1933), no. 7, pt. 1, pp. 842, 847.

51. *JC*, March 29, 1935, p. 5; ibid., April 5, 1935, p. 26. The words were spoken by Antonio Jaen, a delegate to the Cortes, who proposed in 1932 that the ancient synagogue, supposedly dating back to the time of Maimonides (but which actually was built in 1315), should be returned to the Jewish organizations. See Baroja, *Los Judíos en la España*, vol. 3, p. 209.

52. *Actas del primer simposio*, pp. 592–610. The agreements are mentioned in the 1948 order by General Franco. See also *AJYB* 38 (1936–37): 271.

53. Baroja, *Los Judíos en la España*, vol. 3, p. 194. Lapuya's reference to Drumont appears in *JP*, November 11, 1886, p. 438.

54. F. Robles Dégano, *La conspiración Judía contra España* (Ávila, 1932), p. 30. See also Juan Machimbarrena, *La crisis mundial: el oro, el socialismo, los Judíos* (San Sebastián, 1932), pp. 65–91, which is based on the *Protocols*. Baroja, *Los Judíos en la España*, vol. 3, p. 210, n. 37, quotes a pamphlet that appeared in Barcelona in 1932, linking the *Protocols* to conditions in Spain.

55. Pío Baroja, *Comunistas Judíos y demás raleas*, 2d ed. (Valladolid, 1939), pp. 27, 37, 67. The first articles in this anthology were written before the Civil War.

56. *JC*, December 7, 1934, p. 25; JCA, minutes of meeting, May 4, 1935: report from W. Schah, JCA emissary to Spain, April 1935.

57. Amador, *Judíos de España*, p. 568, provides the names and origins of sixteen Jews who were naturalized between 1869 and 1875, of whom only one was naturalized in 1871. Lichtenstein, "Reaction of West European Jewry," p. 162, relying primarily on publications in the Jewish press, provides the names of nine additional Jews, all of whom were naturalized in 1871. As the names are not identical, both lists may be combined.

58. Lichtenstein, "Reaction of West European Jews," p. 96; *AZJ*, October 12, 1886, p. 666. In addition to recognized Jews, there were in Spain many other Jews who hid their Jewishness or converted. See Baroja, *Los Judíos en España*, vol. 3, pp. 186–87.

59. *JC*, November 16, 1877, p. 7; *JP*, September 29, 1886, p. 384.

60. Lichtenstein, "Reaction of West European Jews," pp. 70–76.

61. J. Sanua, *Univers Israélite*, January 16, 1890, p. 279, claims there were thirty families in Seville. See Pulido, *Españoles sin patria*, pp. 342–46; Pulido's descriptions and information are repeated in Mario Méndez Bejarano, *Histoire de la juiverie de Seville* (Madrid, 1922), pp. 231–37.

62. Pulido, *Españoles sin patria*, p. 346, mentions only five families in Cádiz. See also Yahuda, "Prakim," p. 770.

63. Yahuda, "Prakim," pp. 773–78.

64. *Report of the Executive of the World Zionist Organization to the 12th Zionist Congress*, vol. 3, p. 170; see also *AJYB* 21 (1919–20): 299.

65. JCA, minutes of meeting of the Executive Council, May 10, 1924, p. 34.

66. *Report of the Executive of the World Zionist Organization*, organizational report, p. 170; *Report of the Executive of the World Zionist Organization to the 13th Zionist Congress*, financial report, p. 46; *Report of the Executive of the World Zionist Organization to the 16th Zionist Congress*, p. 140. The biblical name "shekel" was given by the first Zionist Congress (1897) to the fee and card of Zionist membership; the shekel was a unit of weight used for payment in ancient times.

67. CZA, KKL5B, file 246, letter from L. Cohen, April 19, 1929.

68. Ibid., correspondence between the Jerusalem office and Ignacio Bauer, January 8, 17, 1931, and esp. August 6, 8, 1931.

69. Roth, *History of the Marranos*, p. 230, discusses the rumor that Prime Minister Alcalá Zamora, Minister of Justice Fernando de los Ríos, and Interior Minister Miguel Maura were of "Jewish ancestry." Baroja, *Los Judíos en la España*, vol. 3, p. 184, repeats this rumor but refers to a distant and doubtful "Jewish origin," such as that of Maura, who actually was a descendant of the Majorcan Marranos. Baroja (p. 211) mentions Margarita Nelken, a Jewish woman who served as a Socialist deputy. Regarding emigration from Salonika to Spain, see CZA, KKL5B, file 246, correspondence between the office in Jerusalem and the JNF representative in Salonika, May 31, June 14, 1932.

70. JCA, minutes of meeting, May 4, 1935, pp. 269–90: report from W. Schah, April 1935 (the report was compiled by a head of the HICEM in France); YIVO, Spain 12/1, letter from HICEM Paris to John L. Bernstein in New York, April 16, 1935. See also JCA, *Rapport de la direction générale au conseil d'administration,* 1935, p. 196.

71. CZA, S5/2233, letter from Maurice Stern to the Organization Department of the Jewish Agency in Jerusalem, June 16, 1936.

72. Ibid., circular letter no. 1, May 1936; ibid., KKL5B, box 949, letter from Stern to the Jerusalem office, June 6, 1936. Mrs. Olga Bauer was descended from the Baron Horace Günzberg family of Russia.

73. OHD, 52 (1), Joseph Nahum, pp. 1–6; *JC*, January 4, 1935, p. 23, evidence provided by journalist Israel Cohen, who visited Barcelona at the end of 1934; CZA, KKL5B, box 949, letters from Joseph Fischer (Ariel), February 4, March 18, 1936.

74. CZA, KKL5B, file 246, correspondence from Ernst Necheles to the office in Jerusalem, April–October 1934; ibid., letter from Walter Goldstein, December 28, 1935; ibid., letter from Stern to Fischer, April 28, 1936.

75. Ibid., letter from Stern to Fischer, April 28, 1936. Birobidzhan, in far eastern Soviet Russia, was the "Autonomous Jewish Region" that the Soviet government attempted to establish for Jews in the 1930s. The program received enthusiastic support from Jewish Communists throughout the world.

76. Ibid., letters between Stern and Fischer, May–June 1936; ibid., S5/2233, minutes of the founding meeting of the Federation, June 6, 1936.

77. Ibid., letter from Stern, June 16, 1936; *Davar* (newspaper of the Israel Labor party), July 21, 1936, p. 3.

78. CZA, KKL5B, file 246, letter from Stern to Fischer, July 22, 1936.

79. Ibid., head office of the JNF to Werner Bloch, April 8, 1937; ibid., letter from Stern to Fischer, July 24, 1936.

80. *JC*, August 14, 1936, p. 16; ibid., September 4, 1936, p. 29, concerning the Jews who returned to Germany. See also YIVO, Spain 12/1, report on the activities of HICEM in Spain, July 1936–April 1938; JCA, *Rapport de la direction générale,* 1937, p. 174.

81. OHD, 52 (1), Nahum, pp. 7–9, regarding the Jewish anarchist who came to pray, rifle in hand, at the synagogue on one of the holidays; see also *JC*, January 22, 1937, p. 20; ibid., April 30, 1937, p. 24.

82. *AJYB* 39 (1937–38): 187–88; *JC*, April 30, 1937, p. 24.

83. *JC*, February 19, 1937, p. 20, letter from L. de Armas; ibid., February 26, 1937, p. 35, reply from A. N. Levy of London to this letter. There was much news concerning the incitement of the Arab populace against the Jews and the imposition of limitations on the Jews under pressure from the Nazis, as well as conflicting reports on the situation in Melilla and the extortion of large "contributions" from the communities in Tétouan and Ceuta. See *JC*, August 7, 1936, p. 16; ibid., August 21, 1936, p. 24; ibid., September 4, 1936, p. 27; ibid., March 26, 1937, p. 21; see also *AJYB* 39 (1937–38): 323; ibid. 40 (1938–39): 187. There were also reports of Moroccan Jews voluntarily joining the Nationalists. See Haim Beinart, *Ha-yishuv ha-yehudi he-hadash bi-sefarad: reka, metziut, ve-ha'arakhah* [The new Jewish settlements in Spain: background, reality, evaluation] (Jerusalem, 5729/1969), p. 23.

84. *JC*, October 2, 1936, p. 23; ibid., April 30, 1937, p. 11. Attitudes of the Jews in the United States toward the Spanish Civil War are discussed briefly in Allen Guttmann, *The Wound in the Heart: America and the Spanish Civil War* (New York, 1962), pp. 65–67. In a survey, 2 percent of the American Jews polled supported Franco, compared with 9 percent of the Protestants and 39 percent of the Catholics. For further details, see Robert Singerman, "American-Jewish Reactions to the Spanish Civil War," *Journal of Church and State* 19 (1977): 261–78.

85. Thomas, *The Spanish Civil War*, pp. 796–97, estimates that 40,000 volunteers served in the five International Brigades, including 3,000 Jews. Cf. David Diamant, *Héros juifs de la Résistance française* (Paris, 1962), p. 12, who estimates that 5,000 Jews served.

86. Salvador de Madariaga, *Spain: A Modern History* (New York, 1958), pp. 156–60.

87. In the elections of February 1936, the rightist parties were supported by 3.8 million out of 8.8 million voting. If the 680,000 voters for the moderate parties—many of whom were closer to the right than the left on the matter of religious legislation—are included, then half voted against separation of church and state. See Thomas, *The Spanish Civil War*, p. 134.

CHAPTER 2

1. According to conservative estimates, 70,000 Nationalist soldiers were killed, including 2,000 Italians, 300 Germans, and 15,000 Moroccans. On the Republican side nearly 100,000 were killed, 90,000 Spaniards and the rest volunteers. Political murders claimed between 40,000 and 50,000 lives but may have been two or even three times more. See Stanley G. Payne, *Franco's Spain* (London, 1968), pp. 23–24; cf. Hugh Thomas, *The Spanish Civil War* (New York, 1961), pp. 789–90. Samuel Hoare, *Complacent Dictator* (New York, 1947), p. 76, places the death toll at 1,000,000.

2. Dante A. Puzzo, *Spain and the Great Powers, 1936–1941* (New York, 1962), p. 213.

3. Payne, *Franco's Spain*, pp. 110–12, arrives at this figure after discussing other estimates almost twice as high. The number of prisoners is taken from Spain, *Annuario Estadística, 1944–1945* (Madrid, 1946). See also OHD, 1 (1), Yehuda Ansbacher, p. 16, who testifies to the execution of Republican fighters in Pamplona in 1943.

4. Payne, *Franco's Spain*, p. 109. See also Zosa Szajkowski, *Analytical Franco-Jewish Gazetteer, 1939–1945* (New York, 1966), p. 19, for a detailed bibliography for the period of Spanish imprisonments. Bartoli Molins y Fabrega, *Campos de concentratión, 1939–194* . . . (Mexico City, 1944), describes, with drawings and photographs, France's betrayal and its steadfast position regarding Spanish refugees.

5. *Ya* (Madrid daily), May 2, 1940; ibid., June 30, 1940; Payne, *Franco's Spain*, pp. 51–81.

6. AFSC, Spain, 1943, file no. 6, report from Philip A. Conard on his visit to Spain in November 1943, p. 10. See Payne, *Franco's Spain*, p. 62.

7. Payne, *Franco's Spain*, p. 7, maintains that in February 1936 Franco refused to proclaim martial law; Puzzo, *Spain and the Great Powers*, p. 48, offers evidence to the contrary.

8. The full name of the united party is Falange Española Tradicionalista y de las Juntas de Ofensiva Nacional Sindicalista (FET y de las JONS).

9. Payne, *Franco's Spain*, pp. 22, 45, table 1.

10. Puzzo, *Spain and the Great Powers*, pp. 202–9.

11. Ibid., pp. 202–20.

12. Hoare, *Complacent Dictator*, p. 312, memorandum from Eberhard von

Stohrer to the Foreign Ministry in Berlin, August 8, 1940, in which he outlines the advantages to be gained by Spain's entering the war. See also Winston Churchill, *The Second World War: Their Finest Hour*, vol. 2 (Boston, 1949), pp. 519–23.

13. Arnold Toynbee, *Survey of International Affairs, 1939–1946: The War and the Neutrals* (Oxford, 1956), p. 277.

14. Hoare, *Complacent Dictator*, p. 127; Raymond Lambert Proctor, "The 'Blue Division': An Episode in German-Spanish Wartime Relations" (Ph.D. diss., University of Oregon, 1966), pp. 1–20, 148–76.

15. Emilio Esteban Infantes, *La División Azul (donde Asia empieza)* (Barcelona, 1956), pp. 7–57, esp. p. 50. General Esteban Infantes took command of the Blue Division in December 1942 from his predecessor, General Muñoz Grandes; both were senior colleagues of Franco.

16. Ibid., pp. 252–69, 293–95, 298–301; cf. Puzzo, *Spain and the Great Powers*, p. 235. See also Proctor, "The Blue Division," pp. 219–44.

17. Dwight D. Eisenhower, *Crusade in Europe* (Garden City, N.Y., 1952), p. 92.

18. Carlton J. H. Hayes, *Wartime Mission in Spain, 1942–1945* (New York, 1946), pp. 88–95; Hoare, *Complacent Dictator*, pp. 163–74; Toynbee, *Survey of International Affairs*, pp. 295–98.

19. Hayes, *Wartime Mission*, pp. 139–43.

20. The tungsten issue resulted in a brief crisis in U.S.-Spanish relations at the beginning of 1944; this was not resolved until April 29, after oil supplies had been halted for months and a rift had developed between Britain and the United States. For a history of the episode, see John Paul Willson, "Carlton J. H. Hayes in Spain, 1942–1945" (Ph.D. diss., Syracuse University, 1969), pp. 163–99.

21. Toynbee, *Survey of International Affairs*, p. 301; Hayes, *Wartime Mission*, pp. 175–76.

22. Hoare, *Complacent Dictator*, pp. 190–98. Cf. Walter Schellenberg, *The Labyrinth* (New York, 1956), pp. 113–15, who attests to the extent and power of the German secret service in Spain; see also Toynbee, *Survey of International Affairs*, p. 279. The Germans exploited their almost total control of the Spanish news media with a psychological campaign of rumor and malicious gossip. For their influence see, for example, Willard L. Beaulac, *Career Ambassador* (New York, 1951), pp. 190–91.

23. Hayes, *Wartime Mission*, pp. 56–57; Hoare, *Complacent Dictator*, pp. 129–30, 154–56; Toynbee, *Survey of International Affairs*, p. 294. Cf. François Piétri, *Mes années d'Espagne, 1940–1945* (Paris, 1954), p. 83. Hayes and Hoare show that Serrano Suñer's powerful influence over internal and external affairs, an influence that sometimes overshadowed even Franco's, was the real reason for his removal. Piétri attributes his downfall to the deliberate pro-Western turn of Franco. The attack on Varela took place on August 15, 1942, in the Basque city of Bilbao, as he was leaving a memorial service for members of his party who fell in the Civil War.

24. Hayes, *Wartime Mission*, p. 31; Hoare, *Complacent Dictator*, pp. 156–61; Piétri, *Mes années*, pp. 82–84.

25. For opinions of José Félix Lequerica, see Hoare, *Complacent Dictator*, p. 276; Hayes, *Wartime Mission*, pp. 250–51. Hayes writes that because of his pro-Nazi past, Lequerica was likely to elicit a stronger interest in American

demands. On the matter of refuge for Nazis, see U.S., Department of State, *Foreign Relations of the United States, Diplomatic Papers 1944*, vol. 1, general (Washington, 1966), pp. 1419–20, 1432–33.

26. Hoare, *Complacent Dictator*, p. 31, discusses Franco's Jewish ancestry as an established fact.

CHAPTER 3

1. See Canton A. Bernandez, *Legislación eclesiástica del estado (1938–1964)* (Madrid, 1965), p. 3.

2. For the laws enacted between 1938 and 1967, see Spanish Information Service, *Fundamental Laws of the State* (Madrid, 1967). On the situation of the Jews, see *AJYB* 42 (1940–41): 435; YIVO, Spain 12/2, letter from Natt Lieberman, early 1942; OHD 52 (1), Joseph Nahum, pp. 9–12; ibid., 1 (1), Yehuda Ansbacher, p. 16; ibid., 18 (1), Avraham Bock, pp. 26–27.

3. Ministerio del Trabajo, Dirección General de Estadística, *Zona de protectorado y de los territorios de soberanía de España en el norte de Africa: anuario estadístico 1941* (Madrid, 1942), pp. 26–27. See also *Sefarad* 2 (1942): 221–23, which quotes the statistics concerning the Jewish population and Jewish pupils that appeared in *El Mundo*, July 20, 1941, pp. 470–72. According to this source there were 11,000 Jews in Tangier; another source gives 7,942, including 840 refugees, for the same year. See Juan Batista Vilar, "Emigrantes Judíos del norte de Marruecos a Hispanoamerica durante el siglo XX," *Maguen-Escudo* (Caracas), no. 21 (February 1972), p. 21.

4. Nehemia Robinson, *The Spain of Franco and Its Policies toward the Jews* (New York, 1953), pp. 9–10; Julio Caro Baroja, *Los Judíos en la España moderna y contemporanea*, vol. 3 (Madrid, 1961), p. 212. *La garra del capitalismo Judío* (Madrid, 1943), published anonymously, is but one example of anti-Semitic propaganda.

5. YIVO, Spain 3, secret report from Augusto d'Esaguy, chairman of the Assistance Committee of the Lisbon community, to HIAS, New York, April 5, 1940; ibid., file 2, evidence from Lieberman on the situation of the Jews, late 1941.

6. AFSC, Refugees, Portugal 1942, letter from Moore Bowden to the Friends in Lisbon, October 12, 1941; JDC, Spain 1943, letter from the JDC office in Lisbon to New York, August 7, 1943, pp. 3–4.

7. *Sefarad* 1 (1941): 1. The school for Hebrew studies was established under the auspices of the Instituto Benito Arias Montano, formerly a research institute for the study of Arabic culture. Today this institute is part of the Consejo Superior de Investigaciones Científicas, established by order of General Franco, November 24, 1939, and affiliated with the Ministry of Education. On November 9, 1944, Arabic studies were separated from Hebrew studies, and the Arias Montano Institute devoted itself solely to Jewish scholarship.

8. After reforms in university education in 1941, Jewish studies in the universities were expanded. See *Sefarad* 1 (1941): 461.

9. Pío Baroja, *Comunistas Judíos y demás raleas*, 2d ed. (Valladolid, 1939), pp. 71–80. The fact that this book went into a second edition by 1939 is one indication of its widespread interest. Baroja's antipathy toward Ashkenazic Jews did not stop him from writing enthusiastically on Walter Rathenau (pp. 81–92). Julio Caro

Baroja, *Los Judíos en la España*, p. 208, writes that he gave permission for the publication of his uncle's book but did not participate in its editing.

10. YV, AA-JM 2257, K-343821, report from the German Embassy, November 7, 1941, following instructions issued September 30, 1941.

11. SFM, Europe, Romania, arch. bibl. leg. R-1192, no. 69.

12. Arie Tartakower and K. R. Grossman, *The Jewish Refugee* (New York, 1944), p. 157.

13. YIVO, ser. 2, France 2/26, report from Rafael Spanien on his visit to the Spanish border, September 10, 1940, which quotes the cable from the governor of Gerona.

14. Zosa Szajkowski, *Analytical Franco-Jewish Gazetteer, 1939–1945* (New York, 1966), p. 30.

15. YIVO, ser. 2, France 2/26, information provided to the HICEM representative by an official in the Spanish Consulate in Marseille, October 8, 1940; ibid., announcement from the Marseille Consulate, November 11, 1940.

16. Ibid., ser. 1, Portugal 12/A2, HICEM report for the period July 1, 1940–December 31, 1941; ibid., file A16, HICEM report for the second trimester 1942; ibid., France 2/169, cable from Sequerra to HICEM France, July 2, 1942.

17. Claude Vigée, *La lune d'hiver* (Paris, 1970), pp. 110–26. Vigée, an Alsatian Jew and fifth-generation French citizen, relates the hostility he encountered when he requested a transit visa from the Spanish consul in Marseille, even though he held documents exempting him from military service in France because of ill health. After a consulate doctor verified the medical report, the consul granted the visa.

18. YIVO, Portugal 12/A4, HICEM Marseille report for the third trimester 1942; Henri Amouroux, *La vie des français sous l'Occupation* (Paris, 1961), p. 117; Szajkowski, *Franco-Jewish Gazetteer*, p. 91.

19. OHD, 42 (1), Samuel Federman, p. 1; YIVO, ser. 2, France 2/169, cable from Samuel Sequerra to HICEM France, May 31, 1942.

20. YIVO, ser. 2, France 2/26, report from Spanien on his visit to Cerbère, September 10, 1940; WJC, Portugal, reports from Knopfmacher to Goldman, August 30, September 1, September 24, 1940, including mention of a family with a ten-day-old infant that crossed the border near Cerbère. See Donald A. Lowrie, *The Hunted Children* (New York, 1943), p. 48, for the fate of people like Leon Feuchtwanger.

21. YIVO, ser. 2, France 2/27, cable from HICEM Lisbon to Marseille, March 25, 1942, concerning refugees who acquired visas at the Cuban consulates in Paris, Brussels, and Antwerp. For a personal account of the experiences of a refugee who passed through war-torn Spain, see the notes of Zalman Shneur, *Ha-olam*, nos. 13–16 (1941–42), pp. 102, 110, 119, 126.

22. François Piétri, *Mes années d'Espagne, 1940–1945* (Paris, 1954), p. 190.

23. YIVO, ser. 3/342, letter from Dr. Drenger, chairman of the Maccabi World Union in Luxembourg, on behalf of twenty prisoners, November 24, 1940. Drenger and several friends, including Federman, stayed in the camp for more than two years. See OHD, 42 (1).

24. YIVO, Portugal 12/11B, letter from Bernstein to HICEM New York, December 22, 1940; AFSC, Portugal 1937/45, letter from Mrs. M. P. Schauffler, March 1, 1941; ibid., report from a conversation with Col. Cary I. Crockett, September 19, 1941.

25. AFSC, letter from Mary M. Rogers, November 29, 1940; ibid., report from Philip Conard on a visit to Spain, July 19–28, 1941.

26. Ibid., Spain 1943, file 2, letter from Virginia Weddell, September 30, 1941; ibid., Portugal 1942, letter from Philip Conard, June 20, 1942.

27. Ibid., Spain 1943, file 2, report from Conard on his second visit to Spain in June, August 10, 1942; OHD, 10 (2), second testimony of Joseph Schwartz, pp. 5–6. See also JDC, *Annual Report: Aiding Jews Overseas* (1941–May 1942), p. 25.

28. YIVO, ser. 3, file 342, letter from the agent of Norddeutscher Lloyd of Bremen in Spain, November 23, 1940; OHD, 35 (1), testimony of Samuel Sequerra, pp. 4–6; ibid., 19 (47), Schwartz, October 24, 1967, pp. 5–7.

29. See Federico Ysart, *España y los Judíos en la Segunda Guerra Mundial* (Barcelona, 1973), pp. 117–19, where the documents are quoted, and p. 126 for the competition between the Nationalist and Republican delegations in Bucharest.

30. SFM, Europe 1940/41, Romania, arch. bibl. leg. R-1261, letter from the chargé d'affaires, July 2, 1940; ibid., letter from José Rojas y Moreno, April 2, 1941, and copy of a letter from Ion Antonescu; ibid., I5-E2 (1), letters from Rojas, April 24, 1941, August 10, 29, 1942. See also Ysart, *España y los Judíos*, pp. 127–30, who quotes from Rojas's letter to Antonescu, March 27, 1941, and other documents.

31. Figures given here were taken from Michael Molkho and Joseph Nehamah, *Shoat yehudei yavan, 1941–1944* [The destruction of Greek Jewry, 1941–1944] (Jerusalem, 5724/1964), pp. 223–24 (rev. and enl. ed. of Michael Molkho, *In Memoriam: hommage aux victimes juives des Nazis en Grèce* [Salonika, 1948]). Compared with other sources, these figures are maximal.

32. Of a total of 640 nationals, 367 from Salonika were transported to Spain, 155 from Athens were sent to Bergen-Belsen, approximately 80 remained in Athens, and 38 from Salonika and northern Greece were sent to Auschwitz. These figures are minimal.

33. YV, AA-JM 2218, K-213082–93, a list of 511 names of Spanish nationals in Salonika, including their Spanish passport numbers and dates of issue between 1941 and May 1942. The list contains several duplications: numbers 290–91 duplicate 274–75, 194/5 duplicate 415/5, and 484 is the same as 511. It is thus possible that this list represents only 506 names.

34. SFM, I5-E1 (1), a list of Spanish Jews deported by the Germans. For example, the family of the widow of Alberto Toledo, from Dhidhimótikhon, comprised five persons, only one of whom was registered in the consulate.

35. SFM, arch. bibl. leg. R-210, no. 133, "Informe sobre la colonia Sefardita," letter from Eduardo Gasset, March 13, 1942, who mentions the report of his predecessor, José María Doussinague, May 8, 1941. Gasset, the first secretary of the consulate, was appointed consul general on May 16, 1941, after Doussinague was made director of the Department of Foreign Policy in the Foreign Ministry.

36. Ibid., Europe 1941, Greece, arch. bibl. leg. 1261, no. 27, letter from the Italian Embassy in Madrid, which carries Gasset's cable, November 1, 1941, and the response by Ramón Serrano Suñer.

37. Ibid., arch. bibl. leg. R-2252, no. 27, letter from Gasset, March 6, 1942, with a letter from Salomon Ezraty, February 25, 1942; ibid., reply from the head of the financial office in the Foreign Ministry, April 8, 1942.

38. See above, n. 35.

39. YV, AA-JM 2218, K-213095, letter from Walter Schellenberg to Geiger in the German Foreign Ministry, June 22, 1943. This letter mentions the names of some of the large contributors. Similar evidence regarding Casset's efforts is discussed in his friend Georg Vogel's memoirs, *Diplomat unter Hitler und Adenauer* (Düsseldorf-Vienna, 1969), p. 97.

40. SFM, I5-E2, cable from Lequerica in Irún, November 8, 1940; ibid., "Informe: Estado en que se encuentra el problema Sefardita," signed Pelayo García y Olay, October 2, 1942. See also Spain, Bureau d'Information Diplomatique, *L'Espagne et les juifs* (Madrid, 1949), p. 21.

41. SFM, I5-E2 (1), cable from Bernardo Rolland, October 24, 1940, no. 880. Spanish policy is quoted in the above García y Olay report from a cable sent on November 9, 1940, no. 637, to Lequerica, and from other documents not attributed.

42. Ibid., letter from the Bordeaux consul, February 26, 1941, no. 52; ibid., note from Jordana to the Director General of Foreign Currency, May 5, 1941. See also CDJC, 75/82, letter from the Administration Department of the German Army Command in France, February 13, 1941. The information is related by Blanke, who connects this Spanish agreement to a direct order from Franco.

43. SFM, Europe 1941, Spain, arch. bibl. leg. R-1260, no. 73, "Repatriación de familias Sefarditas, petición 'Association Culturelle Sephardite de Paris.' "

44. CDJC, 33/79, letter from Rolland, July 31, 1941, to the Commissariat Général aux Questions Juives, and the latter's reply, August 1, 1941.

45. Ibid., 6/127, memorandum, September 14, 1941. Initially, the consulate believed that eleven of its protégés had been imprisoned, but the Germans knew of twenty; it was evident later there were fourteen. See SFM, I5-E2 (1), letter from Rolland, no. 698, September 3, 1941. A note in the margin on September 16 indicates that this matter was under consideration. Ibid., letters from Rolland, October 27, 1941, January 6, 1942, in which he requested instructions and assistance from Lequerica and Ginés Vidal. For the German response, see Christopher Browning, *The Final Solution and the German Foreign Office* (New York, 1978), p. 66.

46. Ibid., letter, no. 417, June 18, 1941; ibid., letter from the border department of the Security Police, July 9, 1941.

47. Ibid., letter from Rolland, September 30, 1941, with a memorandum on "The Problem of the Spanish Nationals in France." See also Baroja, *Los Judíos en la España*, p. 212, who quotes the portion of the memorandum pertaining to the achievements made so far in defending the Jews. It is possible Baroja read Spain, *L'Espagne et les juifs*, pp. 23–24.

48. SFM, Europe, I5-F3, arch. bibl. leg. 1715, no. 21, letter from Rolland, February 20, 1942; ibid., letter from the president of the Spanish Chamber of Commerce in France, February 23, 1942, with a handwritten summary of the requests. See ibid., response of the Foreign Ministry to Lequerica, March 7, 1942.

49. CDJC, 32/180A, reply from Rolland, July 23, 1942, to the letter from the Commissariat Général aux Questions Juives, July 22, 1942.

50. SFM, I5-E2, letter from Manuel del Moral, no. 305, August 19, 1941; Biblioteca Nacional de Madrid, Sección Africa, *Miscelánea García Figueras*, vol. 3, p. 468, memorandum from the High Commissioner in Morocco to Serrano Suñer, October 5, 1941.

51. SFM, I5-E2 (1), letter from García y Olay to del Moral, September

11, 1941; ibid., report from del Moral, December 12, 1941; ibid., letter from Lequerica to Jordana, April 26, 1942; ibid., letter from Lequerica, September 16, 1942.

52. According to Lequerica's proposal, only Jews who were born in Spanish territories before the 1880 Spanish-Moroccan agreement would be considered Spanish citizens; SFM, I5-E2 (1), letter from the High Commissioner in Morocco to Serrano Suñer, asking whether anything had been done, May 21, 1942; ibid., no. 1076, from the High Commissioner of France in Morocco to del Moral, October 4, 1942, and del Moral's letter to Lequerica, October 14, 1942.

53. See above, n. 40.

54. YIVO, ser. 1, Portugal 12/A2, report from HICEM for the period July 1, 1940–December 31, 1941.

55. The following figures are taken from JDC, *Annual Reports: Aiding Jews Overseas* (1940–May 1941, 1941–May 1942); idem., *The Rescue of Jews in a World at War* (1943): (a) During the period June 1940–May 1941, 30,000–40,000 Jews passed through Spain and Portugal (ibid., 1940–May 1941, pp. 16, 23). (b) During the overlapping period January 1941–May 1942, 35,000 refugees passed through Casablanca and the Iberian peninsula to the Western Hemisphere, of whom 23,500 were helped by the JDC (ibid., 1941–May 1942, p. 14). (c) In the months January–May 1941, when 17,000 Jews sailed from all ports of exit to all lands of refuge (ibid., 1940–May 1941, p. 16, table), approximately 4,000 sailed to the Western Hemisphere from the Far East (ibid., 1941–May 1942, pp. 14–15) and another 4,000 reached Palestine through Europe and the Near and Far East, that is, roughly half the total during the entire period of the JDC reports; thus, the number of refugees sailing from the Iberian peninsula during the overlapping five months January–May 1941 was $17,000 - (4,000 + 4,000) = 9,000$. (d) If this number is subtracted from the figures given, $35,000 - 9,000 + (30,000-40,000) = 56,000-66,000$. Deducting the 3,000 refugees known to have sailed from Casablanca, the statistics included in the JDC reports show that between 53,000 and 63,000 refugees crossed Spain and Portugal on their way to safety.

56. One example of such unreliability: a correspondent from the *New York Times* estimated the number of refugees in Lisbon in December 1940 at 8,000 (*AJYB* 43 [1941–42]: 203); the JDC report states that in that month there were 12,000 Jewish refugees there (JDC, *Annual Report* [1940–May 1941], p. 23). See WJC, Portugal, file 4, letter from Augusto d'Esaguy, who claims to have handled 32,000 Jewish refugees from the summer of 1940 until January 1941.

57. An internal report summarizing HICEM's activities from the fall of France until the end of 1941 gives 8,350 refugees who sailed from Portugal after having crossed through Spain; this includes 2,000 who came directly from the Axis countries or from occupied countries through the Trans-Migration project of the JDC. A series of reports sent by HICEM to the Security Police in Portugal, containing complete details of those sailings from Lisbon for which they were responsible, raises this figure to 9,381 by March 31, 1942; two quarterly reports from HICEM Lisbon increase the figure again to approximately 10,500 by the end of September 1942. See YIVO, Portugal 12/2A, report from HICEM, July 1, 1940–December 8, 1941; ibid., ser. 3, file 332, letters from Moses B. Amzalac to the commander of the Security Police in Portugal, which give a total of 1,033 persons; ibid., Portugal 12/A16, reports from HICEM for April–June and July–September 1942.

58. Cf. OHD, 10 (2), second testimony of Joseph Schwartz, p. 4.

59. JDC, *Annual Report* (1941–May 1942), p. 26.

60. Rolland was prompted also to defend the reputation of the Spanish surrealist painter Salvador Dali. On September 9, 1941, during a visit to the anti-Semitic exhibition "Le Juif et la France," organized by the Institut des Etudes des Questions Juives in Paris, Rolland found that Dali was presented as a Jew exercising a decadent influence on French culture. The consul wrote to the organizers of the exhibition that "its organization is praiseworthy, and the documents, pictures, and figures displayed are of great interest and serve the purpose intended," but that Salvador Dali's painting should be replaced with one by a real French Jewish surrealist to avoid insulting Dali. The letter was discovered after the war and was reprinted in *Le Monde Juif* (Paris), August 1946, p. 14. When Rolland wrote this letter he was busy trying to free the prisoners from Drancy; he sent the catalogue of the exhibition to Madrid as part of his reports on the deteriorating situation for Jews in France.

CHAPTER 4

1. Donald A. Lowrie, *The Hunted Children* (New York, 1943), pp. 203–17; Zosa Szajkowski, *Analytical Franco-Jewish Gazetteer, 1939–1945* (New York, 1966), pp. 34–38; Henri Amouroux, *La vie des français sous l'Occupation* (Paris, 1961), pp. 380–425.

2. Amouroux, *La vie des français*, p. 515; Szajkowski, *Franco-Jewish Gazetteer*, p. 76.

3. OHD, 2 (1), Joseph Gabel, pp. 1–2; ibid., 20 (1), first testimony of Andrée Salomon, p. 34, second testimony, p. 21.

4. CDJC, 11/18, "Résumé de mon activité en faveur des juifs persecutés, 1940–1944," also published in *Livre d'or des congregations françaises, 1939–1945* (Paris, 1948), pp. 305–7. See also Arieh L. Bauminger, *Les justes* (Jerusalem, 1971), pp. 33–39.

5. OHD, 20 (1), Salomon, pp. 22–24; ibid., 50 (1), Asher Michaeli, p. 14. See also Ze'ev Kahal, *Barahti mi-tzarfat* [I fled from France], *Davar*, afternoon eds., May 21–July 9, 1944.

6. CZA, L31/9, questionnaires of 154 candidates for immigration, of whom 65 reached Spain between August and the beginning of November 1942. Because the questionnaires contained both the fictitious and real identities of the immigrants, the information is accurate.

7. These figures are according to JDC, General and Emergency Spain 1941–42, an undated memorandum prepared by Samuel Sequerra and sent as an addendum to letter no. 1357 from the JDC in Lisbon to the Executive in New York, ca. October 1942.

8. SFM, Europe 1942–45, arch. bibl. leg. R-1715, no. 14, letter from the Italian Embassy, no. 7062, August 22, 1942, received August 26, 1942. A note in the margin reads, "Procedure: Return." See WJC, Spain, Rescue, letter from Sumner Welles to James A. Wise, August 6, 1942, which constitutes the reply to the appeal by the American Jewish Congress, July 23, 1942. This date proves that the appeal could not have come on the basis of the flight from France, which was begun only later. See also ibid., cable from the American Embassy in Madrid, August 14, 1942.

9. See above, n. 7; JDC, cables from Joseph Schwartz, October 26, 29, November 6, 1942.

10. SFM, I5-E1 (2), letter from Willard L. Beaulac, November 9, 1942. See his *Career Ambassador* (New York, 1951), p. 181.

11. For the history of the intelligence unit that organized and supervised many of these underground networks, written by the man who headed the unit for a long time, see Airey Neave, *Saturday at M.I. 9* (London, 1969).

12. Lowrie, *The Hunted Children*, pp. 103–10; Lucien Steinberg, *La révolte des justes: les juifs contre Hitler, 1943–1945* (Paris, 1970), pp. 243–44.

13. Samuel Hoare, *Complacent Dictator* (New York, 1947), p. 149; Arnold Toynbee, *Survey of International Affairs, 1939–1946: The War and the Neutrals* (Oxford, 1956), pp. 291–92; Ben-Zion Kalisher, *Ba-derekh le-eretz yisrael* [On the way to the Land of Israel] (Tel Aviv, 5705/1945), pp. 156–58. Kalisher describes his flight from Barcelona to Portugal on July 3, 1942, with the aid of the British Consulate in Barcelona and the British Embassy in Madrid. See also OHD, 19 (47), Schwartz, p. 4.

14. Amouroux, *La vie des français*, pp. 104–6; OHD, 78 (1), Msgr. Boyer-Más, p. 6, testifies that in December the entire staff of the cavalry unit stationed in Tarbes fled to Spain, including the two colonels in command.

15. CZA, L31/9, questionnaires of the Schildkraut brothers, ages 18 and 21. The Schildkrauts crossed the border at the end of October 1942, were captured in Figueras, and were returned to Pertuis, France, on November 1; both brothers succeeded in reaching Spain again that same day and secretly arrived at the British Consulate in Barcelona. Many others like them obviously did not try or did not succeed in returning.

16. François Piétri, *Mes années d'Espagne, 1940–1945* (Paris, 1954), pp. 193–95, OHD, 78 (1), Boyer-Más, p. 8. Hoare, *Complacent Dictator*, makes no mention of his intervention in this matter. Carlton J. H. Hayes, *Wartime Mission in Spain, 1942–1945* (New York, 1946), writes that he assisted French refugees in December. John Paul Willson, "Carlton J. H. Hayes in Spain, 1942–1945" (Ph.D. diss., Syracuse University, 1969), p. 220, describes in detail Hayes's activities but does not connect Spain's actions to any intervention by Hayes. All these sources confirm Piétri's evidence.

17. Szajkowski, *Analytical Franco-Jewish Gazetteer*, p. 148, map of France 1940–44, indicating the areas from which Jews were deported; Amouroux, *La vie des français*, p. 105; Neave, *Saturday at M.I. 9*, p. 151.

18. U.S., Department of State, *Foreign Relations of the United States, Diplomatic Papers 1943*, vol. 1, general (Washington, 1963), p. 276, cable from Hayes, March 29, 1943, containing a summary of the letter from the Spanish Foreign Ministry, no. 182, March 25, 1943; ibid., p. 290, aide-mémoire from the British Embassy of a conversation between Winston Churchill and the Duke of Alba, April 16, 1943; ibid., p. 298, report from the U.S. State Department on a conversation with Ambassador Juan F. Cárdenas in Washington, May 5, 1943.

19. Ibid., cable from Hayes, April 8, 1943, regarding an oral promise made by Francisco Gomez Jordana on April 1; cf. Hoare, *Complacent Dictator*, p. 318, memorandum on the conversation between Hans Dieckhoff and General Franco, December 15, 1943, in which Dieckhoff said that Spain had not acquiesced to Germany's request in the matter of French refugees. See also OHD, 78 (1),

Boyer-Más, p. 8, who provides evidence of expulsions beyond the border; M. Fluch (the former Mme. Guérin), *La Résistance à Pau: passages des Pyrénées* (Pau, 1944), p. 59, testimony concerning a Jewish woman captured at the border and returned to France in May 1944.

20. U.S., *Foreign Relations 1943*, p. 250, cable from Hayes to U.S. Secretary of State Cordell Hull, January 4, 1943; ibid., p. 260, cable from Hayes, February 15, 1943, according to which the Spanish government agreed to the departure of the French refugees from its soil.

21. Piétri, *Mes années d'Espagne*, pp. 196–99, concerning his removing 200 refugees on February 27, 1943, to North Africa; OHD, 78 (1), Boyer-Más, p. 8, confirms this. Piétri's relations with Boyer-Más were still intact at the time (Piétri, *Mes années d'Espagne*, p. 199, still mentions him as one of his confidants on February 27), but he later tried—unsuccessfully—to have Boyer-Más and his colleagues expelled from Spain.

22. OHD, 3 (1), Giora Szenes, p. 9; ibid., 35 (1), Sequerra, pp. 16–17, the story of a refugee who declared his name was Adolf Hitler, hoping to spread the rumor that Hitler had fled to Spain.

23. AFSC, Spain, file 2, letter from Knut Behr (a Polish prisoner in the camp), January 5, 16, 1943; ibid., file 1, report of a meeting in the JDC office in Lisbon with Florian Piskowski, a member of the American Polish Relief Council, February 5, 1942. According to these sources, the strike was started by the Poles, who then were joined by the other prisoners. See also OHD, 2 (1), Gabel, p. 6, then in the Polish group.

24. OHD, 35 (1), Sequerra, pp. 9–11; CZA, L31/9, immigration question-naires of nineteen women who arrived on different dates after November 11, 1942. These sources contain no further information on the imprisonment of women after January 1943.

25. U.S., *Foreign Relations 1943*, p. 263, message from Hayes to Hull, March 8, September 28, 1943. See also Toynbee, *Survey of International Affairs*, p. 292; cf. OHD, 78 (1), Boyer-Más, p. 11; AFSC, Spain 1943, file 1, memorandum from Landsberger, October 15, 1943.

26. U.S., *Foreign Relations 1943*, p. 301, letter from Hayes, May 13, 1943, which reveals his suspicions concerning England's desire to stop dealing with the Canadians; ibid., p. 308, extract of memorandum from the British Foreign Office, May 15, 1943, which summarizes the evacuation of British, Belgian, and Dutch subjects from Spain. See also OHD, 31 (1), Avraham Pach, p. 15, who tells of having received a passport and visa for Curaçao.

27. JDC, Spain 1943, report no. 6, Sequerra, addendum to general letter 312 of the JDC Lisbon to New York, July 8, 1943, p. 3.

28. AFSC, Spain, file 1, letter from David Blickenstaff to Philip Conard, August 23, 1943; report from Blickenstaff to the AFSC Lisbon, October 16, 1943. The problem of financing the support of the refugees was a permanent feature in Hayes's letters to the U.S. State Department; see U.S., *Foreign Relations 1943*, pp. 267, 269, passim. Support for the prisoners while they were imprisoned in camp cost five pesetas per day per person; their support while in pensions in assigned residences cost twenty-five pesetas per day per person.

29. Steinberg, *La révolte des justes*, pp. 139–48, 243–44. Thérèse Mitrani, *Service d'évasion* (Paris, 1946), is the account of a Jewish woman who, with her

husband, was active in the Underground in the south of France; Major Victor Gerson is mentioned. Jean-Pierre Bloch, a socialist member of the French parliament and later a cabinet minister, tells how Gerson saved him from prison; see Jean-Pierre Bloch, *Le vent souffle sur l'histoire* (Paris, 1956), pp. 233–36.

30. OHD, 28 (1), Alfred Fraenkel, p. 6; ibid., 31 (1), Pach, p. 17, testifies about a group of Dutchmen (including three or four Jews) who left Spain through Gibraltar on August 14, 1944.

31. OHD, 6 (1), Joseph Fischer (Ariel), p. 1; ibid., 10 (1), Shimon Hammel, p. 1. Concerning the Boy Scout instructors who passed through Spain, see *L'activité des organisations juives en France sous l'Occupation* (Paris, 1947), pp. 61, 67; Jacques Lazarus, *Juifs au combat* (Paris, 1947), p. 17. For the flight of Pierre Dreyfus Schmidt and other Jews in November 1943, see Amouroux, *La vie des français*, pp. 97–100.

32. WJC, Portugal, file 1, signed testimony by Avram Sjeshak in Lisbon, August 6, 1943; OHD, 1 (1), Yehuda Ansbacher, pp. 8–16; YV, testimony 01/76, Ansbacher, pp. 1–4. Amouroux, *La vie des français*, pp. 95–102, relates several instances of the dangers that confronted refugees from smugglers and other go-betweens: the intermediary in Paris who murdered several refugees after they paid him for their transport to Spain, the smuggler who killed one refugee on the road because he was unable to continue the journey, another smuggler who guided escapees directly into the hands of the German border patrol, and a smuggler who extorted extra payments en route. Books about the flight to Spain contain testimonies of hundreds of similar incidents. See, for example, Lucien Greffier, *La mésaventure espagnole* (Paris, 1946).

33. OHD, 3 (1), Szenes, p. 2. This witness, brother of Hannah Szenes, used the connections of a leader of one of the Zionist youth organizations with some people in Perpignan; they made the connection with the smuggler, who later abandoned the group while they were still on French soil. See CZA, file L31/9, questionnaires of the candidates for immigration.

34. Szajkowski, *Analytical Franco-Jewish Gazetteer*, pp. 25, 93, on anti-Semitism in official circles and in the Polish army in France; OHD, 35 (1), Sequerra, p. 12, on a confrontation with the chief of the Polish mission in Madrid, who also headed the Polish Red Cross; AFSC, Spain 1943, file 1, report of the meeting between the representatives of the welfare organizations (AJDC, AFSC, Unitarians) in Lisbon and Florian Piskowski, February 5, 1943; ibid., open acknowledgment to the effect that the Poles consider Polish Jews as a separate group.

35. OHD, 28 (1), Fraenkel, p. 6; ibid., 26 (1), Yigal (Kurt) Benjamin, p. 15.

36. OHD, 2 (1), Gabel, p. 6; ibid., 1 (1), Ansbacher, p. 19; AFSC, Spain 1943, file 1, report from Miranda de Ebro, September 21, 1943; YIVO, Portugal 12, file 17A, report from James Bernstein and Rafael Spanien to the Executive in New York, November 8, 1943, with the letter from Roger Lachowetzki and Jean-Jacques O'Lery to the Free France representative in Barcelona, September 16, 1943.

37. OHD, 19 (47), Schwartz, interview, October 24, 1967, pp. 5–7; Conard, who visited Sequerra in October 1943, expressed his gratitude for the success of his activities (AFSC, Spain 1943, file 5, report of November 20, 1943, p. 12); OHD, 35 (1), Samuel and Joel Sequerra on their activities. Until June 1943 the JDC continued to pay its protégés in Madrid through Moshe Eizen; see AFSC, Spain 1943, file 1, report from Blickenstaff, August 23, 1943.

38. AFSC, Spain 1943, file 5, summary report from Conard, November 20, 1943; ibid., Spain, 1944, file 1, letter from Hayes to Hull, January 24, 1944, containing a report on Blickenstaff's activities; YIVO, ser. 3, file 418, letter from Blickenstaff to all the organizations, July 26, 1944, containing the breakdown of the portion of each of them in the administrative budget of his office. Blickenstaff's activities were outlined and supervised by Ambassador Hayes and his aides, Willard L. Beaulac and Niles W. Bond, all of whom regarded the problems of the stateless refugees as insignificant. See WRB, box 71, report of James Mann to John W. Pehle on his visit to Madrid, August 30, 1944, pp. 71–83.

39. CZA, S25/5207, letter from M. Shertok to L. K. Pinkerton, November 21, 1942. For Wilfrid Israel and his work, see H. G. Reisner, "The Histories of the Kaufhaus N. Israel and of Wilfrid Israel," *LBI* 3 (1958): 227–56; remarks on this article, ibid. 6 (1959): 335. For Fritz Lichtenstein's work, see Peretz Leshem, "Rescue Efforts in the Iberian Peninsula," ibid. 14 (1969): 231–56; OHD, 33 (1), five testimonies of Lichtenstein.

40. U.S., *Foreign Relations 1943*, p. 284, letter from Hull to Hayes, April 6, 1943, in which he mentions a conversation with Sir Ronald Campbell, British chargé d'affaires, on March 24, 1943, three weeks before the Bermuda Conference; ibid., pp. 176, 295, 296, 299.

41. Ibid., p. 179, memorandum from Franklin D. Roosevelt to Hull, May 14, 1943.

42. Ibid., p. 309, memorandum of a conversation between Breckinridge Long and Campbell, June 4, 1943; ibid., p. 319, memorandum from Long to Hull, June 29, 1943.

43. Ibid., p. 307, memorandum from Welles, May 27, 1943; ibid., p. 313, memorandum of a conversation between Hull and Campbell, June 17, 1943; ibid., p. 321, cable from the British Embassy, June 30, 1943, containing Churchill's cable no. 339 of the same day to Roosevelt.

44. Ibid., pp. 322–25.

45. Ibid., pp. 297–98, 311, 332, 339.

46. Ibid., pp. 359, 367, 375.

47. OHD, 33 (1), second testimony of Lichtenstein, p. 6; YIVO, Spain 12, file 14, report from Spanien on his visit to Spain at the end of February 1944; ibid., file 16, summary report from Blickenstaff, December 27, 1943.

48. AFSC, Spain 1943, file 5, report from Howard Wriggins, January 27, 1943, on telephone conversation with Blickenstaff; ibid., report from Conard, November 20, 1943, p. 7; YIVO, Portugal 12/17A, letter from HICEM Lisbon, November 8, 1943.

49. Canada agreed to accept 500 refugees (JDC, *JDC in 1944* [1944], p. 9) and to see that regulations for selection were implemented. YIVO, ser. 3, file 659, memorandum of discussion with the Canadian official, November 10, 1943.

50. OHD, 3 (1), Szenes, p. 5, regarding this manner of release; the entire system is exemplified by the instance of one Jew who, on June 23 and 30, 1943, asked Blickenstaff's office to expedite the handling of stateless refugees. When he did not receive satisfaction, his wife, who was already in Madrid, applied to the Belgian consul and requested his assistance. Two weeks later her husband was freed through intervention from the Belgians and joined the rest of the stateless refugees in Madrid. See CZA, L31/3, L31/9, immigration questionnaire no. 79.

51. AFSC, Spain 1943, file 5, extracts and summary of report from Conard,

Madrid, November 20, 1943, p. 12. Conard accompanied Blickenstaff during his visit and testifies that Blickenstaff wanted to free 27 prisoners after he had secured the release of 500 refugees. CZA, L32/9, letter from Lichtenstein to Crosswell, the representative from the British Embassy, June 6, 1944, on the refusal of the authorities to free 29 candidates for emigration to Palestine. See also YIVO, ser. 3, Spain 12, file 9, report on the visit of Blickenstaff and his wife to the north of Spain, August 18–23, 1944.

52. AFSC, Spain 1943, file 1, letter from Blickenstaff, November 8, 1943; ibid., letter from the commander of the Nunclares de la Oca camp, on stationery bearing the heading "Dirección General de Seguridad, Campo de Concentración Detenidos, Nunclares." See YIVO, ser. 2, Spain 12, file 9, report of Blickenstaff on his visit to the north of Spain, August 1944; Blickenstaff writes that one prisoner, an anti-Nazi German who was arrested at the entrance to the American Embassy, was beaten by the wardens under orders from the Gestapo. Ibid., Blickenstaff's description of the condition of the refugees imprisoned in the Vitoria prison.

53. Ibid., on Blickenstaff's visit to Leiza and the discussion regarding the transfer of the refugees to Madrid. See OHD, 14 (1), Israel Salomon, p. 4.

54. For the efforts of the welfare groups and complaints regarding some of their ill effects, see JDC, General and Emergency Spain, report no. 8, Sequerra, addendum to letter no. 312 of JDC Lisbon to New York, August 7, 1943. This is confirmed also by Lichtenstein (CZA, Immigration Department files, file 3874, letter from Lichtenstein in Barcelona to Linton, December 25, 1943), as well as by one of the refugees (OHD, 13 [1], Shlomo Steinhorn, pp. 22–23, 27).

55. U.S., *Foreign Relations 1943*, p. 332, letter from Hull to Robert D. Murphy in Algiers, July 27, 1943.

56. CZA, L31/7, summary sent by Wilfrid Israel to Hoare, May 22, 1943.

57. YIVO, ser. 2, Spain 12, file 3, report from Spanien, December 1943, with letter from Bernstein to New York, January 17, 1944.

58. YV, 01/76, Ansbacher testimony, 1944. Although it is possible this evidence was based on Spanien's estimate, the figures were acceptable to Ansbacher, who was closer to the events both in time and place.

59. YIVO, ser. 3, file 702, correspondence during 1942–44 regarding JDC assistance, including detailed statistics and the budget required to support these refugees. See U.S., *Foreign Relations 1943*, p. 358, letter from the U.S. consul in Algiers to Hull, September 29, 1943, containing the request by the Dutch consul in Casablanca to accommodate 1,500 Dutch refugees temporarily in the Lyautey camp.

60. OHD, 78 (1), Boyer-Más, p. 16, who testifies that he assisted 23,315 French refugees. For the extent of the escape from France throughout the war, see Amouroux, *La vie des français*, pp. 112–13. For the extent of the rescue of Allied soldiers, see Neave, *Saturday at M.I. 9*, pp. 20–22.

61. At the meeting of the Executive of the Jewish Agency in Jerusalem on September 29, 1944, Eliyahu Dobkin, reporting on his visit to Spain and Portugal, stated that 3,000 refugees arrived in Spain in the months January–August 1944; see CZA, minutes of meeting, September 29, 1944. Dobkin's estimate, based on his impressions only, may be taken to indicate the importance of this escape.

62. See Haim Avni, "The Zionist Underground in Holland and France and

the Escape to Spain," *Rescue Attempts during the Holocaust: Proceedings of the Second Yad Vashem International Historical Conference* (Jerusalem, 1977), pp. 555–602.

CHAPTER 5

1. SFM, I5-E2 (1), Europe no. 754, letter from Bernardo Rolland to Francisco Gomez Jordana, October 6, 1942; ibid., letter from Gategno to Rolland, October 2, 1942, attached to the "research," a sixteen-page pamphlet. See also Henri Amouroux, *La vie des français sous l'Occupation* (Paris, 1961), pp. 416–17. Zosa Szajkowski, *Analytical Franco-Jewish Gazetteer, 1939–1945* (New York, 1966), p. 31, notes similar undertakings by other Jewish groups.

2. YIVO, ser. 2, France 2, file 169, memorandum, October 7, 1942; ibid., letter from HICEM Marseille to Samuel Sequerra, October 29, 1942, asking him to examine the veracity of the rumor.

3. SFM, I5-E2, "Informe: estado en que se encuentra el problema Sefardita," signed Pelayo García y Olay, October 2, 1942.

4. Ibid., letter from Rolland, politica no. 942, December 14, 1942; ibid., letter from the Spanish consul in Marseille, judiciales no. 569, December 17, 1942.

5. *Les Cahiers Sefardis*, November 5, 1946, p. 4; ibid., January 7, 1947, p. 85.

6. YV, documents of the Adolf Eichmann trial, prosecution document 142, Heinz Röthke report, September 1, 1942; ibid., document 9.

7. YV, AA-JM 2298, K-2130670, letter from Franz Rademacher to Hans-Adolf von Moltke, March 10, 1943; ibid., cable from Günther Altenburg, April 6, 1943.

8. Ibid., AA-JM 2263, K-349351.

9. Ibid., K-349468, announcement from Otto Hunsche (Department IVB4b), August 26, 1943.

10. Ibid., K-349497, letter from Eberhardt von Thadden to the German Embassy in Paris, June 19, 1943, stating that Germany should ask Sweden to rescind the citizenship it had recently granted to many Norwegian Jews.

11. Ibid., K-349629, letter from José Rojas y Moreno, no. 313, March 25, 1944; ibid., cable from Manfred von Killinger, no. 1855, May 31, 1944; ibid., letter from Rolf Günther (Jewish Office of the Gestapo), May 31, 1944; ibid., memorandum from von Thadden, June 13, 1944.

12. Ibid., K-349447, internal memorandum from von Thadden, July 23, 1943; ibid., K-349381, two drafts for Eichmann, one signed by Horst Wagner, the other by von Thadden, August 17, 1943; ibid., JM-2218, K-213150, draft of letter to Hans Dieckhoff, December 27, 1943; ibid., JM-2263, no. E-510565, cable to von Killinger, June 14, 1944.

13. Ibid., AA-JM 2218, K-213058, cable from von Moltke, February 24, 1943; SFM, I5-E2 (2), letter from Rolland to Jordana, February 10, 1943; ibid., letter from the Spanish Embassy in Berlin to Rolland, February 19, 1943.

14. Ibid., cable, March 18, 1943.

15. Carlton J. H. Hayes, *Wartime Mission in Spain, 1942–1945* (New York, 1946), pp. 123–24; U.S., Department of State, *Foreign Relations of the United States, Diplomatic Papers 1944*, vol. 1, general (Washington, 1963), p. 998, letter from Hayes to Cordell Hull, February 28, 1944. Hayes summarizes his proposals

to the War Refugee Board, of which one was to persuade the Spanish to reach a similar agreement with the Germans for rescuing additional groups of Jews. Philip Conard, who visited Madrid at the end of 1943, knew that the Sephardic refugees were Spanish nationals or full citizens. It is thus very difficult to assume that what was known to a visitor was unknown to the ambassador. See AFSC, Spain 1943, file 6, sections of Conard's report on Spain, November 20, 1943, p. 5. Hayes's sympathetic and often apologetic position toward Franco Spain is evident in his memoirs as well as in his book, *The United States and Spain: An Interpretation* (New York, 1951). John P. Willson, however, in "Spain and the Refugee Crisis: 1942–1945" (*American Jewish Quarterly* 62 [December 1972]: 106) attributes to Hayes himself the initiative for the rescue of Spanish Jews, quoting a memorandum written by Willard L. Beaulac in January 1944 in the wake of the dispute concerning the activities of the War Refugee Board.

16. Samuel Hoare, *Complacent Dictator* (New York, 1947), p. 233.

17. SFM, I5-E2 (2), letter from Rolland to Ginés Vidal, February 23, 1943; ibid., letter from Vidal to Jordana, February 26, 1943; YV, AA-JM 2218, K-213006, cable from the German Embassy in Madrid, March 6, 1943.

18. SFM, I5-E2 (2), letters from Vidal, February 26, March 5, 1943.

19. Ibid., letter from Rolland, February 19, 1943, with petition, February 15, 1943.

20. Ibid., letter from Rolland, February 26, 1943; ibid., letter from the Spanish Bureau of Commerce in Paris, no. 555 PM-RA, February 26, 1943.

21. CZA, KKL5B, file 246, letter from the Jewish National Fund in Jerusalem to Rabbi Yehuda Leon Halfon in Tétouan, April 9, 1930, announcing the inscriptions in the JNF Gold Book "of the names of the noblemen, the duke from the House of Jordana and Don Diego Saavedra."

22. SFM, I5-E2 (2), March 18, 1943.

23. Hayes, *Wartime Mission*, p. 123; SFM, I5-E2 (2), note from José María Doussinague to Carreño, March 22, 1943; ibid., letter from David Blickenstaff, March 24, 1943; OHD, 35 (1), Sequerra, pp. 20–21.

24. YV, AA-JM 2218, K-213075, note from the Spanish Embassy in Berlin, March 22, 1943.

25. SFM, I5-E2 (2), cable from Jordana, no. 204, April 2, 1943; ibid., letter from José Pan de Soraluce to Rolland, April 10, 1943, informing him that, under Jordana's orders, Ricardo Sadacca Bitti, who had not been registered according to the Primo de Rivera decree, could not be considered a Spanish citizen. "You may apply this rule to all similar cases that arise in the future."

26. Ibid., letter from Vidal to Jordana, no. 245, April 3, 1943; ibid., letter from Conde de Toronton, chargé d'affaires in Berlin, to the Foreign Ministry in Madrid, no. 370, May 29, 1943, referring to cable no. 249 from Madrid as the authorization for their entry into Spain; ibid., letter from Alfonso Fiscovich, judiciales no. 405, May 29, 1943.

27. Ibid., letter from Fiscovich to Ramón Serrano Suñer, Europe no. 72, March 18, 1942.

28. Ibid., cable from Jordana, no. 204, April 2, 1943; letter from Doussinague to the director of the Security Police, no. 587, May 6, 1943.

29. SFM, I5-E2 (2), report from the director of the Security Police, including the list of names of those who arrived on May 10 and June 28, 1943; YV, AA-JM

2263, K-349497, letter from the Spanish Embassy in Berlin, no. 652, June 2, 1943; ibid., cable from Rudolf Schleier in the German Embassy in Paris, June 18, 1943, and the reply from von Thadden, June 19, 1943.

30. JDC, Spain 1943, report from E. Canetti in Zaragoza, August 18, 1943.

31. SFM, I5-E2, letter from Doussinague to German Baraibar, August 13, 1943; CZA, L31/7, copy of letter from the Spanish Foreign Ministry, no. 1162, to Blickenstaff, August 16, 1943.

32. Ibid., report of Paul Block on his travels on September 28–29 and October 5–7, 1943.

33. CDJC, 36/76, letter from the Foreign Minister of the Vichy government to the Commissariat aux Questions Juives, with a list of forty-two Spanish nationals, October 11, 1943. See YIVO, Portugal 12/A17, letter from HICEM, which confirms the arrival of forty-five refugees, November 8, 1943.

34. SFM, I5-E2 (2), list of seventy-three Spanish Jews from France planning to leave from Málaga for North Africa on December 10, signed December 6, 1943. See also OHD, 78 (1), Msgr. Boyer-Más, p. 14.

35. For the fate of those mobilized, see JDC, Spain 1943, report from Canetti on the arrival of the seventy-nine Spanish Jews from France, August 18, 1943; YV, AA-JM 2218, K-213150, personal letter from Hayes to Jordana, December 8, 1943, in German translation and with a letter from the German Embassy, December 29, 1943; SFM, I5-E2 (2), letter from Jordana to Carlos Asensio, stating that the twenty-five mobilized refugees and their families who had arrived in August 1943 were allowed to remain in Spain temporarily, December 28, 1943; WRB, box 71, letter from Blickenstaff to Boyer-Más, December 7, 1943.

36. YV, AA-JM 2263, K-349537, Spanish note, December 6, 1943; ibid., AA-JM 2218, K-213136, November 27, 1943, report of the conversation between von Thadden and the secretary of the Spanish Embassy in Berlin, December 27, 1943; ibid., K-213156, cable from Wagner, December 27, 1943; ibid., K-213155, letter from von Thadden, January 6, 1944.

37. SFM, I5-E2 (4), report from Fiscovich, no. 495, July 17, 1944.

38. Federico Ysart, *España y los Judíos en la Segunda Guerra Mundial* (Barcelona, 1973), pp. 205–23, documents the actions of the Spanish consul in Nice, Alejandro Pons, on behalf of Pedro and Matilda Rosanes, who (according to their daughter) voluntarily relinquished the opportunity to cross into Spain. They were arrested by the Germans on October 22, 1943, and transferred to Drancy, and their property was looted by the police. Pons and Lequerica intervened, and they were freed and included in the group destined to leave from Paris. See also Michel Borwicz, *Vies interdites* (Paris, 1969), pp. 229–37, the story of the Polish Jew Shmuel Skornicki, who worked in the Spanish Consulate in Sainte-Étienne under the alias Santos Montero Sanchez, at first as an aide to the consul and later as the consul himself.

39. Ysart, *España y los Judíos*, pp. 111–12, quoting the petition of March 9, 1943.

40. SFM, I5-E2 (2), permission for forty-five Jews to enter Spain on October 1, 1943; CZA, L32/9, letter from Fritz Lichtenstein, June 6, 1944; ibid., L32/32, memorandum of second meeting with Baraibar, July 14, 1944.

41. For a summary of the process of destruction, see Michael Molkho and Joseph Nehamah, *Shoat yehudei yavan, 1941–1944* [The destruction of Greek Jewry, 1941–1944] (Jerusalem, 5724/1964), pp. 60–100.

42. Ibid., photograph 5, order from Max Marten, commander of the German army in the Salonika area, to the Jewish community, February 6, 1943.

43. Ysart, *España y los Judíos*, pp. 64–70, passim, quotations from Schönburg's letter (the German consul-general in Salonika) and from Eduardo Gasset's testimony.

44. YV, AA-JM 2218, K-213078, cable from Wagner, April 30, 1943; SFM, I5-E2 (2), note from the German Embassy in Madrid, no. 1099/43, April 30, 1943, received in the European Department May 12, 1943.

45. Ibid., letter from Sebastian Romero Radigales to Jordana, April 15, 1943, thanking him for his transfer to Athens, which was a "lifesaver" to his aged mother-in-law. The devotion Radigales showed in his struggle on behalf of the Spanish Jews under his protection might have come from family connections with Greek Jews.

46. Ibid., cable from Radigales sent through the Italian and German embassies; YV, AA-JM 2218, K-213080, cable from Altenburg, April 30, 1943.

47. Ysart, *España y los Judíos*, pp. 66–67, testimony of Raul Saporta, who was deported to Auschwitz on April 7, 1943; ibid., appeal by Radigales. See SFM, I5-E2 (2), list of the deportees and dates of their transport.

48. YV, AA-JM 2263, K-349417, K-349431, cables from Altenburg, June 5, July 7, 1943; ibid., K-349441, Spanish note no. 859, July 14, 1943.

49. Ibid., K-349423, cable from Altenburg, June 12, 1943; ibid., K-349420, memorandum from von Thadden to his superiors; SFM, I5-E2 (2), report no. 9 from Radigales, June 9, 1943.

50. Ibid., K-349435–7, cable from Altenburg, July 10, 1943; ibid., K-349380, cable from von Thadden, July 15, 1943; ibid., K-349442, cable from Altenburg, July 17, 1943.

51. Ibid., AA-JM 2218, K-213099, cable from Heberlein to Altenburg containing the cable from Vidal to Radigales, July 16, 1943.

52. Ibid., K-349444, memorandum from von Thadden, July 23, 1943; ibid., K-349445, report of von Thadden's conversation with Serrat of the Spanish Embassy.

53. Ibid., AA-JM 2218, K-213122–5, cable from Altenburg, July 26, 1943; ibid., AA-JM 2263, K-349380, letter from von Thadden to Eichmann, July 28, 1943.

54. Molkho and Nehamah, *Shoat yehudei yavan*, pp. 92–93; Ysart, *España y los Judíos*, pp. 84–85, testimony of Father Typaldos, who served as secretary of the Spanish Embassy in Athens for twenty-five years.

55. See above, n. 51.

56. Ysart, *España y los Judíos*, pp. 79–80, instructions from Jordana to Vidal, August 5, 1943, and similar instructions conveyed by Doussinague to Baraibar, asking him to handle the matter of repatriation personally. Ysart's attempt to connect Spain's hesitation in accepting Jewish nationals with the German plan to conquer Gibraltar is groundless; according to his own account, these plans were eventually scrapped more than a month before Spain dissociated itself from its Jewish nationals in Salonika.

57. SFM, I5-E2 (2), cable from Vidal, August 12, 1943; YV, AA-JM 2218, K-213124, cable from von Thadden to the German Embassy in Madrid, August 13, 1943; ibid., K-213103, Spanish note no. 1103, August 31, 1943.

58. Ibid., K-349527, Spanish letter no. 1406, December 9, 1943.

59. One member of the group died on the way to Bergen-Belsen, and another died in the camp, reducing the number of survivors to 365. CZA, L32/36, list of the 575 who left for North Africa on June 21, 1944.

60. SFM, I5-E2 (4), letter from Radigales, July 14, 1944, stating that after 155 Spanish nationals were deported from Athens to Bergen-Belsen another 80 still remained. YV, AA-JM 2263, K-349466, cable from von Thadden to the German Embassy in Athens, September 1943. See also Ysart, *España y los Judíos*, pp. 87–88.

61. YV, AA-JM 2263, K-349408, note from von Thadden to the Spanish Embassy in Berlin, September 1, 1943, including the cable from Radigales on August 31, 1943; ibid., K-349513, note from the Spanish Embassy in Berlin, September 30, 1943, containing the cable and requesting that it be conveyed to Radigales in Athens.

62. Molkho and Nehamah, *Shoat yehudei yavan*, pp. 138, 148; YV, AA-JM 2218, K-213152, cable from the German Embassy in Athens to the German Foreign Ministry, November 5, 1943.

63. Ibid., AA-JM 2263, K-349546-7, Spanish note no. 1440, December 21, 1943; ibid., prosecution documents in the Eichmann trial, no. 105, Eichmann's letter of November 15, 1943.

64. Molkho and Nehamah, *Shoat yehudei yavan*, pp. 153–54. See *JC*, September 12, 1969, containing material on the extermination of the Jewish community of Yanina on March 25, 1944.

65. SFM, I5-E2 (4), letters from Radigales, July 14, September 30, 1944. Radigales saw to the lodging of several people hiding in a hotel whose Jewish owners were deported. Molkho and Nehamah, *Shoat yehudei yavan*, p. 145, point out that some—it is not known how many—Spanish nationals were among those who managed to reach Turkey on their own.

66. YV, AA-JM 2263, K-349601, Spanish note no. 361, April 11, 1944. See CZA, L32/9, letter from Fritz Lichtenstein to Crosswell at the British Embassy in Madrid, June 6, 1944.

67. SFM, I5-E2 (3), cable from the Foreign Ministry to Vidal, July 10, 1944. See OHD, 40 (1), Eliyahu Dobkin, p. 2; CZA, L32/32, cable from Lichtenstein and Dobkin to Jerusalem, July 15, 1944. Because they did not know the exact number of prisoners in Bergen-Belsen, their cable mentions 180 people.

68. YV, AA-JM 2263, K-349705, letter from von Thadden to Eichmann, July 14, 1944. See CZA, Immigration Department, file 3874, cable from Eliyahu Dobkin to the Immigration Department in Jerusalem, August 16, 1944.

69. SFM, I5-E2 (4), copy of the cable from Sequerra to Blickenstaff, August 25, 1944; ibid., letter from Salomon Ezraty to the Spanish Foreign Ministry, September 11, 1944; ibid., memorandum from the American Embassy in Madrid, November 15, 1944.

70. Molkho and Nehamah, *Shoat yehudei yavan*, p. 221.

71. SFM, I5-E2 (1), letter from Rolland to Vidal, no. 28, April 29, 1943, stating that of the approximately 250 Spanish nationals whose permits he was handling nearly 100 had fled to Vichy France. Some of the refugees who survived in Vichy apparently had come from Paris, a fact that further limited the number of those who had been rescued among the 1,000 Spanish nationals and protégés living in Vichy at the beginning of the war. See CDJC, 6/127, report from the German Embassy in Paris, September 14, 1941, showing that although the Spanish Embassy

claimed it had 2,000 nationals, only 304 were registered with the police. It is possible that had Spain demanded the rescue of all its Jewish nationals it would have had to fight for them, but Spain's policy kept the Germans from opposing the rescue attempt. In view of this, Ysart's contention (*España y los Judíos*, p. 101) that the number of Spanish nationals in France was originally 637 and increased to 2,000 during the period 1941–44 is untenable.

72. See above, n. 62, based on statistics from the census of Spanish nationals kept in the embassy in Athens.

73. Also included in the tally of the groups from France were the thirty-six refugees who may have reached Spain in August 1944. See YIVO, ser. 2, Lisbon 1, file 156, list of Spanish Jews who were in Spain in October 1943, prepared by Rafael Spanien. The Spanish nationals who reached Spain by July 1943 were included, as well as those whose date of entry was not listed. This list accurately reflects the number of those refugees who reached Spain; because it does not include very wealthy or marginal Jews, the estimate may be increased slightly.

CHAPTER 6

1. Raul Hilberg, *The Destruction of the European Jews* (Chicago, 1961), pp. 473–80.

2. SFM, Europe, 1940–41, Yugoslavia nacionales, arch. bibl. leg. 1344, no. 33, notes from the Spanish Legation in Belgrade, including the names of Spanish nationals in Skopje, October 30, November 13, November 30, 1940.

3. SFM, I5-E2, (2), letter from Julio Palencia y Álvarez to Francisco Gomez Jordana, no. 257, September 14, 1942.

4. Ibid., letters from Palencia, March 17, May 20, 1943.

5. YV, AA-JM 2218, K-213079, cable from Adolf Beckerle to the German Foreign Ministry, May 28, 1943.

6. Ibid., K-213120, cable from Beckerle, June 16, 1943.

7. Ibid., K-213113, cable from Eberhardt von Thadden to the German Embassy in Madrid, August 14, 1943; ibid., K-213107, cable from Beckerle, August 26, 1943.

8. Palencia's fate after his return to Spain is related by his colleague, José Rojas y Moreno. See Federico Ysart, *España y los Judíos en la Segunda Guerra Mundial* (Barcelona, 1973), pp. 121–22; Ysart's description of the event does not tally in several places with the documents of the German Foreign Ministry.

9. SFM, I5-E2 (3), note from Ginés Vidal to Jordana, October 25, 1943. Ysart, *España y los Judíos*, p. 123, claims that most of the Spanish nationals from Bulgaria reached Spain; this is not confirmed by other sources, however.

10. YV, AA-JM 2263, K-349624, note from the Spanish Embassy in Berlin, March 25, 1944; ibid., K-349431, letter from Rolf Günther in the RSHA to von Thadden, May 31, 1944.

11. Ibid., K-349636, memorandum from von Thadden, June 13, 1944; ibid., K-349637, cable from von Thadden to Rojas, June 14, 1944.

12. Ysart, *España y los Judíos*, p. 132. No sources are given.

13. Hilberg, *European Jews*, pp. 509–54. For an account of the rescue of the Jews of Hungary, see Jenö Lévai, "Die Vernichtung der Juden in Ungarn" [The

destruction of the Jews of Hungary], *Fourth World Congress of Jewish Studies*, vol. 2 (Jerusalem, 1968), pp. 3–13; idem, "Aus welchen Gründen überlebte das Budapester Ghetto als einziges die Ausrottung" [Some reasons the Budapest Ghetto survived destruction], *Fifth World Congress of Jewish Studies*, vol. 2 (Jerusalem, 1972), pp. 99–115.

14. See Ysart, *España y los Judíos*, pp. 134–41.

15. SFM, I5-E2 (4), appeal from the heads of the communities in Tétouan and Tangier, May 22, 1944; ibid., exchange of letters on the same matter. See also OHD, 79 (1), Moshe Edrei, pp. 6–7, on people of Hungarian origin in Tangier. For Angel Sanz Briz's activities in screening candidates for rescue, see the report sent from the German Embassy in Budapest to Günther and von Thadden, October 24, 1944, in Randolph L. Braham, *The Destruction of Hungarian Jewry: A Documentary Account*, vol. 2 (New York, 1963), p. 756.

16. SFM, I5-E2 (4), note from the American Embassy, November 14, 1944.

17. Ibid., note from the British Embassy, no. 912, July 18, 1944, and the reply from the Spanish Foreign Ministry, July 22, 1944; ibid., appeals from the American Embassy, July 25, 1944, and the Spanish response, August 2, 1944.

18. Ibid., memorandum from the American Embassy, July 22, 1944, and U.S. notes no. 2908, August 11, 1944, no. 3012, August 30, 1944; ibid., note from the British Embassy, no. 1051, August 18, 1944, and the Spanish response, September 16, 1944. Marginalia in each of the notes disclose the fact that the Germans did not consent to the Jews' leaving.

19. Ibid., report and letters from Sanz Briz, July 24, July 29, August 26, 1944.

20. See Jenö Lévai, *L'eglise ne s'est pas tué* (Paris, 1966), pp. 21–48; SFM, I5-E2 (2), report from Sanz Briz on the meeting of the ambassadors.

21. See Sanz Briz's testimony in Isaac R. Molkho, "Un hidalgo Español al servicio de Dios y la humanidad" [A Spanish nobleman in the service of God and humanity], *Tesoro de los Judíos Sefardis*, vol. 7 (Jerusalem, 1964), pp. 32–37, which concerns the period after October 15, 1944, when Horthy was in jail and Szálasi came to power (i.e., after the deportation of 500,000 Jews to Auschwitz). Sanz Briz attempts to attribute all rescue activities to direct orders by General Franco. Molkho counts 200 Spanish Jews whom Sanz Briz received permission to protect; other sources speak of 300. Despite their tendentiousness and inaccuracies, some details of Sanz Briz's activities may be accepted at face value.

22. See documents in Braham, *Hungarian Jewry*, pp. 755–59.

23. Ysart, *España y los Judíos*, pp. 150, 227–28; SFM, I5-E2 (4), report from Sanz Briz, December 14, 1944.

24. See Lévai, "Aus welchen Gründen," p. 109, on Perlasca's activities, based on archival material. According to this account, Perlasca signed the appeal to Szálasi on November 17, 1944 (Lévai, *Geheime Reichssache* [Cologne, 1966], p. 61), although Sanz Briz was still in Budapest at the time. The number of refugees can not be established accurately at present; only a systematic comparison of the names of the Spanish nationals with the lists and testimonies of other refugees in Hungary will provide this.

25. See Ysart, *España y los Judíos*, pp. 126–27, which quotes Lopez Rey, the representative of the Burgos government in Bucharest, March 17, 1938, and p. 119 on the situation in Sofia; the reference is to the Spanish nationals, most of

whom sided with the Nationalists. See also SFM, I5-E2 (1), report summary of Pelayo García y Olay, who wrote that in view of the persecution of the Jews in Romania, the foreign minister Jordana permitted the minister in Romania on August 3, 1933, to provide an unknown number of Jews with temporary papers as Spanish nationals. These new protégés, in addition to a few in Bulgaria and Romania, thus remained separate from the groups handled by Spain's foreign representatives.

26. The number of Jews saved in Hungary includes 2,295 holders of various Spanish documents and 500 whose transport to Tangier was authorized but whose names have not been discovered to date; it is not certain whether the members of this group were included among those who received documents. Thus, an estimate of 2,795 should be considered maximal. See WJC, Spain, file 2, official announcement from Juan F. Cárdenas to Rabbi Maurice L. Perlzweig, stating that the Spanish Legation in Budapest provided 1,889 letters of patronage and 397 temporary passports—a total of 2,286. In light of this, Ysart's claim (*España y los Judíos*, p. 133) that Sanz Briz effected the rescue of 5,000 Jews in Hungary is exaggerated.

CHAPTER 7

1. Spain, Bureau d'Information Diplomatique, *L'Espagne et les juifs* (Madrid, 1949), p. 17. See also Manuel Blanco Tobio, "Una brecha en las alambradas" [A breach in the barbed wire], *El Español*, December 22, 1945; the title is from Federico Ysart, *España y los Judíos en la Segunda Guerra Mundial* (Barcelona, 1973), p. 99.

2. An interesting and as yet unexplored story is the attitude of the soldiers and officers of the Blue Division toward the plight of the Jews in eastern Europe. There were no Jews on the Leningrad front, but Spanish units in the hinterlands doubtless came in contact with Jewish villages. On its way to the front in the summer of 1941, the Blue Division passed on foot through the towns and villages of Lithuania and northwestern Russia, where the German murder squads were killing Jews. See Bobbe Mendl, *Yidn in Letland* (Tel Aviv, 1972), p. 218, who tells of several Jews who were helped by a senior Spanish officer to flee from the Riga ghetto to Spain.

3. Spanish Embassy, *Spain and the Sephardi Jews* (Washington, 1949), p. 3. The success of the rescue is attributed to the Spanish Embassy in Vichy, where José Félix Lequerica, who was Spanish Foreign Minister in 1949, served during the war. The rescue of the Spanish nationals in Bergen-Belsen is offered as one of the interventions Spain made on behalf of thousands of Spanish Jews in Salonika and elsewhere.

4. SFM, I5-E2 (2), letter from Francisco Gomez Jordana, December 28, 1943.

5. Ysart, *España y los Judíos*, pp. 110–11.

6. Ibid., pp. 114–15; SFM, I5-E2 (2), letter from the German Embassy in Madrid, no. 1175/43, May 10, 1943; ibid., letter from Ginés Vidal, no. 322, May 7, 1943 (in the margin the recipient wrote: "Mr. Carreño, obviously we must maintain our view that property belonging to Spanish subjects can not be confiscated"); ibid., memorandum containing a draft of the Spanish reply with Jordana's approval, May 19, 1943.

7. YV, AA-JM 2298, note from the Spanish Embassy in Berlin, no. 128, February 1, 1943; ibid., reply from the German Foreign Ministry, no. 846, February 24, 1943; ibid., announcement from the Reichskommissar in Holland, April 20, 1944, and comments from Eberhardt von Thadden, May 5, 1944. See SFM, I5-E2 (2), letter from Vidal, no. 298, April 29, 1943.

8. WRB, box 112, 4 D-1, "Cooperation with Other Governments: Neutral Europe, Spain"; ibid., cable from Madrid to the WRB, no. 1195, April 6, 1944; ibid., box 113, cable no. 997, March 22, 1944; ibid., box 71, "Report of WRB Assistant Executive Director James H. Mann from his visit to Spain and Portugal (May–June 1944)," August 30, 1944, pp. 50–86. Mann describes in detail the hostility Niles W. Bond showed toward the WRB and writes that Willard L. Beaulac (under whose supervision Bond dealt with the problems of the stateless refugees until Beaulac was transferred to the American Embassy in Paraguay) "was well known for his anti-Semitic views." In his book, *Career Ambassador* (New York, 1951), Beaulac goes into much detail of little importance but says almost nothing about the stateless refugees. John Paul Willson ("Carlton J. H. Hayes in Spain 1942–1945" [Ph.D. diss., Syracuse University, 1969], p. 214) writes that Hayes complained on February 9, 1944 that of the eight employees the Office of War Information had assigned to Spain, six were Jews—a disproportionate number, in his view, for service in a Catholic country. Attitudes toward Jews prevalent in the American Embassy in Madrid during the war merit special study. For WRB activities in Spain, see WRB, *Final Summary Report of the Executive Director* (Washington, 1945), pp. 36–37.

9. OHD, 35 (1), Samuel Sequerra, p. 24; AFSC, Spain 1944, file 1, summary of meeting between Moses Leavitt and Loïs K. Jessup, March 3, 1944.

10. CZA, L22/152, letter from Wilfrid Israel in Lisbon to Richard Lichtheim in Geneva, April 28, 1943. From his remarks on "the work of Henrietta Szold," which is "delicate" and "complex," and other clues, it may be inferred that Israel is discussing underground activities. For support for this, see OHD, 33 (1), third testimony of Fritz Lichtenstein, p. 4, fifth testimony, p. 7.

11. CZA, Rescue Committee, file 1452, unsigned memorandum, nineteen pages, in German. From the contents it is clear that the memorandum was written by Joseph Croustillon after December 15, 1943, and sent to Palestine before February 1944. See OHD, 65 (1), Croustillon, pp. 24–27; cf. OHD, 13 (1), Shlomo Steinhorn, p. 6.

12. CZA, Rescue Committee, file 1196, unsigned letter (by Croustillon), August 11, 1943. The letter was sent by courier to France and from there transmitted via Geneva to the Rescue Committee in Palestine, where it arrived on October 28, 1943. Cf. OHD, 35 (1), Sequerra, p. 29, on his first meeting with Croustillon.

13. CZA, Rescue Committee, file 1452, memorandum from Croustillon, p. 11. See AJ, file 4, letter from Steinhorn to France, January 3, 1944; OHD, 65 (1), Croustillon, pp. 46–50.

14. YIVO, Spain 12/9, document 25, memorandum from Rafael Spanien on the situation of the refugees in Barcelona, with a memorandum from David Schweitzer to James Bernstein, undated.

15. CZA, Immigration Department, file 3874, letter from Lichtenstein to Joseph Linton, December 25, 1943, p. 6. See YW, file 6, letter from Yitzhak Weissman to Lichtenstein, March 24, 1944, which discusses the expenses involved in transferring four people from France.

16. OHD, 33 (1), third testimony of Lichtenstein, pp. 3, 6; OHD, 65 (1), Croustillon, pp. 52–53; CZA, Rescue Committee, file 1453, testimony of Kurt Binyamin, February 1944.

17. See Yitzhak Weissman, *Mul eitanei ha-resha* [Against the forces of evil], ed. Gershon Alimor-Wilkowsky (Tel Aviv, 5728/1968), pp. 91–96; OHD, 38 (1), Weissman, p. 27; ibid., 13 (1), Steinhorn, p. 28; AJ, file 4, letter from Steinhorn, January 3, 1944.

18. AJ, file 1, list of names of 98 children who were rescued; ibid., file A/40, list of names of 134 children. See YW, file 4, list of children according to their places of absorption in Palestine, containing 79 names.

19. AJ, file A/40, list of the names of refugees passing through Switzerland and Spain; 452 refugees passed through Spain. Cf. ibid., file 1, report of the Zionist Underground in France, 1942–45, which states that 500 young people passed through Spain; OHD, 34 (1), testimony of Jacques Roitman, reply B/19; ibid., 12 (1), testimony of Leon Roitman, p. 7. The Roitman brothers were responsible for the flight to Spain.

20. CZA, Immigration Department, file 1678, letter from David Shaltiel to "Ehud and the comrades," April 2, 1944.

21. YIVO, ser. 3, file 658, letter from Herbert Katzki, no. 143, May 24, 1943; ibid., ser. 2, Lisbon 1/52, cable from Bernstein to the Jewish Agency, September 22, 1943; JDC, Spain 1943, cable from Katzki, August 16, 1943, and reply from Leavitt, August 21, 1943. Evidence that an emergency operation was not needed is found also in the testimonies of Joseph Schwartz, OHD, 10 (2), pp. 40–41, and Sequerra, OHD, 35 (1), p. 21.

22. WJC, Spain, file 2, letter from Arye Kubowitzki to Juan F. Cárdenas, May 5, 1944; CZA, draft of minutes of meeting of the Jewish Agency Executive, September 21, 1944, no. 1, p. 4.

23. JDC, Spain 1943, letter from Cárdenas to Jonah B. Wise, JDC New York, no. 869, December 1, 1943; WJC, Spain, letter from Cárdenas to Kubowitzki, no. 477, May 11, 1944.

24. SFM, I5-E2 (2), letter from Cárdenas to José Pan de Soraluce, no. 149, March 9, 1943.

25. See Weissman, *Mul eitanei ha-resha*, pp. 107–9; WJC, Spain 2, letter from the Duke of Alba to Ben Rubenstein, from the Jewish Congress in England, April 19, 1944; ibid., letters from Cárdenas to Kubowitzki, no. 477, May 11, 1944, no. 540, June 12, 1944. Weissman's assumption that 400 Spanish Jews were saved in Greece by virtue of his intervention he offered as fact at the conference of the World Jewish Congress in Atlantic City, New Jersey, in 1944, and cited in the pamphlet of the Spanish Foreign Ministry, *L'Espagne et les juifs*, p. 26. The number should have been 155 Jews, whose fate is discussed in detail above. See also WJC, Spain 3, memorandum from Maurice L. Perlzweig to his colleagues in the World Jewish Congress, June 22, 1943, praising Spain's assistance to Jewish refugees, which Perlzweig presented in a round-table discussion broadcasted throughout the United States. He previously brought the matter to Cardénas's attention for confirmation.

26. CZA, draft of minutes of meeting of the Jewish Agency Executive, September 21, 1944, no. 1, p. 1; WJC, Spain, file 2, memorandum from Perlzweig to the leadership of the World Jewish Congress, May 4, 1943; ibid., file 5, cable from Marc Yarblum, December 18, 1945.

CHAPTER 8

1. Canton A. Bernandez, *Legislación eclesiástica del estado (1938–1964)* (Madrid, 1965), pp. 81, 251, 263, 452. For Spain's political position after World War II, see Shlomo Ben-Ami, *Spain: From Dictatorship to Democracy, 1936–1977* (Tel Aviv, 1977) (Hebrew).

2. Spanish Information Service, *Fundamental Laws of the State: The Spanish Constitution* (Madrid, 1967), p. 32.

3. *Ha-kesher* (Madrid), no. 23, May 1967.

4. Ibid., no. 29, January 1968; ibid., no. 30, February 1968; ibid., no. 32, April 1968.

5. Sergio Nudelstejer, "La abolición del Edicto de Expulsion," *Tribuna Israelita* (Mexico City), November–December 1974 (special reprint).

6. The Democratic Union of the Center won 165 seats out of 350 in the Lower House and 106 seats out of 207 in the Senate. The Partido Socialista Obrero Español (Socialist Workers' Party) was supported by nearly 30 percent of the voters and won 116 seats in the Lower House and 60 in the Senate. The Alianza Popular (extreme right-wing party) received 7.5 percent of the votes and won 17 seats; the Communists received 8 percent of the votes and won 19 seats. See Ben-Ami, *Spain* (1977), pp. 313–14.

7. Felipe Halioua, president of the Madrid community, in a conversation with Viktor Malka, *Semana*, March 9, 1976; Samy Toledano, interviewed by Mordejai Barkai, *Semana*, June 21, 1977. See Spanish Constitution (Madrid, 1978), article 16. Other articles relating to the legal status of the Jewish citizens of Spain are nos. 1, 10, 14, and 27. In March 1980, the Catholic church was granted substantial government funding for education. See *New York Times*, March 18, 1980, p. 14.

8. *Ha-boker* (Tel Aviv), August 30, 1950; cf. interview with Ignacio Bauer, *Herut* (Tel Aviv), January 10, 1951; see Haim Beinart, *Ha-yishuv ha-yehudi he-hadash bi-sefarad: reka, metziut, ve-ha'arakhah* [The new Jewish settlement in Spain: background, reality, evaluation] (Jerusalem, 5729/1969), pp. 28–29.

9. Natan Lerner, "Report on a Visit to Spain," Tel Aviv, January 23, 1974 (unpublished); Mordejai Barkai, *Semana*, June 21, 1977; *Ha-aretz* (Tel Aviv), December 18, 1977, p. 2; *Ba-tefutzot* (WJC news bulletin, Tel Aviv), January 1977, p. 4.

10. Yitzhak Weissman, *Mul eitanei ha-resha* [Against the forces of evil], ed. Gershon Alimor-Wilkowsky (Tel Aviv, 5728/1968), pp. 135–39.

11. *Ha-tzofe* (Tel Aviv), November 20, 1946; *Ha-kesher*, no. 37, November 1968.

12. S. Kolitz, "Masa bisefarad, eretz lelo yehudim" [A voyage through Spain, a country without Jews], *Ha-boker*, August 10, 1951.

13. *Ha-kesher*, no. 31, March 1968; ibid., no. 36, October 1968; *Arriba, ABC, Madrid, Ya, Pueblo* (Madrid newspapers), December 17, 1968.

14. Consejo Superior de Investigaciones Científicas, *Actas del primer simposio de estudios Sefardís*, ed. Ya'akov M. Hassan (Madrid, 1970), pp. 592–611. The decree was signed on December 29, 1948, and published in the *Boletin Oficial* on January 9, 1949.

15. Spain, Bureau d'Information Diplomatique, *L'Espagne et les juifs* (Madrid, 1949), pp. 45–58. Julio Caro Baroja, *Los Judíos en la España moderna y contem-*

poranea, vol. 3 (Madrid, 1961), p. 214, writes that the decree of December 29, 1948, "conferred Spanish citizenship upon a larger number of Jews than had enjoyed the protection of the Spanish consulates throughout the world in previous periods." Jerry Goodman, *AJYB* 68 (1967): 339, writes, "In 1949, General Franco again proposed Spanish citizenship to all Spanish Jews."

16. *Ha-tzofe*, October 9, 1951; *Yediot Aharonot* (Tel Aviv), October 26, 1951; *Ha-boker*, July 27, 1953.

17. Consejo Superior, *Actas del primer simposio*, pp. 613–15, 497–537. During the symposium the Jewish Museum in Toledo was inaugurated, and a statue of Maimonides was unveiled in Córdoba, the city of his birth; the site where the statue was erected was named Plazuela de Tiberiades, expressing the union between the city of his birth and Tiberias, the city of his death.

18. *Ha-kesher*, no. 4, March 1965, p. 3.

19. Federico Ysart, *España y los Judíos en la Segunda Guerra Mundial* (Barcelona, 1973), pp. 153–56.

20. United Nations, *Official Records of the Fifth Session of the General Assembly, Plenary Meetings* (New York, 1950), p. 380; idem, *Official Records of the Tenth Session of the General Assembly, Plenary Meetings* (New York, 1955), p. 436.

21. *Ha-aretz*, December 7, 1976; *News and Views* (WJC bulletin), January 1977. In this respect the pressure from Libya is particularly noteworthy.

22. Vicente Serrano, "El dialogo Judeo Cristiano en España, datos para una Historia," *El Olivo* (Madrid), January–March 1977, pp. 9–18. Serrano was one of the founders of the organization. Sister Esperanza de Sión and José Francisco Riaza Saco actively supported him; on the Jewish side, Max Mazin, then president of the Jewish community of Madrid, and Samuel Toledano, his deputy, were most outstanding.

23. Amistad Judeo-Cristiana, *Paraliturgica Judeo-Cristiana* (Madrid, 1967).

24. *Amistad Judeo-Cristiana*, no. 44, January–February 1973, p. 8, order of Cardinal Viconte Enrique y Tarancón, archbishop of Madrid-Alcalá, on the establishment of the Center for Christian-Jewish Studies.

25. Jacob Tzur, *Maariv* (Tel Aviv), June 3, 1977, p. 28; Eliahu Maisy, *Semana*, October 18, 1977, and *Ha-aretz*, October 30, 1977.

26. Serrano, "El dialogo Judeo Cristiano," p. 9; José Francisco Riaza Saco, "Ceremonias de Confusion," *Amistad Judeo-Cristiana*, no. 45, April–June 1973, p. 1; Max Mazin, "El Extremismo y Nosotros," ibid., no. 46, July–August 1973, p. 3; José Maria Iglesias Romero, "Grupusculos de Orientación Nazi?" ibid., no. 47, September–October 1973, p. 6.

27. José Amador de los Ríos, *Historia social, política, y religiosa de los Judíos de España y Portugal*, vol. 3 (Madrid, 1875–76), pp. 566–67.

BIBLIOGRAPHY

OFFICIAL RECORDS

Hebrew Sheltering and Immigration Aid Society. *HIAS Activities in the U.S. and Overseas Countries.* 1940.

———. *Rescue through Emigration.* 1941.

Jewish Colonization Association. *Rapport de la Direction Générale au Conseil d'Administration.* 1935.

Joint Distribution Committee. *Annual Reports: Aiding Jews Overseas.* 1940–May 1941, 1941–May 1942.

———. *JDC in 1944.* 1944.

———. *The Rescue of Jews in a World at War.* 1943.

———. *So They May Live Again.* 1945.

Nazi Massacres of the Jews and Others. Some practical proposals for immediate rescue made by the Archbishop of Canterbury and Lord Rochester. London, 1943.

Spain. *Constitución de la República Española.* Madrid, 1931.

———. *Constitution of the Parliamentary Monarchy.* Madrid, 1978.

———. Bureau d'Information Diplomatique. *L'Espagne et les juifs.* Madrid, 1949.

———. Ministerio del Trabajo. Dirección General de Estadística. *Zona de protectorado y de los territorios de soberanía de España en el norte de Africa: annuario estadística 1941.* Madrid, 1942.

Spanish Embassy. *Spain and the Sephardi Jews.* Washington, 1949.

Spanish Information Service. *Fundamental Laws of the State.* Madrid, 1967.

United Nations. *Official Records of the Third Session of the General Assembly.* Pt. 2, Plenary Meetings of the General Assembly: Summary Records of Meetings, April 5–May 18, 1949. Lake Success, N.Y., 1949.

———. *Official Records of the Fifth Session of the General Assembly.* Plenary Meetings. New York, 1950.

———. *Official Records of the Tenth Session of the General Assembly.* Plenary Meetings. New York, 1955.

U.S. Department of State. *Foreign Relations of the United States, Diplomatic Papers 1943.* Vol. 1, general. Washington, 1963.

———. *Foreign Relations of the United States, Diplomatic Papers 1944.* Vol. 1, general. Washington, 1966.

———. *The Spanish Government and the Axis.* Washington, 1946.

War Refugee Board. *Final Summary Report of the Executive Director.* Washington, 1945.

PUBLICATIONS

L'activité des organisations juives en France sous l'Occupation. Paris, 1947.

Adler, E. N. "Auto-da-fé and Jews." *Jewish Quarterly Review* 13 (1901): 392–437.

Adler-Rudel, S. "A Chronicle of Rescue Efforts." *Leo Baeck Institute Year Book* 11 (1966): 213–20.

Agar, Herbert. *The Saving Remnant: An Account of Jewish Survival since 1914.* London, 1960.

Alcheh y Saporta, Isaac. *Los Españoles sin patria de Salonica.* Madrid, 1917.

Amador de los Ríos, José. *Estudio sobre los Judíos de España.* Madrid, 1848.

———. *Historia social, política, y religiosa de los Judíos de España y Portugal.* Vol. 3. Madrid, 1875–76.

Amouroux, Henri. *La vie des français sous l'Occupation.* Paris, 1961.

Attias, Moshe. *Romancero sefaradi.* Jerusalem, 5721/1961.

Baer, Yitzhak. *A History of the Jews in Christian Spain.* 2 vols. Philadelphia, 1961.

Baroja, Julio Caro. *Los Judíos en la España moderna y contemporanea.* 3 vols. Madrid, 1961.

Baroja, Pío. *Comunistas Judíos y demás raleas.* 2d ed. Valladolid, 1939.

Beaulac, Willard L. *Career Ambassador.* New York, 1951.

Beinart, Haim. *Ha-yishuv ha-yehudi he-hadash bi-sefarad: reka, metziut, ve-ha'arakhah* [The new Jewish settlements in Spain: background, reality, evaluation]. Jerusalem, 5729/1969.

———. "Judíos y conversors en España despues de la Expulción de 1492." *Hispania* 23: (1964): 295–301.

Bernandez, Canton A. *Legislación eclesiástica del estado (1938–1964).* Madrid, 1965.

Ben-Ami, Shlomo. *Spain: From Dictatorship to Democracy, 1936–1977.* Tel-Aviv, 1977 (Hebrew).

Bloch, Jean-Pierre. *Le vent souffle sur l'histoire.* Paris, 1956.

Borwicz, Michel. *Vies interdites.* Paris, 1969.

Braham, Randolph L. *The Destruction of Hungarian Jewry: A Documentary Account.* Vol. 2. New York, 1963.

Braunstein, Baruch. *The Chuetas of Majorca: Conversos and the Inquisition of Majorca.* Scottdale, Pa., 1936.

Browning, Christopher. *The Final Solution and the German Foreign Office.* New York, 1978.

Cadier, Henry. *Le clavaire d'Israël.* Geneva-Paris, 1945.

Churchill, Winston. *The Second World War.* 6 vols. Boston, 1948–53.

Consejo Superior de Investigaciones Científicas. *Actas del primer simposio de estudios Sefardís.* Edited by Ya'akov M. Hassan. Madrid, 1970.

Dégano, F. Robles. *La conspiración Judía contra España.* Ávila, 1932.

de Gaulle, Charles. *Mémoires de guerre: l'unité 1942–1944.* Vol. 2. Paris, 1956.

Diamant, David. *Héros juifs de la Résistance française.* Paris, 1962.

Eijan, Samuel. *Hispanidad en Tierra Santa: actuación diplomática.* Madrid, 1943.

Eisenhower, Dwight D. *Crusade in Europe.* Garden City, N.Y., 1952.

Esteban Infantes, Emilio. *La División Azul (donde Asia empieza).* Barcelona, 1956.

Feis, Herbert. *The Spanish Story: Franco and the Nations at War.* New York, 1966.

Fernandez Rodriguez, Manuel. "España y los Judíos en le reinado de Alfonso XII." *Hispania* 25 (1965): 565–84.

Fluch, M. (Mme. Guérin). *La Résistance à Pau: passages des Pyrénées.* Pau, 1944.

Fry, Varian. *Surrender on Demand.* New York, 1954.

La garra del capitalismo Judío. Madrid, 1943.

Greffier, Lucien. *La mésaventure espagnole.* Paris, 1946.

Guttmann, Allen. *The Wound in the Heart: America and the Spanish Civil War.* New York, 1962.

Hamilton, J. Thomas. *Appeasement's Child: The Franco Regime in Spain.* New York, 1943.

Hayes, Carlton J. H. *The United States and Spain: An Interpretation.* New York, 1951.

———. *Wartime Mission in Spain, 1942–1945.* New York, 1946.

Heredia, Angel Tineo. *Los Judíos en España.* Madrid, 1881.

Hilberg, Raul. *The Destruction of the European Jews.* Chicago, 1961.

Hoare, Samuel (Viscount Templewood). *Complacent Dictator.* New York, 1947.

Ippercourt. *Les Chemins d'Espagne: mémoires et documents sur la guerre secrète à travers les Pyrénées, 1940–1945.* Paris, 1946.

Isaacs, A. Lionel. *The Jews of Majorca.* London, 1936.

Jackson, Gabriel. *The Spanish Republic and the Civil War, 1931–1939.* Princeton, 1965.

Kalisher, Ben-Zion. *Ba-derekh le-eretz yisrael* [On the way to the Land of Israel]. Tel Aviv, 5705/1945.

Knout, David. *Contribution à l'histoire de la Résistance juive en France, 1940–1944.* Paris, 1947.

Lacalle, José Maria. *Los Judíos Españoles.* Barcelona, 1964.

Laredo, Isaac. *Memorias de un viejo Tangerino.* Madrid, 1935.

Latour, Anny. *La Résistance juive en France, 1940–1944.* Paris, 1970.

Lazarus, Jacques. *Juifs au combat.* Paris, 1947.

Lea, Henry Charles. *A History of the Inquisition of Spain.* Vol. 3. London, 1922.

Leboucher, Fernande. *Incredible Mission: The Amazing Story of Père Benoît, Rescuer of the Jews from the Nazis.* New York, 1969.

Léon, Henry. *Histoire des juifs de Bayonne.* Paris, 1893.

Leshem, Peretz (Fritz Lichtenstein). "Rescue Efforts in the Iberian Peninsula." *Leo Baeck Institute Year Book* 14 (1969): 231–56.

Lévai, Jenö. *L'eglise ne s'est pas tué.* Paris, 1966.

———. *Geheime Reichssache.* Cologne, 1966.

———. "Die Vernichtung der Juden in Ungarn." *Fourth World Congress of Jewish Studies.* Vol. 2. Jerusalem, 1968.

————. "Aus welchen Gründen überlebte das Budapester Ghetto als einziges die Ausrottung" [Some reasons the Budapest Ghetto survived destruction]. *Fifth World Congress of Jewish Studies*. Vol. 2. Jerusalem, 1972.

Loeb, Isidore. "L'Espagne et les juifs." *Bulletin de l'Alliance Israélite Universelle*. Ser. 2, no. 12 (1887).

Lowrie, Donald A. *The Hunted Children*. New York, 1943.

Machimbarrena, Juan. *La crisis mundial: el oro, el socialismo, los Judíos*. San Sebastián, 1932.

Madariaga, Salvador de. *Spain: A Modern History*. New York, 1958.

Marie-Benoît, Pierre. "Résumé de mon activité en faveur des juifs persecutés, 1940–1944." *Livre d'or des congregations françaises*, 1939–1945. Paris, 1948.

Méndez Benjarano, Mario. *Histoire de la juiverie de Seville*. Madrid, 1922.

Mirelman, Victor A. "A Note on Jewish Settlement in Argentina, 1881–1892." *Jewish Social Studies* 33 (1971): 3–12.

Mitrani, Thérèse. *Service d'évasion*. Paris, 1946.

Molins y Fabrega, Bartoli. *Campos de concentración, 1939–194 . . .* Mexico City, 1944.

Molkho, Michael, and Nehamah, Joseph. *Shoat yehudei yavan, 1941–1944* [The destruction of Greek Jewry, 1941–1944]. Jerusalem, 5724/1964.

Molkho, Y. R. "Temurot be-yahasei sefarad ve-ha-yehudim" [Changes in relations between Spain and the Jews]. *Gesher* (5729/1969): 68–74.

Neave, Airey. *Saturday at M.I. 9*. London, 1969.

Nordau, Max. "Dr. Yahuda and the Madrid University." *Jewish Chronicle*, April 9, 1920, p. 6.

————. "Hafta'ah sefaradit" [A Spanish surprise]. *Ktavim tziyoni'im* [Zionist writings]. Vol. 4. Speeches and Essays, 1915–1920. Jerusalem, 5722/1962.

Ortega, Manuel L. *Figuras ibéricas: el doctor Pulido*. Madrid, 1922.

Patee, Richard. *This Is Spain*. Milwaukee, 1951.

Payne, Stanley G. *Franco's Spain*. London, 1968.

Piétri, François. *Mes années d'Espagne, 1940–1945*. Paris, 1954.

Plenn, Abel. *Wind in the Olive Tree: Spain from Inside*. New York, 1946.

Prato, Jeonathan. "Spain." *Encyclopaedia Judaica*. Vol. 15. Jerusalem, 5731/1971.

Pulido, Martin Angel. *El dr. Pulido y su epoca*. Madrid, 1945.

Pulido y Fernandez, Angel. *España en Marruecos: penetración, pacífica, y colonización en su protectorado*. Madrid, 1922.

————. *Españoles sin patria y la raza Sefardí*. Madrid, 1905.

————. *La reconciliación Hispano-Hebrea*. Madrid, 1920.

Puzzo, Dante A. *Spain and the Great Powers, 1936–1941*. New York, 1962.

Reisner, H. G. "The Histories of the Kaufhaus N. Israel and of Wilfrid Israel." *Leo Baeck Institute Year Book* 3 (1958): 227–56.

Reitlinger, Gerald. *The Final Solution: The Attempt to Exterminate The Jews of Europe, 1939–1945*. London, 1955.

Riaza Saco, José Francisco. "Los Judíos y las cortes Españolas de 1869." *Amistad Judeo-Cristiana*, no. 12 (December 1966–January 1967), p. 1.

Robinson, Jacob. *And the Crooked Shall be Made Straight: The Eichmann Trial, the Jewish Catastrophe, and Hannah Arendt's Narrative*. New York, 1965.

Robinson, Nehemia. *The Spain of Franco and Its Policies toward the Jews*. New York, 1953.

Romanatxo, Hector. *Ils ont franchi les Pyrénées.* Paris, 1955.

Roth, Cecil. *A History of the Marranos.* New York, 1959.

Sanchez, José M. *Reform and Reaction.* Chapel-Hill, N.C., 1964.

Schellenberg, Walter. *The Labyrinth.* New York, 1956.

Singerman, Robert. "American-Jewish Reactions to the Spanish Civil War." *Journal of Church and State* 19 (1977): 261–78.

Situation d'Israël. (Fascicule de Catholicité.) Lille, 1948.

Steckel, Charles. *Destruction and Survival.* Los Angeles, 1973.

Steinberg, Lucien. *La révolte des justes: les juifs contre Hitler, 1943–1945.* Paris, 1970.

Szajkowski, Zosa. *Analytical Franco-Jewish Gazetteer, 1939–1945.* New York, 1966.

Tartakower, Arie, and Grossman, K. R. *The Jewish Refugee.* New York, 1944.

Tenenbaum, Joseph. *Race and Reich: The Story of an Epoch.* New York, 1956.

Thomas, Hugh. *The Spanish Civil War.* New York, 1961.

Toynbee, Arnold. *Survey of International Affairs, 1939–1946: The War and the Neutrals.* Oxford, 1956.

Unity in Dispersion: A History of the World Jewish Congress. New York, 1948.

Vigée, Claude. *La lune d'hiver.* Paris, 1970.

Vilar, Juan Batista. "Emigrantes Judíos del norte de Marruecos a Hispanoamerica durante el siglo XX." *Maguen-Escudo* (Caracas), no. 21 (February 1972), p. 21.

Vogel, Georg. *Diplomat unter Hitler und Adenauer.* Düsseldorf-Vienna, 1969.

Weissman, Yitzhak. *Mul eitanei ha-resha* [Against the forces of evil]. Edited by Gershon Alimor-Wilkowsky. Tel Aviv, 5728/1968.

Wilfrid Israel. London, 1944.

Wischnitzer, Mark. *To Dwell in Safety: The Story of Jewish Migration since 1800.* Philadelphia, 1948.

———. *Visas to Freedom: The History of HIAS.* Cleveland, 1956.

Yahuda, A. S. *Ha-haganah al ha-yishuv ha-yehudi bi-yemei milhemet ha-olam ha-rishonah* [The defense of the Jewish community during World War I]. Jerusalem, 5712/1952.

———. "Prakim mi-zikhronotai" [Chapters of my memoirs]. *Talpiot* 3, 4 (5709–10/1949–50): 600–7, 770–78.

———. "El Rey Alfonso XIII y los Judíos." *Judaica* (Buenos Aires), July–December 1943.

Ysart, Federico. *España y los Judíos en la Segunda Guerra Mundial.* Barcelona, 1973.

UNPUBLISHED

Lichtenstein, Joseph Jacob. "The Reaction of West European Jewry to the Reestablishment of a Jewish Community in Spain in the 19th Century." Ph.D. dissertation, Yeshiva University, 1962.

Proctor, Raymond Lambert. "The 'Blue Division': An Episode in German-Spanish Wartime Relations." Ph.D. dissertation, University of Oregon, 1966.

Willson, John Paul. "Carlton J. H. Hayes in Spain, 1942–1945." Ph.D. dissertation, Syracuse University, 1969.

INDEX